PENGUIN BOOKS

LEARNING TO FLY

Victoria Beckham was a member of the Spice Girls, who sold over 30 million records worldwide. Her debut solo album was released in autumn 2001. She is married to Manchester United footballer David Beckham and they have a son, Brooklyn.

VICTORIA
BECKHAM

learning to fly
THE AUTOBIOGRAPHY

PENGUIN BOOKS

PENGUIN BOOKS

Published by the Penguin Group
Penguin Books Ltd, 80 Strand, London WC2R ORL, England
Penguin Putnam Inc., 375 Hudson Street, New York, New York 10014, USA
Penguin Books Australia Ltd, 250 Camberwell Road,
Camberwell, Victoria 3124, Australia
Penguin Books Canada Ltd, 10 Alcorn Avenue, Toronto, Ontario, Canada M4V 3B2
Penguin Books India (P) Ltd, 11, Community Centre,
Panchsheel Park, New Delhi – 110 017, India
Penguin Books (NZ) Ltd, Cnr Rosedale and Airborne Roads,
Albany, Auckland, New Zealand
Penguin Books (South Africa) (Pty) Ltd, 24 Sturdee Avenue,
Rosebank 2196, South Africa

Penguin Books Ltd, Registered Offices: 80 Strand, London WC2R ORL, England

www.penguin.com

First published by Viking 2001
Published in Penguin Books 2002

2

Set in Monotype Bembo
Printed in England by Clays Ltd, St Ives plc

dedication

I dedicate this story of my life to my family: Mummy, Daddy, Louise and Christian. Over the last six years (the last eighteen if I'm being honest) I have turned your lives upside down. And I don't just mean having to live behind security gates. As difficult as it has been for me, it has been even more difficult for you – not just coping with my personality, with its ups and downs, but your whole lives have been changed.

While I have fame and the money that comes with it, all you have, apart from being proud, is the upheaval. So *Learning to Fly* is an attempt to try to make sense of it all, to give a little bit of insight, I hope, into the people who made it all possible. It happened to me, but it happened to you, too. Perhaps this will help you understand.

And then there is my new family who have given me a depth of love and support that I never imagined possible.

Without David I wouldn't have had the confidence to even think that my life would be interesting to anyone else. He gave me the courage to just do it. And as for

Brooklyn, what can I say except that every day he gives me a sense of real worth and real values. So here's to you, my two boys: I love you lots and lots and I'm very proud of you both. And Brooklyn, when you're old enough to read this book, you'll see that Mummy and Daddy were really famous once.

contents

acknowledgements

I would like to thank everyone at Michael Joseph who made writing this such a pain-free but therapeutic experience: Tom Weldon, Lindsey Jordan, Martin Bryant, my agent at William Morris, Stephanie Cabot, and my friend Pepsy for coming up with the title.

At the Outside Organization, Alan Edwards and Caroline McAteer, whose constructive criticism was greatly appreciated, in spite of jogging my memory on certain things I tried hard to forget, and Lucy Barnicot who had all my press cuttings (even the nasty ones) safely filed.

All at Spice HQ: Julie, Julia, Jo and Jamie, especially Rebecca Cripps who has been with the Spice Girls since the beginning and whose memory I tapped into all the time, not forgetting the lady who makes the Victoria Beckham machine run, Nancy Phillips, who kept me sane and made sure I kept to my deadlines. And Nancy – now the book's finished, maybe I will have that day off.

Andrew Thompson, Mike Brookes, Gordon Williams and Charles Bradbrook, who guided me through the intricacies of the law and other hard-to-grasp matters.

My mum for always being there at important moments with her camera and for her amazing collection of press cuttings, not to mention her incredible memory and for the sheer stamina of standing for thirty hours at a photo-processing machine getting copies of the pictures for this book. Thank you. I love you.

And of course Melanie B, Melanie C, Emma and Geri. Five girls said they'd conquer the world and we did.

Thank you.

1 i'll walk with you

'Daddy! I'm going to be killed.'

'No, you're not, Victoria. I'm right behind you. I'll look after you.'

I can't see him. We're too close together, jammed in by the crowd. But I can feel his hand on my shoulder, and his hand and his voice are just enough to keep me from screaming. Calm, in control, like he always is. Not like my mum who lives off her nerves. When people say, who do you take after, I say, my dad. But when I panic like this I know I'm like my mum.

Another lurch from the crowd. I need space, air. I'm being pushed, my dad behind, me in the middle, the bodyguard in front, so big that all I can see is his back, wet with sweat. I can hardly breathe. Only one thing is louder than the roaring of the crowd and that's my heart thumping in my ears. Even when I'm about to go on stage it's never this bad.

Without my glasses, I'm half blind. But I can sense the crowd towering up on my right, painted faces that loom up from nowhere, red, white and blue. A hand reaches out and pushes my baseball cap down over my eyes. I'm shaking.

'Over 'ere, Posh, Posh.'

They're drunk. I can smell the beer. Laughing and shouting. Their hands sticking out, jabbing their fingers in some drunken impression of Posh Spice.

'Oi, Posh.'

'Get yer tits out.'

Don't make eye-contact, one of the Spice Girls' security once told me. That's why celebrities wear dark glasses. Like me today. So head down. A flash of a camera. Little red lights everywhere, infra-red auto-focus. Like they have on guns. A lens pokes through the wire fence on my left that separates the crowd from the pitch. There are people the other side. Fingers are poking through the wire trying to touch me. That fence shouldn't be there. Haven't they heard of Hillsborough, these morons? The semi-final of the 1989 FA Cup when ninety-six people were killed, crushed against the wire? Only this week they'd had the pictures on the television again. A court case was just starting against the two policemen in charge.

'We love you, Posh.' Then laughter. 'Only kidding!'

We're on the strip of concrete that runs around the pitch at Eindhoven trying to get back to our seats. I know it's concrete because I saw it on our way up; now I can't see anything. Just a blur of bodies and arms reaching out. Trying to touch me.

It's Monday 12 June 2000. The Football Association had organized everything as they always do for all England away games: a chartered plane from Stansted to Brussels, then a coach to Eindhoven. The driver parked in some backstreet, so we'd had to walk a good twenty minutes to the stadium. But we'd still got there two hours before kick-off. Our seats were about five rows from the front, in the middle, opposite the tunnel where the players come out and when people saw me sitting there like a bloody lemon, out came the cameras. Some of them were press: Sky zooming in on my face. Some were just ordinary people, taking a snap to show their friends. Show them what? A moody cow with a baseball cap pulled down over her eyes. I felt a complete idiot, just sitting there with hardly anyone else about. Wasn't there somewhere we could go until kick-off, I asked my security. I mean, what were we supposed to do for two hours. Read the programme?

It was then that we heard about the VIP lounge. We asked Ted and Sandra, David's parents, who were in the row behind if they wanted to come along, but they said no thank you, they'd rather stay.

It was the other side of the pitch, but as the place was practically empty getting there had only taken five minutes. They'd got us champagne and we'd been so busy chatting with Doreen, my mum's friend who was over from Athens and had never been to a football match in her life, we hadn't noticed the stadium filling up. Now with only ten minutes to go the place was absolutely rammed. Thank God I'd decided not to bring Brooklyn. He was safely back at my mum's house in London with my sister Louise.

I'd never wanted to come to Eindhoven. I was booked into the studio in London all week, working on my solo album. But it wasn't just because of that. Everybody was expecting so much from David that I thought it better

3

all round not to go. It's like when he takes an important free kick, or a penalty, sometimes I think it's better not to look.

And David was already out there, kicking the ball around, as they always do before a game. I'd seen him as I walked down the steps into this nightmare. Even without my glasses I can pick him out on the field just by the way he moves even if I can't see the big number 7 on his back. But he hadn't seen me. He'd been looking the other way, across the pitch where the wives and families are always put. He always looks for me. It calms him down to know I'm there, he says. I knew he'd be worried now, not seeing me. I shouldn't have come. I should just be sitting at home, with Brooklyn watching his daddy on television. Then at least David would know his family were safe.

You have to have been to a football match to know what the noise does to you. I'd seen football on television before I went near a stadium and what you hear on television is nothing, even in those pubs with big screens and wraparound sound. Mark, my first boyfriend, would sometimes take me to watch football in pubs, with his friends – his idea of an evening out. Funnily enough, I'd even watched the semi-final against Germany in Euro 1996 in a pub in Enfield; that time when Gareth Southgate missed the penalty. If anyone had told me then I'd be married to a footballer I wouldn't have believed them. It's the noise that's as frightening as an express train when you're standing on a platform. It engulfs you. It's a noise that makes you want to scream.

Dress down, David had said. I knew all the other wives would be in their Away-Day best – first England match in Euro 2000 and all that. And bring security. My dad and a bodyguard – that would be enough, he'd said. But it wasn't.

It was the Friday before that the *Daily Mail* found out my name wasn't on the list and said I was snubbing the other England wives and girlfriends by not going. It was picked up by the radio. I heard them talking about it on Capital as I drove in to work. They were talking as if my going would make the difference as to whether England won or lost. Phil Neville's wife wasn't going, nor Gary Neville's girlfriend. No one said anything about them. Just went on about how I thought I should be treated differently.

But didn't they understand, I *was* treated differently. Were the other wives having fingers poked at them now? No. Even if they were dressed up in their England-Expects best, nobody knew who they were. But Posh Spice. Who everyone knows wants to take their precious Golden Boy away from Manchester United, everyone knows who she is. The most hated woman in England, that's what I've been called. Nice.

And what do football supporters do when they hate? They shout abuse. When I was little my mum used to say that old thing about sticks and stones may break your bones but words will never harm you. That was when I was being bullied at school. But she was wrong. It wasn't true then and it's not true now.

I remember not long after I started going out with David, my mum came up to Manchester to a match and when they saw me the crowd began chanting 'Posh Spice takes it up the arse'. And she said, 'What's that they're singing, Victoria?' She'd heard the Posh Spice

5

bit, but not the rest. I mean, how embarrassing is that? I just said I didn't know and could she please pass me another bag of crisps.

The abuse that me and David get at Old Trafford is hideous – at least it never gets physical, unless you count banging on the glass of a corporate box – but since Euro 2000 started all we'd heard about in the English press was football violence and yob culture. People think I read the papers just to find out what they're writing about Posh and Becks. And I would be lying if I said I wasn't interested – it's the lies they print that mean I have to read that crap. Lies and things that are only too true, photographs you literally had no idea were being taken. Photographs of you and your baby and your husband and your sister and your sister's little girl, and your mum and your dad and anybody else whose lives they feel like poking their lenses into. Yes, I read the newspapers. But I also watch the news every night. No matter how tired I am. It's the only television I do watch. And I knew what was going on in Belgium, how the England fans were a disgrace and were already cluttering up police cells. But David wanted me to come. He says he plays better when I'm there.

The game had just started by the time we got back to our seats. Stadium security had eventually turned up, about six of them, and, just like bull bars on a 4WD, didn't ask any questions, just pushed everyone back. It turned out they'd roped off where the players came through, which was why the place was rammed.

When David saw me, his face broke into that smile and it was like it always is. Like Marilyn Monroe says in

Some Like It Hot 'my spine turns to custard' and I forget everything except how much I love him and how lucky I am that he loves me.

I knew how important this game was to him. So many people were saying that Beckham was going to do it for us. But they were saying that at the World Cup when he ballsed up, and then they turned on him completely. Jeremy Clarkson said he would like to get David in a padded cell with a baseball bat. The *Daily Mirror* had a pull-out dartboard with David's face in the middle. The *Sun* got a dummy, dressed it up like David, put some naff sarong and a number 7 shirt on it and hanged it, not hung it, hanged it with a rope round the neck on a gallows outside a pub in South London, took a picture and put it on the front page. No footballer has ever had such negative press, which is why it was so important that he had a good game.

And he did. Even though it ended in a draw, that first match against Portugal was the best of the three games England played in Euro 2000. And David played so well, I was so proud of him. I kept looking at my dad to check that I was right. He just smiled. David created two goals – which means he kicked the ball to the person who kicked the goal. And I was nearly crying I was so happy, and for me that is unheard of, as any Manchester United supporter will tell you, I'm not really into football at all. My interest in football is limited to David. I don't watch the ball, I watch David. If the two coincide, then fine.

Everybody knows that before an England match players are banned from seeing their families, but what most people don't realize is that they're banned from seeing them afterwards as well. Football teams, whether Manchester United or England, are run like concentration camps. All I wanted to do after that game was to hug David, and tell him how proud I was. But when the final whistle blew, and they did the thing of taking off their shirts and giving them to the other side, we were already being led back to our coach in a crocodile like good little schoolchildren, back to the airport and home.

As we were making our way out of the stadium I tapped out a text message on my mobile. There was no point calling him, I knew he'd be in the shower or the bath, being boys together after the game. We spend half our lives sending messages to each other. The other half we're on the phone. David's physio even says his back trouble comes from having his ear glued to his phone. But sometimes there are things you want to say that you don't want anyone else to hear, whether it's your mum or your dad, or the driver or security or make-up or hair or one of the girls. Or perhaps other people are talking or listening to a CD and it would be rude to just pick up the mobile and chat. There are some people in the music business who think that just because they're up there, they can behave how they like. I suppose it's all about how you are brought up. Some people find sending text messages fiddly, but I don't. I'm like a mobile phone touch typist, though long nails mean I use the side of my finger. I don't even have to think where the letters are.

Then just as my screen flashed *Sent* I get an alert – a message from David. *Call me asap Love you lots XXD*. I punch the keypad, a number I could do in my sleep, then it's two rings and 'Hello'.

Other people can mock David's voice if they like. I love it.

'Hi, Babes,' I said. 'I know you think I know nothing, but you really did well. I feel so, so proud of you.'

'I don't think you will be when you hear what I've done, Victoria.'

I felt my heart do what seemed like a double beat.

'What's that, then?'

'I've just heard the press have got a picture of me sticking my finger up at the fans.'

I couldn't believe I was hearing this.

'You're kidding me, David.' We'd been over it again and again. Don't react. Just don't react.

'I just couldn't help myself.'

'But why? We've been over and over this. Why did you do it?'

Stupid question. I knew why. It's the abuse and David's short fuse. But he knows there is such a spotlight on him.

'It was the things they were shouting about you and Brooklyn. I couldn't handle it any more.'

'Like what were they saying?'

'You know.'

'I want to hear.'

'Brooklyn takes it up the arse.'

That wasn't a new one. But it still made me sick when I heard it.

'Well, we've heard that one before.'

'And then they said they hoped Brooklyn died of cancer.'

I just closed my eyes and said nothing. A picture of Brooklyn flashed in front of my eyes, as I had left him,

9

wandering around the kitchen just wearing his nappy, holding his football.

'Are you still there, Victoria?'

'I'm still here.'

'I just couldn't help myself. I had run my bollocks off for ninety minutes and then there were just these three or four blokes shouting abuse. And I just gave them one finger. I didn't think anyone had seen.'

'And you're sure they did?'

'Gary said they did.'

Gary Neville is David's best friend at Manchester United. They've both been there since they were sixteen.

Another silence. It takes a lot to shut me up, but I didn't know what to say.

'How's Brooklyn?' David said.

'He's fine. Louise just called. She said he watched his daddy on television and he's fine.'

'Don't be angry, Babes. I know it was stupid, but I couldn't help myself.'

I lost him as the coach went into a tunnel. I decided he could call me if he wanted and I opened up another stick of chewing gum, folding the old bit in the new wrapper and putting it in the ashtray in the seat in front. I've always been brought up to be tidy.

He was right. I was angry. I just wanted to get him by the neck and throttle him. No prizes for guessing the picture on the front page of every paper in England the next day.

My mum and dad were up at the front of the coach talking to David's mum and dad. I didn't feel like telling them. They'd find out soon enough. I just curled up in the seat, chomped on the chewing gum and stared out at the sky, still streaked with red. Red for Manchester United. Red for England.

There had been so much talk since Euro 2000 started as to why the England fans were more violent than anybody else, worse than Scottish fans, worse than Welsh fans, worse than Irish fans. I couldn't understand it. I'd grown up with these people, so had David. Both English, both the same age as these stupid louts. So what was different? Why weren't we going around kicking the shit out of anybody who got in our way? And we knew they wanted to be like us, copying everything we did, or everything they could, like the way we looked, the way we dressed, our hairstyles and so on.

David and I have both got very strong personalities. We both knew where we were going, right from when we were very young. Of course I didn't know David when he was little, but the other day, when Brooklyn was rushing around kicking a football, David's mum Sandra said that he reminded her of David when he was that age, that she'd forgotten just what a menace he had been. We were talking about whether Brooklyn looked more like me or David.

'When his hair's spiked up,' she said, 'he looks like David but when his hair is flat I think he's more like you. But how he behaves is exactly how David did as a baby, into everything, he'd never sit still and always kicking a ball. As long as he was free to run around, he was happy. Give him a set of steps to climb up and down and he'd be quite content.'

As for me, I wanted to be a dancer. Not from as early as eighteen months perhaps, but from when I was about eight. So maybe it was easier for David and me, we both had a dream. There was nothing different between us and the football hooligans, except that we had ambition. We knew who we were and who we wanted to be, and nothing was going to stop us, it was only a question of time. Whereas they were so lacking in identity they had to paint red, white and blue stripes on their faces when they punched and kicked and drank. And now they would blame it on David.

Brooklyn was asleep by the time I got home. I still think of my mum and dad's house as home, because it's where I've lived ever since I can remember. Brooklyn's room wasn't there then: Dad made it a couple of years ago by going into the roof space, and putting in a dormer window.

My baby boy had kicked off his duvet and was lying spread out like a starfish, on top of Postman Pat. I lifted him up, moved Postman Pat to the top of the cot, then kissed his head with its silky brown hair, like David's. He smelled like toast. I covered him, then just sat there in the dark, listening to his breathing, like I used to do when he was first born, terrified he was going to stop.

The next morning David Beckham's one-finger salute to the England football supporters was front page on every newspaper, as I knew it would be. His 'yobbish' behaviour had taken over from football violence as the topic of media interest. Stuck in his hotel room in France I must have spoken to him twenty times that day. There was still no word from the FA. The last time he'd put two fingers up at the fans he'd been fined £25,000. But Kevin Keegan was being very supportive, he said. It turned out the manager had heard every word.

The next day, from the moment I got up the phone never stopped ringing. Press. Luckily I left the house around nine and missed the worst of it as I was in the recording studio most of the day. I keep telling my mum that she should change the phone number. But, as she always reminds me, apart from anything else, it's my dad's work number. There's no point in talking to them – it's not as if it made any difference to what they write. Inaccuracies, my mum calls them. She could have been a diplomat. Lies would be the word I'd use.

Next day, my call wasn't till the afternoon so I was in the kitchen just having a bowl of Crunchy Nut Corn Flakes and giving Brooklyn his cereal when the phone rang. The *Daily Mirror*. It was about ten o'clock.

'I've nothing to say.'

'We were just wondering if you'd seen the *Mail* today, Victoria.'

'Can't say I have.'

'Well, we're sending someone over with one, and a copy of the *Mirror*. Take a look at both. Perhaps we can talk later.'

In fact we did have a copy of the *Daily Mail*. I just hadn't read it.

Twenty minutes later, the buzzer went. Someone at the gate. I pressed the intercom.

'*Daily Mirror*. Newspapers for you.'

A woman's voice.

I looked at the screen. No cameras. Mum was upstairs having a bath.

'OK. I'll open the gates. Then if you can bring them to the front door. Over on the right.'

I tied the belt on my old Spice Girls Tour dressing

13

gown that David had got for all of us with our names on, but only opened the door a few inches.

'How do you feel about the way David's being hounded, Victoria?'

They always tried it on.

'Like I said, I don't want to say anything.'

'Well, perhaps you'll feel differently when you've read Roy Hattersley's piece in the *Mail*, and then ours supporting David.'

I smiled and took the newspapers.

'Thank you.'

And shut the door. I was taught always to be polite.

'Who was that, Victoria?'

Mum had come down, her hair in a towel, looking for the dryer.

'*Daily Mirror.*'

'What did they want?'

I was reading Roy Hattersley.

The phone went. Mum picked up the one on the wall. I didn't listen. I carried on reading what this Roy Hattersley person had written about David.

It began on the front page: right at the top, a picture of David with his finger up and the words *So, is this man a national liability? Turn to page 12.*

I turned to page 12. It went on and on – a whole page of it, but basically it said how can we expect England's young people to behave properly when they have such terrible role models as David Beckham and his Spice Girl wife? And I'm thinking, who is this prick?

'Daddy?'

'Yes, Victoria.'

My dad had just walked in and was making a cup of tea.

'Who is Roy Hattersley?'

'An MP I think.'

'What's he doing writing about football, then?'

Mum was holding the phone out to me.

'It's Alan. Says what do you want to do about Roy Hattersley?' Alan Edwards is the Spice Girls' PR and he handles anything to do with the press for me and David.

'Tell him I don't want to do anything *about* Roy Hattersley, but I know what I'd like to do *to* him.' But I took the phone anyway.

Over the next few days Roy Hattersley got what was coming to him. Not only from me, but it seemed from every other journalist in the country and 90 per cent of the population. Several newspapers ran dial-a-verdict lines for readers to phone in and vote for or against David. In the end it was something like 98 per cent for David. Kevin Keegan had decided to tell the papers exactly what he had heard these so-called England fans say, though the words were toned down a bit. I mean you wouldn't want to read what they really said over your Shredded Wheat.

Ted, David's dad, had also spoken to the press, something he never does. About how this was not the first time and how the abuse David got from so-called fans had been going on for years. Even a spokesman for the FA said they were 100 per cent for David and then had a go at Roy Hattersley – apparently the *Daily Mail*'s rent-a-quote was no longer an MP but a life peer – saying he didn't know what he was talking about. But then this was a man, I had found out, who wrote novels about what it's like to be a dog. If I hadn't despised him so much I might even have felt sorry for him. Joke. No, I wouldn't.

Suddenly everything had changed. When it came out what David had put up with he went from being 'a national liability' to a national hero, literally overnight, 'our greatest footballing hope for the future', blah blah blah. From hurling abuse at David, people would smile, and tap on the car windows, giving him the thumbs-up sign.

In all the time since we had known each other it had never happened before.

David is the most amazing footballer and I want him to be the best that he can. I will support him in anything he wants to do. I just want him to be happy. Although it was disappointing when England failed to reach the next round of Euro 2000, at least it meant David would be coming back to his family a little earlier than expected. We had so little time anyway – only three weeks before he had to be back in Manchester for pre-season training.

Just to make life easy I had my single coming out. In the same way as I support David over what's important to him, he supports me. In actual fact, it was David who persuaded me that the best way of stopping the constant caning I was getting – the only Spice Girl not to have gone solo – was to do something no one expected me to do. And this was definitely it.

Dane Bowers, a really bright young guy from the boyband Another Level who had recently gone solo himself, had this idea of having me sing with him on 'Out of Your Mind', a follow-up he'd written to 'Buggin'', which had been a surprise hit for him earlier in the year.

As soon as I heard the track, I was really excited. Because 'Out of Your Mind' like 'Buggin'' was dance music – a completely different world music-wise from pop – it had credibility. No one would be expecting Posh Spice to do anything like it. Then when Dane suggested we launch it at Party in the Park, The Prince's Trust charity show in Hyde Park at the beginning of July, everything fell into place. The record company were prepared to back us totally in what we wanted to do with the song: costumes, dancers, a great video. As Posh Spice I'd rarely had to do more than totter around in heels I could barely walk in. Most people probably had no idea I was a trained dancer.

Which was why I was so tired when I walked into the kitchen that evening, the day after David had come back from Belgium. Every morning that week I'd left home at seven, spent three hours rehearsing with the dancers, then gone to the other side of London to the Olympic Studios in Barnes working with Andrew Frampton and Steve Kipner, who had come over from LA specially to work with me on my new album.

So I was still hyped up when I got home and, while David carried on with his Jamie Oliver impression involving a piece of halibut and assorted chopped vegetables, I put on the tape of 'Out of Your Mind' and started doing the routine, with Brooklyn jigging around my feet singing 'Mind, Mind' – only eighteen months old and ready to boogie.

'So. What d'you think, Babes?' I said, peering over David's shoulder, my arms around his waist as he stood at the stove.

'Much smoother.'

'It's not meant to be smooth, you nutter,' I said whacking him over the head with a baguette. 'It's meant to be jagged, jerky, futuristic.' Suddenly exhausted, I flopped down on a chair by the kitchen table and began to pick from a bowl of grapes. Brooklyn put down his football, and ran over to me.

'Do you want some grapes, big boy?'

I lifted him up on to my lap. My God, he was getting so heavy.

'What do you say?'

'P e e s.'

'There's a good boy.'

David came over with my plate piled high. I was starving.

'Give Daddy a kiss?' he said, and Brooklyn turned his face up, his mouth in a kiss-shape.

'Now Mummy,' David said. And Brooklyn turned round and I put my face to his as David kissed the top of my head.

Happy families. Yeah. It nearly killed me this life – but it was all worth it.

Just then my mobile rang. Did I want to talk to this person? Probably not. The only person I wanted to talk to was right here cooking my dinner. I looked at the number. My lawyer. I listened and said nothing, then flicked the off key and closed my eyes.

'Anything wrong?' David always knows.

'Ever heard of Andrew Morton?'

'Don't think so.'

'Well,' I said, 'you have now.'

2 girl with a dream

'I'm going to be the richest, best-known and most beautiful model in the world.' No, not me – I never wanted to be a model, all that standing around being told what to do. It's what Jerry Hall is supposed to have told her mother when she was fourteen. But at least she probably looked the part, whereas when I said a similar thing to my mum I was a skinny, sallow-faced eight-year-old, with pigtails and a gap in my teeth big enough for a pea to get stuck in.

But what did that matter? I was a girl with a dream. It all started when my mum took me and my sister to see *Fame*, the Alan Parker film about the Manhattan school for performing arts. It was 1982 and I was eight and a quarter.

Sitting there in the dark was like being in a cartoon and a light bulb going on in my head. Suddenly I knew what I wanted to do – just like that – I wanted to be Coco, who not only danced like no one I had ever seen before, but looked fantastic, with wild frizzy hair and sang as if she would explode – 'I'm gonna live for ever, I'm gonna learn how to fly! High!'

'Mummy,' I said as we drove back home.

'Yes, Victoria.'

'Can I go there?'

'Where?'

'That school.'

'No, you can't.'

'Please, Mummy.'

'No.'

'Why not?'

'Because it's in New York.'

Didn't my mum understand? I had to go there, I just had to. How would I get to be a star otherwise? I would ask my nan. She would give me the money to get there. And I had £12 saved from Christmas and birthday money.

I got the record instead. I wasn't the only one. On 17 July 'Fame' sung by Irene Cara went to number 1 and stayed there for three weeks. It was in the top ten for sixteen weeks. A few weeks later the spin-off from the film began on BBC TV. Irene Cara wasn't in it any longer, there was a new Coco. But my other favourites were: a great dancer, a street kid called Leroy who never had any money, and a good-looking boy called Bruno with curly hair who played the piano and wrote songs. Even the teachers were nice. The only one I couldn't be bothered with was Julie, who played the cello and was a bit smug.

That Christmas, *The Kids from Fame* came over from America and Mum took me and Louise to see them at the Albert Hall. And this wasn't some touring cast, it was the real thing: Gene Anthony Ray as Leroy Johnson, Erica Gimpel as Coco Hernandez, Lee Curreri as Bruno

Martelli. I know as I've still got the programme. The night before I didn't sleep. Louise did, but then she was three years younger than me. Just because she had red hair, people were always smiling at her. I knew the truth, she was really boring, she didn't understand anything.

I lay in bed that night thinking that they might have a bit where the audience go up on the stage like they did at the Broxbourne pantomime every year, and then Coco would see me and might ask me to go to New York. I had literally never been so excited.

We nearly missed the beginning because we couldn't find anywhere to park and by the time we got to our seats I was near to exploding. Sometimes things you have been looking forward to that much are a let-down, but not this. Apart from the Broxbourne pantomime, which we went to every year – my mum and dad were always big on family traditions – it was the first live show I had ever been to. The energy of the dancers, and being so close to them, totally hooked me. On the way out my mum got me and my sister *Kids from Fame* velour tracksuits with gold lettering on the back. Mine was blue and Louise's was red.

It was then I began to pester my mum about learning to dance. I'd started ballet when I was about three but had left after only a few weeks, so she wasn't about to waste her money again, she said.

'But I'm older now,' I said, jumping from one sofa to the other and leapfrogging over Louise. 'And I promise, promise, promise, promise, I won't give up. And I promise I'll be nice to Louise. Please, Mummy. *Pleee-eee-eeese.*'

That Christmas when we went to the pantomime,

which was about four miles from where we lived, my mum noticed how all the children in the show came from a local dance and drama school. The next day she phoned up and I was enrolled to start in January. They told us we could get everything we needed at a shop called Danceworks in Hoddesdon, one town further north. Danceworks was just off the market and my mum got me ballet shoes, jazz shoes, leotard and leg warmers. I was on my way.

It was at a Barry Manilow concert about six months later that I first informed the world (in the shape of my mum, her friend Pam Davies and my best friend Amanda Davies) that I was going to be famous. Amanda and me were always being dragged along to concerts by our mums – Amanda's mum was a massive Barry Manilow fan and a member of the Barry Manilow fan club.

As usual I hadn't much wanted to go, but this was in Blenheim Palace and I quite liked the idea of going to a palace. It turned out to be a field full of sheep-shit and we had to watch this giant nose from about twenty miles away, stuck behind a giant electricity pylon.

'One day I'm going to be doing that,' I said. Strange considering Barry Manilow was not exactly Michael Jackson. But I just loved the whole stage thing. For my next birthday Amanda bought me a pair of Barry Manilow laces. They were grey and they said Barry Manilow all over them. I put them in my trainers. Sad.

In actual fact, I quite liked Barry Manilow and still do, not like Cliff Richard who I couldn't stand even then. He should have stayed on that bloody bus and carried on with his summer holiday. But both our mums were really into him. I knew my mum had pictures of the old lizard stuck on the inside of her wardrobe before she met my dad. We went to a concert of his in October 1983 at Wembley when he'd just brought out his *Silver* album, which as Cliff Richard albums go is probably the best. (Silver for twenty-five years in the business, don't you know.) It was a very new image, very eighties. He had the suit, and the tie undone and the shirt undone. And we're all sitting there and I turned to my mum and said, 'I'm going to be up there one day.' Watching Cliff prancing about with his shoulder pads and puffed-up hair giving the coachloads of mums at Wembley the old razzle-dazzle, I thought, Yeah, I could do that.

Like I said, we are great ones for family traditions and every year just before Christmas we'd go up to Oxford Street to see the lights being switched on. And I just knew one day that it would be me up there, high above the crowd.

'Someday I'm going to do that,' I blurted out as we watched whoever it was that year from down below. Weird or what?

I must have been a right pain.

'She'll have her work cut out,' Christine Shakespeare told my mum when I started classes. 'Dancing is 90 per cent hard work and 10 per cent talent. You'll have to work till you drop, Victoria.'

What was she talking about? Work? Work was reading and sums. Dancing was like Maltesers and ice-cream, like popcorn, like strawberry milk shake, like the seaside.

I was about three years older than any of the other girls in the beginners class and Miss Christine, as we were allowed to call her, told my mum that one class a week wouldn't be enough if I wanted to get into the pantomime next year. So at first I went twice a week – ballet and jazz – later this was doubled.

The ballet was the most difficult. At home I practised hour after hour in my room, using the rail at the bottom of my bed as a barre.

'Are you doing your homework, Victoria?' my mum would shout up from downstairs.

'Yes, Mummy,' I shouted back over the beat of my Walkman.

I wasn't afraid of hard work. I'd always had to work hard at junior school just to keep up: I was never one of the clever ones. Looking back at my dancing, I was never the best dancer either. The difference was that it never felt like work because I absolutely loved every minute.

When my mum first said she'd got me into the Jason School of Dance and Drama, I imagined something a bit like the school in *Fame*: locker rooms, noticeboards, a big gym with wall-to-wall mirrors. In fact our classes were held anywhere they could find in Broxbourne that had a wooden floor: church halls and even a scout hut. Only one place had a barre and mirrors. But my disappointment only lasted about two minutes because Miss Christine was a really nice person. She had been a professional dancer but was now rather pear-shaped, although she still had tiny dancer's feet and a lovely face.

'Prepare.'

Feet in first position at right-angles to each other, left arm on the barre, right arm held out to the side, or as Christine called it *'port de bras en seconde'*.

A nod to Mrs Hawkins at the piano, and one, two, three, four . . .

'To the side, two, point, four, and again, six, stretch, eight.'

And over and over, the leather soles of seven or eight pink ballet pumps swishing across the wooden floor. Up, hold, down, hold. Up, hold, down, hold. And point, point, point.

Then plié. I was so thin my tights bagged at the knees.

'Back straight, Victoria.'

'Bend those knees, Lindsay.'

'Chin up, Lorraine.'

'Point those toes!'

'Stomach IN!'

'Knees OUT!'

'Bottom IN.'

'Head STILL.'

'Once more from the top please, Mrs Hawkins.'

With Christine Shakespeare, the more I did, the more I wanted to do, though I never understood why she had to use French words for everything. Soon I was going every day after school. But at least I was never bored. Not like my ordinary school, Goff's Oak Primary, which had gone wrong from day one.

My class teacher was horrible, which was a bit unfortunate because she was the only teacher I had the whole of that first year. We had her all day, every day. She was like the Wicked Witch of the West, only worse. She looked almost as old as my nanna, my mum's mum, all wrinkled up, but not in a comforting way. She wore grey suits and salmon-coloured blouses with ruffles on them. But her being horrible was nothing to do with her age. My nanna was wrinkled and old but she was lovely. Even if she wasn't that old, Mrs Horrible certainly wasn't one of those teachers that let you experiment. Reading was the worst. The books we learnt to read from were Janet and John.

'Oooh, Janet and John, Victoria,' my mum said when I brought the first one home. It must have been quite nostalgic for her: these were the same books she learnt to read from in the fifties. Janet and John had a mum and a dad and a dog and went to the shops. And that was about it. We used to read Janet and John every day. And when one Janet and John was finished you moved on to the next Janet and John. Janet and John didn't only dominate my life at school, they dominated my life at home, too. I remember sitting down with my mum for painful hours and hours reading bloody Janet and John. This went on for months. By now no one else was still reading Janet and John – they were reading Roger Red Hat and Billy Blue Hat and Jennifer Yellow Hat. Finally came the great moment when I reached the back page of the last book.

I went into school the next morning really excited. Everyone got a star when they'd finished Janet and John. Now I would get a star. I remember standing at Mrs Horrible's desk in front of the class, in a queue waiting my turn, jigging from foot to foot. Mrs Horrible takes the book with its sheet inside that my mum has ticked and signed. I feel so excited: I've reached the back page and now I'm going to get a star like everyone else.

But Mrs Horrible, the old witch, says no.

'No.' She repeats it when I just stand there, still holding my book out, not understanding, the blood flooding into my face, as she hands the book back. 'If you've read it once, you'll have no difficulty reading it again, will you, Victoria?'

The class went quiet. All the early morning chattering has stopped, no squeaking of chairs. I can feel them all looking at me, thinking how clever they are – they all had their stars – and how stupid I was.

'So, now, back to your seat and you can start from the beginning again. And then you can have a star.'

Even now I can remember that walk back to my desk, the other children's heads bent low over their books trying not to look at me.

I blinked hard. I felt something in my eyes. The next playtime, even my friend Amanda didn't play with me. She joined in a skipping game with some of the other girls. There was an old hopscotch game marked out in chalk at the other end of the playground and I found a stone and played it on my own.

Mrs Horrible was a witch, I decided. And she'd put a spell on me. And I knew that at her house she'd got a witch's hat and a broomstick and she collected things like spiders and ants and made spells with them.

I can't have been even six. Not old enough to ever have hated anybody. But I hated Mrs Horrible. And I think she must have hated me. But I don't know why. I was never late. I was always neat and tidy. I never forgot my indoor shoes. She told me that I was backward. How traumatizing is that?

'It's a pity they don't have a remedial class here, Victoria, because that's where you belong.'

So Mrs Horrible put me at the back of the class so that I wouldn't be a bad influence on the others.

These days if they see you are a slow reader they might think you are dyslexic and give you extra help, or at least be nice to you. I don't think I was dyslexic, I think I was just bored out of my mind.

Although I had one or two good teachers over the years, teachers who encouraged me and didn't make me feel a total inadequate, Mrs Horrible was my first teacher and she completely destroyed my self-confidence, because after that I refused to do anything that reminded me of her. Like reading. And I think that's what stopped me reading – because I was starved from a really young age.

Goff's Oak Primary School was like an old-fashioned village school, although Goff's Oak was not exactly a village. It had been once, but by the time we moved there it was what it is now, a comparatively well-off suburb of the commuter towns (thirty minutes to Liverpool Street) that stretch north out of London along the A10, past the M25 as far as Hertford, like Waltham Cross, Cheshunt, Broxbourne and Hoddesdon. Although it was so close to Central London, there were no black people in our school. Not one; in fact, nobody foreign at all. We were all nice little white girls and boys. And looking back on it, we all led a very sheltered life.

My best friend, Amanda Davies, was very pretty, with short blonde hair, nice hands, nice fingernails, perfect skin, and glasses. She was the sort of girl who, as we got older, would bend the school uniform to make it look cool. We had to wear a brown knee-length skirt with thick pleats, a golden-coloured shirt and a tie that was gold and brown, and a brown jumper and a brown blazer with a crest on it. Her skirt was always slightly shorter. She always had a very cool pencil case, a very cool school satchel and she even had high-heels. I was always neat but never cool.

Once a week, after mid-morning break, we had Show and Tell, where you brought some interesting thing into school and talked about it to the rest of the class, like a bird's nest. Other people always seemed to have more interesting things than me for Show and Tell, particularly Amanda.

I can still remember things she brought in – like a beetle, bright red, a Roman coin her dad had found near the Roman road you could walk along in Broxbourne Woods, an old green bottle with a stopper like a marble.

One of the most interesting things I found to bring in was a wiggly piece of plastic, which looked like part of a puzzle you might get in a cracker. My mum had just come home from hospital with my new brother Christian and she showed this wiggly thing to all her friends who came to visit her and said how he had come out waving it in his hand. They all seemed very interested.

'Come here, Victoria. What's that you've got?'

'Just something for Show and Tell.'

'Open your hand.'

I open my hand.

'You're not taking that to school.'

'But, Mummy, why not?'

'Because it's not suitable.'

'Why not?'

'Because it's my coil.'

'What's a coil?'

'It's to stop having babies.'

'But you've just had a baby.'

Sometimes grown-ups were hard to understand, even my mum. Instead of being cross with me, she seemed to be laughing.

'No more questions. If you don't hurry up there won't be time to do your plaits and it'll have to be bunches.' My mum always did my hair until I was about fourteen.

As I got older I stopped just standing around in the playground watching the other children playing hop-scotch, or skipping or just whispering together in the playground, and did what I enjoyed, dancing. I didn't just dance around, I would make up whole dances that had a story. Sometimes it was ballet, sometimes modern. Then, when afternoon registration was over, our teacher, who was then Mrs Hardy, would say, 'And do you have a dance for us today, Victoria?' And I would say yes. Then she would tell the rest of the class to sit down and I would take my place in front of the form, put on the tape of whatever I was going to do, then begin. This would happen literally every day. Or so I seem to remember.

I was so eager to perform – I felt more at home on the stage than sitting behind a desk. If I didn't make them smile, I'd make them laugh, and that's what performing is all about. Every Christmas we did a school show and I would do anything to be in it, if at all possible the main part. One year we were told it was going to be *Frostie the Snowman*. And Mrs Hardy said, 'Does anybody have anything that looks like a snowman outfit?' Up shot my hand. 'I have.'

Well, I would have by the next morning. My mum was brilliant with costumes. Whenever there was a fancy-dress competition, she would make something really special for me and Louise. She loved competitions – our Yorkshire terrier had even won Prettiest Dog prize. I knew she would make the best snowman outfit you could imagine. And she did, out of lining material left over from some curtains. It was shaped like a ginger-bread man, with big black buttons which I wore with a top hat, and a scarf.

We lived about a mile from the school in the house that had been Goff's Oak village school until the sixties when the new one was built. It was a black and white arts-and-crafts-style Victorian building. My mum saw the ad in a newspaper she had put on the kitchen floor. Our dog at the time, a Yorkshire terrier called Samantha, was very old and she did a wee on it. That's how she noticed the ad: 'A magnificent detached character residence standing in a third of an acre in a pleasant rural position.'

At the time we were living in a small house in Hoddes-don that my mum and dad had bought when they got married and where I was born on 17 April 1974. I wasn't actually born in Caxton Road, I was born in a hospital in Harlow, but for years I tried to forget about that because Harlow is in Essex. Spice Girl yes, Essex Girl no.

The Old School House was more than they could afford but they bought it anyway. There were no other houses there in 1977, just the church and the pub at the end of the road, but it wasn't rural rural. If you believed the newspapers, you would think we were in the middle of the country. It was nothing like that. We were surrounded by old nurseries – hundreds of greenhouses wherever you looked, left over from the time when the Lea Valley grew more tomatoes and cucumbers than anywhere else in England. Most of them have gone now, turned into mini-estates of detached executive-style houses. Dad thinks the greenhouses were an eyesore anyway and says the new houses aren't so bad because they're only allowed to build four to the acre. But I miss them. The greenhouses. Sometimes the glass glinted so much it was like being at the seaside. And I've always wanted to live by water.

The people who did the conversion had put in an upstairs, but even they knew it wasn't very well done and so my dad decided to rip everything out and start again. He was a great one for ripping houses apart. He even did it in the house in Hoddesdon and that was brand new. What people really wanted was Georgian-looking windows, he'd decided, so if he put some in he'd get a better price when they sold, even if it was on a seventies estate.

My earliest memories are seeing my sister crawling through piles of cement. I was three and a half and she was one. For the first few years it was like living on a building site; it was hideous, with the inside walls half knocked down. I remember climbing over radiators and sinks and planks of wood and having doors with no handles. The only room that was done was a bedroom which Louise and I shared.

My dad had just started up his own business as an electrical wholesaler so they couldn't afford to get workmen in. My dad is amazing, did most of the work himself, helped by builder friends and my grandad, my mum's dad, who was a retired docker.

He had crinkly hair swept back from his forehead, and was a bit bald on top. Grandad was a complete gentleman. Even when he was doing the garden, he would wear a suit, and even on a hot day he'd ask before he took his jacket off. Underneath he always had a V-necked sleeveless jumper – 'so as not to catch his death', Nanna said. For years I was worried that death was something you could catch.

My mum's family came from Tottenham, in North London, which in those days was quite posh, at least compared with Edmonton, which was a bit further to the east, where my dad came from. And they were quite well off. Grandad worked very long hours and my nan used to let out a room to footballers from Tottenham Hotspur, funnily enough, which was just down the road. This was way back, when footballers used to earn about £9 a week.

Since Grandad worked in the docks he was always bringing back weird animals – his little stowaways, Nanna called them. They had a penguin that they kept in the bath and a monkey called Jackie. I loved listening to my nan telling me stories of Jackie, how he was really naughty and how he loved jam and how once he had taken a jar of jam out of the cupboard and was running around the kitchen with it, on the dresser, up the curtains. This was in the war and my nan had saved up all her ration coupons to get this jam. And she was saying, please Jackie, give me the pot of jam. And Jackie just threw it on the floor and smashed it. In the end they gave Jackie to a zoo when he got out of hand.

Then when my mum was born they called her Jackie. I once asked my mum if she minded being called after a monkey. She said she had never thought about it.

My grandparents waited until the war was over before they had my mum. By then Nanna was thirty-nine and it was too late to have any more children, which is why my mum doesn't have any brothers or sisters.

I loved my nan and grandad. Tottenham wasn't that far by car, and they often used to babysit. Sometimes we would go over to them, but usually they came to us. I remember sitting at the window waiting for their old Ford Zephyr to come racing up the road. And racing was the word. Death on wheels, Mum called him. There was no indicating, no slowing down. It got so bad that when I was about ten she stopped us going in the car with him.

When we saw the car swerve into the drive, all three of us would race downstairs and fight to be the first to open the front door. Nanna always had something in her pocket for us. My mum being an only child, they had really spoilt her, and now they did the same to us. This was at a time when my mum and dad didn't have anything. They couldn't even afford an oven – my mum did all the cooking on a Primus stove. I remember once going to buy her a birthday present with my dad and we got her shampoo and conditioner and soap because he couldn't afford anything else. And I remember getting really angry and wanting to buy her something myself.

But my nan always had a little something for us in her pocket. 'Here's some money, don't tell your mum or your grandad,' she'd say. Or else it might be sweets. Not like my other grandmother. Once I saw her hide a box

34

of chocolates that someone had given her, just so she didn't have to give any to us. But I still loved her, after all she was my nan.

The Adams family weren't anything like my mum's, the Cannons. When my mum started going out with my dad, my nan said she had thought he was 'a bit of a yob' but once they got to know him she thought the world of him. He was like the son she never had, she said.

In fact, my dad's childhood had been rather sad. His earliest memories were having to collect dog-ends from the ashtrays in the pub for his father to smoke. My dad was one of those kids who had to hang around outside the pub for hour after hour waiting for his dad to come out. And I think his mum was pretty much the same. They used to get him to do all the work around the house. He never had toys or anything like that. One Christmas they got him a bike and he couldn't believe it. He was dead right. They forgot to tell him that he had to keep up the repayments. When they heard he was going to get married, the first thing they said was, 'So who's going to do our decorating now, then?' But even knowing this didn't stop me loving them. After all, they were my grandparents.

My parents got married in the church opposite where my mum lived in Westbury Avenue. They had met at a party. My mum was going out with somebody else at the time. 'A real good-looking bloke of about six foot four,' Dad says. And Dad is only about five foot nine. Anyway, this bloke went off somewhere and Jackie and Tony – that's my dad's name – ended up having a snog. But then this bloke came back and emptied a cup of coffee over both of them. My mum still went off with him, but the next week my dad got her phone number and that was that.

My mum was only seventeen when they started going out. She was working for the Phoenix Assurance company in Pall Mall. I wasn't born till nearly ten years later, but I still remember her as being very glamorous, with long dark hair and blue eyes. She's still glamorous, perhaps even more so these days because now she has the clothes. She's just as skinny but her long dark hair is now blonde and short.

We lived about a mile from the school so Dad used to take us in the car, a bright green Hillman Avenger estate, but he took all the seats out to use it as a van. So we had to squeeze in among a tangle of cables and boxes of plugs and switches, and long neon tubes. Some of the cables came wound round things like massive cardboard cotton reels and I would always try to sit on one of those, so as not to mess up my uniform. But if we thought that was bad, it was nothing compared to having to ride in my dad's Rolls-Royce.

3 a certain age

Like me, Dad is a complete workaholic. He never stops; if he's not in the office, he's out delivering. If he's not out delivering he's in the garden in his wellingtons getting weeds out of the pond, or taking flies off the swimming pool, or mending locks, or a squeaky door. Then his mobile phone will ring and you'll hear just one side of the conversation. Things like:

'You're making me cry, Keith.'

'Are you waiting for me to start playing the violin, Tel?'

As well as more obvious things like: 'Tell Ray if he brings the unit price down by 15 per cent, then it's a deal.'

Photographers standing outside my parents' house waiting to snatch a picture of me or David think we're always having things delivered: vans pulling up, boxes being handed over and signed for. They don't realize most of it is just electrical components destined for the garage. You won't find any cars in the garage in the house in Goff's Oak, just cables and boxes of plugs and sockets. Upstairs is Dad's office. People have this vision of a big wholesaling company, with drivers and salesmen. But it's just him.

Whenever Dad had a rush order on he'd bring all the bits he needed into the lounge and we'd have this mini production line.

'Come on, children,' my mum would call. And we'd run in and sit in front of whichever pile we'd been given. It was made into a game: we all had our special thing to do. Christian, my brother, because he was littlest, would get one of these things out and pass it to me. I'd then add some part from my pile of screws or whatever it was, then pass it to Louise. Louise would then add something else and pass it to Mum, who would add something else. Dad would then check over what we'd done and pack it all up. We were the Von Trapps of the light fittings and electrical components world. We did this for years.

From when I was very young, I always remember my dad saying the same thing over and over again: 'If I want things done properly, I have to do it myself.'

'But you work so hard, such long hours,' we'd say. 'You're tired, you don't have as good a social life as you could have. You've worked so hard for what you've got. You should go out, go on more holidays.'

But he'd always come back with the same thing: 'If I want anything done, I have to do it myself, because I can't rely on anyone else to do it.'

Dad is a perfectionist. It drives my mum mad because he can be very stroppy if he doesn't get his own way and that's such a pain. It takes one to know one.

During the eighties the business was doing so well that he bought a second-hand Rolls-Royce, a Silver Shadow Mk 2, a browny colour, but the press prefer to call it gold. My dad had a difficult childhood and he was determined to do better for himself and having a Rolls-Royce was always his dream. Funnily enough, he isn't that interested in cars, the total opposite of David who's a car-a-holic. So there's David talking about engine size, delivering this b.h.p. and that torque, and Dad's looking completely blank. Most of the time he wouldn't know how to undo the bonnet and look in the engine.

I hated that Rolls-Royce right from the word go. The people round us might be quite wealthy compared to other parts of the country, but that didn't mean they had Rolls-Royces. We had the mickey taken out of us so much. Me and my brother and sister used to beg my dad to please take us in the van but it was like talking to a fridge.

He says now that we didn't go in the Rolls very often, only when he was on his way to see a client. But that car blighted my life. Why couldn't we have a Maestro like Amanda Davies? With her glasses and her high-heels she had everything I wanted, whereas me and Louise looked like that advert for Startrite shoes, all polished and matching.

My mum had always wanted twins so me and Louise were the twins she never had. We would go shopping for clothes in the Harvey Centre in Harlow and come back with two of everything in different colours. One Christmas we even had to wear identical knickerbockers, except for the colour. Once I remember my mum even crocheted matching outfits for us. It was all right for Louise, she was three years younger than me, as well as being pretty and cute, whereas I was this ugly duckling with no teeth. With her freckles and curly red hair and perfect skin, Louise was the sort of little girl that won beautiful baby competitions. When she was little complete strangers would come up to her in the street.

'What lovely hair.'

My mum would smile and Louise would smile.

'Such a pretty baby.'

And Louise would chortle.

I know I'm not pretty. Everyone likes Louise. They don't like me. And who can blame them, with my pinched face and scraped-back hair I look like one of those children who get put up for adoption.

Sometimes, even my mum was horrible. Like telling me I couldn't have high-heels.

'I won't have you looking like a tart, Victoria.'

What did she mean, a tart? What kind of tart? My nanna made blackberry and apple tarts sometimes. And in Broxbourne there was a shop which had tarts, with lovely strawberries and raspberries all in patterns.

So what about glasses, then? Would they make me look like a tart?

'Don't be so stupid, Victoria.'

'So can I get some, then?'

'Not unless there's something wrong with your eyes.'

Before I started dancing, my mum had sent me to have piano lessons. My nan was a brilliant piano player. She couldn't read music, but she could play anything, from 'Roll Out the Barrel' to Beatles' songs and even 'Fame'. She only had to hear something once, and she could do it.

Funnily enough, my teacher was called Mrs Adams.

She was a widow and lived in Broxbourne in a big semi-detached house in a wide street. Even though there were big windows, she always had the lights on inside, even in the summer, because the shrubbery and trees around the house were so overgrown. Inside it was horrible; everything was old and dirty. It smelled of mould and mothballs and cats. Not just one or two cats but hundreds of them. I think she must have collected them – she was one of those people who never threw anything away. The piano was dark brown and the lid squeaked whenever it went up or down. The only light was a chandelier high up in the ceiling that was missing half its bulbs. It was a junk house. And Mrs Adams was probably as old as the house, with crinkly grey hair that was so thin you could see her scalp through it. I remember saying to my mum once, what do I do if she dies when I'm having a lesson there? Who do I ring?

And just like with reading I was bored stiff. We did scales and silly tunes like 'Old MacDonald Had a Farm' and Mrs Adams was a right miserable old cow, always moaning at me. There was this thing called a metronome that was supposed to help you keep time. It was a triangular brown box that you took the front off and then wound up with a key on the side and this big hand would move from side to side, like a windscreen wiper. Tick, tick, tick, tick. You could change it from faster to slower. But however slow she put it, I could never keep up. And my fingers were never high enough for Mrs Adams. They were supposed to be curved like claws. She used to put a ruler under my fingers to keep them from flopping on the keyboard. Sometimes she would whack them with the ruler.

There was nothing modern about her way of teaching, nothing to get someone of my age interested. Even my dad's old Beatles' songs that Nanna played would have been better than the stuff I had to do. One day I was staring at the same sheet of music for so long it started to go blurred. So I told Mrs Adams I couldn't go on because I couldn't see the music. So then she told my mum that I had something wrong with my eyes. I didn't know that's what happens if you stare at something long enough.

So finally I was going to get glasses. Just in case they didn't think my eyes were bad enough, I decided it might be safest not to see all of the letters that they hold up in front of you. Even the big ones. My mum became really worried.

'See that Escort, Victoria?' The idea was that I had to read the numberplate.

We would be on our way to dancing. My mum would pick me up from school then the driving started. Down Newgatestreet Road to the crossroads, through the village, into Cheshunt, under the A10, and down to the Methodist Hall or the Scout hut. About fifteen minutes.

'It's too far away, Mummy.'

'No it's not. Just try.'

But by this time the Escort would have turned left or right, or overtaken a bus. So she'd try another one.

'What about that Astra?'

I made something up.

Or we'd stop at traffic lights so that a car or lorry was so close a mole could read it.

But not me. My mum thought I was going blind. She

was so painstaking. They ended up taking me to an eye specialist in Harley Street, having this test and that test. The man in the white coat put these heavy frames on, then different lenses were slotted in, first the right eye, then the left eye, one lens on top of another, until it was so heavy I felt my nose would drop off.

'Now, Victoria. How's that?' the man said, putting yet another lens into the holder.

'Oh yes. I can see much better now, thank you.'

I felt very smug. And this time it wasn't a lie. I really could see much better. It was only a question now of choosing the frames. I had seen a pair I really liked in a shop in Harlow.

My excitement was short-lived. It turned out the last lenses he had put in were clear glass. There was nothing wrong with my eyes at all. So I never got the spectacles, at least not till years later. But at least it was the end of the piano lessons.

I didn't mind all the travelling to Broxbourne and back because it meant I could be with my mum. I don't know if it was because I didn't really have any friends but I had to be near her to feel safe. I used to think there was a string attached to the top of my head joining me to my mum. If we were walking in the street and there was a bin, say, then I would have to go round the bin the same way as my mum because if not I'd feel like this string would get messed up and my head would get messed up. Sometimes I'd walk to the end of the street and realize I'd gone the wrong way round a lamp-post or something, not the way my mum went, and I'd have to go back and go round the lamp-post the same way my mum had, otherwise I'd feel all knotted up inside.

It was like mental torture. A bit like you hear of people who have obsessive-compulsive disorder and go, God, did I lock the door? and go back to check, then it's the same thing, God, did I lock the door? and they go back again. It was like that but I'd be thinking, did I go the right way round the bin? or the right way round the car? I was never like my brother or sister. They never had any trouble staying away from home, always going on school trips and things. Not me.

One night we went to stay at my Auntie Sheila and Uncle Eric's house. My mum and dad were having a dinner party or something. Auntie Sheila is my dad's sister, she's quite a bit older than him, and she and Uncle Eric have a daughter, Karen. Anyway, my mum and dad drove us to their house in Tottenham and it was the first time I had ever been away from home and I really didn't want to go. So it was all done like it was a bit of an adventure, and after we'd unpacked Auntie Sheila and Uncle Eric took us all out to a big old-fashioned restaurant on the A10 – like a Beefeater kind of place.

It was split level and we were upstairs. And although they'd only been gone for about half an hour I was really feeling homesick and before the food arrived I went to find the toilet. And I'm standing there on the landing and what do I see coming up the dual carriageway but my dad's Rolls-Royce and I felt totally panicky at the idea of not being with them.

So I go back to the table and everyone else is looking happy but I am just all nerves and when I'm like that I get really clumsy and I somehow knocked my steak knife, one of those wooden-handled ones with a serrated edge, off the table. The next thing, there's a shriek from downstairs, and we look over the side to the floor below, and my knife is sticking up like a dagger in the middle of a table.

That was it. The waitresses were freaking out, I was freaking out. My auntie and uncle had to call my mum and dad and get them to come and collect us. That was the last time I stayed away from home until I went to college.

Compared with junior school, secondary school was hell. I was an outsider from the very first day. Most of my old class had got places in Goff's, the school for clever kids where they did what was called total immersion – like having history and maths classes taught in French and German. My parents claim that they decided St Mary's would be better for me, more caring. But the truth is I wasn't clever enough to go to Goff's.

If I had gone there, things might have been different; at least most of the kids came from the same kind of background I did. But St Mary's was right in the middle of two huge council estates in Cheshunt. 'London over-spill' as people who didn't live there called it. These kids had never come across anyone like me and I had never come across people like them.

About a week before I started at St Mary's a girl from junior school thought it would be nice for me to meet somebody else who was going whose name was Angelina Foley. She had all this blonde hair, and was very grown-up and everything. I remember her coming round to my house in the holidays and saying, 'Are you bussing it?' What did she mean – are you bussing it? I didn't know what she meant, so I didn't answer. But of course that's what everybody did, it meant getting the bus every day. I had never been on a bus in my life. So it's like, No. I'm going in the Rolls-Royce.

Then there was the uniform. They'd given us this list and I turned up on the first day with the exact uniform, the St Mary's bag which my mum had even sewn a badge on, the right shoes, the right socks, the right tie. Now I realize that no one else could afford them. They had any old grey skirt and jumper and a Tesco's carrier bag. You had a choice of a grey pleated skirt or a kilt. Most kids had one or the other, I had both. Then you had a white shirt; most people's was a bit crinkly. Mine was always ironed. And I always had the correct tie, not tied the short trendy way or the thick trendy way. I was so not a rebel. In the winter, you had a choice: you either didn't have a coat and froze or you had a mac, a grey-looking horrible thing that went below the knee. Or you could have a duffel coat with a great hood that did up like Paddington Bear. Believe it or not, I thought the mac would be much more trendy. But no. I had the Paddington Bear because my mum and dad said I would be warmer 'standing around in the playground'. How right they were. Because while everybody else was mucking about and gossiping with their friends, I was stood on my own in a corner of the playground in a puddle with this Paddington Bear coat, the toggles all done up, looking like a complete geek.

I was a total misfit. No one would talk to me. When it came to PE lessons I'd be the one standing up against the wall that no one would pick for their team. I was the one that no one wanted to sit next to in class.

What did I care? I didn't need friends, I had my family. I mean, look at them. Who would want to be like them anyway, all dirty, shirts hanging out, buttons missing, shoes scuffed. What do they think they look like? Don't they have mothers to look after them?

I might have tried to look as though I didn't care. But it hurt, even though I pretended that it didn't. For them going out into the playground was the best part of the day. For me it was like being sent out on to the ice at the North Pole. At least in class, even if no one wanted to sit next to me, I could get on with my work. But out in the playground with everyone else rushing around, it was like hell. At my junior school at least I'd been able to practise my dancing at breaktime. Here I couldn't do that – at least, not so anyone could see. But I did them in my head, planning new dance ideas. Going through routines till I was move perfect. When I was dancing my body seemed to belong to me but standing in the playground on my own, none of me felt connected and everything felt clumsy and too big; like sometimes just before you fall asleep every bit of you feels like it's double its real size and made of lead. Other people seemed to be happy with what they looked like, as if every bit of them was them. I felt that every bit of me was a spare part that didn't really fit. Every bit of me was ugly. It must be, otherwise why did no one want to be my friend? One day I'd show them. One day I'd be famous. And then they'd be sorry.

I didn't seem to have anything in common with any of them. In fact I thought they were silly. And it wasn't just me finding a way of coping with the loneliness. I really felt that. I didn't find the work easy so when I was in class I wanted to concentrate, not muck around like most of the other kids. I worked hard even then.

It wasn't a cool thing to work hard and do your homework. Even so I was never in the top stream, I never got straight As. But in my last year I was made a steward, St Mary's version of school prefects, and that was only because I was a swot and grassed on other children to the headmaster and I really didn't care. I might not have been clever, but I was always responsible and the teachers knew it. I had to be organized the amount I was having to cram in my life outside school.

It was also very much not cool to be into dancing or singing. By the time I started at secondary school, I'd be at some dance class or rehearsal every single night: tap, ballet, modern, jazz, and national – Irish, Scottish, Polish – the kind of thing where you had to wear some dodgy long skirt and clogs.

After school most of the kids would hang around the chip shop or off-licences, smoking or snogging boys. Whereas as soon as the bell went, I was off, down the end of the drive and just praying that my mum would be there and that I wouldn't have to wait. Because some days the boys who teachers used to call 'the rough element' would threaten to 'get me' and the teachers had to walk with me up to the road, so that I didn't get beaten up.

Another reason I didn't have friends, apart from the uniform, the Rolls-Royce, the dancing, the grassing on other kids, was spots. The ugly duckling with pigtails was now an ugly duckling with spots. Anybody notice that whenever I describe someone I'll always mention their perfect skin? That's because if you haven't got one, it's something you notice. I've had spots for years and years and years. You'd have thought I'd have grown out of them now that I'm a wife, mother and half of that oh-so-glamorous celebrity couple Posh and Becks. But no. Out they come, just to remind me that money can't buy you everything. I'll go to bed, brush my teeth, wash my face, look in the mirror and – nothing. Then in the morning, there they are, like bloody mushrooms on the lawn saying: that'll teach you.

Spots began to dominate my life from when I was about thirteen and I never went out of the house without make-up. I had all the creams and lotions, the blemish disguisers, the spot shrinkers, the concealers, not to mention cover-up foundation, as thick as paint. Boots must have made a fortune out of me. I would get up at least an hour before my sister to do it properly. But every day after registration I was told the same thing. To go to the toilets and 'scrub that make-up off '. So, being the good little girl I was, I'd go off to the toilets and scrub that make-up off. Then, at lunchtime I'd be back there putting it all back on again. And the toilets would be thick with smoke, packed with girls puffing away on their fags, risking lung cancer, not to mention pregnancy and assorted sexually transmitted diseases down the back of the field. Yet I was the one getting told off.

The other thing I always notice is boobs. Same reason. This time because I don't have any and never did. I was completely flat until I was twelve, a stick.

St Mary's was a Church of England school and once a week we had to go to church, which was right next door. That first term it was an Indian summer, really hot, and we were all just walking around in shirts rather than blazers or toggle-coats. The boys had this game where they used to run their fingers down your back to see if you had a bra on. And of course I didn't. I was so embarrassed I asked my mum if I could get one. It was called a training bra, it came in a box marked Double A and consisted of two cotton triangles. It was a complete waste of time and money – I had nothing to put in it.

But I never really worried as much about my boobs as I did my spots, because at dancing nobody had boobs. In fact it was important *not* to have boobs. At dancing I wasn't an outsider at all. I even had friends. There was myself, Louise Pickering, whose mum ran Danceworks in Hoddesdon, Lindsey Gritten and Lorraine Weather-hog. Although they lived in Broxbourne, and I lived in Goff's Oak, we were all quite similar and our parents would mix socially. The Weatherhogs are friends of my mum and dad even now.

By this time I was sometimes doing three classes a night. And my mum was like a chauffeur, because the classes weren't always in the same building. No sooner had she gone home to cook my dad's dinner, when she'd have to turn round and come back again. She did so much travelling it was ridiculous: miles and miles and miles. She knew what I wanted to do, she was so support-ive. No wonder I feel I owe her everything. By that time she had my sister dancing, too – although Louise never took to it like I did, she was more docile. Mum had registered us both with a model agency. They loved Louise with her cute freckles, her perfect skin and her curly red hair. But not the moody old cow with spots.

Myself and Lindsey were probably the best in our group and we used to compete against each other in competitions and things. In actual fact, she's done very well. She's got a great voice and is a really good dancer and has been in a couple of West End shows. Our dancing lives were driven by exams. You did Grade 1 through to Grade 6. Then pre-elementary, elementary, intermediate and advanced. I went through all of them. If you hadn't finished your exams by the time you left, you could finish them off at college. Then you could take teaching exams in ballet, tap and modern. I suppose it's still the same now. I am a qualified teacher in all three. I was probably better at tap and modern. But even in the ballet exams I always came out with Honours (the top) or Highly Commended.

Twice a year the Jason School put on a show, called *Let Us Entertain You*, some bits of which we choreographed ourselves and I always enjoyed that; after all, I'd been doing it since I was eight in the school playground. In fact, in my last year I won the Senior Choreographic Award and the Shakespeare Shield and the Personality Cup. (But not, as you can see, the shrinking violet cup.) They were presented to me by the Principal, Ms Joyce Spriggs.

The drama bit of the Jason School of Dance and Drama was very limited – and to be honest I wasn't that bothered: all that improvisation, pretending to be an egg. But when the local amateur dramatic society needed a chorus or walk-ons for their musicals, like *The King and I* or *The Wizard of Oz*, that was completely brilliant. The Broxbourne Civic Centre sounds nothing, but in fact it was a proper theatre, brand new, with wings and flies and tabs.

In *The Wizard of Oz* I was a Munchkin and a Jitterbug. My Munchkin outfit was a pink hooped suit and a red top hat. As a Jitterbug I had a purple catsuit, with a bright green neck and gloves and a little skirt, made of this really shiny, horrible material which almost looked plastic. As these were full-length shows, there were loads of rehearsals, even though most of the time you were just hanging around. But I loved it all. Exams were hard work, but performing, being up there on a real stage, hearing the audience clap and knowing that some of it might be for you – made everything worthwhile.

When I was thirteen my mum saw an advert for YST in the *Stage*, the showbusiness newspaper that came out every week. YST was short for Young Stars of Tomorrow. It was a dance showcase for young people – three performances for charity in the West End. To get into YST you first had to get through the audition. These were open auditions which meant anybody could go and they were held at the London Studio Centre in York Way near King's Cross. It was the first big audition I had been to. Most open auditions follow the same pattern: first someone at a desk takes your name and address then gives you a number. Then – at least for YST – you'd be asked what you wanted to do dance-wise, like tap, or jazz or ballet. Then you'd go into a class, and they'd start weeding you out.

Once you dropped out of one class, you'd start on another. All through this my mum would be waiting in a room with some of the other parents. The kids who were experienced came on their own.

I was so excited when I heard I'd got in. In fact I got in two years running: once at the Prince of Wales Theatre and once at the Mermaid in Blackfriars. The first year I got into the jazz and the tap. I didn't get into the ballet.

Ballet was the elite, full of girls who looked as if they had never picked their noses in their lives. One year I got into the National, and did some Portuguese dance with a basketful of fake fish.

Rehearsals were every Sunday and went on for about two months. Some people would travel a long way, one girl I remember came from Nottingham, another from York. Even though our journey wasn't that bad, my mum would have to get up really early every Sunday and drive me all the way to King's Cross. I'd rehearse all day, then she'd come back to pick me up and take me home again. She was a complete saint. Once she put me on the train but I was terrified – remember I had never even been on a bus.

It turned out that Emma, later in the Spice Girls, was also in the jazz section that year – with me in a number called 'Reet Petite' – but I never knew her there. Because she had her little group of friends, and I had my little group of friends. You wouldn't know everybody.

The second time I got into all the sections, including the ballet where I was a cloud. So there's this huge long ballet lasting about twenty minutes, and then there's me, just a big piece of fluff in the background, who comes across right at the end. But who cares? I was in the ballet and getting into the ballet was a Big Thing.

Looking the part was the easy bit. I didn't want to know all the positions, I didn't want to know the French names for sticking your hand up in the air, I just wanted to dance.

I don't know how many parts I went up for, but there's no denying that auditions are hard when you're that kind of age, in fact when you're any kind of age, always being slapped down, never feeling good enough. 'Next please. We'll call you.' All that.

No matter how many times it's happened to you, it always hurts when you get told No. I didn't often cry, at least not until I got in the car, but that was because I would always prepare myself for the No – which wasn't difficult because it happened so often. But some people used to get terribly emotional. And back in the dressing rooms where you changed, there would always be red eyes and at least one person crying.

But in some ways it was a good lesson: you learn that nobody has any time for also-rans. Only the best get through and it doesn't change however high you climb the ladder. If you can't take being knocked down, you shouldn't be there.

My ambition at that time was to dance in a musical in the West End. Being at the theatre was such a good feeling. Christine Shakespeare was mad about the theatre and she took me to see them all: *Starlight Express*, *Miss Saigon*, *Cats*, *Les Mis*. She always made me feel special, as if I was worth it. We'd go and have something to eat first, in somewhere like the Pizza Express by the British Museum. She'd always pay. Then off to see the show. Whatever we went to see, that would be my favourite until the next one. I loved *Starlight Express*, because it was so modern and very fast. I knew all the songs and bought the sheet music so that I could sing them when I was at home. At least those terrible piano lessons with Mrs Adams meant that I could recognize the notes. Louise and me also learned to roller-blade, but the nearest I got to *Starlight Express* was the Waltham Forest rollerskate gala at Waltham Cross. (Later I was cast in a

BBC1 series called *Bodymatters* where I played an anti-body on skates, dressed like a medieval knight with pointy armour.)

Then there was my other favourite, *Cats*. I must have seen it five or six times, first with Christine Shakespeare, then with my family. Of course what I really wanted to be was the white cat. But this was complete fantasy. The white cat is always a ballerina who has come up through the Royal Ballet and has to be an amazing dancer. At that time me in a white catsuit would have been the most disgusting sight: I would have looked like a beached whale. Because the skinny eight-year-old had somehow turned into a porky fifteen-year-old. No one knew why. Puppy fat, my mum called it, though later we discovered that I had polycystic ovaries – which meant they had lots of little cysts around them and this had some kind of hormonal effect, which was why I was so big.

Not that in those days I really cared about how I looked. But that was set to change.

4 message to the underdog

Just the sight of 'back to school' signs in the shops in August made me feel sick. Sometimes I would be really ill – I was always getting ear infections. Sometimes I'd just get my mum to write a sick note. I can honestly say I hated school, the teachers, the kids, everyone. I was called names because of my spots, and names because I didn't have anything to do with boys (frigid and tight) and I was even told I couldn't belong to my mum and dad because I had a 'black person's nose' and dark skin.

I never had that many friends at St Mary's, except for two: Brenda Ecclebosh and Sara Buckle. But even they used to giggle about boys and play netball at break.

It wasn't until I was fourteen that I started to take an interest in how I looked. It began with make-up then spread to my hair. The original dull, brown, thin hair was now dull, brown, big hair. This was my contribution to the eighties. My mum's friend Sue, a hairdresser, had come round one evening and done the perm, but to get the look I wanted I had to wash it every morning, crinkle-dry it with a diffuser, then put on so much hairspray it wouldn't move. Now not only did I get the usual 'scrub off that make-up', it was 'and get rid of that muck on your hair'.

I had also started to get a bit more trendy in what I wore. To achieve the dancer/leg warmer look that I lived in at home I started the fashion of wearing two pairs of socks. As they had to be white, there wasn't much scope for originality. First came a pair of over-the-knee socks pushed down to mid-calf. Then another, shorter, pair on top which you'd push lower down so you had loads and loads of crinkles, that looked like socks and leg warmers. Some socks were better at achieving this look than others, and every morning me and my sister would fight over which socks we would wear.

My skirts began to get slightly shorter. Not by much because the headmistress used to make us kneel on the floor and our skirts had to touch the ground perfectly.

The girls at my school had always been obsessed by boys. But I was never that interested. It seemed to go with smoking and I wasn't interested in that either. They'd always be giggling and puffing and whispering in corners, but boys were things to avoid, I'd decided – until Franco arrived at the beginning of the spring term in 1990. He was American, the son of the new vicar at St Mary's, Cheshunt.

He was quite tall, had shortish dark hair and brown glasses and everybody really fancied him, partly just because he was American and had the accent but also he wasn't bad-looking and he was quite cheeky.

Because I'd never had a boyfriend, Valentine's Day meant nothing to me. I'd certainly never had a Valentine Card, apart from the ones that my mum used to send me and Louise so we didn't feel left out.

Boys didn't come near me any more than girls did – not that I can blame them because I really was a bit of a minger. I mean, acne, permed hair, make-up like pebbledash – how attractive is that?

This particular Valentine's Day, 14 February 1990, I didn't only get one card, I got seven, one for every classroom I went into. The way it worked at St Mary's, you went from room to room for the different lessons and you always had your set desk. And every desk I sat in, when I opened it up, there was this envelope: TO VICTORIA in capitals and a line underneath. And it was like, Oh My God. This was the first time anything like this had happened to me. Nobody knew who had sent them. Then the rumours started that it was Franco. Then right at the end of the day, the last lesson, there was the last Valentine's Card. Not just a question mark like the others, but a question: *Would you go out with me on Saturday?*

So I ended up talking to him after school. I could hardly remember even talking to a boy and I felt so clumsy. We were outside and it was quite dark; even so, I felt my spots glowing.

Why didn't we go to the pictures in Waltham Cross? he said. He'd come round to pick me up. I said Yes to the pictures but No to him picking me up. I'd go round to his house. There was no way I was having him come round to me, to be stared at by my brother and my sister, not to mention my mum and dad, like he was an alien.

Being the new vicar's son, he lived virtually opposite the school, which was next door to the church. I thought a long time about what to wear for this momentous occasion and finally decided on a pair of jeans, a pair of boots and a shirt.

My mum drops me off, all smiles and little looks. I walk up to the front door and ring the bell. I'm just willing her to go, and I practically fall inside the door when it opens, give my mum a little wave and at last she drives off.

'Hi. Is Franco there?'

It's Franco's dad, the vicar. Behind him Franco runs down the stairs, so *Saved by the Bell* and – Oh God. I can't believe it. He's wearing a pair of big baggy Wrangler jeans – totally uncool to start with – white socks, hideous trainers that turn up at the toes and worst of all, a *Star Wars* T-shirt TUCKED IN and a lumberjack shirt, tucked out. Until that moment I had only seen him in school uniform.

Then came the next horror thought. Because nobody believed he had asked me out, my so-called friends had said they were going to turn up at the cinema just to check up on me.

So how are we getting there? By bus. I had never been on a bus in my life. I hadn't a bloody clue what a bus was, where you got the ticket, how much it cost – anything. And I had to sit next to this complete dweeb. So when we got to Waltham Cross, there they were, doing what they spent their lives doing, hanging around bus stops.

'Awright, Vic?'

'Awright, Franco?'

I could feel them all smirking. I could have died. After the pictures he wanted to take me to McDonald's, but I was so embarrassed, I just wanted to go home. So then it's back on the bus again, back to Cheshunt, and then he says do you want to come in until your mum gets here? I'd called her from the cinema to come and get me.

So I go into the house and just sit there in the lounge in front of a video Franco's put on. No sign of the vicar or Mrs vicar. So I'm just sitting there and I'm thinking, just don't kiss me. Please, whatever you do, just don't try and kiss me. I haven't kissed anyone in my whole life, and you I do not want for my first experience. I was so tense, I felt as if I might crack.

And then he says, 'I've got a present for you.'

'Oh.' A BOY has bought ME a present.

'What is it, then?'

And he pulls out this little jewellery box, the sort with a snap lid. And inside is a gold cross on a gold chain.

'Oh, thank you, Franco.' Aaaah.

Then I hear my mum *poop-pooping* outside the house. So I put this gold cross on, give him a quick kiss on the cheek and go.

'So how was it then, Victoria?'

Mum.

'So how was it then, Victoria?'

Dad.

'So did he snog you or what?'

Louise.

I had just come out of the bath and my little sister was trying to discover the secrets of romance.

'What's that, Tor?' she said, pointing at my neck.

'Franco gave it to me.'

'Not the cross, you idiot, the green mark under it.'

'There can't be a green mark, it's gold.'

'No, it isn't. His dad gets hundreds of them free for

confirmations, everyone knows that. He'd be a million-aire if they were all gold.'

I wiped the condensation off the mirror and looked for myself. Oh my God, I don't believe it. A big green mark the shape of a cross.

'But it is real gold, and it isn't one of his dad's,' I protested. 'Franco bought it for me. It's just my skin has a funny reaction to it.'

So that was my one and only school romance. One evening at the pictures. Is this a record?

It was coming up to GCSEs and I was having extra tuition for French. One day I was just having my tea and this boy comes into the kitchen. I'd seen him before, he was the son of the man who did the burglar alarm and I really fancied him, he looked just like the Karate Kid. So my mum's rushing around, and telling me I've got to get ready if I'm not going to be late for my extra French lesson in Broxbourne.

So then this boy says why doesn't he take me, because he lives in Harlow so Broxbourne is on his way? But my mum says no, that's all right, she has to go out anyway.

'Why did you do that, Mummy? Why didn't you let him take me?' I said once we got in the car. I was so frustrated. I couldn't believe it. My one chance to get alone with this boy who I really fancied and my mum had totally ruined it.

His name was Mark Wood and he was about three years older than me. He wasn't bad-looking, about six foot two with really dark hair that he gelled right back. But the real appeal was that Mark was different. Since Franco I had been out with a couple of other boys, but just boys from school. Mark wasn't some spotty fifteen-year-old local boy, bragging about which girl's knickers he'd been in, like everyone else at my school went out with. Mark was practically a grown-up and it was like, Wow, he can drive.

I can't remember exactly how it happened, whether he phoned, or if he came round to do something with the alarm again, but a few weeks later, he asked me out.

The van he drove usually had ladders on the top of it, but as this was a special occasion he had taken them off, though there was nothing he could do about the name of the company on the side: Telmark. His dad was called Terry. We went to a place called Villa, a wine bar, somewhere in Walthamstow I think, near Epping Forest. I can't remember what I wore, my dress sense wasn't the best in those days, but I was so excited. Forget Franco and the bus. This was a car. Well, compared to a bus it was.

'So, what are you having, Victoria?'

Total panic.

'Vodka and tonic please, Mark.'

It was the only thing I could think of. It was what my dad always had when we went to a pub.

Of course I got completely drunk. I was so nervous, and so every time Mark said 'Do you want another one?' I said 'Yes.' And the more I drank the less nervous I seemed to get. Now just one vodka and tonic and I'd be on the floor, but I was much bigger then, quite round really, and it took a few more. I don't remember any of what happened after that, but anyway, I started going out with him. I waited for about six or seven months before I slept with him and he never put pressure on me to do it.

Not only was I having to do extra French and work hard at school, I was also having to decide what to do next. Ever since I had started dancing, I had longed to go to a stage school, like the Italia Conti, or the Arts Educational at Tring or Sylvia Young. These were schools where you went at eleven and did all the usual lessons, as well as singing and dancing and acting. Emma from the band went to Sylvia Young. Even now I think I should have done the same. I would have been surrounded by people like me and I would certainly have been much happier. But my mum was totally against it; she wanted me to have 'a proper education'. And, at the end of the day, they probably couldn't have afforded it.

The alternative was college. Here again there was a choice. Italia Conti and the Arts Educational had college courses as well as being stage schools, then there was Doreen Bird, Stella Mann and Laine Theatre Arts. I'd been to see all their summer shows and the one I wanted to go to was Laine's. In actual fact, Laine's ran a summer school and I'd stayed there for a week the year before. There was this really cool boy there called Christian Horsfall, really good-looking and talented.

The next spring I auditioned for all of them. That winter Christine Shakespeare really pushed me, because, as she kept reminding me, out of the hundreds and hundreds who audition, some of these colleges will only take ten.

It was Christine who told me: 'If you get into Laine's that's the one you should go to.' Laine's was the most professional, I can always tell a Laine's girl even now. Always very pretty, tall and thin, very well groomed, always have their make-up on when they leave the house. But I didn't get in. I was put on their reserve list. But I did get into Doreen Bird, which was my second choice.

I left school with five GCSEs and the cookery prize. (Yes, you cynics who believe that poor old Posh can't even boil an egg, the cookery prize, do you hear?) But the best news came a few days later from Laine's. Someone had dropped out and I was in. As well as this I was lucky enough to get a grant from Hertfordshire to pay my fees.

College turned out to be a lot like school, worse in a way because I had to live away from home. What made it especially difficult was that it wasn't long since my nan and grandad had died. It's quite sad actually. I only really remember them as being old. Nanna had senile dementia. She had always been so smart and immaculate, but it got to the stage where none of her clothes would match and she'd have bra straps showing and one leg of her tights in and one leg out. And she'd forget to put her false teeth in.

Poor Grandad used to get so embarrassed. He tried to look after her but it really was a twenty-four-hour job. People think that senile dementia is just being forgetful, like – what day is it again? – but it had got to the stage where she'd say to my mum, 'Who's that young lady over there?' And that young lady was me.

I remember one Christmas there was some pro-gramme on television where they were shooting at each other and she turned to Grandad, grabbed at his arm like she was drowning, and said, 'That man with a gun. He's going to shoot me.' Really, really frightened.

Mum was devastated. I remember standing in the

kitchen when she was cooking Sunday dinner obviously very stressed and very upset and my nan's in the lounge going absolutely loopy and I'm asking my mum something, something really basic. And she says, 'Oh, I can't remember.' So I say, 'You're going just like Nanna.'

And she burst into tears. Bear in mind this is her mother I'm talking about. And at the time I thought, what are you crying for? What are you getting upset for? It's only now that I understand. She was obviously paranoid she was going to go the same way, because senile dementia gallops in my family. Just gallops. You don't realize what you say when you're younger.

Laine's was a three-year course. For the first year I lived with a family in Epsom and I used to go home every weekend. As much as I was enjoying doing my dancing all day every day, I longed for the weekends. The family I stayed with were very nice, but it's not the same as being at home. Little things, like the kind of biscuits they had, even the kind of fish fingers and breakfast cereal.

I only had one real friend, Sarah Stewart, a very pretty Irish girl with long blonde hair. But not having lots of friends didn't bother me particularly. I was used to it. And when I saw a whole load of girls together, giggling and smoking, I certainly didn't feel that I wanted to be one of them. The only thing I wanted to do was work. I never forgot Christine Shakespeare's words. 'She'll have to work at it if she's to get anywhere.' And I was going to get somewhere. Just you wait.

What I lacked in talent I made up for with hard work. I've never had a problem about getting up and I was always down in the rehearsal studios an hour before class began, and when the favourites had packed up for the day, I was always the last to leave.

Anywhere else it should have been enough, but at Laine's, to really get on, to be in all the shows and be seen, you had to be a favourite. And Betty Laine, the principal, never made any secret of who her favourites were. I was not one of them. I was never the best dancer, or the best singer, or the best at drama. My crime was being fat. And in those days I must have been nearly ten stone, more of a twelve than a ten. But I wasn't that bothered. Other girls were always going on about calories and things but I used to eat anything: Mars Bars, McDonald's, chips. I'd eat chocolate till it came out of my ears. I might have had a bit of a double chin, but at last I had boobs. And I was perfectly happy with that. And so was my boyfriend.

It was nice being able to say 'my boyfriend'.

'So what are you doing this weekend, Victoria?'

'Going out with my boyfriend.'

OK, so it was down the pub with his friends, watching football and doing quiz nights. What I don't know about musicals of the forties and fifties you could write on a beer mat.

We often went over to Harlow where Mark lived with his family and spent most of the time at this pub, the Harlow Mill.

Mark had had a completely different upbringing from me. His parents were both a lot older than mine and were real East Enders. Whenever we all went out together to the pub or a dinner and dance, his mum used to sit there drinking pints while his dad was up at the bar. His father, in particular, had very funny mood swings.

I never particularly got on with them and his sister was always hostile. She used to look at me going out in my short skirts and all the rest of it, and make comments. She was much more of a sensible skirt-and-cardigan type. Even when I was a lot bigger I could always get away with wearing short skirts because I had long skinny legs.

A couple of years after we started going out there was some big argument in their family. It didn't involve me but it left Mark with nowhere to live.

My mum had always liked him ('Such a nice boy, Victoria') and welcomed him with open arms. As I was away in Epsom during the week, he could sleep in my room. My mum did his washing, she did his ironing, she did his cooking.

During my second year at Laine's my parents bought a flat in Epsom. I lived there for the next two years with three other girls and they all paid my mum and dad rent. I could choose my own kind of cereal (Frosties) and my own kind of biscuits (Marks & Spencer's), but I wasn't any happier. It was increasingly apparent that my weight was becoming an issue.

Although I told everyone I had a boyfriend, I don't think anyone believed it, because he never came to see me. I'd be literally crying on the phone, pleading with him to drive over to see me. Epsom wasn't that far – only about an hour round the M25 – it wasn't like you had to cross London. Whereas for me, going by train, it was really complicated. First a train to Victoria, then tube to King's Cross, then another train up to Oakwood, then someone would have to pick me up from the station.

One weekend it was snowing and none of the trains were working, so I couldn't get home. And I begged him to come, but he didn't. The other girls in the flat had gone out or gone home and I don't know how I got through it. I bought a bottle of wine and some tins of peaches, then spent the whole evening squeezing my spots and just cried and cried and cried.

He said he didn't have the money for the petrol. Although he'd had to leave home, he was still working for his father's company and he wasn't paying my mum any rent. I said to him, 'Ask my mum, she'll lend you the money for the petrol.' But he still wouldn't come. It wasn't as if I was earning. As I saw it, being at college was my choice, so every time my mum or dad offered me money I wouldn't take it.

I don't know what it was about Mark but when he wasn't the centre of attention he would just sulk. You wouldn't even know what would set him off. He would go into a mood and not talk to me for days. Just before my eighteenth birthday we all went skiing. There were loads of us, about thirty all together in this hotel in Switzerland. Peter and Marie Featherstone, friends of my parents, had invited some of their friends who we didn't know. We knew their children Danielle and Maria-Louise, but the children of the friends were quite different. They were very well off, all very pretty and always in very expensive designer clothes, things like Naf Naf and Ton Sur Ton.

Me and my sister never had clothes like that. Since I'd been at Laine's my mum had given me money to buy my own clothes, but I put most of it straight in the bank. There didn't seem any point spending money on clothes when I lived in jeans and leggings. But my mum would always like to surprise me with bits and pieces, like little tops she thought I'd like that she'd bought at Top Shop or Dorothy Perkins.

Although I don't remember ever saying anything to my mum in Switzerland, she must have noticed me looking a bit longingly at what these rich kids were wearing, because the first thing she did when we got back was to go out and buy us a Ton Sur Ton cardigan each. Mine was very thick in pale orange, with appliqué on the front and a plain back with Ton Sur Ton embroidered on it. Louise had one in mauvey-blue. My mum would completely go without for me and my sister and my brother to have something.

That cardigan was the first thing I ever had which you could call 'designer'. I'd had clothes that had names on them – things like leggings and T-shirts that I'd got from Pineapple Dance Studios in Covent Garden, but not 'designer'.

I can't say that was when I began to be obsessed by clothes, because I have never been obsessed by clothes, in spite of what people write about me. But suddenly I saw that you could get nice things, and that nice things made a difference.

When we got back from skiing I discovered this different world. Although we were better off than most people we knew, it was nothing compared to Maria-Louise's friends. There was one girl I remember who had horses. She had left school, didn't want to work and so her parents just let her look after her horses all day. I used to think, God how lucky. I don't think that now.

They didn't only have expensive clothes and expensive make-up (Dior versus Rimmel) they also had expensive cars, Golf GTIs or Peugeot 205s. One boy had a Porsche, whereas my car was a seen-better-days Fiat Uno that my mum and dad bought me for my seventeenth birthday along with driving lessons. But to me it was better than ten Porsches because it was MY OWN CAR and I just loved it and cleaned it religiously. It was red and had a brown interior, and to make it look more sporty my mum had painted red hub caps, red wing mirrors and a silver stripe down the side. It also had a red aerial and a red sun roof. Everyone knew it was mine: one of the hub caps fell off a few streets away and someone actually brought it back to our house because it was so obvious whose it was.

My parents were so generous. They treated Mark as one of the family, not only had they paid for him to come to Switzerland with me; for my eighteenth birthday they paid for him and me to go to EuroDisney and stay two nights in Paris at a really nice hotel. It should have been so romantic, but he totally ignored me. I kept asking him: What have I done? What have I done?

Probably I hadn't laughed at one of his jokes. He used to think he was a real laugh. A lot of the time he didn't realize that people were laughing at him rather than with him. He tried to give me the impression that I was the odd one out, that he was Mr Popular. But he actually wasn't popular at all, or if he was, only among a bunch of dweebs, a big fish in an incredibly small puddle.

So what do you do when someone treats you like shit? You get engaged. It was just before I left Laine's, and I suppose I was feeling a bit frightened about the future. I never for one moment thought that I would marry Mark; getting engaged was just getting engaged: you had a party and you got a nice ring. All the girls at college were getting engaged. I don't even think Mark asked me to marry him, it was more, did I want to get engaged? So I thought, why not?

The only person who wasn't happy with this development was my sister, who absolutely hated Mark Wood.

'You can't marry him, Tor, he's a complete and utter wanker.'

'What do you know, you're only fifteen.'

'Right, I'm not staying here to see you mess up your life.' And she left, packed a suitcase and went to stay with a friend from school.

But what did Louise know anyway? It wasn't like I was going to marry him. For the party mum ordered a cake with two shoes made out of icing, my half was a ballet shoe and Mark's part was a football boot.

The best thing about my last year at Laine's was Maureen and Gwyn Hughes. Gwyn was a music teacher and one day he saw me fiddling around at the piano and he asked if I could play. I told him that I had started but given up but that I would really like to learn. So he began to teach me to play the piano again. I really wanted to do it because of my nan. And for my mum who I know always wanted to learn.

Gwyn and Maureen actually taught on the musical theatre course, but for some reason they took me under their wing. They must have felt sorry for me. I remember there was an audition for *Starlight Express* and when I asked permission from Miss Laine to go up for it, she said, 'Don't bother.' But Maureen and Gwyn said take

71

no notice and try for it anyway. So I did. And OK, I didn't get it, but then no one from Laine's got it. And while they were all crying their stupid eyes out – because Miss Laine had built them up so much – I just enjoyed the experience.

Everything in those last few weeks at Laine's was gearing up to the end-of-year show, when agents, cruise directors and casting directors would be out there looking for new talent. We'd all been told a hundred times that 'It's a jungle out there' and that hardly any of us would get jobs. When it came to casting it was always the same people who got picked to do the solos, or the pas de deux, or whatever. People like Victoria Adams and Sarah Stewart just got put in the background. Literally. Christian, the boy I had fancied that first trial week, was in nearly everything and one girl, I remember, called Zoe Smith, was in every single number.

At the end of every Laine's production there was this massive tap routine, and all I did in the entire show – the showcase for the rest of my career – was run across the back of the stage waving a top hat. And I didn't even do that every night; if they decided you weren't that great then they would alternate you with someone else they'd decided wasn't that great. So half a number, right at the back every other night, was all I got for three years of very hard work. Blink and you'd miss me.

It was always the very tall leggy beautiful girls who would start off the finale, and we'd all join on the line, high-kicking all the way back. There we were, wearing our different colour catsuits and silver high-heeled sandals, waving our bowler hats like Liza Minnelli. And I'll never forget that last dress rehearsal. I was standing, at the back of course, and Betty Laine came up to me and said, 'You're so fat I'm going to have to fly you in. I'm going to have to get you in on a crane because you're such a roly-poly.'

As the prospectus puts it: 'The college demands from its students self-discipline, a sense of responsibility, personal grooming and a respect of values – all of which will become an integral part of their characters.' Blah blah blah.

Message to the underdog: I am the most successful person who has ever come out of Laine's. It doesn't matter what you look like, it's all about hard work, determination and self-belief.

5 we'll be in touch

That last term at Laine's was enough to make anybody want to jump in the Thames. Just knowing that no matter what I did, however hard I practised, however many hours I spent at the barre, when it came to the final show I wouldn't be in anything. No Mr Big would see me and say, 'That girl, the one with the star quality, have her call me as soon as she gets offstage.' No *42nd Street* scenario for Victoria Adams. I was on my own.

From very early on my mum had registered me with child agencies (these were different from model agencies) and I was always going to castings for commercials, but I'd never got anything. Louise had – she'd even done a children's TV serial for the BBC – but not me, the gap-toothed ugly duckling with spots.

The main source for work was, as ever, the *Stage*, a weekly newspaper that covered everything from Shakespeare to cabaret – a mixture of jobs, reviews and news. It came out every Wednesday and that last term we'd all be sitting around, chewing our felt tips and circling anything that wasn't topless dancing in Taiwan or shooting ping-pong balls from where the sun doesn't shine.

Three years of having somewhere to live and something to get up for were coming to an end. Most of the girls were happy to get a job with a cruise: regular money, no expenses, and a tan. But I didn't want to spend months on a boat and I didn't want to dance with a load of feathers all over me and silver sandals. I'd had enough of silver sandals at Laine's. I wanted to work in musicals in the West End, I always had.

Bertie was a brand-new musical based on the life of Vesta Tilley, who made her name dressed up in top hat and tails singing 'Burlington Bertie'. In her time she was a really famous music-hall star, but unlike Marie Lloyd, Dan Leno and Charlie Chaplin, she'd been more or less forgotten.

My nanna and grandad had always loved the music hall and I remember Nanna was always playing those kind of songs on the piano. I remember all sitting round the television watching *The Good Old Days* when they were babysitting us.

Bertie was an open audition and the favourites were out in force. For some reason I was really nervous: with *Starlight Express* and *Cats* at least you knew what they were looking for. *Bertie* was a brand-new show, so who knows what they wanted.

No audition for a musical was exactly the same and you could never be sure what you'd be asked to do. Sometimes they'd get you to sing 'Happy Birthday' all together, then they'd go down the line pointing or tapping you on the shoulder saying yes, no, no, no, yes, no. I found it easier than some of the other girls when I got the 'No' tap, because it was what I was expecting. Only when I was back in the flat on my own did it sometimes get to me, and I would call up my mum and howl down the phone, about how I couldn't bear it any more and how I couldn't go on.

'Come home,' she'd say. 'And we'll go out and buy a pair of shoes.' My mum has always had a great belief in shopping therapy. Whereas my dad would come on the phone and tell me, 'No, you cannot give in to these people.' Yet all I wanted to do at times was to give up. It was my dad who really made me carry on.

This time we'd be singing our own song they told us. You'd always have one audition piece prepared and mine was 'Mein Herr' from *Cabaret*. It was good for me because the register was quite low. Most of the other girls at Laine's did things like 'The Wind Beneath My Wings', or something from *Miss Saigon*. Much more technical. Girls with really fantastic voices would do something from *Phantom of the Opera* or *Les Mis*.

Because I'd been on the dancing course rather than the musical theatre course at Laine's, I hadn't done a lot of singing but I've always been able to belt something out and with 'Mein Herr' I could make up for the fact that I wasn't the best singer by doing all the moves and drawing attention away from my vocals. I didn't want to showcase my voice, I wanted to showcase my personality.

I dressed as I always did for an audition in black tights, black leotard, black leg warmers, black jazz shoes. All very black because somebody once told me that black makes you look thinner.

First we were taught a tap routine in batches of about fifteen. Then there was an acting piece – I did something from *Shirley Valentine* by Willy Russell. And finally the song. You handed over your music to the pianist and just prayed they wouldn't race it. When I finished, they just said, 'Thank you, we'll be in touch,' the usual brush-off. But for once I left feeling really pleased. I had actually got through to the end, to the song. About a thousand had been there at the start, only about fifty made it to the song.

The audition must have been just before a weekend because I was at home when I got the call.

'For you, Victoria,' my mum yelled up the stairs.

It never occurred to me that it might be about *Bertie*. I really wasn't expecting to hear, I was just pleased I had got so far.

'We'd like to offer you the part . . .' the voice began. And I was so excited I didn't hear anything else – what they said about rehearsals or even what the money was. My hearing just switched off. I mean, I'd never been picked for anything. I had to ring back later, say I was really sorry but I'd been too excited to take it in and could they please tell me again?

I felt I was about to explode: all those pent-up hopes, all the times I'd pretended I didn't care. I ran downstairs two at a time shouting out *Y-e-e-e-e-e-s!*, which came out sounding like *eh-h-h-h-h* and I saw my mum's face looking so worried. It was only when I hugged her so tight she could hardly breathe that she realized what had happened. So often I had called my mum and dad from college in tears – I'm never getting anything, I'm not getting anywhere, I want to give up – and through the whole thing it was them who kept me going.

And then it was just so great telling everyone that I'd got the job, especially Maureen and Gwyn Hughes.

Next best was seeing the favourites open their prissy little mouths like fish in an aquarium and not know what to say. It would be nice to think that Miss Laine ate her words. But it didn't go that far – I think she said to me 'Well done'. And it was well done. That part was one of the best jobs anyone got that year.

Rehearsals were due to start in London at the beginning of August at Sadler's Wells. For anyone who has ever wanted to be a dancer, Sadler's Wells is one of those names that are like magic. I had been there so many times with Christine Shakespeare to see the ballet. I thought of all the great names that had danced on this stage: Alicia Markova, Margot Fonteyn. That's where all the greats of English ballet started off. And now it was me. Sadler's Wells has recently been rebuilt, but then it was a really old-fashioned theatre, musty and dusty and all the things that I don't usually like. But I didn't care.

Bertie starred Anita Harris as Vesta Tilley and her father was played by Ron Moody, who I remembered from *Oliver*, the film, when he played Fagin. The book and lyrics were by Anita Harris's husband Mike Margolis, the director was Stephen Tate and the choreographer was Irving Davies – a really huge name in the business.

We opened at the Alexandra Theatre, Birmingham, on 6 September for a pre-London run of six weeks; then the plan was to tour before transferring to the West End. The company – as you call everyone involved in a theatre production – was great. Everywhere I'd ever been before – at school, at college, even at Jason's – people had always been jealous. Now everyone just wanted to help each other, and be positive. Of the five other girls, one – Kate, the head girl – had been to Laine's, but she had left before I got there. She'd been in *Cats* and *Starlight Express* in the West End so I was very much in awe of her. Another of the girls had been in *Bugsy Malone*. I was one of the only ones who hadn't done a lot. But they were all very talented and really nice people.

One of the girls – Camilla Simson – became a really good friend. She was very tall, very slim with lovely curly strawberry-blonde hair and had trained at Elmhurst as a ballerina and only stopped because she got too tall. She'd had a very different upbringing to me; her family was really well-off, but understated in an old-money kind of way. She was very well spoken and never showed off, even though she had a house just off the King's Road in Chelsea that her father had bought her. Camilla was a really nice girl, really talented and really good fun and when the time came to move up to Birmingham we shared digs.

Theatrical digs are where actors or dancers stay when they are on tour. The theatre gives you a list and then you're on your own. Ours were in Edgbaston, and our landlady was called Marlene P. Mountain, if you can believe it. She was the theatrical landlady to end all theatrical landladies. In the lounge she had all these flyers and playbills and signed photographs of the show people who'd been her lodgers over the years. And if you weren't careful she'd be telling you all about them, and how she was everyone's best friend. But she was a really nice, kind lady. I can't remember now if there were six or eight of us staying there from the company, but one was someone who became a really good friend – David Harington. As well as dancers, the cast had all these other multi-talented people who you might have had in the music hall. David played a character called Little Tich. Although he was tiny – in fact he was a dwarf – he looked quite mature with long moustachios and wild out-of-control hair – but he was really cute and such a nice bloke. He was quite shy when doing normal things, but was transformed when he was on stage.

My entire life from the moment I woke up to the moment I passed out at night was the show. Food was the Chinese chippy down the road and tea made by the ASM (Assistant Stage Manager). We had dance rehearsals and company rehearsals and singing rehearsals. As well as being one of the dancers, I also had a solo as the clockwork ballerina and had diaphanous wings and a tiara that looked like little silver flames. The dress was a real fairy dress, white with lots of glitter and I had pointy shoes and white tights. They had to fold me into this wooden musical box and then the doors would open and the wings would spring out behind me. It wasn't that easy because they were surprisingly heavy and changed your sense of balance.

I also learned to juggle. We started the number with our backs to the audience, then we turned, singing 'What You Need is a Little Advice' and juggling at the same time. Or in my case trying to juggle. My balls were always all over the place. (There might be a better way of putting that.) But there were more serious problems. The show was very slow in rehearsal and, even though we were due to open in a couple of days, there were still things that weren't right or weren't ready. And the running time was four hours. And this wasn't *War and Peace*. Stephen, the director, blamed the script, but as the script was written by the leading lady's husband it was a no-win situation. Then just before the first performance he left. Whether pushed or jumped nobody knew.

I will never forget that dress rehearsal. There was this one scene, towards the end, where we're all dressed up as First World War soldiers in front of that famous poster with the finger pointing and the words Your Country Needs You. I hated that scene because our uniforms were made of this horrible scratchy material. At the end we walk up a ramp and then comes the whole pyrotechnics thing. And just before the big explosion, I look out into the auditorium and I see two people dressed in a similar kind of outfit to the one I am wearing. And I realize that it's my nanna and grandad. Curiously I don't remember feeling surprised. Then came the great *Pffafff* and all the smoke that went with it. I looked again, and they were gone.

Something like that happens and you don't know if you're just seeing things. It can't have lasted more than a few seconds, but I remember it so clearly – looking up and thinking, it's them. Watching me high up in the gods.

I didn't tell anyone else, not even Camilla. People don't usually believe things like that and I didn't want anyone taking the mickey. But as soon as we'd rehearsed the final curtain, I was feeding ten ps into a payphone at the stage door telling my mum. Because throughout the whole thing, she was saying, 'Oh your nan and grandad, if only they could be here, they'd be so proud of you.'

In actual fact we were quite used to ghosts in our family. My dad, who is so not like that, saw a woman in a brown gingham dress on the stairs one Sunday lunchtime. My mum came in from the kitchen and said the hairs were standing up on his arms. A few years later she met an old lady whose husband had actually gone to school in our house and got her to ask him what the teachers wore. And this old man wrote back and said there were two teachers and one of them, the head-mistress, Miss Broad, used to wear a brown checked dress.

For the first night of *Bertie* ('the World Première') the whole family came up, including Mark, and I was so excited. I remember rushing down to the stage door and seeing all their smiling faces. Except one. When everyone else had said all their congratulations, I remember walking next to Mark, so up and feeling really, really happy. My first professional show, a real milestone.

'So,' I said, giving his arm a squeeze, 'did you enjoy it then?' All he said was, 'It was OK.' Suddenly it was like the world went dark.

Have you ever noticed how people who are mean with money are also mean about things that don't cost them anything? What would it have cost Mark to just say something positive? Or anything at all? I don't want non-stop praise – there's no point in that – but some kind of reaction would have been nice. The truth was, he was mean.

And although I didn't like to admit it, I think I knew by then that Mark was taking money from my mum to buy me presents rather than spending his own. But what really hurt me was the engagement ring. A ring is a symbol of how much you love somebody. So when we found a ring that we liked in Hatton Garden, I was really happy. He was going to give it to me at the engagement party. But then he discovered that he could get something similar a lot cheaper through one of his friends. So he got the other one. I never felt the same about that ring. And when we finally broke up, I gave it away. Like I said, a ring is a symbol.

OK, so the show was long and perhaps it wasn't a candidate for an award, but was it so much to ask that my fiancé said something nice? But then Mark always hated it when someone else was the centre of attention.

The trouble was, he really wanted it to be him up there on the stage. Mark Wood was a member of the Harlow Amateur Dramatic Society and didn't we all know it. I remember one show he did was *Mr Something and the Amazing Pizza Pie*. It was a kids' show, but even kids deserved better than this. And it wasn't just me who thought so. I'd gone with a load of his friends, and they all thought it was crap. I spent the whole night sticking up for him. Mark thought he was the next Laurence Olivier but in actual fact he was more Timmy Mallett. But he just didn't see it. And I begged him not to do it, but he said I was only saying that because I was jealous.

Bertie ran for six weeks and I loved every minute of it. I was earning £250 a week – a fortune – and as a treat to myself I went down to London and bought myself a Prada handbag and a pair of Patrick Cox shoes. Patrick Cox Wannabes were the new thing, and everyone wanted them. So Louise and I got up really early one Monday morning, and we waited for the shop to open. We both tried them on (we take the same size) but I only had money for one pair.

In the meantime, another director was brought in to try to knock the show into shape, so as well as performing every night (with script changes) we were rehearsing during the day. Right till the end we all believed we'd be going into the West End – after all, we'd had good reviews. ('Brings vaudeville back to life with wit and fizz' *The Times*.) Even after the last performance we said, 'See you in Shaftesbury Avenue.' We were put on a retainer for a few weeks after the Birmingham run, but nothing happened and the whole thing just folded. Back to the dole queue.

One thing I had got from *Bertie* was my Equity card. In those days the actors' union was a closed shop – meaning you couldn't work in the West End without it. This also meant that I had to change my name – the rule is that you can't use the same name as another member of the union, even if it is your real name. And it turned out there was someone called Victoria Adams already registered with Equity. So Mark Durr-Brain Wood suggested Victoria Wood. Now why didn't I think of that? But adding the Wood wasn't such a bad idea and so I became Victoria Adams-Wood. It was on my cheque books and everything, which was handy for him.

Getting a job without an agent is as difficult as driving a car without a clutch. You can do it, but it's bloody hard work. I must have written to fifty agents asking them to come and see the show, but not one bothered to reply. Camilla's agent came up and she very sweetly took me on – but nice as she was she was more about straight plays, and that wasn't what I wanted. I wanted to do musicals.

Contacts is only about a quarter-of-an-inch thick but it is the showbusiness bible. It's full of lists: agents, casting directors, production companies, theatres, everything.

So every weekend during my last term at Laine's I sat down in my parents' study and wrote to every single name in the book. I started at the beginning and worked my way right through to the end. It took me weeks and weeks at this old-fashioned desk sitting on a swivel chair with a bendy back, done in the same dark green leather as the desk with brass studs.

I'd had a few replies of the 'thank you but no thank you' variety and that was it. Give up? No. Although I wanted to do musicals, I was ready to do commercial work, pop videos, trade shows, anything.

First, I did the rounds of the dance agencies and got into one, Dancers. They used to send me on auditions, but there was always such a bitchy atmosphere; I was straight out of college and most of these other girls were real pros. I'd turn up in my leotard and they'd be there with their low-cut tops, plastered with make-up. And they'd be making comments about bad skin and brown hair and 'Look at the double chin on that'. They needn't have worried – I used to get turfed out straight away. I was never that quick at picking things up and the atmosphere was so intimidating.

Then there were modelling agencies; although I knew I wasn't tall enough to be a catwalk model, I'd had a Z-card done before I left college. The only agency who actually asked to see me was called M O T – Models Out of Town. Funnily enough, it was the one Geri belonged to. They were very nice, but No.

As well as every other kind of agency, I joined a promotions agency. This was nothing to do with dancing, just about earning money. To do promotion work you didn't have to be able to do anything except look a bit of a bimbo. I handed out leaflets for the Carphone Warehouse in St Albans. I was at the opening of Wickes in Cheshunt where I gave out balloons to all the kids. I gave out leaflets at the Harlequin Centre in Watford. I worked in a department store at the Lakeside shopping centre in Thurrock, spraying perfume on shoppers. It was Champagne by Yves Saint Laurent and it's really strong. I used to work for hours and hours and hours, from the minute the shop opened to the minute it shut. There was a video machine on the counter which had the same adverts going round and round on a loop – all the perfumes and aftershaves of Yves Saint Laurent. And I knew all these bloody adverts off by heart. When anyone walked past I had to say the same thing:

'Good morning, madam. Would you like to try Yves Saint Laurent's latest fragrance?' Smile. Spray. Smile. Over and over and over again. And some people were so rude. As if I wanted to fill my lungs with this stuff. That's why now, when I'm in Harrods or Harvey Nichols or wherever, even though I really don't want any perfume I'll always say no thank you politely and smile. Because I know what it's like to stand there and do that hour after bloody hour.

I got £35 a day. My mum and dad always made me put a third away in a separate account for when the tax man came asking for money. In fact, I never had to pay any tax because I never earned enough. But it taught me what I need to know now.

A typical week began on Wednesday when the *Stage* landed on the mat. I circled all the open auditions that I was interested in, then cross-checked with my time-table. I did a new one every week. I was so organized.

My dad was the lead vocalist in a couple of bands before he met my mum. This one was called the Calettos.

Joan Collins was a very early influence. In fact I bought a pair just like this in early 2001.

Me aged two months with my mum and my dad. I would stay, the 'tache (thank God) would go. My dad's, that is.

Nothing like starting early.

Grandad was a true gentleman and I absolutely adored him.

This Pierrot outfit was probably the first my mum ever made for me. Not sure if Louise's hat is fancy dress or just a fashion mistake.

Perhaps it was always wearing the same as my sister that made me determined to be totally individualistic in how I dress.

Life in a half-built house was difficult for all of us.

Frostie the Snowman.

My nanna and grandad's anniversary.

You only have to look at our expressions
to see which car we preferred.

Emma and a kid from *Fame*.

Barry Manilow and young fan snapped in secret assignation at Blenheim Palace.

Louise had personality but no rhythm.

First day at St Mary's: right kilt, right blazer, right tie, right badge, right bag, right idiot.

I wasn't the best dancer but I learnt early on that hard work can make up for a lot.

We always had Yorkshire Terriers. This one was probably called Samantha, but to be honest they all looked the same.

South Pacific comes to Hertfordshire.
Louise, Alison, Lorraine and me
Washing That Man Right Out of
Our Hair.

My guru, Christine Shakespeare,
pushed me to the limits. I owe
her so much.

Darcey Bussell eat
your heart out.

The original dull, brown, thin hair
was now dull, brown, big hair.

Spot the future Spice Girl (clue: back row).

The timetable would already have auditions arranged through agents marked on it. Then I would slot in the open auditions and work the promotions around that. Auditions were usually held in the West End, so audition days were also class days, as I always tried to fit in a class at Pineapple or Dance Works.

Once they trusted me, the promotions agency got me to find other girls to work with. In other words, my friends. I remember handing out leaflets for steel girders at Romford Market with a friend of Louise's called Simone, a really funny girl with bright red hair and a fiery personality. And I'm standing there, smiling like a gibbon and I'm thinking, I don't want to do this, I want to be a dancer, when it started pissing down and the standard 'Awright, darlin'' became 'Look at the tits on that'. We were soaked.

And I'm thinking, Listen, you pricks, one day you'll see. I'm going to be famous.

Then Simone says, 'What are we doing standing here handing out these leaflets, Victoria?'

'It's the job, you know, Simone. It's what we get paid for.'

'So why don't we just dump them? Take them down the tip?'

'We can't do that.' I was so shocked.

'Of course we bloody can. Just put them back in the jeep and take them all down the tip.'

So we did. But I never did it again – too scared I'd be found out.

With the money from *Bertie* I'd traded up my Fiat Uno for a Suzuki jeep – not a Vitara, one of the old ones. A friend of my dad's drove it once and described it as a sewing machine on wheels. It wasn't fast, it wasn't practical, but it was a convertible – black with a white hood with a windsurfer on the side and in immaculate condition. I mean, how cool is that?

The best job was working for the *Daily Mirror*. (Bet you never realized that one, Piers.) Real bimbo work this was: we had to wear little tight T-shirts with *Daily Mirror* plastered all over them in red letters, a white cap with red letters, tight black trousers and black boots. They liked to use dancers because they always looked quite respectable – nice but dim. So the *Mirror* gave me a list of newsagents and I had to go and check if they were advertising the current *Mirror* promotion. If they were, they'd get a T-shirt or a pen. I got my sister to come with me.

The first day wasn't too bad; at least we knew roughly where we were going. But from then on it was like doing a jigsaw puzzle without the picture. Every day we'd go to a different area, every day we'd get lost, every day we'd end up not talking.

My life at certain points was quite surreal. One week I had a call from Dancers. A job, a little unusual, they warned, but it paid good money. 'You've got to be flexible and you've got to have dance ability.'

They had me put on a skin-colour catsuit, then I had to go on all fours and arch my back and imagine that somebody was having sex with me – while they filmed. What they were doing was making a risqué cartoon, which is why they wanted all the back arching and the strange positions, so that the artist could use me as the model.

This was art. There was no second party here – I have

to admit that my acting ability, as well as my back, was being stretched to the limit.

The next time I was asked to be a model was only a couple of years ago. A plastic surgeon contacted me saying he'd spent years searching for the perfect ears and they only happen to be on Posh. So he asked if he could take some photographs to show in lectures, and for use as a template for replacement ears. No one would even know it was me, he promised, he purely wanted my ears. But in the end I thought, No. My ears are originals, after all, and there are enough people walking round looking like me anyway, why make it easy? Just think, after all these years of worrying what I looked like, I never realized I had an outstandingly perfect pair of ears. Why couldn't I have had the perfect complexion, hair or chest? Let's face it, who gives a monkey's about what your ears look like?

Perhaps I should get them insured, Jennifer Lopez has insured her backside, so why not Posh's ears?

You don't usually do auditions for promotion work, but the next job was ridiculously good money, £150 a day, and for that the guy wanted to see what he was getting. (For that I'd have given him 'Mein Herr'.) All I had to do, he said, was to spend the day with him and his friends at Kempton Park racecourse. I'd be picked up in a car and taken back in a car, so I thought why not? To this day I don't know what he was up to, or what he was paying for. There were six pretty young girls and me. Then at some point he gave us £50 each just for betting. As far as I know nothing else was involved, but perhaps I was just so naive I didn't get it. If it was now, I'd be far more cynical. I mean, what the hell was he doing paying us all that money? You can kind of understand how young girls can get themselves into funny situations.

Then one Wednesday, just after Christmas it must have been, I saw this advert in the *Stage*, so small you could have easily missed it. 'Girl singers wanted for pop group.' And a London phone number. Not exactly the West End and not exactly a musical. But why not?

6 wanted

I'd sent in a picture and CV like the ad said. Then a couple of days later the phone rang. Could I come for the audition and bring some music to dance to?

The tape I took with me was 'Let Me Be Your Fantasy' by Baby D; it was a club tune that had become a hit that November. It was very housey, so when they put it on I just jigged about. As for the song, 'Mein Herr', it must have given everyone a good laugh.

Most auditions are run on similar lines but this was so unprofessional. It was just these couple of guys watching, they didn't even look at my portfolio. The main one, the one with the dream of having this band, was Steve Andrews, real *Sarf* London, but good-looking in a cheesy kind of way, tanned, quite well-built, dark hair, the sort you could just hear your mum saying, 'Oh, what a handsome boy.' And he was – from a distance. But close up you could tell that most of it – especially the tan – was fake.

'So, righ', Victoria. Fanks fa comin'. We'll call ya.'

Usual thing.

But a couple of days later, he actually did phone.

Could I come for a recall? A club in the Uxbridge Road just beyond Shepherd's Bush.

Clubs are pretty sad places in the daytime. You feel a stripper's about to come on at any moment and start letting it all hang out, literally. Funnily enough, it turned out Steve was a stripper – his day job, as it were.

There must have been about ten of us. So we're all there, disco lights going, giving it everything around this seedy dance floor, singing 'Band of Gold'. But nobody's looking at us, the nightclub crew and the barmen are all wandering around doing all that clearing up/getting ready thing. And I'm thinking, This is what it must be like being a Redcoat at Butlins. And Steve's out front doing his Mick Jagger strut, Cuban heels, leather jacket with the collar turned up with no top underneath and a shaved chest and jeans so tight that his packet looked massive. Then it was, 'We'll call ya.'

And the next day he did. If I was interested he'd like to have me in the band, he said. No mention of a job as such. Or money. But that didn't matter. A band! I'd been picked for a band! I was really excited. My promotion work would keep me going until this took off.

The studio we rehearsed in was up in Park Royal. There were five of us, three girls and two boys, including this Steve. There was Natasha, who I'd known at Laine's. She was the usual Laine's type, tall and thin. Then there was another Natasha, a black girl who was a really good singer. (Funny that, two Natashas.) And as well as Steve there was Nick, a good bit older than the rest of us, in his thirties. He'd done a bit of dancing, and a bit of modelling. Everyone was OK, but not outstanding.

We'd meet up about three times a week in this crappy little studio to rehearse. I was the lead singer. The only song I remember was a ballad that some black guy Steve knew had written. It went: 'I wanna be the one, be the one, who takes you home. I wanna be the one, be the one. I wanna be the one, be the one that takes you home, I wanna be the one, be the one.' It was called, surprisingly, 'Be the One'. The band was called Persuasion. It would take more than Persuasion for anyone to take us on.

Then in the middle of March I was reading the *Stage* over breakfast, and spotted an ad for another band.

WANTED
RU 18–23 with the ability to sing/dance?
RU streetwise, outgoing, ambitious, dedicated?
Heart Management Ltd are a widely successful
Music Industry Management Consortium currently
forming a choreographed, singing/dancing
all female Pop Act for a Record Recording Deal.
Auditions on 27 March 1994 at Dance Works
opposite Selfridges, 11–4

It was clear from the moment I stepped through the door that this was a totally different set-up from Persuasion. For a start Dance Works was a professional studio; in fact, everything about the audition was totally professional. There were literally hundreds of girls there. And this wasn't the only audition. They were auditioning all round the country.

They'd get about fifty of us in at a time and then we were taught the routine. Then ten would come on and do it, then the next ten and so on. It wasn't anything too difficult – more like street dancing and quite relaxed. But right from the start I knew getting through to the next round would be hard. There were some fantastic dancers there, and later on, when we got to that bit, some fantastic singers.

I couldn't help noticing that some of the best voices weren't getting through. I had to keep reminding myself that this wasn't an audition for the West End and that being in a pop group is not about having the best voice, it's about image and personality. Without me even noticing it happening, the coats and bags that had littered the floor at the beginning were slowly disappearing. And I was still there. How many were they looking for? The ad hadn't said.

When it came to the individual song I knew my luck had run out. What chance did I have with 'Mein Herr'? It had got me *Bertie*, but a pop group? There was no way I was getting through against these girls doing 'I Will Survive' and Whitney Houston.

So I stood there, head lowered, hands on hips, and just gave them Liza Minnelli, Judy Garland and Elaine Paige rolled into one.

'Thank you – er – Victoria. We'll be in touch.'

The 'we' were two men, father and son, and a young woman. But to be honest I didn't take that much notice of them. I'd got to sing my song and I really hadn't thought I'd get that far. Perhaps I ought to consider finding another one if I was going to think seriously about trying the pop route.

So it was back to tight T-shirts and push-up bras with some company's name plastered across my chest and handing out leaflets and rehearsing a few times a week with Persuasion. More than two weeks had passed and I hadn't heard anything from the girl band, so that was probably that.

It was about a month after the original audition that they phoned again. Seven days after my twentieth birthday – April 24th. Was I free for a recall?

I was just so excited. I tried to think back to how many of us had been left at the end. About thirty. So how many would there be at the recall?

It was held in Nomis Studios, in a side-street between Shepherd's Bush and Olympia. One by one we were called in to go through our portfolio and CV with Bob and Chris Herbert, as the father and son were called.

They're already halfway through seeing people when this girl comes crashing through the double doors, half tripping up on what look like Vivienne Westwood platform shoes, an original sixties handbag spilling make-up and keys all over the place. We all turn and stare. She's wearing this purple coat with marabou feathers round the neck and underneath she's got on a pair of really really tight deep-purple seventies-style Farrahs, slightly flared. And this auburny hair half up and half down, loads of make-up, very high cheekbones, sparkly eyes, brilliant skin. She was really really tiny, really skinny and obviously very very scatty. In fact a bit bloody weird. This was Geri.

I recognized her from a month or so before when we'd both done an audition for a film called *Tank Girl*. *Tank Girl* was originally an advert, but there was all this publicity about how it was going to be made into a big Hollywood blockbuster. The ad in the *Stage* read: *We're searching for the star of this futuristic action feature film.* They even had ads for it on the radio.

Again it was an open audition and there were literally hundreds of girls queuing up at a cinema in Leicester Square. Most of them were dressed as Tank Girl: a sort of tarty punk look, ripped tights, loads of make-up. Miss Sophisticate was wearing a smart suit and heels. I hadn't thought they'd want the whole method acting thing. Anyway I'm standing next to Geri in the queue and we started chatting immediately, she was really bubbly and friendly. She was wearing ripped shorts, ripped fishnet tights and hair tied in knots like a cannibal from an old Rupert Bear annual.

It was like a mini screen test. We were divided into groups of ten, then they'd ask us something about ourselves on camera. So ten people would go into this room where they were filming and the rest of us would wait outside till our number was called.

So I'm sitting in the foyer waiting with Geri, and we're having a chat and all of a sudden she disappears and then comes back with a box of popcorn. And she's stolen it. She had to do it, she tells me, because she has a low sugar level and no money. So she offers me some of this popcorn, and I say, 'No, thank you.' Not because I don't want any, but because I'm just too scared.

So then this woman comes over and starts shouting at me, for some reason thinking that I had nicked it. And I can feel my face go bright red, and obviously I can't say anything about Geri, so I just say, 'No, I didn't. It wasn't me, I swear.' Over and over. Then she goes and Geri carries on popping the popcorn into her mouth, grinning. And there's me, so square I wouldn't even take any of this popcorn because I don't want to be seen eating stolen property.

So after about a couple of hours we're in. They had us standing in a line and then one by one you had to say why you thought you should be Tank Girl straight to camera.

'I think I should be Tank Girl because I love shagging kangaroos. And I've got the best pair of tits you've ever seen.' This was the girl in front of Geri. Then she lifts up her top and starts shaking her tits about in front of the camera. (I later found out that Tank Girl in the cartoon apparently used to have amorous liaisons with kangaroos.)

And I'm thinking, what am I doing here? Here's everyone trying to be outrageous and I am so not outrageous. I'm just totally embarrassed. This is so not my character. Before I had time to decide whether to walk out there and then, Geri had started.

'I should be Tank Girl because . . .'

I can't remember what she said, but she was so loud. And it was like, Get your panto outfit out, dress up in these big high-heels and be ALL GIRL.

Then it was me, Morticia Addams with spots.

I stepped forward, looked straight to camera and said, 'How can I follow that?' Pause. 'I can act.' And I shrugged my shoulders. 'That's it.'

I didn't get the part. Geri didn't get the part, the girl who liked shagging kangaroos didn't get the part. None of the thousands who queued up got the part. It turned out Tank Girl had already been cast. All just a publicity stunt, probably to raise finance they didn't have – a scenario that would become very familiar a few years later.

Now here was Geri again. And we gave each other big smiles of recognition and I suddenly felt that I wanted her to be my friend. I thought at the time it was because I didn't know anyone else. But I later realized that everybody felt like this around Geri; she had a daring streak in her that everyone wanted to be part of. The same as Melanie Brown, I later discovered.

After seeing Bob and Chris individually, we were split into three groups of four and given a cassette player and a tape – 'Just a Step from Heaven' by Eternal, who when we started out were the only other girl group around. We were told we had forty-five minutes to choreograph a routine.

In a situation like that, it's like musical chairs. You know that there aren't enough chairs for everyone and you spend half your time watching what the others are doing. And I remember thinking I'm in the group with the prettiest girls. Was that just chance, I wondered? Or did it mean something? Geri wasn't in our group, but there was this mad mixed-race girl called Melanie Brown. I remember thinking she was really really beautiful: lovely little figure, nice pair of boobs, perfect skin, all this black curly hair. She was wearing a cream-coloured top and a little cream A-line skirt with buttons up the front. She had a very strong North Country accent and was very outgoing and confident. In fact she was a bit frightening, if I'm really honest.

Then there was a Welsh girl, who looked older than the rest of us. She was very slim, short dark hair, with a fantastic voice. Finally there was Michelle Stephenson, tall with mousy-coloured corkscrew hair but again really pretty – the sort of girl you can imagine on a Flake advert, clear complexion, a few little freckles and an all-year tan. She was one of those who didn't need much make-up. Just a flick of mascara and a bit of lip gloss.

After a while it dawned on me how the other three were all wearing these little short skirts and I looked totally different. Long straight dark hair, my usual slimming black: leggings, tight top and a pair of big black boots, a cross between calipers and things with gold buckles that Michael Jackson might wear. Then gold-coloured earrings and a leather choker with a brown stone hanging from it that looked a bit like a pebble you'd dug out of the garden, but which in actual fact I had bought from Oasis.

'Have anything you want, girls,' Bob Herbert said, waving his hand towards a counter piled high with cans and bottles and food. We were in the reception area waiting our turn. 'There's a tab.'

We all looked at each other. You didn't usually get this at auditions. And we were all broke. So, it's like, This is all right. I had a sandwich and a Diet Coke. Melanie Brown on the other hand picks up a bottle of wine. In anybody else it would be like taking advantage – but with her it was just a cheeky, Forget the Diet Coke, anybody want a glass? Right from the beginning, Melanie always had the courage to say what she thought, do what she felt like, go that bit further. It was just part of her personality and part of what made people love her.

Then we were on. Melanie had set the ball rolling on the choreography and it was quite funky – we were all good dancers except for Michelle who had trouble picking it up.

The stage was quite low, only about a foot off the ground. It was the same people watching us: Bob Herbert, the father, totally *Miami Vice*: the suit, the hair, the medallion. His son Chris, in his twenties, quite slight, more casual, denim and Timberlands and Chris's girlfriend – who was introduced as the stylist – Shelley.

'That was great, girls, great, great,' Chris said when we'd finished, with all the been-there, got-the-T-shirt, I'm-in-the-music-business confidence. 'What we'd like now is for you to teach your routine to Geri here,' he said and nodded to where Geri had come in at the door. She gave me a cheeky grin.

'Think you can do that?'

So it was back to our little rehearsal room; not the best place to learn a dance, particularly when the person learning isn't a dancer. It turned out Geri hadn't even come to the original audition. She was a complete blagger – just said she was ill and pleaded to be fast-tracked to the recall. But you could see what it was about her – all this marabou around her neck and all this red hair – she was completely mad, completely over the top. The kind of Yes-I've-climbed-Mount-Everest-I've-done-everything kind of person you'd want to hang out with. And, in actual fact, she had lived a lot more than the rest of us. She'd lived in a squat, she'd worked in Turkey and Majorca. She'd been around. The rest of us were fresh out of college.

So we did the routine again, this time with Geri, if you can use 'with' to describe someone who was not really with it at all.

This feeling of superiority didn't last long. Next we

were told we had to sing solo and it had to be a pop song, Chris said, looking straight at me. So, not 'Mein Herr', then.

As I didn't have one, they made a couple of suggestions and I had to choose one of them. I can't remember now what it was, only that it was terrible. The pianist played in his key and I sang in mine. It started OK but then it went far too high. And I remember standing there on this little stage trying to sing this bloody song and knowing that I wasn't singing, I was squawking. It was so far beyond bad that I didn't even feel nervous. It must be like when you're in the war, and you know you're going to die anyway. About halfway through I totally gave up.

'Look,' I said, 'I can't do this. I sound like a cat.' The other girls were looking at the ground. I was desperate. I had done so well getting this far with the audition and it was slipping away from me like a piece of soap in the bath. 'But I can sing, I promise you, I really can sing. This is just not in my key.' I stood there, hands on my hips, like a school prefect. And that's where my personality came through. I didn't look away, I wasn't apologetic, I just stared at them, willing them to believe me.

When I was up there, talking to them, it didn't feel so bad, because in actual fact I am quite good at convincing people about things. But afterwards I had to stand at the side and listen to the others who — apart from Geri — were all really, really good. Geri at least had a song that worked for her voice. And it was so embarrassing to realize that I'd had the nerve to stand there and tell them that I could sing. I just thought,

Well, that's that. From all those hundreds of girls I'd got to the last five and then blown it.

'We'll phone you.'

Like, Thanks, but no thanks.

The call came a few days later. It was Chris.

'Victoria. Hi. Would you be free to come back to see us next week?'

Was I free? As a bloody bird I was free.

'I'll be sending you a tape. Stevie Wonder's "Signed, Sealed, Delivered". Perhaps you know it. We'd like to see how your voices blend.'

Stevie Wonder – I couldn't believe my luck. I had been brought up on Stevie Wonder by my dad. I was so excited. Forget Persuasion. Well, not completely. I had to keep reminding myself, it was only a recall, after all. Nothing more than that. But a recall out of five. How big did they want this group to be? Four and I'd be out.

A week later we were back again in Shepherd's Bush. I had expected it to be the same five, but it wasn't. The Welsh girl with the great voice wasn't there, instead there was a girl who said she knew me called Melanie Chisholm. She had a Liverpool accent and I genuinely couldn't remember ever having seen her before. She told me that she'd been to Doreen Bird's, the college I would have gone to if I hadn't got a place at Laine's. She was soft, and seemed like a really nice caring person. She was wearing a black A-line skirt with buttons on the front, a tight black top, hair all scraped back and a bright red lipstick.

This time I was really scared. At the beginning it had been just another audition. How many auditions had I done over the last ten or so years? Thirty? Forty? But this was different. The solo I'd done last time was like some terrible obstacle that somehow I had overcome, but I knew I had no slack left. With Stevie Wonder at least I could just belt it out.

So we're standing round the piano and first we sing it individually. Melanie B was very confident, but then she was already quite a professional; she'd been in *Coronation Street* and *Emmerdale Farm*. Melanie C, who had been at the original audition but missed the recall because she'd had something the matter with her tonsils, was a good natural singer, generally a lot more controlled and sounded a lot more trained than the rest of us. Whereas Geri was more Here-We-are-Standing-in-a-Pub-type thing with the husky voice to go with it. I was more Take Me to the Music Hall. Geri didn't have an outstanding talent, but she could belt something out, and she was louder than me. Pure personality. Michelle had a good voice, but it was not poppy at all. And I remember thinking, Well, if it's four, then I stand a better chance than Michelle, my main reason being that I could dance and she couldn't.

A soulful Stevie Wonder song like 'Signed, Sealed, Delivered' works through your feelings which affects your phrasing. Put five different people together and they're going to feel completely differently.

Our first effort was terrible. Apart from anything else, we all wanted this job. We weren't a team, we were five sprinters going for gold. It was a case of all wanting our own voice to be heard and f*** the others. We were really strong characters so we were all just belting out what should be a controlled, soulful song. Well, four of us were – Michelle was really quite quiet.

When we arrived we'd been introduced to this other

man. The backer. His name was Chic Murphy and he had a face you could describe as lived in and he sounded as if he had just walked out of *EastEnders*. He must have been over sixty. He was tall, silver haired and tanned – real, not like Steve – the kind of tan that comes from spending three months in Marbella, not three hours under a lamp. He dressed quite smart but quite casual and spoke with a real East End accent. On the lobes of his ears he had tattoos of little stars. And he never stopped smoking. He smoked ordinary cigarettes but stuck them into these see-through filters that he always had with him. He was one of those people who, wherever he is, gives the impression that he owns the place.

'We'll call you.'

We needed to work more together to see if our voices could blend, Chris said when he phoned a few days later.

'We'd like you to spend a week together,' he explained. They had booked rooms in a guest house just outside Windsor, and there was a studio not far away. Everything would be paid for. As for Persuasion, I told Steve that I wouldn't be able to make rehearsals for about ten days, as I was going away. Well, it was true.

That week I was happy in a way I had never imagined possible. Every morning we'd pile into a car that came to collect us and go to Trinity Studios in Woking where we'd spend the whole day working on our dancing and our singing. For the first time in my life I was with people who wanted to know me and liked me and I had something in common with. We never stopped laughing. I'd always been quite quiet and reserved. And already I'd had more laughs with them than I'd had with anyone I could remember.

That was when we first met our singing teacher, Pepe Lemer. She was all Moschino jeans and Versace gold belts – very Dorian from *Birds of a Feather*. She was one of those people who you could tell had had elocution lessons, very theatrical with lots of shaggy looking high-lighted hair, but she wore it well.

Although she had been teaching for years, she had started off as a session singer, she told us, and so really knew what she was talking about. The song we had to work on was 'Take Me Away', a mid-tempo ballad. Our main problem was blending. A perfectly blended five-part vocal group with no lead singer is one of the most difficult things to get right and so perhaps it wasn't surprising that when we first heard ourselves recorded on the cassette player we sounded awful. We still didn't know if we had got the job. Obviously everyone wanting to Do Their Own Thing made Pepe's job really difficult. You weren't interested in blending, you just wanted to take the song and do it. You wanted to be in a pop group, not a bloody barber-shop quintet.

When it came to the dancing – again, it was a question of balance. Three of us could dance, no problem, the other two were frankly a disaster. Michelle's main prob-lem was timing. But Geri was the weakest: however you look at it, a few months as a podium dancer in Magaluf just isn't the same as ten years at the barre, and it showed.

A week had never passed so quickly. Forget Jason's, forget Laine's. This was what I always thought it would be like to be a Kid From *Fame*, a complete adrenalin rush. It was like falling in love, everything felt new and fresh.

At the end of the week we went into Windsor to a Pizza Hut for our final meal. While the rest of us made pigs of ourselves with pizzas and ice cream, Geri attacked the salad bar. Until then I didn't even realize Pizza Hut did salads.

On our last day we did our number for Bob, Chris and Chic and Shelley. It all seemed to go well. Everyone smiling. So, were we in?

'Great, girls. Great. We'll give you a call.'

My dad came down to pick me up. As Geri lived quite near us, in Watford, we gave her a lift back. Me and Geri had shared a room and, although she was completely mad, we got on really well. Although our taste in clothes was different – I was designer, Geri was vintage – we were both into style in our own way.

The great thing about Geri was that she never did things by halves – she would almost become a character. Like eighties, seventies, or sixties. It made no difference if we were going to the studio, Tesco's, or out to a club. Geri would dress in whatever character she had decided she was going to be that particular day. She was totally styled all the time, and almost knew how to dress like a pop star even before she was one. In fact it was only as time wore on that she got more casual because we barely had time to go to the toilet, let alone go shopping.

We said goodbye with promises to keep in touch 'whatever happens'. Geri was the first person I had ever felt I could say, this is my best friend.

I got back to the house around eight. During the week there had been a bit of a heatwave and my mum had done a barbecue in the garden. My mum and dad have always been very sociable and barbecues in the garden were something they'd done ever since I could remember.

Everyone was there – Louise and Christian, my parents' friends Dee and Del. And, of course, Mark. It was baking, everyone was in the pool. I remember sitting on my bed and listening to the familiar sounds outside – voices, splashing – and suddenly feeling very unreal. I'd come from having this great week with four amazing girls who wanted to do the same things as me, felt the same as me, shared the same vision as me. I'd never had many friends and suddenly it was as if I had found the people I belonged with. Sitting there on the bed on my own I felt I didn't want to break the spell, because I knew Mark was waiting for me downstairs like a black cloud in my new blue sky.

They taught me how to have fun. They taught me about myself, they showed me that I had a personality. For the first time I didn't feel embarrassed to be Victoria Adams. All my life people had taken the mickey about how I dressed. They liked the way I dressed. It was almost as though they were picking up the pieces that Mark had demolished, even in that first week. It was like all my life I had been pretending to be me, but now for the first time I really was me. Almost a feeling that I was coming home. Then again through the open window I heard Mark Wood being loud about something. I went downstairs.

He was sitting by the pool with a can of lager.

'So,' he said, 'what's the little pop star been doing all week, then?'

He was looking towards the barbecue to see if the chicken pieces were ready. He really didn't care what I had been doing all week. But I told him anyway. How these girls I'd been with were so fantastic, how they had all this energy and enthusiasm and how we all had the same dream, how everything was moving so quickly, and how I really thought we could do it.

Mark was so not impressed.

'Girl bands, forget it. It's a complete waste of time.'

He was only saying what everyone believed then.

7 the famous five

Maidenhead was another try-out, Chris explained when he called me, but this time longer. We would work on our voices and routines during the day and live together in this house to see how we got on together.

I still didn't know if I'd got the job, none of us did. It meant we could never really relax: we knew that at any time we could be told, 'Sorry, but it just hasn't worked out.'

Vocally we were still all over the place, but Pepe had told Bob and Chris that with a little more time she thought she could knock us into shape. She hinted that everything hinged on getting our voices to blend. There was no mention of how long we were going to stay in Maidenhead. 'A few weeks,' Chris had told me on the phone. 'A month or two,' Bob had told Geri.

The house belonged to Chic. It was on a typical sixties estate, a bit rundown, but it had recently been decorated, so at least it was clean. The two Mels and Geri were oohing and aahing every time a cupboard door was opened as if it was the Ritz, although the house was really very small compared with anywhere I had lived. I think this was the first time I realized how different my background was to theirs.

There were two and a half bedrooms; I shared the biggest with Michelle. It had a light blue carpet and a yellowy floral wallpaper, white wardrobes and white sideboard. Nice, but not matching quilts. The two Mels had to share a double bed. We called it the 'sex room' because it had pink walls, a reddy coloured carpet and Mel B put a red bulb in the main light. No lampshade. Geri had a room that was little more than a cupboard. It didn't even have a proper bed, only a mattress. There was only one bathroom and Mel B used to irritate us all because she hogged it, lying in the bath for hours singing Zhane songs such as 'Groove Thang'. She had at least two baths a day. And there again I was different. She'd be in there having a bath and she'd never lock the door and the other girls would go in and have a wee. I was the only one who would lock the door. But towards the end I was just the same and used to wee in front of them all. That's how close we actually got.

The thing I liked about the house was that it was light. It had big windows. I still have this thing about light. Light and sunshine can make everything seem better if you're feeling a bit sad.

Somewhere to live and somewhere to rehearse – what more could a girl want? Well, a bit of money to live on, actually. For a few weeks we survived on the dole – none of us wanted to be pushy and ask for money at this stage. It was only after about a month that we said we had to have something. They agreed on £60 a week.

Nobody was saying how long this would go on for,

but I decided it was crunch time for Persuasion. I knew I was where I wanted to be. Sorry, Steve.

We worked a five-day week. Up at eight, in Trinity Studios by ten. Two days a week Pepe came for four hours, the other three days we were on our own. The guy who owned Trinity Studios was called Ian. He was forty-five and balding on top with a beard and not like somebody who was in the music business at all – more like your uncle, very uncool but a nice enough bloke. He loved us being there because we were the first people to use it as studios – I think it once might have been an old school – and he was trying to transform it into a professional recording studio. He had a dream. We had a dream and he really picked up on that and got a real buzz out of watching us rehearse. Even Bob and Chris had a dream. There were so many people who were working together.

By this time we had found out a bit about Bob and Chris. We weren't their first project – it turned out they had discovered Bros, but just when Bros were going to make it big they'd signed with somebody else.

Chic never stopped telling us how he had managed the Three Degrees, the seventies all-girl group. Because of the Three Degrees, he knew everything there was to know about the pop world. What we had to have was a set. A set? A set was what my nan had done with her hair and went hand in hand with a purple rinse. That was way back in the old days, we said. What about getting us on *Top of the Pops*?

'Don't you effing forget,' he said, 'I managed the Three Degrees and the Three Degrees 'ad an effing set.' But then he'd light up another cigarette, wave it in the air and with a twinkle in the eye say: 'Well, gehwls, I fink we've got somefing 'ere,' and ask us down to his house in Bray, which backed on to the Thames, to have a swim in his pool. No one really knew where he made his money. We decided it was better not to ask.

Tracy, his wife, was a really nice person, very pretty and much younger than Chic. They had two beautiful little kids – really well brought-up. Chic was a real romantic – he had their initials T and C entwined in mosaic at the bottom of the pool.

It was when we were swimming at his house that he first had a go about my weight.

'Do us a favour, Vic,' he said, giving me the once-over in my swimming costume. 'Lose a couple of pounds, will ya?'

I wished I could just disappear, I felt so terrible. But anyway, I told myself, I wasn't any bigger than Mel C was I? A few days later, Mel C told me he'd said the same thing to her.

For our 'set' we had these three songs to learn from a tape recorded by a session singer. They weren't crap but they weren't great either.

It didn't help that we didn't have a lead singer, everyone said. Everyone except us. We didn't want a lead singer. We were like, Why? We all wanted to have a go. That's how we started and that's how we've stayed. We'd sing a line or two each, then we'd blend together for a chorus, then somebody would – say – do the first part of the verse, then back to the chorus, then someone else would sing the bridge, and two of us would split the middle eight, for example.

Our problem was still blending. Basically it was back

to the drawing board, learning to use our ears, Pepe said. Listening to what everyone else is singing is really important, listening to their tones, to their timing. And it's all really quite difficult, you have to be very disciplined, learning to push forward for the solo, then to pull back and blend when somebody else is at the mike.

The dancing came easily to me and the two Mels, but for Michelle and Geri it was uphill all the way. Michelle had a real problem with rhythm. Nothing we did seemed to make it easier. So when we were dancing we'd be shouting at her, and clapping at her legs.

'Five, six, seven, eight.'

'Pick. Your. Legs. Up.'

'Listen to the bloody music, Michelle.'

But it was hopeless: she had less rhythm than a cement mixer. She had an all-right voice, but it wasn't poppy – it was what you might call cruise-ship operatic.

In a way we were a bit cruel to Michelle, but then she set herself up for it. When things got tough, instead of knuckling down, she'd remember her tan needed a top-up and go out into the garden. Also it didn't help that she came from a very different background from the rest of us. My family might have been better off than the other girls' families, but basically we had a lot in common. Michelle was different. She lived in Oxford and had a place at university. She didn't think the same way we did. She didn't have the dream.

Geri had the dream but she didn't have the training – to be honest, she didn't know what she was doing most of the time and would just wing it, hoping that no one would notice. What she did have was more ambition than the rest of us put together, she was totally focused, totally single-minded. Sometimes you just wanted her to shut up, but that was just Geri.

Melanie C was fantastic, so patient, spending hours after rehearsals really helping her, and Geri did work really really hard. Back at the house, when the rest of us just flopped down in front of *Home and Away*, Geri was going over and over the dance routines. Yes, it was frustrating knowing we could have moved on more quickly if we hadn't been held back by two of the group, but we could forgive Geri – at least she was trying. Whereas Michelle just couldn't be arsed.

First we talked about it amongst ourselves, but in the end we decided we had to say something to Bob and Chris. By now we knew that although Bob could look quite stern, a flutter of eyelids and he'd turn to jelly.

They agreed. The sun-worshipper, as we called her, would have to go.

Michelle left during the summer break. She had a place at university to go to, so we didn't feel too bad, though I wish I'd had the chance to say goodbye. I felt particularly shitty – after all, I had been sharing a room with her for something like two months – but in fact getting rid of Michelle made us feel more like a gang. And it wouldn't be the last time that losing someone brought the rest of us closer together.

We knew we had to find somebody else. Even though Michelle hadn't worked, five felt right. Michelle had looked the part but inside she had been wrong. What we needed was somebody like us – loud, gutsy, ruthless workaholics – but blonde.

Did we know anybody like that? No we didn't. But Pepe did. A couple of years back she had taught a girl called Emma Bunton. And during the break she got hold of her address from the school where she'd taught her, and asked her to get in touch. Then Emma met Bob, Chris and Chic. They asked her to come and spend some time with us to see if she fitted in and if her voice sat comfortably with the rest of us. Finally it was Us. Or 'Touch', as Bob, Chris and Chic had decided we should be called.

We'd been on and on at them to give us a name.

'But there's no point in having a name,' they said. 'You're not doing anything yet.'

I quite liked Touch.

We decided we should meet Emma at the station, so we all piled into Geri's car. It was a really sunny afternoon and Geri had on hot pants, and this tight little white and red stripey top that she still wears now, her hair up in pigtails, black and white stripey socks and big platform shoes. This was a French day; all she needed was some onions around her neck and a bike and she'd be away.

Anyway, typical Geri parks on a double yellow line and says she'll run in and get Emma while we stay in the car to fend off traffic wardens.

It's funny now to think that's where the five of us first met. I can see it now: Emma walking towards us with her mum, wearing a little white dress, white knee-socks and trainers, blonde shoulder-length hair, really clear skin and a really big smile – like she'd been to stage school, and she had: six years at Sylvia Young. And she looked so young. In fact, she was the youngest, although she had more working experience than the rest of us put together. She'd done *Grange Hill* and *EastEnders*. Within a few hours of meeting Emma we all gelled. A few looks, a few nods. We knew this was right.

When Emma moved to Maidenhead it was the first time she'd lived away from home. She and her mum were very close – the first time I saw them that time at the station they were holding hands. She took over Michelle's place in my room. Like me, Emma found it hard being away from her family and we both used to go home every weekend. As she lived in Finchley I always gave her a lift.

That was the only bad thing about being with the girls – it meant I couldn't be with my family. At least during the week. I sold the jeep and bought a Renault Clio. It was black and it was automatic – a lot more sensible for long journeys.

Me and Geri were the only ones with cars and every day we used to pile into her beaten-up old Fiat Uno to go to work because Geri liked driving and I didn't, especially when I had Mel B in the front telling me what to do and everyone singing and being generally loud. I couldn't handle it. Also I was very proud of my new car, cleaning it all the time, and didn't want any mess. Any mess in my car used to drive me potty.

How we ever got anywhere, I don't know, because Geri is the worst driver. She has no concentration what-soever and the amount of times she used to bang into things and have crashes you wondered how that car ever got through the MOT.

Even more tidy than me was Melanie C. She was very house-proud (the David Beckham of the Spice Girls). At the beginning she used to do all the tidying and cleaning. We ended up having a rota: who would do the clearing up, who would sweep the stairs, who would do the hoovering and who would clean the toilets, and we would take it in turns, although Mel C always ended up doing more than anybody else. If she saw that the washing-up needed doing, she'd just do it, even though it wasn't her turn. She couldn't stand mess.

The fridge was covered with posters, pin-ups from *Smash Hits* or *Top of the Pops* magazine. Mel C was a massive Take That fan and she had stickers and fridge magnets of Robbie Williams while I had Jason Orange. Geri was George Michael mad.

We didn't have mobile phones in those early days but Chic had got us a payphone and we soon worked out that if you unplugged it and put an ordinary phone into the socket, you could make free calls. We just had to make sure that whenever Chic came round we had plugged the payphone back in.

We went shopping once a week at Tesco's but we never really cooked communally because we all liked different things – like I'd live on cheese and packets of crackers and I went through a stage of liking bagels with honey. Emma lived on babyfood. Seriously. Geri seemed to live on nothing.

Me and Emma never thought of the Maidenhead house as home, it was more a Monday to Friday thing. For Geri and the two Mels it was different. Geri, being the oldest, had lived on her own for years and the other two came from up north – too far away to go home at weekends, though Mel C would often go to Sidcup in Kent where she still had friends at college – so Mel B and Geri used to spend their weekends together and were very much partners in crime. In those days I thought they were both quite mad. If they decided they wanted to go to a club at two o'clock in the morning they'd be up and off.

I used to come back after a weekend at home and find all my clothes lying around that had been borrowed and not put back. I didn't mind if they borrowed my clothes – we all borrowed things from each other – but I just wished they'd take care of them, not leave them with make-up smeared all round the neck, or the sleeves baggy from being tied in a knot. Just because I had more things than they did didn't mean I didn't care.

In those days when Geri was really thin and I was much bigger, she used to lend me her bras because we had the same size bust. They were called Cross Your Heart, made by Playtex, and you wore them under tight little T-shirts. Geri was always so completely styled, she never wore anything normal, and she was the one who started the baby T-shirt thing.

'Who the hell does this bloody bra belong to?' my mum said when she found one in my washing. Geri's bras were really frumpy-looking – all frayed and grey. 'It's like one left over from the Second World War.'

She was right. These bras were complete passion killers, which was just as well as passion was something I was trying to avoid. Going back home for the weekend was always a bit uneasy. I wanted to go because of my family, but there was a dark cloud over everything, called Mark. He was still living there – in my room. I kept saying that I thought he ought to get a place of his own, but he would then turn it round and say I wanted to get rid of him. As much as it was the truth, I was so terrified of not having a boyfriend that I would say, no, no.

But what's the point of having a boyfriend if you

never go out? Mark's excuse was that we needed to save. And he certainly was saving – my mum and dad were always offering to pay and Mark never seemed to have a problem about accepting. So what was he saving for? A romantic holiday for two? No. New wheels and a bigger exhaust for his Escort RS Turbo. After all, he couldn't afford to lose face with the other boy-racers at the Sunday meet down at Southend.

But I did go out with the girls during the week. There was a nightclub we went to in Maidenhead called the Avenue and Wednesdays was student night when you could get in for a pound. And I remember once Geri going up to the DJ and getting the microphone and shouting out, 'Just to let you know that tonight Touch are in the house' – as if we were a top band people had heard of.

We were all so wired. The rest of us would be on the dance floor and Geri would be up on the podium dancing. Or rather jigging, which continued to be her speciality. We danced until they chucked us out.

At the time Emma had a boyfriend called Chris who was Greek, and on Friday nights going home in the car we'd talk girls' talk: me about my problems with Mark, Emma about her problems with Chris and she'd be chatting away about this club and that DJ and I'd laugh and pretend I knew what she was talking about. But I didn't. All I knew was the Harlow Mill and Quiz Night.

'Don't you want to know what we thought of him, Tor?' the girls said when Mark came down to see me one time.

I had a good idea. They treated him as if he were like somebody on *Harry Enfield*.

'He's a prat.'

You couldn't accuse the girls of not being honest, particularly Mel B. She would always say what she thought and sometimes that would get her into trouble – like getting expelled from college.

'Now listen to me, Vic-keh.' She was the only one who called me Vicky. Usually I hated it, but somehow even this didn't matter. Any of us could do anything and it would be all right.

'That dickhead totally suppresses you. Just get shot of him. Give him his P45 and get back a bit of your self-respect.'

Then one of the others would join in.

'I mean, Vee. Take a grip. Armani shoes don't make up for that nose you know.'

Mark didn't have the best dress sense and they all used to take the mickey, particularly the way he'd wear his trousers pulled up really high.

'So, what chest size are your jeans, sir?'

Then they'd all collapse with laughter.

But as much as I knew they were totally right about him, that he did suppress me, he was still my boyfriend and I felt that I had to stick up for him. In fact, I was now quite embarrassed being with him. He'd always been really skinny and gangly but I was finally beginning to see how everything about him looked awkward. He had no coordination and when he danced he looked like Herman Munster. What made it worse was that he was so cocky and thought he was the world's best dancer.

Even though I was still quite reserved, now that I was one of the girls, I was gradually getting on their vibe, but when I was with Mark it was just like I hadn't met them – I was Mrs Just-Sit-There-Shut-Up-and-Do-as-You're-Told.

Our three-song 'set' was now a five-song 'showcase'. The idea was that Chris and Bob would invite people like record producers and writers and publishing companies to see what an amazing talent we were so they'd be desperate to work with us. So that's what we were rehearsing for, week after bloody week.

'If we're going to do this showcase, let's do it,' we'd say.

'Not till you're ready,' was always the reply. We never got much encouragement – in fact, the reverse. But we were getting bored with the same old songs, the same old routines and we knew we didn't want to get stale. As well as rehearsing till we were as slick as hairgel, we still had Pepe twice a week with her scales and breathing. Didn't she realize that it wasn't being able to sing scales that got you to the top, it was hitting the right groove?

The kind of singing we wanted to do we did back at the house. Not having a lot of money, we'd mainly sit round and entertain each other. And Geri would say let's do a Madonna medley, and someone would start 'Like a Virgin', then we'd all sing along, then someone else would segue into the next one – 'Papa Don't Preach' – and then someone else might say Tina Turner or Bros or Stevie Wonder. It was great practice. Mel C even had a Take That video and we used to put it on and copy their routines. We had this big full-length mirror in one of the bedrooms that we brought down and stood up in one half of the lounge, so when we were practising we could all have a go at looking in the mirror – we'd have to take turns because it was a long thin thing and you could only see one person at a time.

The two new songs we'd been given for the showcase were just as boring as the original three – bottom-drawer stuff that we reckoned a writer had given to loads of bands and no one wanted. We'd tried to improve the lyrics of one of them but this didn't go down very well. However, if they thought by knocking us back they'd make us easier to deal with, they had another think coming – it just made us stronger. If that's how they wanted it, we'd just have to write our own songs.

It became like a mission. Geri had a little Casio and I remember us all sitting on this old wooden table in the other half of the lounge – and I mean on – and we'd start humming melodies and writing down lyric ideas and keyboard ideas and we'd be up till really early in the morning trying to write stuff ourselves. None of us could really play, but the Casio kept us in tune. Our first song was called 'Just One of Those Days' and we wrote it on that old table.

'We want to do our own songs,' we told Chic on one of his rare visits. We might have been speaking Hindustani. He just raised his hands.

'Gehwls, gehwls.'

'And we don't like the name Touch.'

'So what's wrong with Touch?'

'It's not us.'

Touch, like the name of Bob and Chris's management company, Heart, was too touchy-feely, we had decided. We wanted something with edge.

What about High Five? Plus Five? Five Alive? One sounded druggy, one sounded extra-large and one had copyright problems as it was a fruit juice. But the idea stuck. Later Bob and Chris went on to manage a boy-band: 5ive.

It was Geri who had the brainwave. She and Mel C had just come back from the gym – Mel C was a fitness fanatic and Geri was a thinness fanatic. Geri came bursting in through the lounge door.

'I've got it.'

'What?'

'Spice.'

'Spice what?'

Was this a knock knock joke?

'Our name. Spice. It's got five letters and it's us. One word for five different tastes. So? What do you think?'

Our showcase was set for late November back in Nomis Studios in Shepherd's Bush. Chic gave us £50 for outfits ('get somefing smart, gehwls'), so Geri and Mel B went to Camden Market and came back with matching Adidas T-shirts to wear with our own jeans and trainers. We didn't want to dress the same – we didn't in real life – but Bob and Chris said we had to, just like we had to sing their songs.

When you're performing you're so concentrated, you don't notice the audience until it's all over – and we did it like a proper performance with mikes and lights and proper playback. People came throughout the day so we must have done the showcase about four or five times. I don't know how many people saw us, but it could have been as many as a hundred – with twenty or thirty there every time we did a show. And I remember at the end when we took our bow, as it were, feeling quite surprised that they genuinely seemed to like us, clapping and making quite a bit of noise. Afterwards, when we sat on the edge of the little foot-high stage, everybody was coming up and telling us we were great. We didn't know who any of them were, but you could tell they really meant it.

When they did the bit about has anybody any questions, I just sat there and said nothing because I felt embarrassed that my questions were going to be crap. Geri was very outspoken and totally fearless. And that's where she was good. Good for all of us.

Since the autumn and Emma joining us, we'd been on and on at Bob, Chris and Chic, trying to get some kind of agreement or contract out of them, but they always put us off. None of us had even been told that we were in, that we had the job. We just got our £60 every week, and that was that. Now that they saw other people were interested, it was a different story. Suddenly it was, 'Shit, we didn't get them to sign.' Whereas for us it was, 'Shit, thank goodness we didn't sign.'

'Wait till I've talked to my dad,' I told the others when, a few days later, legal envelopes landed on our doormat.

What I haven't mentioned yet is that I wasn't the first one in my family to have a dream. My dad was actually in a couple of groups in the sixties, called the Soniks and the Calettos, and knows all about contracts from bitter experience. Somehow or other the Soniks got an introduction to Joe Meek – Joe Meek was to London what Brian Epstein was to Liverpool. He was a manager and a writer – he made most of his money from a huge hit called 'Telstar' by the Tornados in 1962. Anyway, he auditioned the band, and said he wanted to sign my dad.

Not the band, just their singer, Tony Adams. So of course he signed. His first demo was a song called 'Redder on You' and he recorded it with a group called the Riot Squad. My dad was rehearsing the B side when he heard the news that Joe Meek was dead. Joe Meek's studio was in a converted bedroom above a leather goods shop in Holloway that his landlady owned; and in actual fact my dad had been there the night before.

Nobody knows exactly what happened but Joe Meek kept a shotgun in the flat, which was owned by another of his pop stars called Heinz who sang with the Tornados. He had it because he was having trouble with fans showing up at all hours. Joe Meek must have had an argument with his landlady – my dad says it was more like a mother/son relationship, they were always giving each other presents – and when they argued that night he shot her, then went upstairs and killed himself.

Now because my dad had signed the contract with Joe Meek – even though Joe was dead the contract didn't end – he couldn't sign with anybody else. Tony Adams couldn't do anything until the end of the contract – and it was a five-year contract. Another band who had the same problem were the Honeycombs. Their girl drummer Honey wanted to go solo, but she was in exactly the same position as my dad.

If he hadn't auditioned for Joe Meek, who knows what might have happened. The Soniks even played the Lyceum and had a booking in Hamburg just like the Beatles. But one of the band hadn't wanted to go – he was the only one with a proper job, he worked at the post office. So that was that. They never got to Hamburg, which was why my dad auditioned for Joe Meek and why after Joe Meek died he went into the electrical wholesaling business.

A couple of years ago my dad told me that somewhere he still had the tapes of that original demo. My mum said she thought they were in the attic, and (without telling my dad) I found these tapes and searched through reel after reel and actually found 'Redder on You' and put it on to a CD as a surprise for his birthday. It's really crackly and very old and poor quality, but at least he has it, which he is really happy about. The Soniks still get together now and then to do charity dos.

So what did my dad say about Bob and Chris's contract?

'It's like throwing hundred pound notes on the fire. Forget it.'

The whole point of the showcase had been to introduce us to writers and other people in the industry who would be interested in working with us or writing songs for us. We were still telling Chic, Chris and Bob that we wanted to do our own thing, but they took no notice – but that didn't stop us working on our own stuff most nights. Matt and Biff were two writers who came to us via the showcase and they were different from the others in that they seemed happy to work *with* us, rather than just writing *for* us. Their real names were Matt Rowe and Richard Stannard and they had worked a lot with East 17 – proper pop stars. We got on really well from the very first meeting. They picked up very quickly where we were coming from – didn't tell us what to do, but listened to what we wanted to do and didn't think our ideas were crap. Nobody had treated us like that before. And for them we were really something different.

Until we came along, there were boybands, there was grunge, there was Madonna, and there was Kylie, but that was about it. We were five wild women, equal but different. And we were going to conquer the world.

Their studio was called The Strong Room, in Curtain Road – right in the centre of the City. To get there from Maidenhead we had to drive across London and you could feel the sense of excitement in the car. It was a quite scruffy looking building from the outside, and the studio itself was small, totally different from places we would work in now.

Biff (Richard) was mainly lyrics and melody. Quite camp, blond hair, always smiling, always happy – the kindest person you could ever want to meet. At first he comes across as quite shy but is really good fun when you get to know him. He's a really lovely guy; we're still great friends and he came to our wedding. Matt was the musical side and he's fantastic on piano. In looks they are quite different; one's short and tubby, and one's tall and thin. Matt looks like Postman Pat without the glasses. (Sorry, Matt, I love you really.) That's the trouble with having a baby, you begin to see the whole world through their eyes.

So how did it work? Working with Matt and Biff was a bit like brainstorming and things haven't changed much since we first met them. We get into the studio and they put on the music that Matt has been working on, a backing track if you like, which sets the key, the rhythm, chord structure – things like that. Then we'll start humming melodies. What about this? Yeah, some-one else will say. Sounds good? OK, so into the dicta-phone. We'll all have pads and pens for writing ideas, words, images – whatever. Then somebody might say, What about this? – and sings a line. It might be just a phrase, something setting the mood perhaps. With seven of us around, it could get really buzzy.

In those early days I still felt a bit left out. I knew that I wanted to be part of the mix, but the others were so much more confident than me: Emma with years of work under her belt, Mel B being so totally fearless, Mel C taking a melody and making it really sing, Geri I'm-all-girl-look-at-me – she was even flirting with Matt. It was so intimidating – like standing in a room with no clothes on. And particularly during the early sessions, I didn't have as much input as I did later. In fact with 'Wannabe' I missed most of it.

We'd been working with Matt and Biff all week, but by the time Friday night arrived it was only half done – so everyone agreed to carry on over the weekend. But I had a problem. Some relation of Mark's was getting married and he put so much pressure on me to go to this bloody wedding. I said to the girls that I really didn't want to miss anything, but they said, 'No, no, no, you must go.'

'I'll call you,' Geri promised. (Geri and I had just bought these mobiles, which were so big that they could have done duty as coshes.) 'Don't worry. I'll let you know exactly what we're doing. You won't miss out on anything.'

But I did. The wedding was somewhere near Torquay and from the moment Geri calls me I'm thinking, What am I doing? It wasn't as if it was anything to do with me. It was Mark's bloody family.

She was great, calling me every five minutes saying,

'What do you think of this idea, what do you think of that idea?' But I just couldn't bear not being there. Because whatever they said about how it didn't matter, it did matter. Saying 'Yes, I like that' or 'Not sure about that' down the phone is not the same. I could have cried. I did cry, later. Because I knew, we all knew, that this song was so perfect. That 'Wannabe' was us, that this was it.

And it did make a difference, because by the time it came to recording, performing and singing it, all the parts had been divided up between the rest of them. Yes, I did a few backing vocals but nothing major. And every time we performed it I just felt like a gooseberry standing at the back not doing anything.

And I used to say to my mum, 'God, they'll say I'm the one who doesn't sing.' And she'd say, 'Don't worry, Victoria, no one will notice.' But they did notice. And to this day it's what always gets thrown at me: Posh Spice, the one who doesn't sing.

8 bonnie and clyde

'Not celebrate your twenty-first? And 'ave 'em say Chic Murphy don't treat his gehwls proper?'

Chic's treat was in fact a week before my actual birthday, which in 1995 was on Easter Monday, and for that my mum had organized tea at the Ritz followed by *Miss Saigon*.

It was nearly three months since Bob and Chris had given us the contracts to sign. We hadn't said yes, we hadn't said no. We'd just stalled.

OK, so they'd put us together, but everything after that was down to us. We had the energy, we had the personalities, we had the vision of what we wanted to be. We were all of us creative in our different ways and together we could conquer the world. But we could only do that our way: writing our own songs, wearing our own clothes, being in control. It was just a question of finding a way to do it.

Chic and his friend Wally picked us up in his Rolls-Royce and took us to the Cromwell Mint, a members only casino in Kensington. It was all shiny black-tiled floors and mirrors with neon lights running round the walls that changed colour from green, to blue, to purple. All quite eighties, quite *Miami Vice* and quite tacky. But at the time it seemed the ultimate in glamour.

At the top of the building was the restaurant – part of the casino but Chinese. Now I'd been used to eating at Chinese restaurants with my family for years but this was like, Wow. Forget green tea and lager. This was champagne, and as much food as you could eat. Then at the end of the meal they brought up a cake for my birthday.

I don't know who started it, but one of the girls got a piece of this cake – which was more like a gateau – and threw it across the table. And I'm sitting there and I'm thinking, What are you doing? Then the others join in. And soon the whole place is thick with cream and flying cake.

And all I could think about was my brand-new suit. It was from Karen Millen, a really dark charcoal: trousers, little waistcoat and a jacket. And I remember going into the toilet and being devastated because I was covered in cream and desperately trying to wipe it off with toilet paper, which was all there was. I was so not impressed.

They could just throw their clothes in the washing machine. But all I could think about was how disgusting I was going to smell by the end of the night and this was meant to be my party. Which all goes to show how much I've changed: if the same thing was to happen now, I'd be the first one to pick the cake up and throw it and jump on the table.

Sitting there, watching them chuck cake at each other is like a moment frozen in time. I can see us all as clearly as if in a publicity photograph. Emma in her white baby-doll dress, blonde hair and pigtails, over-the-knee socks and boots. Mel B had on a baby-doll black dress, knee-length boots, and big scary hair. Mel C was wearing something a bit more sporty. Geri was in something loud and vampy. And there's me with my straight brown hair and black suit, probably with a worried expression on my face about how I looked. And people say the Spice Girls were invented.

In fact, we were wearing so much make-up that, judging from the looks we got from the men in there, we must have looked like five little tarts. You can wear all the make-up you like when you're a pop star. But we weren't pop stars. At least, not to anyone but ourselves.

If this was a last-ditch attempt by Chic to persuade us to stick with Bob and Chris, he certainly did it in style. It was totally amazing. I prefer to think that it was just Chic being Chic. He was always so generous – like giving us each £100 in chips to play roulette. None of us knew about gambling, and I was still Mrs Sensible. When the others won, they just said 'Sod it' and put it straight back on the table. Whereas every time I won, I kept it: I might be seeing a bit of the good life, but my brother and sister weren't – this way they'd get a share of my luck. Amazingly, I won about £60 – which made £20 each. In spite of the flying cream, I had a really good night.

Funny how things work out. The birthday celebration I'd been really looking forward to, with my family, was a complete disaster. My mum had arranged for us to be picked up by a big limo, and from the moment we got in the car Mark totally ignored me. We'd had a row a few nights before about the shoes he'd got me for my birthday. I'd got them to go with my Karen Millen suit and so obviously I wanted to wear them for the evening at the casino with the girls. But Mark said no. That they were a birthday present and I couldn't wear them till my birthday – which was rich considering he hadn't actually bought them, my mum had. Mark had just bought himself a flat in Hertford and so he didn't have any money left over for presents, he said.

So of course I had worn them, which is why he had the hump.

To ruin my twenty-first was such a mean thing to do. When we got back from the theatre I stood on the steps and said, 'You ruined my eighteenth, you ruined my twenty-first; are you really going to hang around and ruin my fortieth?'

The next day I got my answer. He dumped me. Why? My childish behaviour, he said. I should have been delighted – Louise was like a bloody Cheshire Cat – but I was in total shock.

'What the bloody hell is wrong with you?' Louise said. 'Can't you see the bloke is a complete prick?'

'You're being really horrible, Louise. Mummy, she's being really horrible. Tell her to stop.'

My mum was keeping out of it. She knew it wasn't worth getting involved. The funny thing is I felt as if I was acting when all this was going on. As if being upset was expected of me. But underneath there was this funny feeling that it was right.

'That was clever of you,' my dad said a couple of days later.

'What was?'

'Getting rid of Mark without him realizing it.'

Sometimes it takes somebody outside to see things for you. A few days later Mark was history.

'Mummy?'

'Yes, Victoria.'

'I've got somebody with me. Can I bring them home?'

'Who is it?'

'Corey Haim.'

The name didn't mean anything, but when she met him she recognized him from the picture I'd had up on my bedroom wall from the time when he was in *The Lost Boys* and I'd recently seen him in *National Lampoon's Last Resort*. He was Canadian, and about two years older than me. He had quite cute spiky hair, and he had come over to England to try and make a record. Which is how I met him – through Matt and Biff. We were working on '2 Become 1' and he was there trying to launch a singing career with this awful song that he wrote. All I remember is: 'You are my enemy, my perfect harmony'. Great rhymes. With me being a miserable old cow because of Mark, Geri got Matt to ask Corey over to his flat in Harley Street with some of his friends.

Looking back it's hard to work out whether I really fancied him, or if I was just a bit of a sad fan. Anyway, it was just what I needed – I used to go round to his hotel or he used to come up to our house. We didn't have sex or anything. In actual fact, he didn't seem to even want to try. The most we did was kiss.

But then Mark came round to my mum's house to pick something up – after all, he had lived there for over three years – and he saw a photo lying on the kitchen table that my dad had taken of me and Corey in the garden. He went totally berserk. Suddenly all the stuff about me being childish and him needing his independence stopped. This time it was him crying and bellowing, begging me to give him another chance.

What's that, Mark? Another chance? I don't think so. Funny how much better it makes you feel when you're the one doing the dumping. Not that Corey Haim was about to become Mr Right. For a start he was completely weird. He said it was jet lag, but he never slept at normal times and was often up in the middle of the night.

I remember one evening I arrived at the Hilton, where he was staying in Park Lane, and all he could talk about was how he had to get his nose pierced. Tonight.

'You must know somebody, Victoria.'

Well, er – no.

'But you must. I gotta get my nose pierced right now.'

And then I remembered that one of my sister's friends did ear-piercing.

'So call her.'

So I did.

'Louise, Corey says he wants his nose pierced. What about that friend of yours, the one that does ears?'

So we're there in Corey's suite waiting for Louise and her friend to turn up, and my sister walks in, on her own and carrying this case.

Denise was busy, she said, but she'd lent her the equipment and explained how it worked.

So Louise gets it all set up, but just before she's about to plunge this plunger bit in his nose Corey chickens out. The Canadian wimp.

Corey was quite a nice boy most of the time, but he had really bad mood swings. One minute he'd be all over me, the next minute he was so jealous he'd shout and scream like I was about to get off with his best friend. I only had to smile at the lift-man and he'd think I fancied him. He was a complete split personality.

A couple of nights before he was due to fly back to the States we were at Matt's flat watching television when Take That came on. So I was just watching them, doing a bit of a bop when Corey went mad, saying how I couldn't wait till he left the country so that I could get off with one of those f****** faggots.

That was it. I didn't even wait to find out which one he meant. I went round Matt's flat picking up everything Corey had managed to spread around the place, put it in a carrier bag, dragged him out by his neck, shoved him in my car, drove to the Hilton, opened the car door, pushed him out with my foot, undid the bag of clothes, scattered them in front of the hotel and drove off to the sound of him shouting 'I'm sorry, I'm sorry'.

I had enough on my plate without worrying about some screwed-up film star.

It was two years since I had first met the girls and I had changed. When we started out all the other girls would leap on a table and sing and dance, whereas I'd always be the one to say the table might collapse and perhaps we oughtn't to do that. But they had tapped into my brain and discovered the real me, the person I am now. If I hadn't met the four Spice Girls, I'd be completely different. They brought out the daring side, the say-what-you-think side. If you want something, go and get it. If you want to wear something, so what if no one else is wearing it, just wear what you want to wear. Do your make-up and your hair how you want, and sod everything.

We had stalled for as long as we could with the contracts, changing this clause and that clause. We wanted to get as much work done with the writers we'd met at the showcase as we could before it was crunch time. From hardly ever looking in on our rehearsals, it had got to the stage where Bob, Chris and Chic were our jailers. How could we work like that? The problem was that, like jailers, they had the key. Not the key to the studio, the key to our future – the precious tape of the songs. Bob and Chris guarded it like it was a winning lottery ticket. Which in many ways it was.

Friday. The stars were in perfect conjunction according to Patric Walker – we bought the *Evening Standard* every day just to read him – it was now or never. Geri and the two Mels would go to the management offices in Maidenhead and while the two Mels did the decoy bit keeping Chris and Bob occupied, Geri would somehow manage to wangle the tape. Meanwhile me and Emma would go to the studios in Woking to collect some things we had there till we got the all-clear from Geri. Now we really were a gang.

My phone rang. Geri. The deed was done.

When Geri said meet on the roundabout, I didn't think she meant literally on it. But there was her rust-bucket Fiat Uno, parked on the grass in the middle. As we pulled up, Geri emerged waving the tape in her hand. I don't know how she actually managed to get it – everything was so Bonnie and Clyde, Thelma and Louise – I never asked her. She had hidden it inside her knickers, she said, in case Bob and Chris had given chase. Me and Emma took our stuff out of the Fiat Uno and put it into my Renault Clio and drove off.

The drama wasn't over yet. We knew Bob and Chris had set up a session the following Tuesday with a writer called Elliot Kennedy in Sheffield – he had done a lot of work with Take That. The problem was we'd never met the guy, didn't have his address or phone number or anything. All we knew was that he lived in Sheffield.

So after we'd parted company at the M4 roundabout, Geri and Mel B set off for Yorkshire – Mel C had already arranged to see some friends in Sidcup – and that night they stayed in Leeds with Mel B's mother.

Geri phoned about four on Saturday afternoon. 'We've found him and he's up for it. So get up here as quick as you can.'

They'd given him the whole we're gonna conquer the world and we really, really, really want to work with you routine – and he said great.

We were so lucky. There was always the chance that he would say no dice. Bob and Chris may not have been big wheels in the music business, but they were wheels. For all Elliot knew we wouldn't last five minutes on our own and it was a real risk going with us rather than saying, 'Look ladies. Sorry. But . . .'

Next morning, me and Emma got a coach from Finchley up to Sheffield. We were met at the bus station by three excited girls – Mel C had come up by train – and a mad-professor type with ginger hair and glasses in a red Astra.

'Have you girls got anywhere to stay?' Elliot asked as we drove to his house. Emma decided to go and stay with Mel B and her mum; me, Geri and Mel C ended up staying with Elliot.

Elliot Kennedy was the kind of person you meet and feel you've known all your life. His house was a three-bedroomed semi – quite big and he'd turned the dining room into a recording studio. The next day we're just talking about what we want to do, bouncing a few ideas around, when the phone rings.

'Yup, speaking.' Elliot makes a *shshsh* shape with his mouth and holds up a warning finger. Then there's a long silence with somebody talking on the other end and Elliot just nodding and listening.

'I don't think they have got flu, Bob. They look perfectly healthy to me. I know because they're right here in front of me.'

Then it was squawk, squawk, squawk, Bob shouting so much that Elliot had to hold the phone away from his ear. Poor old Bob. I always liked him. He was killed in a car accident at the end of 1999.

Living and working with Elliot was the best thing that could have happened to us at that time. It took our mind off What Happens Now. The first song we wrote with Elliot was 'Love Thing', which is on the first album – a great song – especially after what I'd just been through with Mark – full of lines about broken hearts and not going down that road again, and how my plans no longer include you, you loser.

Elliot was a total sweetheart. He insisted that Geri and me had his bedroom and he would sleep on the sofa downstairs with his great big fluffy dog. One night we'd just been out to dinner and me, Geri and Mel C said we were going to bed. So we're all sitting there on the bed having a chat, when the door is flung open and Elliot bounces in wearing a pair of truly terrible Y-front things, and just sits on the bed with his chin in his hands just like Jack Lemmon as Daphne in the bunk-bed scene in *Some Like It Hot*, just being one of the girls.

Because we were just working in the house, we were wearing tracksuits and jeans and socks. Although the bathroom was upstairs there was another toilet downstairs, so when we were recording in what had been the dining room we'd go in there and whenever someone was having a wee you'd hear them go 'Shit!' Basically, there was this wet patch by the side of the toilet. And the next thing would be this Spice Girl hopping around, one sock on, one sock off. And it was just so annoying how everybody would always forget. None of us said anything, because we all thought it was Elliot missing his aim or something. But it turned out to be his dog who liked to think he was human.

We couldn't stay up in Sheffield for ever. Now we had two more tracks under our belt and Elliot had other things to do. He was a one in a million. Usually writers won't do anything before you've agreed a fee, but money was never discussed. He wasn't interested in the money; right from the start, he was interested in us. We have always kept in touch, and in fact he's still working in Sheffield where he owns a massive studio now called Steel Works.

Spice's first priority was finding a manager. We'd talked to Elliot and we'd talked to each other, and we'd decided we couldn't do it on our own. Even Columbus didn't discover America without a bit of investment by the King and Queen of Spain, or wherever he came from. But it had to be on our terms – that was one thing we were totally sure about.

Back at the showcase, Geri had spoken to someone called Marc Foxe. He'd given her his card and said if we ever needed help give him a call.

Our calling card, if you like, was 'Wannabe'. It said everything about us, musically and in terms of where we were coming from. For too long pop had been about boys. Spice was about girls, but it was using boys' music – hard, direct – but making it our own.

Our routine was very businesslike. Marc Foxe, who was in music publishing, would make the appointments and we'd take turns driving, either me or Geri. Emma now had a clapped-out Metro, but it was so unreliable we didn't dare take it.

We all now lived in north London. I was at home, Emma still lived with her mum and she'd found a flat for rent in Cyprus Road, just round the corner, for the two Mels and Geri. From there it was straight down the Finchley Road into the West End, the land of managers, record companies, publishers.

So every morning I would drive to Emma's and her mum would give us all tea and toast, then we'd pile into either Geri's or my car, taking the toast with us. Then it was off to whatever office we'd got an appointment at – record company, agent, manager – it was carpet bombing, straight to the jugular with 'Hi, we're Spice', then 'Wannabe', which we'd already put into their music system, would burst into life and we'd just leap around the room, literally – jumping on chairs, desks, whatever was there, the vibe and the lines bouncing between us like a basketball.

'We'll call you,' we'd say, as we left.

No more hanging around waiting for them to call us. Spice were turning the tables, rewriting the rule-book. These guys in suits might not have realized it but we were auditioning them. No control freaks, no Svengalis, no tight-arses need apply.

After a hard day on the town we'd sit in our boardroom (car) and go over the people we'd met. The next morning it would be somebody's job to call the losers and say, 'Sorry, but no.' We didn't want to make enemies, so we let them down as lightly as we could. None of us liked this bit, so we took it in turns – except Mel C who had a real phone phobia, but as she had always done more than her fair share in the house at Maidenhead she was exempt.

Marc Foxe had also put us in touch with Paul Wilson and Andy Watkins, writers and producers known as Absolute. They had worked with people like Mica Paris and Lisa Stansfield. The first song we did with them was 'Something Kinda Funny'. Whereas Matt and Biff were more poppy, Absolute were more soul. They went on to produce 'Love Thing' and 'Say You'll be There', the two songs we did with Elliot Kennedy.

Their studio was on an island on the Thames near Chertsey called Taggs Island. It was a scruffy, rather creepy place, cluttered up with boatyards. One day, when we were chatting on the dock, Paul or Andy mentioned that their agent was in partnership with someone called Simon Fuller who managed Cathy Dennis and Annie Lennox. Cathy Dennis was a Norfolk-born soul queen who had taken America by storm. And Annie Lennox, as they say, needs no introduction. In fact,

Andy told us that they had already sent Simon a tape of 'Something Kinda Funny'.

Simon Fuller started as a publishing scout for Chrysalis Records in the mid-eighties. His company was called 19 Management because he made a lot of money when an unknown called Paul Hardcastle had a huge hit in 1985 when '19' (n-n-n-n-n-nineteen – the average age of American soldiers killed in the Vietnam War) went to number 1 and was nine weeks in the top twenty. It was quite innovative for then – Paul Hardcastle used a lot of sampling and went on to become the most in-demand remixer of the time – so Simon used to tell us when we asked him why Paul Hardcastle hadn't had another hit.

19's offices were very posh, right on the river in Battersea in a modernized wharf complex called Ransome's Dock. Psychologically, we felt very up since before we had got round to calling him he had called us to say he would be interested in meeting.

The first thing that I noticed was how light the offices were – open-plan, a bit like a posh version of *Drop the Dead Donkey* – and full of sunshine. Everyone there looked busy but happy, and the staff were mainly women, girls not much older than us – perhaps six or seven years – and they were all well-spoken.

The first surprise was that Simon himself wasn't there. His PA apologized and asked us to wait in his office – he had a closed-off bit.

This wasn't how it was meant to be – we were supposed to POW into his office and ZAP jump on the table and BOOF hit him with Energy and Excitement and Attitude. Six weeks after leaving Bob and

Chris we could turn Girl Power on like a tap. I looked at my watch. We weren't early, he was late.

We put our CD in the machine, but then all we could do was wait and look at the walls which were covered with Gold Discs for Annie Lennox and Cathy Dennis. Hmm. Impressive.

Knowing Simon as I do now, it's a dollar to a dime that the whole thing was totally planned. If he'd been sitting at his desk, being 'Spiced' would have made him the weaker party. This way he kept the upper hand.

Three minutes later, in walks this man, mid-thirties, five foot eight with fluffy hair – a bit like Paul Young's in his heyday, cut in a stylish way but overgrown. Underneath this Furby-like thatch was a perma tan and very white teeth. He had on a pair of jeans, not just any old jeans – Armani. And a Comme des Garçons shirt the colour where purple meets lilac, perfectly ironed. In fact everything about Simon was very clean, very well pressed, more studied than spontaneous, like his polished DMs. Smart watch – Patek Philippe. The over-all impression was casual but wealthy, underlined by a bit of a double chin, more a sign that he could afford the good life than that he was going to seed.

Compared to most prospective managers we'd seen, there was something soft about Simon, even a bit camp. Everything was understated, including his voice. He knew how to get control of the room in a calm way by speaking really low.

Usually we'd go in and zap whoever it was with sheer energy, introducing ourselves through 'Wannabe'. This time we just did it in the ordinary way. He said he'd heard good reports of us from Absolute, but he gave nothing away – didn't say what he thought of the track they'd sent him, for example – nothing that might lose him the edge.

Eventually, after the introductory chat, we did get to leap around his office and blast him with 'Wannabe'. I had a little black dress on, Geri a pair of mad hot pants, Emma her trademark little white dress, Mel C was wearing her Adidas tracksuit and Mel B was in a leopard-print top. The music, the image, it was all part of the same thing. It was, we were, Spice.

Received wisdom is that Simon Fuller made us. Yet the truth is that we went to him that morning in Battersea with our first album well under way and the image already in place.

We were there for about an hour. Here was someone who was totally professional, sensitive, and who listened. International was a word he kept bringing in. He told us about Cathy Dennis – it was Simon who took her to the States where her career took off. England was just the beginning he said. We had to Think Big.

There was no contest. Simon Fuller it was. We even liked his accountant, Richard, who looked like the father from *Big Foot*.

The next day we were assigned a PA, Camilla Howarth, to organize our schedules. A nice girl, about twenty-four, well-spoken with strawberry blonde, curly hair, fresh-faced, bluey-greeny eyes, freckles. She looked like a student but was incredibly well organized.

So. May 1995. We had our manager. Now all we needed was a record company.

9 top of the pops

Something I've noticed: when good things happen, they spread like butter on hot toast. No sooner had Simon Fuller come into our lives than I met Stuart Bilton.

'You should get out more,' Louise had said when I'd told Mark where he could stick his quiz nights. 'I mean, there you are in a band for God's sake, and what do you do for fun? Hamsters have more fun running around their poxy little wheels.'

D'you know what? I think maybe she was right. It took losing Mark to discover that my sister wasn't such a pain in the arse after all. In fact she was a really nice person, and so funny.

I met Stuart in a bar in Broxbourne where my sister and her friends went all the time. He was a real charmer and he made me laugh. Stuart was one of those boys that everyone fancied: good-looking, wore really nice clothes. He had a real style about him. He wouldn't necessarily go with the fashion, he'd always look a bit different, like wearing a shirt and tie when nobody else was wearing them. Quite a classic dresser really, the sort of person people would turn round and look at when he came into a room – a certain star quality if you like. He'd even been out with famous people – it was like, Wow, Stuart Bilton.

Funnily enough, in the days when I was in the school toilets redoing my make-up and the girls used to hang around smoking and talking about boys, the name Stuart Bilton always used to crop up. I didn't know him myself because he was at a different school. It was quite strange how I ended up going out with him years later.

Stuart's grandparents owned a flower shop in Wormley, on the bend, just before you got into Broxbourne proper. It was a family business – everybody helped out, including Stuart. He was very artistic and enjoyed pottering around the shop arranging bouquets and doing things with flowers. That was one of the really nice things about being with Stuart. Whereas Mark had always been such a miserable sod, Stuart always enjoyed whatever he happened to be doing at the time, always smiling. His family were all very hard-working – getting up in the middle of the night to go down to Covent Garden to pick up the day's flowers. If Stuart had been out late with me, sometimes he never went to bed at all. He was a really nice boy and his family were fabulous. All of them, his mum Andrea, his father David and his sister Shelley – not to mention his nan and grandad. Right from the word go they treated me like part of the family, they really were the complete dream mother- and father-in-law.

Stuart Bilton was a hundred per cent improvement on Mark Wood.

Back at Ransome's Dock, Simon was busy sorting everything out. We all decided it was only fair that Bob, Chris and Chic were paid back what they had invested in us, including the money for the phone bill we'd run up when we unplugged the payphone at the Maidenhead house and what it cost to record our first three demos.

The next time we saw Chris was years later at the *Smash Hits* Poll Winners party where he was with 5ive. It was quite a brief encounter. We just said, Hi – but quite friendly – certainly there was no animosity. As much as they were really pissed off at the time, I think they saw it as a learning experience and accepted they had made a few mistakes – the main one obviously being not giving us a contract. Chris was always enthusiastic and ambitious and like us he had a dream. It's nice to see him now doing so well.

Where the Herberts had poured cold water on our ideas, Simon Fuller not only liked them, he acted on them, then multiplied them by two. On the surface he was as calm as a lake, but underneath he was like a volcano. Anybody else would have had us out there with a single within a few months, but he 'took the long view'. In fact it was all a bit frustrating. Didn't he understand? We'd been together for over a year, we wanted to be out there, conquering the world. NOW. But in fact it would be a year before 'Wannabe' was released.

What was good about Simon was that, although he wanted to get the machinery behind us well oiled, he was very happy to leave us as we were. He wasn't interested in polishing up the rough edges.

Geri was very loud and mouthy. Mel B had a throaty voice and a quality that couldn't be tamed. Mel C really was obsessed by Liverpool football team. Emma really did have this thing about doughnuts. And I'd been playing the Little Madam ever since I could talk.

We were all so different and Simon recognized that this was our appeal. He didn't try and tame down our introduction 'Wannabe' performance. It had sold us to him, so it would sell us to the record label.

So that's what we did. We went to these record companies and literally danced on the tables. And people fell in love with that. Instantly. No one had to push it. Once people had seen us that was it.

Most new bands are so desperate to sign with anyone that they end up getting screwed, but in taking his time, leaking a little bit of information here, a snippet of a track there, Simon had got the whole record industry talking about us. Within six weeks of us signing with him, every record company in Britain (except Warner Bros, who said that a girl group wouldn't work) was gagging for us. We had gatecrashed the pop industry and no one could understand quite how we had done it.

Instinctively we felt we wanted to be with a smaller company. The obvious choice in 1995 was London Records. East 17, who worked a lot with Matt and Biff, were with them; in fact London had a whole string of pop bands. Also Pete Tong, their A & R guy, and Tracy Bennett, their Managing Director, really wanted us. They were people we knew we could work with, really nice guys.

Then there was Virgin. Virgin was a bit of a wild card. Strangely, they didn't have any other British pop bands in those days – but our thinking was that this was an advantage, there'd be no chance they'd get complacent, as other record labels might. They had too much to prove.

In the end we decided to go with them. Everyone

was very impressive. Paul Conroy, Managing Director of Virgin since Richard Branson sold it to EMI a few years before, was similar to Simon in many ways, getting things done without raising his voice, very calm, very friendly, not too aggressive.

The head of A&R at Virgin was Ashley Newton. He was in his late thirties then, good-looking and quite trendy and with it. Ashley's partner in crime, if you like, was a guy called Ray Cooper who was a real party animal, always clubbing, but always kept his finger on the pulse. Even if he'd been out till three, you always knew he'd be at his desk at eight. They were very intuitive – knew something good when they heard it – and although very different, they vibed off each other. They knew what they were talking about and we knew that we could trust them.

Days passed and we still hadn't signed. There was no rush, Simon said. We had to get it right.

London Records thought they were still in the loop – and to be fair, until we signed, they were. So in a final attempt to seduce us away from Virgin, London Records threw us a party on the Thames. The problem was the date, 13 July 1995 – the day we were supposed to be signing with Virgin. So we tell Tracy Bennett what's going on – we'd all decided we didn't want to play those kind of games. And he says, what the hell, come anyway.

So it is just like a seduction: majorly wild – this boat blasting its way up the river, rammed with people we didn't know but everyone a somebody – loudspeakers pumping, wine flowing, fantastic food and us.

Time was ticking on. We were meant to be signing with Virgin. But, hey! We were on a boat in the middle of the Thames having a brilliant time high on adrenalin – all this for us!

I don't remember whose idea the blow-up dolls were, but it was totally spontaneous. We persuaded Camilla, our PA, to go to the Ann Summers sex shop on Charing Cross Road and buy five of these things, spray the hair relevant colours, put them in our cars and take them to Virgin where they'd think it was us, open the doors, and hey presto!

If Virgin didn't know yet who they were dealing with, they would now.

I have no memory of getting off the boat, nor of the journey to Ladbroke Grove where Virgin had their head office, nor signing, nor getting the cheque. But I can remember the party. I can remember chucking the blow-up dolls over the bridge into the canal. I was totally drunk – my inability to drink more than one glass of anything and remain sober was now legendary – and the evening had only just begun.

Simon told our cab driver to go to Kensington Place. He didn't come with us because the driver wouldn't take six. Against the law.

'Five max.'

Five Max, great name. What about it, gehwls?

So in we climb, five max plus flowers and champagne. Round a corner – whoa – champagne everywhere. I was wearing this really tight Lycra dress, red with blue and white stripes down the side like a tracksuit, that came down to just above my knee.

'Hang on to your knickers, girls!' I yelled.

I was so drunk I fell over and the other girls ripped my knickers off and threw them out of the window.

Whoops, another corner. This is as bad as being in my dad's van. Is that my handbag all over the floor? Crunch. Another lipstick bites the dust.

'Can't you see the bloody sign?' the cab driver bellowed, as someone lit a cigarette.

Cigarettes rolled around the floor, soggy white worms covered in dirt and make-up. God, how vile. The back of that cab was like a chorus girl's dressing room – make-up, tissues, champagne, flowers. Everyone was bashing each other over the head with them. Rock 'n' Roll! We were Spice! We were famous. Or we would be. I have a vague memory of hanging out of the window and shouting to the world, 'We've just signed with Virgin!'

Simon was waiting for us outside the restaurant. The cab driver looked and sounded like Danny Baker on a bad day. We all piled out. Rent-a-snarl was shouting at Simon about the state of his cab. £50 shut him up.

Kensington Place was very cool and trendy, darling, very minimalist with these huge panes of glass, like a massive aquarium with us as the fish, and it had really nice toilets. Because, frankly, I spent more time in the toilets than I did in the restaurant. The girls got me there, sorted my hair out, put make-up on. I was completely flopped. A pity really, as it's a really nice place. We were completely, absolutely bladdered. A good night that.

The next day, 14 July, was my mum and dad's twenty-fifth wedding anniversary. And we've got this picture of me standing there holding the cheque with a stupid grin on my face. It was £10,000. More money than I'd ever had in my life.

Those first few months after we'd signed with Virgin were a bit of a honeymoon period with Simon. His way of working was very different from everybody else's in the music business. He was always very polite, never raised his voice. If he didn't know what to do about something then he would go away and think about it. This might sound as if he was a bit of a nerd, but he was never that. Just in control. Always in control. His favourite words were 'sure' and 'no problem'. One thing that we always knew, he was a hundred per cent committed to us.

After signing with Virgin, the next thing on Simon's agenda was finding sponsors. In the meantime there were more songs to write and the tracks that we'd already done before we met Simon needed to be re-recorded and mastered as most of them were only of demo quality. Every few weeks we were being told they were going to be releasing 'Wannabe', but they kept holding it back and holding it back. But the material was only one element of Spice. What was now needed was to spice up the buzz.

Our first public outing was the Brits in February 1996. We were there as guests of Virgin, sitting at a table with two blokes who were part of a band called the Brotherhood. And Michael Jackson did that thing of coming down from the roof and Jarvis Cocker ran on to the stage and ranted. Shock horror. Just being there was amazing. The music industry knew Virgin had this new girl band called Spice, but no more than that. And you could see people turning their heads as we passed, and hear the buzz – who are they? And you'd hear the answer: those Spice girls. That's how the name got changed: people asking if they'd heard 'those Spice girls'. Or saying, 'Are you the Spice girls?' So Spice Girls we became.

It was a bit of a funny time. In a way we were in limbo – like all dressed up and nowhere to go. The plan was to release the album at Christmas, leading up to it by releasing two singles, and working back that meant July for the first single, which we were determined was going to be 'Wannabe' – although we'd had to fight for that. OK, there was the video for 'Wannabe' to shoot, and the second album to write, but what were we going to do until July?

Simon had this idea that we should do a dummy run in Japan. The Far East was too often an afterthought, he said. No one had done it that way round before. So Spice would change the Rules. Yeah!

In the meantime I continued to try to lose weight. If all went according to plan we'd be doing a lot of television and Geri was always telling me that television makes you look fatter. Miss Laine had made clear that she thought I was overweight, but to be honest I didn't care that much. When Miss Laine sent me to the back of the line, I just accepted that I was fat. But the truth was I wasn't. I was just a bit bigger than the other skeletons in the place. Anyway, what did she know? There was nothing about her that I could relate to.

But Geri was different. I will always be grateful to her for bringing out that fun side of me, but there was a downside to knowing Geri.

Geri never told me in so many words that I was fat. She knew that Chic had told me and Mel C that we could both do with 'losing a couple of pounds' so she started encouraging us both to get up early with her and go jogging, to 'get into shape'. So why not? I've never minded getting up early, and it was the summer, so that was easy. We used to jog around this park in Maidenhead for about an hour before going to the studio. Then it moved on to food.

It started gradually. Geri would say things like don't put sauces on food, that low-fat things were just as good and I could try just not eating quite so much. It was Geri who introduced me to Slimfast, a milkshake drink that fills you up and stops you feeling hungry.

The trouble is, when you start thinking like that, it's hard to stop, particularly if you're an all-or-nothing person like I am. You start reading labels. Is that low fat or isn't it? When I first went to Maidenhead I had no idea how much fat was in tomato sauce, how much fat was in mayonnaise. I didn't think of things like that – they never entered my head. Soon the fat content of food was as familiar as my two-times table. While Emma and Mel B were at home watching television, eating chicken kormas, I'd be down the gym, or swimming, or eating a plate of lettuce.

So did this make me any happier? No. In fact it was the opposite. Being with the girls had transformed me from a confused pubescent teenager into a Spice Girl, now I was back to worrying again. Spots I could disguise, but fat was something different. I became obsessed with what I looked like. In the gym, instead of watching to check my posture or position, I was checking the size of my bottom, checking to see if my double chin was getting any smaller.

It was only after we left Maidenhead that I think I

changed from someone who was dieting to lose a bit of weight to being obsessive. I began living on vegetables, and nothing else. I used to chop up bowls of spinach and carrots and mangetout and steam them. Or I'd just eat peas – like a whole family pack of Birds Eye at one sitting. But it never occurred to me for a moment that I might have an eating disorder because everybody knew people with eating disorders were thin, and I was still the same size as I had always been. I was just eating healthily and getting myself into shape.

Even though I was living at home, nobody was really worried because I wasn't losing weight and I had always been a bit of a faddy eater so it wasn't that odd that I had gone off things like yogurt and pitta bread. And there was no logic to it – I would eat ten bowls of Frosties but never dream of having a Chinese.

However, Japan was crunch time. I couldn't get my Frosties, there were no normal vegetables, mainly weird slimy mushrooms. All they had was sushi and that kind of thing. And it was vile.

'You won't believe what they give you here,' I told my mum when I phoned home. 'Half the food we get is not just raw, it's alive.'

So I just stopped eating. And all of a sudden I found I was losing weight. And I'm thinking, if I can't eat the food let's turn it into a positive thing. So every evening when we'd finished working, I'd spend an hour doing sit-ups, crunches, aerobic exercises. I was getting thinner and thinner every day. I was shrinking. And the excitement at getting thinner quite took away the hunger. Even the other girls started to notice, but they were easy to fob off. Because when you have an eating disorder you can fool people. Fooling people becomes part of the buzz.

I was out in Japan that first time for about two weeks. And when the car pulled up back in front of my mum and dad's house I was so thin my mum burst into tears. Dad thought I must have been ill. And I was in a way. My mum realized I hadn't been eating, because of what I'd said about raw fish on the phone, so she started saying things like 'Why don't you have a sausage, or a cheese sandwich?' – things I'd really liked in the past. It's hard to know what to do, it's hard to cope with someone who is eating strangely. You have to treat them very warily.

I agreed to go and see the doctor. The funny thing is he didn't think I was that thin. But when we went through everything, how I had never really had proper periods and my terrible skin, he said it might be something called polycystic ovaries and sent me to have a scan at King's Oak Hospital in Enfield. And there they were, you could see them, little round cysts clustered around the ovaries.

It's some kind of hormonal problem that largely goes undiagnosed. But in America there's now something called the Polycystic Ovary Society. They reckon there are ten million women in America suffering from it – one in every fifteen, and it's the single biggest cause of infertility. I had all the classic symptoms: irregular or absent periods, adult acne, overweight. The only thing I didn't have was excess body hair. If I'd had that I think I really would have been six foot under.

Higher than usual levels of insulin cause the weight gain and polycystic ovaries can lead to a higher risk of endometrial cancer, diabetes, cardiovascular disease, and stroke. Not that they told me any of this then. They just said I might find it difficult to conceive and that when I began thinking about starting a family I should go back and see them again.

I did start eating more, but the damage was done. All I would eat was vegetables, fruit, chicken and fish.

'Wannabe' was released on 8 July 1996. We'd done weeks of promotion – our biggest coup was getting on Cilla Black's *Surprise Surprise* a few weeks before. We did this by cornering the show's producer in a toilet and zapping her with the a cappella version of the song. The following Sunday we were number 3. In fact we'd heard the Wednesday before that we were the mid-week number 3 and we just couldn't believe it. Our first record and we were in the top ten.

We'd just finished a radio interview and we were near Carnaby Street when we got the call. We were so excited, we couldn't just do nothing. So we got the cars to stop at the first restaurant we saw. It was only a little Italian sandwich bar place – but what did that matter? We'd made the top ten! On the way out people were coming up and asking for autographs. This was the first time it had happened. It was a fantasy come true. When I was little I remember wandering round John Lewis with my mum, imagining people were about to come up and ask for my autograph, and here it was really happening.

For years I had dreamed of this moment but, in an odd way, now it was here it still took us by surprise.

To the general public it must have seemed like we were overnight sensations – the reality was we had been working for two years and we never thought it would take so long. But even though we'd had all that time to imagine what it would be like to have a hit record, it came as a real shock. Nothing and no one can prepare you for all the mixture of emotions that you feel.

It was so exciting and what made it even more exciting was that I had four friends who were equally excited to share it with and bounce excitement off.

We were pop stars. It wasn't just a dream any more. People were starting to recognize us when we went out. It was almost as if we were all standing there one minute and the next minute a huge great whirlwind came and swept all five of us up in the air. It was manic.

Sometimes, like when I was being driven back home on my own, with the driver not saying anything in the front, it would just hit me, I'd done it. Without the other girls around it was less of a feeling of excitement, more like triumph. I could just hear all those arseholes at my school, the girls who found it hard to keep their legs together, who called me names, who I could just hear saying to their friends, Oh yes, I was a friend of Posh Spice, we did this and we did that. And the boys who called me frigid, they were probably saying how they'd slept with me. Warning: if you ever hear anybody saying they were friends of mine at school then you will know that these people are lying. I'd always said I'd show them and I had.

And I could just hear Miss Laine telling her girls how I'd been at Laine's and she'd always known how talented I was. And I wondered if any of them would remember the truth, or would they just blank out what they had really said and really done? I wouldn't blank them out. I would never forget. And I thought as well of Christine Shakespeare, who I hadn't seen for years. I owed her so much but she had disappeared, totally disappeared from my life. Unfortunately, it's a lot easier to remember who put you down, but when it comes to remembering the people who got you there, it amounts to so few – just your family and a handful of selected others.

Two days later it was back to Japan where 'Wannabe' was heading up the charts. I remember we were all having dinner in this Japanese restaurant in the hotel. I had a long down-to-the-floor dress that I'd borrowed from Louise to take away with me. It was Sunday and Camilla, our PA, came in and said she'd just heard from Simon we were number 1. That was just totally unbelievable. Number 3 had been amazing enough.

And although it was a great night, with champagne and everything, something was missing. When everyone had gone to bed I sat in my room and rang my mum and dad. And they were all there, so excited and everyone was celebrating, they said, with a barbecue in the garden. And Dee and Del were there, and they'd asked all their friends to come round and listen to the charts.

So I can hear my mum saying 'It's really great.' And I can hear my dad saying 'It's really great.' And I can hear my brother and sister in the background, I can even hear the house, the sounds it makes, the fridge door closing, the squeaky hinge Dad hadn't got round to oiling, the echoes in the kitchen, even splashes in the pool and voices I didn't recognize. And happy as I was, all I could do was cry. Because all I wanted was to be home with my family.

'Wannabe' broke all records for a debut single. It

stayed at number 1 for seven weeks. 'Say You'll Be There' gave us our second number 1 and Ladbrokes were already making '2 Become 1' favourite for that 'all important' Christmas number 1 – a record that hadn't even been released yet. '2 Become 1' became the fastest-selling single since 'Band Aid'. That made three in a row. Jackpot. There was always promotion to do, for each single, then for the first album. Any gaps and we'd be booked into a studio to work on the second album. Our feet didn't touch the ground.

It soon got out that the Spice Girls had got together through an advert and there was all this negative stuff about us being a manufactured band. If Eric Morecambe hadn't put an advert in the *Stage* and Ernie Wise hadn't answered it there would never have been a Morecambe and Wise, but you don't ever hear complaints that they were manufactured. The girls would always take the mickey when I came out with bits of information like this and say, 'Did your mum read that in *Hello!*?' In fact it was probably quiz nights at the Harlow Mill that gave me a taste for useless bits of information. Take me to a quiz night and I'll wipe the floor with the opposition.

Soon it wasn't just teen magazines that were splashing our faces across their pages, they were even writing about us in serious newspapers. The Spice Girls, they said, were a cultural phenomenon, and ' "Wannabe" ', someone wrote, 'fuses cute hip pop with vague feminist gender shift'.

Yeah. Right.

At the other end of the cultural scale it was Peter Lorraine, editor of *Top of the Pops* magazine, who gave us the Spice Girl names. I remember the page so clearly

– a rack of five spice jars, and then our heads with the names: Ginger, Scary, Sporty, Baby and Posh. And everybody loved the names, the kids, the media, us. Although it might seem obvious now, it wasn't then. We were just Geri, Melanie, Melanie, Emma and Victoria. And it was great for us. Everyone loves nicknames – nicknames make you feel closer to someone and it was really something that the kids could identify with – from the start they would pick one of us and dress like us. When we did our concerts later on, there were always kids who looked like us. Later in America there were even mothers who dressed like us. To this day the names have stuck. And – apart from Geri, sadly – we're still all very proud of our Spice Girl names.

The amazing thing is that at the time we had no idea we were so big. We didn't have time to read newspapers ourselves, too busy following the schedule that Simon dished out every day, which just got heavier and heavier. Yes, we did TV shows like *Top of the Pops*, but the kids there yell at everyone and we never had time to see what the press were saying. I remember reading something my mum had cut out: 'I want to bring some glamour back into pop' was what I was supposed to have said. My reputation as being the classy one, the cool one who wore Gucci, was already part of the myth. 'They radiate good humour and joie de vivre . . . Endless energy . . . inexhaustible bounce . . . they love their mothers and are very down to earth . . . but sexually predatory.' Sexually what? 'A cross between Minnie the Minx and Colette's Claudine or St Trinian's. Let men salivate over their sassy sexiness.'

The moment it really hit me that things had changed

for ever was when we turned on the Oxford Street Christmas lights. We went right through those barriers and there were policemen and security guards everywhere. We just drove straight through. We looked at each other and started squealing. It was 7 November 1996. For me, just being invited was amazing, after all those years of going there with my family and looking up at these glamorous people who pushed the switch. I remember standing on that hotel balcony looking down at the street full of people and thinking, that used to be me.

And I thought what I really want is to be down there looking up here because seeing is believing. You try and make it real by looking at other people, at what's showing in their faces. And I was already noticing how people were looking at me differently. I'd met celebrities when I was little, people like David Jason, Bonnie Langford, and I remember going all funny and feeling a bit silly. Sometimes seeing the way people were looking at me was the only way I could believe that I really was famous. Nothing about me had changed. Inside I was still the same gawky little schoolgirl with the gap in her teeth.

Soon it was back into the waiting cars and off to the Oxo Tower on the South Bank where Virgin were doing the launch for the album, which was being released the same day with all those songs on it that we seemed to have written and recorded in another life.

Oxo was a really buzzy new bar and restaurant on the top floor of a converted warehouse just by Blackfriars Bridge. Although they said the party was for us, it wasn't. We were slowly learning that these things never are. No friends, no boyfriends, no families. We'd even had to wait at the hotel in Oxford Street to give the guests time to finish their dinner before we got there.

Christine Shakespeare had this expression – on with the motley. It's that switch you make in your head between standing in the wings and then going on, performing. Another drama teacher said, just remember eyes, teeth and tits. We were there to perform. At the Oxo Tower the wings were the cloakroom. The stage was the bar and restaurant. Our job was to sell and the product was the Spice Girls. Not in a tarty way but in a doncha-want-to-be-in-our-girl-gang way. Doncha just wish you were twenty years younger.

At midnight there was an incredible fireworks display, which we watched from a terrace overlooking the river. I heard later that they'd had to close the Thames for an hour. I looked down at the riverside walkway and wondered if my family were somewhere down there watching.

10 planet fame

From the time we'd signed with Virgin in July 1995 we'd lived on 'wages' which Simon gave us of £250 a week plus expenses. He'd warned us that the real money wouldn't start rolling in until we started selling real records. But with two number 1s, and an album that had gone platinum within five days of going on sale, Spice Girls earnings were no longer financial projections, but a cash reality.

At the time Simon was also managing Gary Barlow of Take That – the beginning of his solo career – and at a party for Gary, Simon took us into a little side room and handed us each an envelope. I thought it must be an early Christmas card but inside was a cheque for £200,000.

This was more money than I could even imagine, but I still couldn't help feeling guilty. Although my mum and dad look as though they've got a lot of money, they've never had anything like £200,000, and what they've got they've worked for and most of that they've spent on us.

Simon had promised us three weeks off for Christmas,

and the one thing I could do as a thank you was take the whole family away on holiday. Unlike the other girls in the band, foreign holidays were something we had always had in my family. The first time I went abroad I was sixteen months old and we went to the Canaries, and there was trouble because we'd left my special bit of blanket behind. I'd been to Florida, to Disney World, and to Spain where my parents had a house, and skiing in Switzerland. But we'd never been to the West Indies, it was just too far and too expensive. Until now. The other girls had the same not-so-original idea, and we all ended up in the Caribbean, though on different islands.

But first I had to do what every pop star does with their first mega cheque. Go shopping. Where? Where else but Bond Street. All the hype about me wearing nothing but Gucci and Prada was just that. I did have my Prada handbag, which I bought with my *Bertie* money, but none of the other stuff was the real thing. How could I have afforded it on £250 a week?

The original little black dress actually belonged to Geri, but she never wore it. She had hundreds of things she never wore. We shared everything from clothes, to knickers, to shoes, to make-up, to hair products. Not boyfriends.

The first time I wore it was out to dinner with Stuart and everyone had said, 'God, what a lovely dress, it really suits you.' But it was only Miss Selfridge or Top Shop or something – none of us had any money to spend on clothes. Anyway, because Geri was smaller than me at the time, it was a bit too tight so I had it copied by a dressmaker who still lives down the road in Goff's Oak called Violet. The original shoes that went with the outfit were black patent and came from a cheap shop in Carnaby Street and one of the heels kept falling off so I was always having to glue it back on. That dress, the one everybody said was a little Gucci dress, was never a little Gucci dress. The material and paying to have it made cost no more than £20.

Second on the more-money-than-sense pop star's shopping list was obviously a sports car. So what was it to be? A Porsche? A Ferrari? Not for Mrs Sensible. I went down to a dealer my dad knew in Waltham Cross and bought an ex-demonstration MGF. So not rock 'n' roll. This is typical; even when I've just been handed more money than my grandparents earned in a lifetime, I don't buy new, I buy an ex-demonstration model and save five grand. But I'd always been careful and I wasn't about to stop now. After all, it could all just disappear. Anyway, I just loved that car, bright purple metallic, nice wheels, all the extras and a roof that went down at the touch of a button.

Everywhere that Christmas was wall-to-wall Spice Girls. Which Spice Girl do you fancy? Which Spice Girl do you want to kiss under the mistletoe? Who is the world's favourite Spice Girl?

That was the funny thing. There were Bob and Chris wanting us to look the same, but the Spice Girls worked because we all brought something different to the party – and not just the fantasy thing for men – though it's probably fair to say that when the Spice Girls were at their peak, every man in the country probably fancied one or other of us.

It went right across national prejudices. We were huge not only in Europe and in America, but in Japan and India and Indonesia and Malaysia and South Africa. There wasn't a single country that didn't have a Spice Girls hit and everybody had their favourite. There was something for everybody and that was attitude-wise as well, not just the way we looked.

Any time I feel sorry for Chris and Bob and Chic having missed out on the pop phenomenon of the nineties, I have to remind myself that if they'd had their way we'd all be dressed the same, and one of us would have been the lead singer. The Spice Girls were so huge precisely because we didn't do any of that. Now you only have to watch MTV to see that everybody's doing it. But what made the Spice Girls different and will always set us apart is that we were the first, like Elvis, like the Beatles, like the Sex Pistols. The ones who do it first make it possible for everybody else.

By Christmas 'Wannabe' had sold three million and was number 1 in twenty-seven countries. I don't think I could even name twenty-seven countries without looking at an atlas.

Our first week in the Caribbean was on Grenada, the second on St Lucia. It was a real family holiday with everyone, even Louise's ex-boyfriend, Sharky, who I still really liked, and Stuart. For me not to think about what I was wearing or what I looked like was a holiday in itself. I can't stand wearing make-up in the sun; the most I'm prepared to do about my appearance is to shove my hair into a ponytail and slap on the suntan oil. It was quite funny really, because everything there is tied in with what's happening in the States, and I kept hearing 'Wannabe' being played – it was released there on 1 January. Soon there was a rumour going around about a Spice Girl being at the hotel. Before long cameras were snapping. I knew I looked vile, but these were just kids and I didn't really care. It wasn't till we got back that I saw just how lucky I was. Poor Emma and her mum had been photographed by the *Daily Mail* going into the sea, just showing their bottoms.

We'd conquered Britain, now came America. This was the big one, as Simon never stopped telling us. However big you make it in the UK, if you make it big in America, it's like gold-plating. It gives you credibility. There's this glamour thing attached to America, the land of dreams, the land of opportunity. If you're successful in England, you're famous, but if you're successful in America, you're a superstar.

The next six weeks were like a nightmare version of a kaleidoscope I remember getting one Christmas when I was little. Mad colours, changing at a twist into a different pattern, but somehow staying the same.

It was everywhere you went. All over the world. You'd go to countries you hadn't even heard of and you'd get mobbed. People would know everything about you, not only your name, but your parents' names. It was weird. I still couldn't really believe how massive it all was. One day I was walking along the beach somewhere in a bikini with my dad and there's this man collecting coconuts to sell to tourists. And instead of trying to sell us a coconut, he says, you wouldn't be a Spice Girl would you? And you wouldn't think this man even had a wireless, let alone knew who the Spice Girls were.

'Wannabe' had gone straight into the Billboard Top 100 at number 11, the highest entry for a debut single ever, British or American. As 'Wannabe' rose in the chart, so too did our daily quota of interviews. America has literally hundreds of radio stations and every one of them wanted the Spice Girls. Now. Fortunately, because it was radio we did the interviews down the line sitting in a New York studio. But being witty and wacky on air can be difficult without the visuals. Sometimes the only thing to do to spice things up was to say outrageous things. For all its in-your-face sex on TV and in films, America really is very strait-laced.

I'd been looking forward to a bit of New York shopping now that I had the elastic plastic – all those names, Barneys, Macy's, Bloomingdale's. Not to mention Tiffany's. Fat chance. It was interviews, photo-calls and more interviews. Good morning, America.

Right from the beginning I said I wanted to be as famous as Persil Automatic. Why stop at selling records? As long as we were careful about who we signed with, we'd decided, then what harm could it do? Now we were famous, we could sell anything. But there were casualties – the first was the Diet Coke that I lived on. The massive deal we'd done with Pepsi, who became our major sponsors, put paid to that. Another deal that came through early on was with Mercedes Benz. In return for doing the launch of the new MacLaren F1, each of us had the use of a tiny little Mercedes SLK convertible for a year. We didn't actually get them for another six months: they were delivered on the last day of shooting of our film *Spice World – the Movie* which we shot that summer.

The MacLaren launch was on St Valentine's Day, when we had just heard that 'Wannabe' had hit number 1 in the American Billboard Hot 100. The news had come just as we were wrapping on the set of the 'Who Do You Think You Are' video, our fourth single. Two days of the three-day shoot were unlike any other video shoot we had ever done before, or are ever likely to do again.

Simon Fuller's brother Kim, who was one of the writers on the film, was a friend of Lenny Henry, one of the founders of Red Nose Day and Comic Relief. We had all agreed that the royalties of our fourth single would go to Comic Relief. For Red Nose Day itself, there would be a spoof video.

We knew that there were already lookalike bands doing the rounds but the Sugar Lumps would be the only ones to get our seal of approval. And guess who they had doing Posh – Dawn French. I was incredibly flattered because she is the most fantastic comic. As she had to give the impression of being me through mannerisms rather than how she looked, it was really interesting watching her get into character. The whole thing was a real laugh. But, Dawn, do I really pout that much?

Jennifer Saunders was Ginger, Kathy Burke did Sporty, Llewella Gideon was Scary, although in actual fact Melanie spent ages trying to get Lenny Henry to play her. Lulu was Baby. The first time I met Lulu was in a shoeshop in Oxford Street. I was out shopping with my mum, Louise and Christian and I must have been very young because Christian was still in a buggy. Anyway, we went over and asked for her autograph. So she did one 'To Victoria' and then one 'To Louise'.

'So, do people call you Lulu?' Lulu asked my little curly-haired sister.

And my mum, who hates shortening names, came back quick as a flash, 'Not bloody likely.' By the time she realized what she had said it was too late.

Although I sometimes see Lulu – she's a very good friend of Elton's – I've never dared tell her that the rude woman in Saxone and the two little girls was my mum, Louise and me. My mum, of course, is still embarrassed.

Then it was off into the skies for more plugging. It was like being on a roundabout. You never knew where you were going to get off.

For all our success in America, and Simon telling us how important this show was, or that show was, the big one for us on a personal level was the Brits. We'd had other awards and would get other awards but the Brits is the equivalent of the Oscars. It's voted for by the music industry. And they're the hardest bunch to impress.

A year before, just being at the Brits as guests of Virgin, getting bladdered in such oh-my-God-look-who-that-is company had been so exciting. But the truth was, we'd been nobodies or should I say Wannabes. Twelve months later, not only had we been nominated for five awards, we were opening the show with a big production number of 'Who Do You Think You Are'.

The big day was Monday 24 February. The previous week Simon had asked me if I wanted to go to a football match on the Saturday before. Ashley Newton, our A&R man at Virgin had tickets, he said. Both Ashley and Paul Conroy were massive Chelsea fans. And that week they were playing Manchester United, and as they knew Simon was a massive Man United fan, they'd asked him if he wanted to go along as well.

So I said OK. It wasn't as if I was doing anything

else: Stuart would be working. Saturday is the biggest day of the week for flower shops.

Simon had been trying to get me to a football match ever since I could remember. He was always saying I needed a famous boyfriend. And I'd say, 'What are you talking about? I'm with Stuart, remember?' And he'd say don't worry about Stuart, I see you with someone famous, somebody like a footballer.

I wasn't impressed. All the footballers I'd ever met were complete wankers who hung around the Epping Country Club shagging any nice Essex girl who walked through the door. They were a very immoral bunch.

'So what should I wear?' I asked Melanie the day before. For 'Who Do You Think You Are' at the Brits I was wearing a white bikini top and a white skirt – more like a pelmet, my dad said – covered with chainmail. I told her I was thinking of going in that. And I think she really believed that I might.

I can't remember anything about the game, the main reason being that I didn't have my glasses on, so it was all a blur. After the match we were taken to the players' lounge, where the VIPs get to meet their heroes. So I'm standing there holding a glass of champagne and there's this man who's really annoying me. He'd had far too much to drink and was swaying all over the place. I tried to ignore him but he kept lurching towards me, saying things like 'Do you come here often?'

'Look,' I said, when he nearly knocked my glass flying, 'I don't talk to people who are drunk.'

Not for nothing am I called Posh.

I was just about to escape to the toilet when Simon came up and put a hand on this piss-head's shoulder. I thought he was about to do his minder act and tell him to piss off. But instead he began smiling and laughing with him. I stood there, staring into space.

'Friend of yours, is he?' I said, as the piss-head finally lurched off.

Simon told me he was a namesake and was surprised that I hadn't recognized him – Simon le Bon.

If he'd thought this would impress me, he was wrong. The pictures I had in my room around teen-time were Bros. (I know. I know. Don't even say it.) I was never interested in Duran Duran, so my knees didn't exactly turn to jelly.

By now the players had come up from the dressing rooms.

Simon took my arm and pointed over to one of them who was standing by the door.

'Who is he?' I asked. He said it was David Beckham. 'Who?'

He said the name again. David Beckham. And that I had said I fancied him.

I was completely mystified. How could I fancy somebody I had never even heard of? What was he talking about? As for this David Beckham person, I supposed he must be a footballer, but whether he had played or not, whether he was Chelsea or Manchester United I had no idea. When it came to footballers Simon was completely starstruck and he was obviously determined to meet this Beckham and was using me as an excuse. I couldn't even see who he was on about. Everything was a blur at the other side of the room. He could have been talking about a hatstand.

By then we were there.

Simon said hello to David and stretched out his arm in a manly handshake. He told him that he managed the Spice Girls then introduced me. At that moment I remember thinking that it was an absurd situation.

I smiled, said hello to the boy with the lank-looking brown hair. Then Simon started on his great-game-nice-cross-shame-about-the-score routine. I just stood there feeling stupid and trying to clock this footballer I was supposed to have fancied as he talked free-kicks and corners. In fact, I decided, he was quite nice-looking. Occasionally he glanced at me with a shy smile, as Simon carried on with what he would have done if he'd been out there on the pitch. Then he left and we stood there, neither of us saying a word.

'Good game,' I finally managed.

'Glad you enjoyed it, Victoria.'

I liked the way he said my name. Yeah.

I smiled. He smiled.

I looked around for Melanie C to help me out but couldn't see her. What were you supposed to say to a footballer? I was just so embarrassed. But the embarrassment was more than just feeling stupid. It was that shy feeling that comes from instant attraction.

I left soon after.

The next day was a heavy rehearsal day at Earls Court. While the crew were doing the technical for 'Who Do You Think You Are', Melanie C came up to me. This was unusual. Even though we were only miming, Melanie always gets her voice into shape doing vocal exercises that drive me completely mad and make me so tense it's never worth going near her.

'So, what do you think of him in the flesh then, Tor?'

In the flesh? What was she on about?

'David Beckham. I saw you talking to him yesterday. Remember? He's the one you picked out for *90 Minutes*.'

And then suddenly it all came back to me. Not David. I still didn't remember him, but the whole business.

Simon, being this obsessive football fan, had organized for us to do an interview with a football magazine called *90 Minutes*. This is not a magazine that features on the hit list of most pop groups. It was about three months before, for their Christmas issue, with a picture of us all wearing football strip. Emma supported Tottenham, so she wore that. Geri wore Watford, because that's where she's from. Melanie B wore Leeds, same reason, and Melanie C wore Liverpool because she's obsessed with Liverpool. Her family have been Liverpool supporters for ever. If anything I should have been Tottenham, I said, because my parents are from Tottenham, and about a year before they had a party where one of the guests was a Spurs footballer called Ian Walker. And then of course my nan used to have Tottenham footballers as lodgers. So I said all this. But it was no good. Emma already had Tottenham, so Simon, being this massive Manchester United fan had said why didn't I wear that?

'Depends what colour it is.'

'Red and white.'

I wasn't over the moon as red and white aren't my favourite colour combination. But the stylist had thought it was a good idea. So that was that. Of course all this had been decided long before the shoot because they had to get the kits in. Although they'd got the smallest sizes for us, we all looked totally ridiculous. The red was horrible and I particularly didn't like having SHARP plastered all over my chest. Everything had to be rolled up (shorts, sleeves) or rolled down (socks) to make it look a bit sexy. It was really very funny with Geri and Emma shrieking, 'Can't you get platform boots? We need to look taller.'

After the shoot we did the interview, which boiled down to which famous footballer did we fancy. To help us, the woman doing the interview had a pack of flash cards with photographs of famous footballers on. The two Melanies were the only ones who had any idea. Melanie C I remember went for Jamie Redknapp. I said that if Jamie Redknapp came and slapped me round the face with a haddock I wouldn't know who he was.

I had never had any interest in football. But I had to choose someone or else it would spoil it, the interviewer said. So I was going through these flash cards and I couldn't see anyone I liked the look of. The other girls were going *Cor* to all of them.

Then I stopped at one I must have missed before.

'He looks nice,' I said. 'What's his name?'

The woman interviewer took a look, then said: 'That's David Beckham.'

I was always happiest when I had something positive to do on stage, and Priscilla, our choreographer, had put together a big production number for our Brits opener. After months of zap-'em-in-three-minutes TV spots and how-banal-was-that-question radio interviews I was back to doing what I'd spent all those years training for. Dancing.

We had worked with Priscilla Samuels since before 'Wannabe'. When I first met her at one of the flash music industry parties Simon used to give, I recognized her from *Top of the Pops* where she was often one of the dancers, the kind of dancer that made you think, Wow, I would love to do that.

Priscilla gives the impression of being taller than she is, because she's very slim with this amazing body and she is literally the most amazing dancer I have ever seen. Completely self-taught, she's absolutely fabulous, dynamic and sharp. If you put Priscilla among a group of dancers in a room and gave them the same dance routine, she's the one you'd watch.

So days of rehearsals over, it was time. Standing at the back of the stage with our backs to the audience we all held hands and looked at each other as we waited for our cue from Ben Elton.

'Yes, we all want to be their lover, we are all more than happy to be their friend. Then get with them, friends. They are, of course, Ginger, Sporty, Scary, Baby and Posh. The all-conquering Spice Girls.'

Then the first bars of 'Wannabe' segued into 'Who Do You Think You Are'. We turn round and GO. Hips and shoulders pumping like pistons, we sashayed and strutted down the ramp between purple silk flames to whistling and cheering like I had never heard before. The Oxford Street crowds had been huge, but up to now audiences for our PAs (personal appearances), like *Top of the Pops*, were basically kids. Fantastic and fun, but still kids. This was the music business in all its cigar-puffing, coke-snorting tacky splendour. This wasn't a studio in Elstree, this was Earls Court. Can you hear me at the back? Let me shout it. EARLS BLOODY COURT. There are certain moments in your life that you remember for ever. There aren't many of them that stay as important and as vivid as they were at the time. This one did.

My dad is a great walker and was always getting us to go up mountains. And you'd reach what you thought was the top, only to find there was another bloody hill to climb. You never got to the top, ever. But now here we were on top of the world, the sun was shining and there were no clouds on the horizon.

Simon was always drumming into us how the music business is a very cut-throat world and you're only as good as your last hit. But that night it was as if I could see the hits stretching out for ever.

Nominated for five awards, we came away with two: Best Video and Best Single. Who do we think we are? We're the Spice Girls. Zig ah zig ah.

As she so often did, Geri got us on to the front of every newspaper, both tabloids and the posh papers, the next morning with her home-made Union Jack outfit. One of our stylists had tried to stop her, saying we'd be branded as National Front. With Geri's remark to the *Spectator* magazine before Christmas that Margaret Thatcher was the first Spice Girl, politicians had seen us as a fast track to the youth vote. With only a few months to go before the May Day election everything seemed to have a political edge to it. Now, thanks to That Dress, the Spice Girls were suddenly the cheerleaders of Cool Britannia. Political commentators wrote that we were to Tony Blair's New Britain, what the Beatles were to Harold Wilson.

11 into my heart

You know when you're dreaming – about winning the lottery or, in my case, about being a pop star – you have this idea about what it will be like. Well I'd imagined I'd always be out at premières, meeting lots of famous people. But it wasn't like that. We knew we had the invitations, but they were never passed on to us. And it was unfair. We didn't mind doing the hard bit but what about the good bits? It was like, Haven't you seen the movie, Simon? This wasn't how it was supposed to be. Not that there would have been time to attend anything anyway, we were so busy. We were on a roller-coaster that didn't have stops. The only time we met people was when they were doing the same shows as we were, like *Top of the Pops*.

I remember a customs man at Heathrow once told me that he had never known anyone travel as much as the Spice Girls. The first few times it was like, yeah, jet-set superstar sort of thing. But we soon realized that it wasn't. We might have been going first class now, but it was just as tiring. We might have travelled the world, but we didn't see it. Planes, limos, radio studios, TV studios, hotel rooms are pretty similar the world over and sometimes it was literally impossible to know what country you were in if you woke up in the middle of the night, which I often did.

What were we doing in America that week following the Brits? I don't remember. Promoting our album probably, or the 'Who Do You Think You Are'/'Mama' double-A-side single. It was hard to keep track. We needed Camilla our PA to tell us where we were, let alone what we were promoting. Every show had to be personalized, we had to say the name of the radio station, or the television station plus the name of the show and the name of the DJ or interviewer. The interviewer gets the teleprompter, you don't.

It's harder than it looks, but I've always loved doing promotion – when we're together it's always such a laugh. The worst thing is being away from home. Almost never sleeping in the same bed for more than one night because you're always on the move, this town, that country.

Depending on the time of year you may never see your bedroom in daylight. Alarm call at 6.00 for the first breakfast show. Radio studio, TV studio, WOW, ZAP, limo to airport. Flight. Touchdown. Limo to hotel. Unpack? Sometimes it's all I can do to brush my teeth and wash my hair. I wash it every night before I go to bed. I can't risk oversleeping and facing the world – or more importantly the camera – with either dirty or wet hair.

I think it was worse for me and Emma because we were so much closer to our families than the other girls and America is one of the most difficult places to stay in touch with your family, because mobile phones work hardly anywhere. It's such a huge place. But the first thing I always did when the bellboy put my bags inside the room was to phone home. But then you'd have to stop and think things like, what time is it in England? The problem was always finding a time when I was in my room and they were awake.

Early March, and I'm back in London. Just. Our double-A-side single 'Who Do You Think You Are'/ 'Mama' is number 1. That makes four in a row. Hope that *The Guinness Book of Records* is listening.

I was shattered. I'd just been for dinner with Stuart but kept falling asleep. He was a really nice boy but after all the things that had happened to me it was hard to get worked up about a delivery of flowers going wrong.

My dad let me in, then my mum called from the kitchen.

'Is that you, Victoria?'

'Yes, Mummy. What do you want?'

'Can you give Melanie Chisholm a call?'

My mum never really liked the names of the Melanies being shortened.

If Melanie felt anything like me, I decided, she'd probably be asleep.

She wasn't.

'Simon's got tickets for the footie on Saturday. That season-ticket holder friend of his wants to know if we want to go. It means flying up to Manchester. Are you up for it, kidder?'

'I can't really think straight, Melanie. I'll call you in the morning.'

I wasn't thinking straight. My heart had suddenly begun beating very fast. Football. Manchester. David

In the flat in Epsom.
A very lonely time.

Who needs a
Porsche when
you can have a
Fiat Uno?

Me and Mark Wood.
Getting engaged
meant a cake and a
party. It didn't mean
getting married.

Me and my dad are both workaholics.
While I work on building up my tan, he
works on cleaning the pool.

The Adams family on holiday.

Backstage at *Bertie*, my first professional appearance.

Marlene P. Mountain (centre) was the ultimate theatrical landlady. Second from my left, my friend Camilla Simson. In front, with the mad hair, David Harington.

With Stuart Bilton it was all hearts and flowers.

Louise, her then boyfriend, Sharky, me and Stuart on holiday in the Caribbean.

A moment of intimacy in the glamorous life of the Spice Girls.

Rehearsing in North London in the run-up to our November 1994 showcase.

Our first-ever concert, sponsored by Preston Borough Council. We stayed at the Midland Hotel, Manchester, where a year later a certain footballer smuggled himself in.

Sporty, Scary, Baby, Posh and Ginger.

With Simon Fuller in Japan.

My first pop trophy: oh, and a car.

Me and Geri somewhere hot, possibly Bali if the hand-positions are anything to go by.

1996, my 22nd birthday. As usual my mum had ordered an appropriate cake, some reference to my eating habits I think.

Beckham. He might not even be there. But then he might be there. Just the thought made me all goose-pimply.

I wondered why Simon hadn't called me himself. Probably because he didn't want to risk getting my mum. I had the feeling he didn't like to think any of us had families.

I kicked off my shoes and pointed the zapper at the television. Just in time for the News. My mum was still rattling around the kitchen.

'Mummy.'

'Yes, Victoria.'

'When's dad off skiing?'

'March the fifteenth. Saturday morning at about six. Why do you want to know?'

'Just wondered.'

Dad still went skiing with his friends. And this year it was an all-male thing and Christian and Stuart were going with them.

Me and Melanie got the plane from Heathrow on Saturday morning. It was just a commuter flight, so there was no first class, but Simon's friend, who Melanie and I had christened Porno Pete for no good reason except that he had this 'tache like a proper porn star, bought us a bottle of champagne. He was the nicest guy you could ever meet, and so funny. He used to wear jeans and a shirt, but the shirt unbuttoned to show off his nice gold locket – inside was a piece of the grass he'd cut from the ground at Wembley. By the time we got to Manchester – which was only forty-five minutes away – Melanie C and I were completely rat-arsed.

I'd be lying if I said I could remember much of what happened that day. So think of this as *Match of the*

183

Day-style edited highlights. Because we were Spice Girls and famous, they'd organized a lunch before the game with the chairman who at the time was Martin Edwards. To me he was just a man in a suit with a dodgy haircut. More champagne, girls?

I was so nervous about the prospect of seeing David again.

Why not.

At half-time at Manchester United there's always a big tombola for charity, and Martin Edwards asked if we would mind doing it.

Why not.

So just before the end of the first half, Melanie C and I were taken down to the pitch. First along the smart corporate corridors, then down in the lift, then along the back of the stands, through all these swing doors until we came to the side of the pitch where the TV cameras were.

In those days I hardly ever wore trousers. But that day I was wearing combats, a tight shirt with a bit of cleavage showing, a tight little leather jacket with the collar turned up and a full face of make-up.

So then, at a nod from the bloke that was with us, we walked out on to this amazing bit of grass. I remember thinking it was so much better than my dad's efforts. If I'd expected cheers I was very much mistaken. Because there had been so much press about the Spice Girls, everyone knew that Melanie C was mad about Liverpool and the crowd started shouting 'You scouse bastard, You scouse bastard'. I couldn't believe it. So she turned round and gave them two fingers. No prizes for guessing what was all over the press next day.

So we're standing there in the middle of this pitch,

and I was handing the bits of paper to the guy to read out the winning numbers. But then came the embarrassing bit. Half-time lasts about twenty minutes, and to pass the time while the ground staff are wandering around putting back the bits of grass that have come up with kicking they read out the half-time scores of the other premiership games. And if they've got a celebrity there, they get them to do it. By this stage, it's clear that getting Melanie to do it is not a good idea. So the guy hands me this bit of paper and pushes me towards the mike.

I remember how I used to hear the football scores on the television at home. Whoever it was had this singsong way of doing it, where you could practically guess the scores by the way he said the first bit. Like *Manchester United 5* – voice up. *Newcastle United 2* – voice down. So I'm thinking, I can do that. But it's not that easy when you've had a glass of champagne and the names don't mean anything anyway. So I was reading them out syllable by syllable, as if I was still in Mrs Horrible's class reading Janet and John. I was doing all right until I reached Derby, which I pronounced *Dur-by*. 'Derby 1' – pause – 'the other team didn't.' That one had Melanie grabbing hold of the official she was laughing so much.

After that it was back through the maze of underground passages to the directors' box.

Me? Get involved with a footballer? No way. I'd seen footballers at the Epping Forest Country Club. I'd read about them in the press. Immoral, drunk, shagging everything that moves, hitting the women they keep at home. Ought to be locked up the lot of them. I want someone who isn't going to have affairs. Who is going to completely devote themselves to me. Anyway, what's so clever about kicking a football about?

I was on my way back to London. Melanie C was asleep beside me. I couldn't sleep. David Beckham had asked me out. I felt like shouting it out. DAVID BECKHAM HAS ASKED ME OUT! In fact, he'd asked me to have dinner that night in Manchester. I'd said no. But it was a near thing. Apart from being scared, it was like, Where do I stay?

This time I'd seen him as soon as he came up to the players' lounge after the game. It's a strange room, long and narrow with a very low ceiling. Luckily, I'd spotted his mum and dad who I'd met at the Chelsea match and they were sitting at a low table at the far end near where the players came out. There was a girl with them. A tall blonde girl, perfect skin, nice-looking. Who the hell was she, I'd like to know? Unlike all the other footballers who headed straight for the bar, David went over to where they were sitting. Someone who appreciates his family. I like that.

The good thing about champagne is that the bubbles seem to make me bubbly, too. I felt very bubbly, not nervous at all. Very Spice Girl confident. Yeah. I was a Spice Girl. Go Go Go. I was wearing combats and a jacket like at Chelsea, but this time with a lower-cut top. No heels to worry about. I sashayed straight over. He was too busy talking to his dad and didn't notice me until I was on top of him.

'Hi. How are you?' I said and gave him a little Posh point. What was I thinking of? God, I was so nervous.

He got up straight away. (Such a gentleman.) Then he introduced me to the blonde girl.

'Victoria. This is my sister, Joanne.'

'His younger sister,' his mother chipped in.

Sister. Ah ha. So that's all right, then. I gave her a smile that nearly broke my jaw. Be nice to the sister, I'm thinking, and you're halfway there. So Joanne and me began to chat. I mean, what was I going to say to David anyway? Nice game? I didn't even know if he'd played.

Then Joanne went off to talk with one of David's footballer friends, and David moved nearer and said how he'd seen me on the Brits – and that was about it.

'Well, I was wondering, Victoria, if you weren't doing anything after the game, I mean, perhaps we could have dinner.'

This was the longest sentence I had heard him say and he said it all without any gaps.

'What, tonight? In Manchester?'

'I've got training tomorrow morning.'

'But tomorrow's Sunday.'

'We train every day.'

'What, even Christmas?'

'Christmas and Boxing.'

'New Year's?'

'That depends.'

'I can't,' I said. 'I've got to get back to London. Flying to America on Monday.'

We looked at each other. We both knew.

'Go on, give me your number, then,' I said. 'And I'll call you when I get back.'

'No,' he said, quick as a flash. 'You give me your number.'

So I did. I opened my bag, found a pen, then looked for something to write on. The tear-off bit of my boarding card, that would do. First I wrote my mobile number. Then I thought better of it. You never know. I scribbled over the top then wrote down my mum's number at Goff's Oak. Simon was making signs at me.

'I've got to go now,' I said.

'I'll give you a ring, then.'

'You better,' I said. 'I'm telling you, Mr David Beckham, if you don't ring me I'm going to kick you in the bollocks next time I see you.'

Then I walked off.

My mum picked me and Melanie up from Heathrow and dropped her off at her flat in Finchley. I was so tired. But with Stuart away skiing I'd arranged with Emma from the band to go on a girls' night out with one of her friends to the Met Bar, where it was all very cool and trendy – even the waiters and porters look like pop stars in their black polos. Louise was coming with me. I should have gone straight to bed, but I was so buzzy.

OK, I'll go out.

So, literally, I get home, don't even shower, just change, re-do make-up and cab it up to Park Lane. Emma was already there with her friend Donna.

'So what have you been doing all day, Tor?'

'I've been at the football in Manchester.'

'Again?' Emma laughed.

'She's given her phone number to some footballer,' Louise whispered loudly.

I'd called her from the airport, but told her not to say a word to my mum.

'What's this about a footballer?' Donna had just come back from getting the drinks. I was on Diet Coke.

'Nothing really. I've just met this bloke who I really like.'

'So what's his name, then?'

'David Beckham.'

Donna shrieked as if she'd been stung by a wasp.

'My God. David Beckham! You lucky cow, I really fancy him.'

Donna, I now discovered, was a huge Manchester United fan.

Emma looked blank.

'Emma, you must have seen him,' Donna went on. 'He's in all the magazines. He's great-looking.'

'Don't worry, Em,' I said. 'I'd never heard of him before either.'

'So what about Stuart?'

Ah yes. What about Stuart? Well, Stuart was away.

Next morning I went down the gym with Louise. When I got back I made myself a cup of coffee and a couple of slices of toast smeared with Marmite. I was just settling down to read the Sunday papers when my mum came into the kitchen.

'Who's David?'

I froze.

'What do you mean, Mummy?'

'Somebody called David called when you were out.'

'Oh. I think it's some guy Louise met at the Epping Forest Country Club. A footballer,' I added.

'Don't talk to me about footballers. I'm not having any of my daughters going out with a footballer. And your dad would go mad.'

The next time the phone rang I went to grab it but Louise must have been sitting on top of it upstairs. I picked it up anyway. His voice.

'It's all right, Louise, it's for me.'

I shut the kitchen door and curled up on the chair, legs tucked up under my bum.

David had just heard that he had to be down in London for a meeting on Monday morning, he said. He'd be driving down that afternoon and wondered if we could meet up for a drink later.

I knew me, my mum and Louise were supposed to be going out with Stuart's mum and sister for a meal.

I thought quickly.

'I'm not sure where I'm going to be,' I told him. 'Tell you what. If I give you my mobile number you can tell me when you know what time you're likely to get here. Then we can arrange where to meet.'

No sooner had I put the phone down when my mobile rang. Simon. He had seen me give my number to David, he said, and hoped I wasn't planning to 'do anything silly'.

'But you're the one who introduced us, Simon.'

I didn't understand. He was also the one who had been on at me to get rid of Stuart and get myself a famous footballer for a boyfriend.

'Anyway, I don't know what you're getting so worked up about,' I went on. 'He only wants to meet up for a drink.'

He said that we couldn't be photographed. And that if people knew we were going out together there would be a lot of interest. Press interest. He said that we ought to keep it quiet and to only go somewhere private. No pubs or bars.

'But, Simon, I can't live my life behind walls.'

Simon told me that it was for my own good. It was nothing to do with the Spice Girls, simply being careful.

And before we were photographed we should really make sure we liked each other, because of the tremendous pressure that would be on both of us. His view was that it could be over in a month and you never knew what might happen. And it wasn't just paparazzi who were the problem; anyone with a camera who took a photo of us, with one quick call to the *Sun* or the *Mirror* they would be £1,000 richer. Or even more. He said that we had to be sensible.

I can't bear it. For once in my life I meet a bloke I really fancy, and I just want to be with him. If we got seen or photographed together, so what? I just wanted to be with him. And there was Simon telling me to be sensible. Who wants to be sensible when you're falling in love? And I already had a quivery feeling I was.

He stressed again that we had to be very careful wherever we went together and that it was for my own sake.

My mum had arranged to meet Andrea, Stuart's mum, and his sister Shelley in a pub in Loughton, Essex. We went in two cars. My mum in hers, Louise and me in my MGF. I told my mum I'd arranged to meet Melanie C later, which is why I needed my own car.

'I hope you know what you're doing, Tor,' Louise said, wagging her finger.

'I'm only meeting him for a drink.'

'He better be worth it. Stuart's a nice bloke.'

When we get to the pub it's even worse. Stuart's only broken his leg, knocked down by a snowboarder of all things. And him such a good skier. So now he's lying in some hospital in France in plaster. I feel really bad and Louise keeps giving me looks.

I order a chicken salad and all I can do is pick at it. They're still talking about Stuart and what bad luck it is, and how miserable it must be for him in some French hospital and all I'm thinking about is that David Beckham is on his way to see me, and that it is only a question of an hour, two at the most, and I'll be sitting next to him.

'What time did you say you were meeting Melanie, Victoria?' my mum asked as she caught me glancing at my watch.

I hadn't said.

'I don't know. I'm waiting for a call.'

It wasn't a lie. I was waiting for a call. Just not from Melanie.

A minute or two later my mobile rang. Luckily the pub was very noisy.

'Sorry, I can't hear you,' I said, getting up from my chair. 'I'll have to find somewhere quiet.'

The two mums smiled, Louise smirked, and I left the table.

Where to meet? Where did we both know?

I explained that it shouldn't be anywhere public. One of the problems of being a Spice Girl, I said, was escaping press photographs.

Did I know the Castle in Woodford?

Yes, I said, I'd been there with Louise a couple of times.

There was a bus stop right outside. He'd meet me there. In about an hour.

I'd never done anything like this. I must be one of the most moral people in the world. I said goodbye, then sat in the car park and re-did my make-up. I had this tight skirt on, and this tight check jacket. Soft and woolly.

In the pub I had it buttoned right up, but it can be worn with the buttons undone and a bra showing, very Posh Spice. And I had these Gucci heels that were pink with a big G on the front which I'd got in New York. He'd seen me in combats twice. Now for something completely different.

Woodford isn't that far from Loughton, and because I was early I drove round and round the cricket green in the middle of the one-way system. This is stupid. I pull up by the bus stop outside the Castle, and watch for him in the rear-view mirror.

And sitting there in front of this pub I remembered something funny. I'd been at the Castle with Louise a few months before and someone was saying that there was this famous footballer in the next bar. David Beckham. Some of them went to have a look. But I didn't.

Then this car pulls up. An M3, top-of-the-range BMW convertible. Brand-new shape, brand-new car. For a moment, I don't realize that it's him. And this man looking completely gorgeous comes over to me and gets in the passenger seat. How dangerous is that? Letting a strange man into your car?

'I'm just going to park in the pub car park,' he says. 'Back in a minute.'

I wait. And suddenly all I can think of is Stuart lying in a hospital bed somewhere in France.

A minute later he was back in the car. I thought he might kiss me on the cheek. But he didn't. There's a big gap between the seats in an MGF. It would have been a bit forced.

'So. Where shall we go then, Victoria? Any ideas?'

I genuinely can't remember what we talked about.

Our families. A bit of football, but not much. David isn't a great talker until he gets to know you. Not a problem I've ever had. I can talk to a dead person.

It's very hard just driving without knowing where you are going, but that's what I did. I just wanted to find somewhere we could sit and talk and get to know each other. First I drove up the main road, which happened to be the way the car was facing. I soon realized we were in Epping Forest.

Every pub we passed the car parks were full. David would look at me and I'd shake my head. So we headed back into London, down into Leyton. Then Stratford. Miserable pub after miserable pub. You just knew that there'd be some bloke there, some wide boy who'd spot a nice little earner when he saw the two of us walk in in our Adidas and our Gucci. We'd have less chance of being noticed at the Met Bar. This was bloody ridiculous and I knew it. But Simon had made me completely paranoid. Then David had a brainwave.

'I know,' he said. 'There's this little Chinese place my mum and dad go to in Chingford. And it's always empty. You hardly ever see anyone in there.'

'You'll have to direct me.'

Twenty minutes later we parked the car under the only street lamp that was working, pushed open the door and walked in.

It was one of those places that have 3-D wallpaper with furry bits like Velcro on it, and red pagoda lampshades. Eleven o'clock on a Sunday night and there was literally nobody in there. Except the two Chinese waiters, and they wouldn't recognize Elton John if he walked in. We sat down at a table at the back.

'We'd like to order some drinks, please,' David began.

'Very sorry, drinks with food only.'

'But we've already eaten,' I smiled sweetly. 'All we want is a quick drink.'

'Look,' David said, 'we'll pay for a meal, but we'd actually just like to have a drink.'

'Very sorry. No. Must order food.'

And he held out the menu, a thing half-an-inch thick with tassels.

'If lady not hungry, fried rice with prawn very nice.'

'Well, you can bring it if you like,' said David. 'But we won't eat it.'

And then we looked at each other and suddenly we just had to laugh. And then we couldn't stop. Just laughing and laughing.

The waiter wasn't laughing.

'Please. This very exclusive restaurant and people like you not wanted. Please to go.'

And I had this headline flashing through my mind. Shock Horror. Footballer and Spice Girl kicked out of poxy little restaurant. Sorry. Exclusive restaurant, in Chingford. And we just looked at each other, got up and left.

Luckily that afternoon I'd phoned Melanie C, told her what was happening and asked her, if I got stuck, could we come round to hers?

We rang the bell. There was a bit of a wait. More than a bit of a wait before a sleepy voice answered.

I looked at my watch. 11.30. We went up anyway.

Not surprisingly perhaps, Melanie's flat is wall-to-wall Liverpool FC. I was so embarrassed. Although Melanie had been at Chelsea and Manchester with me, she and

David hadn't actually met. I did the introductions. Melanie was already in her pyjamas. She said she'd been watching a video, but I knew she used to go to bed very early. She was still very disciplined, always down the gym, healthy eating and the rest of it.

So we're in her flat. And she makes us both a cup of coffee and I know she's thinking, For God's sake go away. But I drag her into the bathroom, leaving David watching the TV with the sound turned low – what else was he supposed to do? And I'm asking her all those girl things.

So what do you think?

Is he good-looking?

Do you like what he's wearing?

What do you think of the way he speaks?

Blah blah blah.

We had nowhere else to go so we stayed there; it must have been for a couple of hours, just the three of us. David and I didn't even sit together. It was really quite embarrassing.

It was getting really late and Melanie obviously wanted to go to bed, so me and David left to go and pick up his car.

Twenty minutes later I pulled up into the Castle car park.

'Where are you staying in New York?'

'The Four Seasons.'

'Call me when you get there.'

Then he kissed me on the cheek, got out and waved before he got in his car.

By the time I was next back in England, a week later, me and David had talked for hours and hours on the phone. I don't think there has been a day in my life since then that we haven't spoken to each other. I told him about Mark. I told him about Stuart. Told him about everything really. He told me that he'd seen me in Russia. In Georgia actually, Tbilisi. It was an England game and he was sharing a room with Gary Neville and they were watching MTV when the 'Say You'll Be There' video came on. And David had said to Gary, I really like the one in the black catsuit, the one with the bob. And he told me how he'd read *90 Minutes* and couldn't believe it when I said that I fancied him. And how he tried to find out the clubs that I went to in London, hoping to just bump into me. And then how he just didn't know what to do when there I was in the Chelsea players' lounge. And how he'd bought a copy of our CD and how he'd got his sister Joanne to look through *Smash Hits* to find out what my surname was.

I got back early on Sunday morning.

I put the kettle on, poured myself some Crunchy Nut Cornflakes and sat down to read the papers. I didn't suffer too badly from jet lag but having something like breakfast at breakfast time always helped.

My mum came into the kitchen and shut the door.

'Don't you think you ought to go up and see Stuart?'

My stomach did a lurch.

'What do you mean?'

'Stuart's upstairs in bed. I think you ought to go up and see him.'

I nearly choked.

'What the hell is he doing in my bed?'

'He came home with your dad. You remember, we had tickets to see Jimmy Nail last night.'

It was all too much. Everything was too much. I was so confused and I didn't know what to do. So much had happened and I had so much to think about. I'd got myself into a right old tangle and I needed to get everyone out of the way until I could sort it out. I mean, I was even keeping things from my mum, something I had never done. I couldn't go back to Stuart just because he was ill. If it was right with Stuart I wouldn't have fallen for someone else in the first place, would I?

'Five whole days and he didn't even call me and now he's sleeping in my bed.'

I had to buy myself some time to get my head together.

'Victoria, you know how hard it is to call you in America. We never know where you are from one minute to the next.'

'Well, somebody else managed to find me.'

'Now, whatever you've got going on, Victoria, the least you can do is go up and see how Stuart is.'

'Don't tell me what to do.'

I punched in a number on my mobile phone. I'd thought of a way of getting out of the house.

'Hi. It's Victoria Adams. Good. Thank you. Look, sorry to trouble you on a Sunday, but it's a bit of an emergency. Right. If you're sure that's no trouble. Thank you. I'll be with you in half an hour then. Bye.'

I flicked the off button.

'Right. I'm off to get my nails filed,' I said, lifting up my hands like I had nail varnish that needed to dry. Grabbed my car keys from the hook by the door and walked out.

I hadn't gone far when my mobile went. My mum.

'Just to remind you, Victoria, that we're all meeting up with Dee and Del for lunch and then Andrea and David are coming back to see Stuart.'

'I want him to go, Mummy. Get his mum and dad to take him with them. I don't want him to be there when I get back.'

'You're making things very difficult, Victoria. Tony thinks a lot of Stuart, you know. He's a very nice boy.'

'I don't care what Dad thinks. It's my bed and my life. And I want him out of both.'

The Biltons' car was in the drive when I got back. So. There was no way of doing this nicely then. I walked straight across the lounge, up the stairs, turned left, along the corridor and into my bedroom.

Andrea was sitting on the bed. Stuart gave me a huge smile.

'Hi, gorgeous. I've really missed you.'

Obviously my mum hadn't said anything.

I couldn't look at him. Just asked Andrea if she could leave us alone for a few minutes. She gave me a bit of a look, and then left.

He looked awful. But the thing was, I didn't care. Obviously I didn't want him to be ill, but everything had changed.

'Look, there's no easy way to say this, Stuart, but I just don't want to go out with you any more.' I just thought, I have to be honest.

He held out his arms, but I was stuck to the floor. I just couldn't move. Certainly couldn't kiss him, not even on the cheek. I just stood there, my arms by my sides, limp. It was like watching a film, a film of a boy being told by his girlfriend that that's it. Stuart was totally devastated. God, when I think about it now. Such a nice bloke and what had he done to deserve it? Nothing.

'Is there someone else?'

'No, nothing like that.'

I mean, what was I to tell him? It was true that I had feelings for David that I had never had for anyone else, but I'd only met him a few times. We hadn't done anything. I hadn't even touched him, let alone kissed him.

'I'm an international superstar now. I wear Gucci. There's no room for you in my extremely glamorous life.'

No, I didn't say that. That wasn't what I felt. But I expect that's what it felt like to him. But I knew it just wasn't right. So I just said that it wasn't working, that my life as a Spice Girl was just too difficult, too complicated to keep up a relationship. At the end of the day I'd rather someone was truthful with me. If they are horrible, at least you can hate them for being cruel.

'So I think it's best you go back with your mum and dad. You'll be better there. I mean I can't look after you properly here.'

My whole body was screaming JUST GET OUT OF THE HOUSE.

And I left the room.

His mum was standing on the stairs in a huddle with my mum. I liked his family so much. I felt terrible. I just walked past them and into the bathroom and ran a bath.

What could I do? Lie? Suddenly Stuart was just a boy who I once went out with. That's all. We'd never talked like me and David had talked. If anything, seeing him had confirmed to me how different it was with David. I tried to feel guilty, but I couldn't. I know me being in the Spice Girls had been difficult for him, but I was in the Spice Girls before I met him. By the time we met it was part of who I was.

Later that evening, I was just sorting my clothes for the next day when my mum came to the door. She was holding the phone.

'That was Andrea. Stuart's told her that you've split up. She asks can you just go over and see him. She knows you're upset. We're all upset. But she said, if you could just go over.'

Like I said, I was so fond of them, the Biltons were like a second family to me. I cried as I drove over to Wormley. I cried when his mum opened the door. I cried when I saw Stuart.

'Please let's give it another go.'

I was just so drained, so exhausted, but I went through it all again, the career thing, needing to spend more time with the band, needing to spend more time away. But that, yes, we could still be friends. In the end I said, 'Look, I'm going home now because I'm very very tired. I haven't slept or stopped since I got up in Palookaville' or wherever it was. And I kissed him on the cheek, and I walked out of the door.

I get into the car, turn on the ignition, and my mobile rings. David.

'How are you, Victoria?'

'Not great.'

'What's the matter?'

'I've just split up with Stuart.'

'Oh. Well, that's a coincidence. I'm in London tonight. Any chance of meeting up for a drink?'

12 a footballer and a gentleman

'Victoria, you've got a delivery.'

I've just got out of the bath. Monday morning – but it's already gone twelve. I'm like that all the time now. Totally exhausted. If I don't have to get up at six (rare) then I just sleep on and on till I wake up with a shock and wonder where I am, where I should be.

We'd not stopped for over six months – up at six, bed at two. How many countries? I don't know. I don't have bags under my eyes, I used to say to the press, I have wheelie bins – and it wasn't a joke. The most important thing in my make-up bag is under-eye camouflage called Yves Saint Laurent Touche Eclat, translated as 'radiant touch'.

It's flowers from Stuart with a card, a balloon and a cuddly toy. I put the flowers in water. I feel really bad.

The front door bell goes.

'Answer that will you, Victoria?'

My mum is on the phone.

I can hardly see the delivery man, hidden behind a

huge bunch of red roses wrapped in enough cellophane to double-glaze a greenhouse.

'Sign here, miss.' He hands me a pad with a cross on it.

Funny. You don't usually have to sign for flowers. Then he bends down and hands me a box. I hadn't seen it behind this massive bouquet.

Oh, my God. The ribbon it's tied with says Prada all over it. What on earth?

'Thank you.'

I rip it open – a handbag. A Prada handbag. A black Prada handbag.

Envelope. I rip open the envelope. Card. David. I realize I'm shaking.

'What's that, Tor? More flowers from Stuart?'

My mum's calling from the kitchen.

I grab everything and race upstairs.

When David phoned me the night before he'd been at his parents' house in Chingford. We could meet at the City Limits car park, he said. We'd passed it the time before when we went chasing all over the East End. Not so far for me to come, he said.

It was late. Gone ten. But my mum would think I was still at Stuart's – so she wouldn't worry or ask questions. And I was only about twenty minutes away.

David was already there waiting. I saw the lights on his car as I pulled in.

He gets out and climbs into my MGF like before. But this time I don't switch on the ignition. We just sit there in the dark, looking straight ahead at nothing, talking.

And so I'm going on about Stuart's accident, and how ill he still is, how his kidneys have been damaged and how bad I feel. And David says how he's got this really bad arm, how he strained it in training.

And I remember how I've got this aloe vera leaf in the car. Not really a leaf, more a spear because aloe vera is a kind of cactus, but leaf-shaped. When I'd had my nails done that morning my nail lady saw I'd cut my arm and had given me this aloe vera leaf thing, told me how it's incredible at healing and how you use it.

So I reach over to the glove compartment to get it and I'm explaining what it is, telling him how you have to break it gently and rub the gungy stuff on your arm, and he takes hold of my head and kisses me. Doesn't say a word, just kisses me. And again.

So that was our first kiss and it was all very romantic. I even remember what he had on, a really nice lightweight cashmere grey jumper, lovely and soft.

Now, just twelve hours later, all those roses and a Prada handbag. I phoned him straight away. He told me he'd read in interviews that I was really into designer clothes, so as soon as he'd got up he'd gone into the West End, to Bond Street, and got me this bag. Was it all right?

All right? Everything David did just astounded me more and more.

'What are you looking for, Victoria?'

It was my mum doing her Gestapo impression. I was in the laundry room.

'A big vase.'

She handed me one that might have taken a quarter of David's roses and gave me a look. I decided I had to tell her, otherwise life was going to get too complicated.

'You do know, don't you, Victoria, that your dad

will go mad.' It would probably be best not to say anything to him quite yet, she said.

The next time David and I arranged to see each other, my mum said she wasn't happy about all this meeting in car parks and driving home alone late at night. She'd take me, she said.

So there's me, my mum and my brother – he just wanted to see what car this new boyfriend would be driving – and we're waiting in City Limits car park when this Aston Martin DB7 drives in – the look on Christian's face; he's only ever seen me in vans. But David didn't get out this time, we were going in his car: I could see my mum trying to sneak a look.

In actual fact, the Aston Martin wasn't his, just borrowed for a test drive, so he wanted to give it a good run. It was only about six and the sun wouldn't be gone for a few hours.

'What about Southend?' I said.

The trouble was that because this wasn't his car it didn't have a map in it. And because David had been living in Manchester since he was sixteen, it was years since he'd been to Southend and then only with his dad driving. I had been there but I was useless with directions. And if that wasn't enough we were talking, talking, talking. We never found Southend. We ended up in Cambridge.

So we pulled up outside this little wine bar–type place. Empty. Well, nearly. And I'm thinking, we really shouldn't be going in here. I mean, what would Simon say? Not that David knew it was Simon I was worried about. I'd made out that it was me that was worried. But it was horrible. I mean, I just wanted to be with him.

David kissed me outside in the car, and then we went in. David had a pizza, just like anybody would. But people were kind of looking at us, with the look that said, Isn't that . . . ? But it was probably the car that did it.

In the wine bar I needed to go to the toilet and when I stood up David stood up. At first, I thought there was something wrong. Then when I got back, David stood up again until I had sat down. And then I understood: he was just being polite. I had never had anyone treat me like that. It was clear from day one that he was a complete gentleman. David had been brought up to have a lot of respect for women – something that's pretty rare these days – and that's all down to his parents.

He dropped me back at my house. It didn't take long, especially in an Aston Martin. I didn't ask him to come in – that really would be dropping my mum in it with my dad still not knowing.

A few days later, he phoned again. I was at a Capital Radio launch. What about going out?

Going out? But what did that mean? Where could we go where we wouldn't be seen? My driver at the time was called Costa. I went to find him.

'If you wanted to go somewhere with somebody, Costa, and you didn't want to be seen, where would you go?'

He looked at me hard.

'What about the pictures?'

Now why didn't I think of that.

'There's this little cinema down the King's Road,' he went on. 'It's quite old-fashioned.'

So I picked up a copy of the *Evening Standard* from reception to see what was on. A comedy starring Tom

Cruise. Good reviews, even been nominated for an Oscar. I called David back and we arranged to meet in a side-street in Chelsea. Costa's car had blacked-out windows, so the idea was that Costa would jump out, get the tickets, wait for the show to finish, wait for the foyer to clear, then me and David would dash in.

So that's what we did. And no one saw us. So the film has just started and I just don't believe what I've done. There's me thinking we're going to see some romantic comedy, and it turns out to be all about football stars and their agents. I feel so embarrassed. And then he started kissing me. And all I can remember about the whole thing is that my glasses were so steamed up I didn't actually see any of *Jerry Maguire* that night.

When we got back to where he had parked his car, David was expecting me to go my way and him to go his way. Instead I told Costa that David would take me home. Halfway there, we stopped at a garage for some petrol. I quickly punched my mum and dad's number.

'Are you in bed?'

'No, why?'

'Well, is it OK if I bring someone back? There's someone I'd like you to meet.'

So we get to the house and my mum and dad are in the lounge in their dressing gowns.

'So,' says my dad, 'you're a footballer.'

David nods.

'What team do you play for, then?'

And David is so shy when he meets people for the first time. So he just sat on the sofa not saying a lot until my mum and dad took the hint and went upstairs.

I had needed something good to happen.

On 2 April the first of three instalments of 'intimate revelations' of Posh Spice, as told by her first boyfriend Mark Wood, took up two pages of the *Star*. So, if you thought I was being a little hard on the little bastard, now you know why. Anyway, I wasn't being hard on him. He was a tight-arse who treated me like shit then sold me down the river for £60,000. (Any chance of paying my mum back some of what you owe her, Mark?) I was just being honest.

All these years later he still feeds off it. In November 2000 he was on *Blind Date* with Cilla Black. He went on as my ex-fiancé. One of the three girls he had to choose from was a Posh Spice so-called lookalike. And Cilla Black says, so was Posh Spice really posh and he turns round and says, if she's posh, Cilla, you're the Queen. Of course the lines are all written for them, but how tacky is that? What are people going to think except, You wanker? He should have stayed in the burglar-alarm cupboard.

These newspapers wanted their money's-worth and made sure they got it, true or false. Like he said how we had had sex in a train going up to Scotland. In your dreams, mate. Talk about not being up to it. But is this really the sort of thing you want your dad to read about over his breakfast?

It was just horrible, like your house being burgled, only worse. Stuart, bless him, was really sweet. He would never do anything like that, he said. And I believed him. He still didn't know about David.

Two days later everyone knew. If I insisted on seeing David, Simon had said, it was sure to come out. And it did. The photographers were waiting outside his house in Worsley. It was like an ambush. Someone must have leaked it, but if I'm honest I was really pleased. Now it was out there was nothing Simon could do to stop us seeing each other. It had got to the point where if Simon had said go and sit in a police cell for an hour together, we would have done it.

While my world suddenly seemed to have shrunk to the size of a pea, Spice World was growing bigger and bigger and it was back to America again, and *Saturday Night Live*. Since it started in 1975 *Saturday Night Live* had become a cult show – it's really a comedy showcase but anybody who is anybody in the entertainment industry gets on it if they can. The *Spice* album had already sold over two million in the States and was still climbing.

Saturday Night Live was exactly what it said: live. This meant we couldn't lip-sync to a backing track as we had always done until then. Hardly anybody sings live on television now – it's such a risk that what comes out will sound totally crap – it's nothing to do with not being able to sing. The days of John, Paul, George and Ringo standing there with their guitars had long gone.

But then when Noel Gallagher picked up an award at Capital Radio for a live performance, he had a go at the Spice Girls, saying, When were we going to do a live gig?

And Oasis being still so big at the time, this went round the world. What he didn't realize was that we were all trained performers and at our best when performing live. We just hadn't done it in public. In live performances it's not the voices you have to worry about, it's all the various sound systems and the balance between you and the musicians.

The tradition on *Saturday Night Live* is that you use the in-house musicians – which was fine; it wasn't as if we had a band of our own whose noses might have been put out of joint. What we did need was time to rehearse. Singing live and singing to a backing track are very different. You can't be as energetic for a start.

The show was on Saturday 12 April. We sang 'Wannabe' and 'Say You'll Be There' – memories of those sessions with Matt and Biff and Elliot Kennedy. And it went fine. Not great, it could have been much better, but the important thing was we'd done it. And psychologically we needed that, especially as next time we sang live it would be in front of Prince Charles and David Beckham at a Prince's Trust concert in Manchester.

I didn't see David for three weeks. Although we spoke all the time on the phone, I could hardly bear it. First America, then on to Taiwan and Bali for more promotion and to meet some prize-winners. In Taiwan I actually got to juggle on TV. For my birthday we went to some really tacky club in the basement of our hotel and danced to Abba and the girls gave me a bracelet from Tiffany's. As for Bali – well, it sounds so romantic, but give me a car park in east London with David Beckham any day.

Simon was still adamant that we should be seen in public as little as possible. But at the same time he was such a Man United obsessive that he was getting off on playing the ring-master role.

A few weeks after me and David met he suggested that we go away for a few days. To a great hotel he knew in Italy. He'd make all the bookings, he said, giving me a look. It would be totally incognito. He was basically arranging the first place we should have sex. I had the feeling he expected me to say, Oh thank you, thank you, Simon. That was one thing I didn't want scheduled.

On 3 May he suggested I went with him to an away-match against Leicester City – Porno Pete providing the tickets of course – and this time I took my sister.

David knew I was coming and he'd explained we wouldn't be able to meet up. I didn't care. Although I'd been at Chelsea and Old Trafford those two times, I'd never really seen him play, not really watched him, knowing it was him, understanding what was going on. And I knew how important football was to him and I did want to understand.

In fact, I did see him. Simon spoke to someone at the Filbert Street ground and arranged for me to 'change' in one of the offices. Then he waited by the coach and when he saw Gary Neville said to tell David that if he wanted to spend five minutes with me, he could.

And it was so strange, alone with the filing cabinets, like an office romance. It was only about five minutes before the knock came. Gary.

'You'd better come now,' he said through the door, 'the gaffer's on the coach.'

On 13 May we had the Prince's Trust concert in Manchester – a big variety show for charity – and we were doing 'Wannabe' and 'Mama'. The other girls were going up on the morning of the show, whereas I said I'd like to go up the night before. With the usual wagging finger, Simon said OK.

Then again he told me to remember to keep a low profile.

Victoria Williamson, who worked with Simon, was

going up early anyway and she would keep an eye on me. Or so he probably thought.

We were booked into the Midland Hotel – a really nice, old-fashioned hotel with a really nice old-fashioned back entrance. I called David, to give him instructions on how to get there.

'Don't forget,' I said, 'keep it low-key.'

So there I am, waiting at whatever time it was we'd arranged, and there's a screech of brakes as this amazing metallic-blue BMW, hood down, stereo blasting out, pulls up at the back. And this man with blond hair flapping over his sunglasses toot-toots on the horn. That's David being low-key.

Nine o'clock. Ten o'clock. It's getting later and later and later. I mean, this is ridiculous. I'm not a thirteen-year-old to be told when I've got to be home. At eleven I phone up Tor.

'Look,' I said, 'if I stay, are you going to say anything?' Because I didn't want anyone to know. Nothing to do with Simon – this was something I wanted to keep really private.

'Just make sure you're back before the others get here,' she said.

So really early next morning, David took me back to the hotel. I crept upstairs to my room and rumpled the bed to give the impression I'd been there all night, just like they do in films.

The Prince's Trust concert at Manchester Opera House was a big black-tie charity do and David and the rest of the football team were all invited. So all the other footballers turn up wearing black tie, except for David. Well, he was actually wearing a black tie, but he was also wearing a black shirt and a burgundy-coloured Gucci suit that I bought him for his birthday the week or so before. No socks and a pair of loafers. The press just loved it.

They'd have loved even more what they didn't see. The next morning Mel C knocks on my door to borrow some shampoo. I'm just about to open it when I remember the body sprawled across my bed.

'I've just got out of the bath, and I'm dripping wet,' I said. 'Give me five minutes, and I'll bring it to you.'

David hadn't been able to come to our after-show party – there was a football thing he had to go to. So when I got a knock at my door at two o'clock in the morning, I was actually asleep. He knew my room number because he's called me there. So there he is knocking on the door and I wake up and I'm thinking, Oh my God. No make-up, no hair done, nothing.

But I let him in anyway.

Four days after the Prince's Trust concert we're on this yacht in the middle of Cannes harbour. Right from when we first met Simon we were talking about doing a film – nothing serious, just a spoof really. We'd been working with Simon's brother Kim on the script since well before Christmas and we were about to start shooting in London.

This was the whole promotional razzmatazz. Not that we needed to engineer anything: the whole of Cannes was going absolutely berserk about the Spice Girls. *Spice* had just been made the number 1 album in the American Billboard Top 100 and the atmosphere was unbelievable.

We were in the South of France to do a show – an outdoor show right by the sea – and with the roads being so clogged up it was actually easier to go by boat. So we put scarves over our heads with big sunglasses, and big roses sticking out of our mouths. Very fifties, very Grace Kelly. And I remember I had a little brown dress on that the press said was a little brown Gucci dress. It wasn't. It was a little brown Oasis dress, very very short, and a pair of high-heeled brown and cream shoes.

What with *Spice* being number 1 in the States and the David and me thing having only just broken the English press were out in force.

'So, girls. What does it feel like to be number 1 in America?'

and:

'Show us the watch, Victoria.'

Somehow they had heard that David had bought me this Cartier watch. God knows how.

So they're zooming along in the launch next to us going, 'Show us the watch. Show us the watch.' They've got their cameras up to their eyes and they're constantly getting banged on the head as the boat hits the wake of another boat. Serves them right.

After the show it was back to our yacht, then off to Cannes itself and Johnny Depp's birthday party, which was being held at Planet Hollywood. It was the first time we'd been in the streets and you couldn't move there were so many people. It was absolutely rammed. We were in a people-carrier thing and not moving and fans were shaking it. One of the PAs was so frightened that she wanted to climb out. It was all security could do to calm her down.

The car drove straight behind the barriers, then it was fast-track up to the VIP area, which was full of faces I recognized, some I could put a name to: Kate Moss, Naomi Campbell. Some I couldn't. I saw this one guy sitting there on his own, really interesting-looking but lonely. Suddenly I realized it was Johnny Depp. So it's like, Wow, Johnny Depp. Back in those days, for me seeing a celebrity was like finding a blue Smartie. It was the first time I'd met someone who was better looking in the flesh than they are on the screen.

In *Spice World, the Movie*, the manager played by Richard E. Grant says, 'You don't have lives, you have a schedule.' He was right. The film was being shot in England, so at least the travelling would stop for a while and I'd be able to sleep in the same bed every night and see David on a more normal basis. The football season was over; he didn't have to be up in Manchester until training started in mid-July.

We'd been working on the music for the film ever since we met Simon Fuller two years before – it was going to be both our second album and the soundtrack – and we'd been working on the script for not much less than that with Simon's brother Kim. This wasn't a film where we played characters, we played ourselves, so it was important that we were involved right from the beginning. It was a spoof really, sending ourselves up, exaggerating our characters and generally having a laugh. The director was Bob Spiers, director of *Absolutely Fabulous*, *Fawlty Towers* and *Are You Being Served?* And he was great. As much as we needed direction we needed someone who would work with us rather than telling us what to do.

But when the rest of the crew wrapped for the night, the Spice Girls went straight to a mobile recording studio at the side of the filmset to work on new tracks. And believe me, after a full day of working on a filmset this is the last thing you need.

I remember one day in particular when me and Melanie C had spent all day in the Thames. We were based in Docklands and the script had us fall in the water. So there we were soaking wet, wet clothes, wet hair, just horrible. We'd spent the whole day either on this boat or in the water and we were both freezing and really tired. Not only that, I was really stressed. There's this disease you can get from being in water that has rats' urine in it. It's called Weil's disease, pronounced *vile*. And it really is vile. You can die of it. And I know that I've always been a worrier, but the husband of a friend of my nan's got it in the war. He was in the navy and he died, so I'm not totally paranoid. Anyway, I've spent the whole day checking that I haven't got any open wounds and everyone thinks I'm a lunatic getting the production office to check up on my insurance. So all I wanted to do was to pull on a tracksuit and go home. But no. We had to get changed and get dry in this derelict warehouse place with no heating. The trouble was when you're on a roll – as we were that summer – the record company really pushes you. Quite understandably they want to strike while the iron is hot – and we were so hot we were on fire.

No one will ever know how hard we worked. So much for thinking I'd see more of David. We didn't see anyone. My family was allowed on the set once. I pleaded with Simon to let Louise and Christian come, they would have loved it so much. No.

On the last day of shooting, our little Mercedes arrived

– we all just got in, turned on the ignition and raced off. Security went apoplectic. We all had limited-edition colours: mine was racing green, Melanie C had a darker green one, Melanie B had a goldy colour, Geri had red and Emma had baby blue. Melanie C's brother smashed up hers by accident. Melanie B gave hers back after the year, and my mum and Emma's mum really liked ours, so after the year was up we bought them for them. I can't remember what happened to Geri's.

I ended up selling my MGF to Cathy Dennis, the dance queen who Simon used to manage. Although she'd had quite a few hits in America, writing your own songs is where the money is and so we'd had a couple of writing sessions with her at her house in Kingston soon after we met Simon. One of the songs, 'Bumper to Bumper', had been the B-side to 'Wannabe'.

By then my few weeks of comparatively normal life with David were over – he was already back in Manchester training and we were back on the Simon Fuller treadmill, recording. Didn't he understand we needed a break?

One afternoon, I'd finished work early – it was a lovely August day and I just really wanted to see David. I'd hardly driven the SLK, so why not just drive up there to give it a bit of a run? The next morning, my call wasn't till ten – I could be back by then. I didn't want to go alone, I'd never driven that far in my life, so I called my old friend Maria-Louise. We were literally going to drive up, spend the night, leave at five and drive back. No one would know.

So that's what we do and the next morning we set off back to London really early. It's a beautiful summer's day, the sun's coming up low over the countryside and we're whizzing along, the roof down, not a thing on the road. Because I'd left in a bit of a hurry, I had literally pulled on one of David's old shirts, one of those striped things, with a little collar and couple of buttons, like a rugby shirt, and that was it, no socks, no shoes. To keep my hair out of my eyes I'd scraped it back and tied it with a pair of knickers – a little black G-string.

The MGF was fun, but the Mercedes was a seriously fast car – it just ate up the miles and chatting with Maria-Louise I can honestly say I had no idea how fast I was going. All of a sudden, I see this flashing light. And I feel totally sick. I'm a complete law-abider. It wasn't an obvious police car, but a dark green unmarked saloon. At first I'm not sure what to do. But with all the flashing going on, I realize that I'm supposed to stop. I'd never even been pulled over before.

'Do you realize, young lady, that it's an offence to drive without shoes?'

I look down at my feet. In the car I was quite comfortable, but here on the hard shoulder bits of gravel are already getting stuck to my toes and I'm thinking what must I look like. I've got nothing on but this massive shirt.

'We've been following you for the last ten miles. Perhaps you would be interested to see how fast you were going.'

I pick my way over the sharp roadside gravel to their car where they've got this little TV screen. It turns out they've been videoing me. So they rewind it and there's my new car and in the corner these numbers clocking up how fast I'd been going. The numbers ranged between 98 and 104.

Oh no. Girly tactics would be best, I decided.

'It's brand new,' I simpered. 'I only got it last week. But doesn't it look lovely?'

So not impressed.

Nothing for it. Go for the damsel in distress.

'The thing is, I'm not actually meant to be here. I'm going out with a footballer in Manchester and I'm rushing back to London, because I've got to get to work.'

'I see,' said the main policeman suspiciously, looking at my oh-so-expensive, special-edition sportscar. 'And what sort of job might that be?'

'I'm a Spice Girl.'

'A Spice Girl. I see.'

I might as well have said I was Cleopatra.

'But I am. I'm Posh Spice.'

Total disbelief.

I couldn't understand it, the Spice Girls were everywhere. Then I realized that I didn't look anything like Posh Spice, no bob, no make-up, no high-heels, no little Gucci dress. Not to mention the glasses.

So I shook my hair out of these knickers, took my glasses off and did a Posh Spice-type pout and pointed my hand.

'See,' I said, imploringly. 'I really am Posh Spice and I'm supposed to be in the studio finishing off the next Spice Girls album and I'm not meant to be here. And if you give me a ticket or arrest me, then everyone's going to know and I'm going to be in trouble.'

Then the other one suddenly springs into life.

'D'you know what,' he says, 'I love Posh Spice. I've put a picture of Posh Spice over Pamela Anderson down at the station.'

'So what about if I sent you some autographed pictures?'

And they started laughing. I took their names and addresses and they let me go.

'Now watch your speed, Miss Adams, and put on your shoes.'

They gave me a wave and roared off.

In actual fact, my shoes were ridiculous high-heels, which was why I was driving in bare feet in the first place. So much safer.

13 spice camp

One night a week or so later we were up in Manchester and David had gone out to get a video and a Chinese takeaway. So I turned on the television. Or tried to, but the remote didn't work. I saw the back was off and there were no batteries, so I went to the drawer in the kitchen where David put everything that didn't belong anywhere else – David is the most tidy person in the world.

At first I couldn't see any. Then I saw two rolling around loose in the front. So I picked them up and suddenly went sick. My hand seemed to lose all its strength and they clattered to the floor. They weren't batteries. Bullets. Silver bullets, with our names on – Posh and Beckham. I felt the blood drain from my face and my knees went weak.

Just then I heard the key in the door. I didn't move. Just stood there, the bullets lying on the floor where they had dropped. David came in, big smile, and then stopped. I just stared at him. I couldn't speak. He came over and hugged me, kicking the bullets away. They'd come the week before, he said. He wanted to find the right moment to tell me. We just stood in the kitchen, clutching each other.

Although most of David's mail went to Old Trafford, a few things did go to the house and he'd just got back from training, he said, and had been standing at the snooker table when he opened the envelope and the bullets fell out.

He went over to the same drawer, took out an envelope and handed it to me. An ordinary brown envelope. Quite thick paper. I sat down and took out this piece of lined paper, very crumpled. There were two lines of writing in bad capitals:

THERE'S ONE FOR EACH OF YOU
YOU'RE BOTH GETTING IT

'It doesn't make sense,' I said. 'None of it makes sense.'

I felt his arm squeeze me and he dropped his head on to my shoulder. I felt cold. I couldn't say anything, just let the paper drop on the floor. David picked it up and put it back into the envelope.

'Security have already seen it,' he said, 'but I said I'd give this back after you'd seen it. I know it's not nice but I think it's important because it affects both of us.'

David had never had any kind of hate mail before, nothing like that, and neither had I.

That wasn't the only thing that was making us both feel nervous and unhappy. As we would be out of England for the best part of a year on our world tour, Simon Fuller had convinced us to take what's called a tax-year-out. This would mean we wouldn't have to pay income tax on the money we earned outside the UK. The downside was that we would only be allowed to spend something like sixty-five days in England during that year, which was to run from 1 September 1997 to 31 August 1998. As we would be abroad most of the time anyway, he said, it wouldn't make much difference. I really didn't want to go and obviously David didn't want me to go. It had been difficult enough seeing each other anyway. But in the end I'd agreed. We all had.

David and I had been together now for six whole months but 'together' is hardly the right word. Most of that time, either I was out of the country or David was in Manchester and I was in London. Now it was going to get worse. Everything seemed to be slipping away from under us, like being in an avalanche or something and having no control. It was as if we both needed something we could hold on to.

With only a week to go before I had to leave the country, David decided we needed time on our own. But the end of August was so booked up with matches we couldn't go away, not even for a weekend. So he asked his agent if he knew of any nice hotels locally, and he told him about Rookery Hall, not far from Nantwich, how it was really nice and private and only two exits down the M6.

It was a beautiful old house, set in beautiful grounds – quite old-fashioned – but that seemed right. We had a lovely light room overlooking the garden and the second night we were there David proposed to me. Went down on his knees and asked me to marry him.

I didn't dare say anything to anybody. I was still terrified of what Simon would say. Well, I knew what

Simon would say, he would go mad. He had this thing he used to repeat time and time again – that a man would split the Spice Girls up. So why didn't I just tell him to go to hell? The truth is I was frightened of what he could do. He had such power he could make it even more difficult for me to see David. And it was going to be difficult enough anyway.

It would have to stay secret. Rings could wait – all that mattered was what we knew, what we felt for each other. We tried swopping rings – but my Tiffany band wouldn't even go on David's little finger. So we just moved our own rings from our right hands to our left. We were like kids, we were so excited.

Saturday 30 August. Just two days before I had to go and I was feeling very confused. But I had to stay cheerful for David. At the beginning of the previous season – before I met him – he had scored this amazing goal against Wimbledon, which he kicked from the halfway line, fifty-seven yards away – the furthest goal anyone has ever scored in the Premiership. We had watched it together on video and even I could see it was amazing. Anyway it had won him the Matt Busby Young Player of the Year Award. So we're all sitting there, my mum and dad, his mum and dad, to see him get it, and I did feel so proud, with the crowds roaring, David holding the trophy high up in the air, turning round so that everyone could see. And I wanted to shout out loud, this is the man I love, this is the man I am going to marry. And I clapped and clapped so much that my hands hurt, as if I wanted him to hear me clapping above all the other 67,000 people in the stadium.

After the awards ceremony, it's the game: Man United

v Coventry City. At half-time we all go back to the players' lounge as usual, and we're just having a drink when my dad's mobile phone rings. He makes a sign for me to go over.

'That was Louise,' he said, giving me an odd look. 'She says the press are on the doorstep saying you and David are engaged or married or something. The place is under siege, she says, and there's bouquets of flowers arriving, and the phone's going mad. What's going on?'

I couldn't believe it. How could they have found out? Because nobody knew. No one, except my mum. I mean, the man of your dreams asks you to marry him – you can't not tell your mum.

Everyone was leaving to go back to their seats for the second half.

'Please, Daddy, not now. I'll talk about it later,' I said.

As usual, when the game finished, David's dad bought a copy of the *Pink Paper* from one of the men selling them outside the ground. This is a sports paper that comes out straight after the match. How they do it so quickly I don't know. Anyway, David's mum and dad were in their own car, so I didn't see it till we got back to the house in Worsley.

And there it is on the front page: a picture of David holding the trophy with a ring circled on his left hand and the headline BECKHAM TO MARRY. We're all standing in the kitchen – Sandra had just put the kettle on – and they're all (my mum, my dad, Sandra, Ted) looking at me, or rather looking down, at the Tiffany ring on my left hand.

Next thing, my mobile rings. It's one of the lawyers who worked for Simon and handled the press in those days. He was a real hard-core lawyer – we used to call him the Grim Reaper.

This was all I needed. His voice sounded colder than a fridge. The press had photographs of David wearing a ring on his engagement finger and one of me wearing a ring on my engagement finger, he said. An engagement would of course be denied. The story he was putting out was that the finger where David usually wore his ring had a slight infection, which was the reason he was wearing it on the other hand. And that I regularly wore rings on my left hand. It was, he would assure the press, of no significance whatsoever.

'Well,' said my mum, after I'd finished talking to him, 'it's going to take something really big to knock this off the front page.'

Early next morning, in a tunnel in Paris, Princess Diana was killed in a car crash.

We didn't know until we left David's house next morning to drive down to London. There were all these photographers waiting outside – we'd had the odd one before, but nothing like this. I had done what the Grim Reaper had told me, and switched the ring back to my right hand. But they didn't shout 'Show us your hand', or anything like that. They said, 'Had I anything to say about Diana?'

Diana? I remember thinking. What are they talking about? And seeing I looked blank, someone else said, 'Haven't you heard? Princess Diana was killed last night in a car crash.' I looked at David. Neither of us said anything. Suddenly I felt afraid.

We got into the car – the first big thing we had ever bought together, a blue Porsche – and I called my mum.

What they said about Diana was true. We drove down to London feeling totally numb.

The night before – our last night alone – we'd gone out to dinner at a nice Italian we knew in Bury and when we got back we sat on the sofa for hours, just crying. And David had made such an effort for our last night alone to be nice, and looked so beautiful in the Prada shirt I'd bought for him in New York.

Back at Goff's Oak I spent the afternoon packing while David paced about trying to pluck up the courage to ask my dad for my hand in marriage. He was determined to do everything properly. He was so nervous.

'It's not like it'll be a total shock, David,' I pointed out. 'He's not going to have a heart attack or anything.'

They were in there together for about ten minutes, talking. I don't know what they said. I never asked. David's smile and the kiss he gave me when he came upstairs were enough.

That evening we had planned a farewell dinner. It was always going to be difficult but Diana's death made it so much worse. Everyone knew that Prince William was a fan of Emma's and I was sure that one day we'd get an invitation for tea at Kensington Palace, and then I'd get to meet her – not just in a line, shaking hands or something, but a proper chat. I was a real admirer. Forget Margaret Thatcher, Princess Diana showed the world what you can do if you put your mind to it. She got out of an unhappy marriage and had begun to live her life as she wanted to. If that isn't girl power I don't know what is.

We went to Smiths, a restaurant in Ongar that we often used to go to for family occasions – it was only about twenty minutes away from my mum and dad's house. And we were all there, the two families, the Adamses and the Beckhams: Sandra and Ted, David's two sisters, Joanne and Lynne, and Lynne's husband, Colin, and Jackie and Tony and Louise and Steven, her then boyfriend, and Christian and me and David. Everyone was feeling so upset and strange. And looking around the table at all these people who meant so much to me I was thinking more than ever how money isn't important and how just being alive and with your family is what's important. And here was I leaving my family for a whole year, and why? For money.

That night I finished my packing. Camilla had bought us big trunks. That was all the luggage we were allowed: one trunk. We each had different colours. Mine – appropriately enough for the mood I was in – was blue. It was the kind of trunk that you would find under the sea with treasure in it. David actually wrote on it *Jolly Roger*. It was all very emotional.

And while all this was happening the girls were on the phone. The pictures of me and David with our rings on our left hands might not have made the front page, but they made page three. Apart from the shock of Diana's death, they all seemed quite bouncy. For them going abroad was different. Mel C didn't have a boyfriend and she hadn't lived at home for years. It was the same for Geri and she didn't have a major boyfriend at the time either. Emma felt like I did – though she didn't have a particular boyfriend she was leaving behind.

Melanie B did have a boyfriend, but she didn't see him that much because he lived in Iceland. She called me at midnight and asked if I'd packed. I said, not really. What about you? She hadn't even started. She didn't want to go.

And, anyway, how do you pack for a year?

'Don't think about a year,' my mum said. 'You'll be back in two weeks, so just pack for two weeks.'

Our first port of call was New York, to shoot the 'Too Much' video and also for the MTV Awards where 'Wannabe' surprised all of us by picking up Best Video. We all wore black armbands for Princess Diana. Unfortunately, we didn't have Jennie and Karin, who had done our hair and make-up ever since 'Wannabe', with us and we all ended up looking like drag queens, in particular, Geri. And I remember we were sitting next to Lenny Kravitz and his daughter, Zoe, and she was dressed like a proper rock chick although she can't have been more than about six at the time. She had a little leather skirt, white T-shirt, and a leather jacket and shades just like her dad's.

Just as my mum said, two weeks later we were back in England, but only for one night. Simon had rented this chateau in the South of France, where we were going to rehearse for our first big concert in Istanbul at the beginning of October. At least Nice was within an hour or so's flying time from London. Not that, as it turned out, it would make the slightest bit of difference. We might as well have been in Siberia.

The chateau was outside a village called Biot. Not that we ever got to see Biot or anywhere else for that matter. In the month that we stayed there we went out to a restaurant once. Everyone lived in the house. As well as us, there was our cook called Cressida, and

Camilla. For security we had Verne and JP plus Alan Underwood, who wasn't so much security in the seeing-the-girls-don't-get-harmed sense as security in the MI 5 sense. Alan Underwood was Simon's ears when he wasn't around, which wasn't often. He looked just like the Equalizer – he even had the bow-legged walk. He always wore a suit and often a long coat – even though it was hot – in fact his face was always pouring with sweat. He carried around this silver-coloured metal case thing that I was convinced had surveillance equipment in it.

When I was little I was a great worrier, always worried about something, and there was this thing I used to do. I would close my eyes and imagine putting whatever it was on a ship and standing on the dock waving it good-bye. The boat was an old-fashioned ship with sails and it would go off towards the horizon taking my worries with it. I tried doing it with Alan Underwood and his horrible case, hoping that they would go away, but this time it didn't work.

I was convinced all the phones were bugged and never dared say anything anti-Simon when I talked to David or my mum and dad. I later found out that it was the same for the other girls.

In the grounds of the chateau was a marquee, which was used as a gym and dance studio where we practised our routines with Priscilla who was back with us again. And outside the grounds, a short drive away, they'd built a mock-up of the Istanbul stage.

Everyone knows you have to be incredibly fit to tour – and so as well as all the rehearsing we also had workouts every day: fitness classes, singing classes and dance classes.

Mel C and Geri were the only ones who enjoyed them. For the rest of us it was hell. Because this was the south of France, and the weather was still baking, even though it was September, so we had to get up at six.

Since I'd been with David my eating had been more or less normal. But now it began to get worse again. I think it was because food was the only thing I had control over. I couldn't see my family, I couldn't see my boyfriend. No one was allowed in there at all. No one. It was only a month but it felt like a year.

Photographs taken for the *Spice Girls* magazine show us all larking around and having fun. But it was not a happy time. None of us were happy. But instead of talking about it like we would have done in the old days we just kept to our rooms.

One weekend, the other girls were all planning to be away and I was dreading the thought of being totally on my own. To the outside world it must have looked like a beautiful chateau on the French Riviera, to me it was a prison. It got so bad that sometimes I felt I couldn't breathe.

One morning Simon said that he had an invitation to the Versace show in Milan that weekend. And that as I was on my own, perhaps I would like to go?

Of course I'd bloody like to go. But, like, who with?

He suggested I ask a friend.

I called Maria-Louise. She had always wanted to be a stylist so had always been interested in fashion. It was like offering her the crown jewels.

It was only a month or so since Gianni Versace had been murdered, shot outside his house at Miami Beach, and his sister Donatella had taken over the fashion business. Simon said he would make all the arrangements with her.

I was so excited. We knew he got all these invitations for us, but he never passed them on and we never went to anything. Literally anything.

Alan Underwood took me to the airport to meet up with Maria-Louise on the Saturday morning. Then we transferred to a helicopter that Versace had laid on. Milan isn't that far from Nice as the crow – or helicopter – flies.

It was then I began to get worried. Everything was very vague. Who was going to meet us? How would we recognize them? What if they didn't turn up?

Standing on the tarmac to the side of the helicopter were four men: black suits, long black coats and black sunglasses, no smiles. Not even anything you might call an expression. One of them had this great big bouquet. For a moment I wondered if they were expecting royalty at this airport. No. It was me.

So then they walked two each side of us. It was like being under guard. We walked straight out of the airport terminal, no customs or passport control, and there were these four chauffeur-driven Mercedes, black with blacked-out windows. Only one had the door open. We got in and drove off. Behind us two empty cars, in front of us one empty car – except for the drivers and security. We arrive at the poshest hotel in town and are met by Daniel – English, thank goodness – who works for Donatella. We weren't staying here, he explained. This was just our base for the day. We were actually going to be staying at the Versace house at Lake Como, about forty-five minutes' drive from Milan.

'Donatella wondered,' he said after we'd got to the room, 'if you would like to go to the Versace shop to pick something to wear tonight.'

We just couldn't believe all this. I really felt I'd strayed into some strange alternative universe. Forget Spice World, this was totally surreal. I'd come from living like a nun in a convent to the ultimate in sensuality. Everywhere beautiful clothes, beautiful food, the best champagne, jewels. It was so full-on, it was almost too much to bear.

'And after the show,' he said, as we were on our way to the Versace shop, 'Donatella hopes you'll come to her party. There'll be a few people there that you'll know. That reminds me,' he said, and handed me an envelope. Inside was a message:

Dear Victoria,
    Please could you write Allegra a little note and give her your autograph. She's a great Spice Girls fan.
    Love Naomi.

I knew Donatella Versace had two children: Allegra, who was eleven, and Daniel, who was about eight. But who was Naomi?

'Naomi Campbell, a close friend of the Versace family,' Daniel added by way of explanation.

Anyway, we get to the Versace shop. And it's like being a kid in a sweetshop and all I'm thinking is the girls will never believe this. I mean, I didn't believe it, and I was actually there.

In the end I got a black leather dress that was all corseted inside. It wasn't even Versus, Versace's ready-to-wear range, it was Gianni Versace – couture – and would have cost thousands and thousands of pounds.

I also got a long white cashmere coat with a furry neckpiece and a handbag and shoes. Maria-Louise got a different dress and the same coat as I had, but in black. Then it was back to the hotel.

'The hairdresser and make-up artist will be with you in about an hour,' Daniel said. 'I suggest you call room-service and have them send up something to eat. It's going to be a long night.'

So I'm wearing my new leather dress – low cut, straight across like a boob tube but with little leather sleeves – and more make-up than I've ever worn in my life. Then it's back to the limousines. First we're taken backstage to meet Donatella. She's talking to someone who turns round when we're introduced. It's Janet Jackson. JANET JACKSON. Then we take our places at the foot of the catwalk and I realize that I'm sitting next to Demi Moore. DEMI MOORE.

After the show it's backstage for champagne and canapés.

'Do you think I could ask Demi Moore for her autograph?' I whisper to Maria-Louise. 'Or is that just too naff?'

Then someone taps me on the shoulder.

'I wonder, Victoria,' this American voice purrs in my ear, 'could I possibly have your autograph for my girls? They're such fans.' And – yes – it's Demi Moore.

Then I get introduced to Donatella's daughter Allegra. And she tells me that the DJ is Boy George, and would I like to meet him? And I say no thank you, because I'm just too scared.

It was all so bizarre, everyone air-kissing – *mwoi-mwoi* – fashion-week, lovely darling. And I'm standing there, as if I wasn't part of it – as if I'm just watching it all on a screen, it felt so remote. Sometimes I see a face I recognize and have this feeling that I should be able to rewind, see it again and work out who it was. No problem recognizing Kate Moss, Naomi Campbell and Amber Valletta, huddled together in a corner, and I can see from the way they keep looking in my direction that they're talking about me. It's such a tight little world and I was very much the new kid on the block. After a few minutes of me and Maria-Louise just standing there like extras, Kate Moss came over and said hi. And she was really sweet and introduced Amber Valletta who is one of my favourite supermodels. Naomi Campbell just stayed where she was. Then eventually she struts over, shoulders going, boobs out, built like a horse, and she stands in front of me, hands on hips. Really belligerent. And without any introduction says:

'So exactly why do they call you Posh?' You could hear the sneer.

And I got as face to face as you can with someone who's about ten foot tall and said:

'Why exactly do they call you beautiful?'

Her face hardened, she turned first her head, then her body and left.

But it was only bravado. In fact I felt incredibly lonely and just wished I was at home with my family. It wasn't so different from being in the school playground really. Everyone else looking as if they're having fun and you feeling that you would rather not be there. Just being stared at.

By this time I didn't really want to go on to the party. I knew it would be more of the same. And it was. A flat that seemed to go on and on, wooden floors, furniture that looked as if it would break if you sat on it, and like you would imagine: lots of gold, and the place thudding to loud music and people posing, air-kissing. I felt like Little Orphan Annie. I ended up talking with Guido, a hairdresser, and to Paul, Donatella's husband, who used to be a model. I felt far more comfortable with them than with the lovely-darling, *mwoi-mwoi*, fashion-week darling, fuck-wit celebrities.

We didn't stay to the end. Paul arranged for the car to take us to the country *palazzo*. We got to the house at Lake Como around three. It was all terraces and urns and statues and hedges and gravel. Although it was pitch dark when we arrived you could tell it was amazing, the long drive lit by lights and security everywhere.

The housekeeper met us – our bags were already there – and took us to our rooms. First Maria-Louise, then me.

My room was amazing. No other word will do. Balcony overlooking the lake, everywhere photographs of Gianni Versace, a phone beside the bed with names next to the speed keys: Elton, London. Elton, Nice. And suddenly I get it. This was his room, Gianni Versace's room.

Then I go into the bathroom with my washbag and hanging on a hook above the mirror is a headband, a stretchy towel headband. With the blood on it. The very one, I realize with a shock, that he was wearing when he was shot. And it's like this place is a shrine: the squashed toothpaste tube just like he left it. His clothes in the wardrobe.

And I'm just totally freaked. Tired as I am, there's no way I'm sleeping there on my own. I open the door and knock on Maria-Louise's. I reckon Versace's bed is big enough for four, let alone two.

We spent the next day with Donatella's two children, the nanny and two security men, really tough-looking, who never let the kids out of their sight. When he died Gianni Versace's fortune went to Allegra, and Italy being Italy they had this real fear of kidnapping. We got a boat and had lunch on an island in the lake. Then we cruised up and down the lake and had dinner back at the house. All very lovely, but what a life.

A helicopter picks us up from the garden early next morning, then it's back to Nice and real life. Or the Spice World approximation of real life.

Surely it didn't have to be like this? The world saw me as Posh Spice, millionaire pop star, but I was so unhappy. Coming back to Spice Camp, as my mum had christened it (she even got baseball hats made with 'Spice Camp' written on them for us all), made me realize how it felt no better than a prison. Usually when I'm feeling low just looking out of the window at a sunny day can make me feel happy. Outside, the chateau was surrounded by sunshine, but it might as well have been winter.

When you're unhappy you are inclined to think that you're the odd one out but some time later that week, I was sitting on the ironing board talking to Geri in a little laundry room that was on the same floor as our bedrooms.

'Tell me, Geri,' I paused looking for the right words, 'are you really happy with Simon?'

There was another pause. Geri walked over to the door and looked into the corridor. Nobody. Then she gave me a look that was just so sad.

'No.'

'So what do you think we should do?'

'I just don't know.'

Just then we heard the sound of a man's footsteps echoing up the stairs of this old chateau. We jumped, I slid off the ironing board as quietly as I could and started ironing my pyjamas.

14 girl power

Divide and rule was one of the few things I remembered from history at school. The teacher explained it with a bunch of sticks. Tied together you couldn't break them – he brought in a bunch and we all tried. But when they were separated, each one broke easily. And as much as we still ate together, worked together, lived under the same roof, and even our periods were coordinated, that's what I felt Simon had in mind. Together we were strong, we had proved that – we had literally conquered the world. There was no way we were going to let Simon come between us.

Simon would get us on our own and tell us things that showed people had been talking. One example – me and food. He made no secret of the fact that he knew exactly what I was eating and not eating. It might have been for my own good, but that's not the point. Some-one was grassing me up. But who? Security? The cook? The PA? The only people we could trust were each other and I became convinced Simon was trying to destabilize us. Because in an atmosphere like that you end up trusting no one.

Yet we were all so vulnerable away from our families and none of us wanted to jeopardize what little freedom we had, and Simon kept us on a short leash. One way he did this was by having favourites, the Spice Girl who at that particular time could do nothing wrong. But the favourite could suddenly change and you never knew why. He had total power over what we could and could not do. He made sure we knew that anything – like a weekend seeing our families or boyfriends – could be cancelled 'in the interests of the group'. He'd promised I could meet up with David – which I did, in Paris – but until I was on that plane, I was terrified he'd turn round and say I couldn't go.

That time in France was one of the most unhappy experiences of my life. Perhaps Simon could sense our unease. For the first time he said that our families could come to see us in Istanbul. At the Prince's Trust concert in Manchester, our first live performance in England, the woman sitting next to my mum recognized her and asked if she was going backstage after the show to see me. Oh no, said my mum. We don't go backstage. Oh, this woman said, Simon Fuller said I could go. And this woman was Sandra, David's mother. It was the first time they had met. So for our first live performance in England David Beckham's mother was invited backstage and my mum wasn't. It makes me so angry now I'm a mother myself. How must she have felt?

Cynics said we chose Istanbul for our first live concert because we hadn't the balls to perform somewhere mainstream. Not true. It was Pepsi's decision: from the start they were our major sponsors and as they were sponsoring the entire thing they called the shots. It had to be somewhere where Pepsi was bigger than Coke, which narrowed it down a bit. But in Turkey, Pepsi is big. And again, Istanbul was good for our image – the whole East/West thing, and not US-UK focused, something unexpected and a bit radical. And from a business perspective it was a really good deal – Pepsi would pay for everything, including the sets, which we could then use again for the world tour.

(As it turned out, somebody totally ballsed-up – they built the set all right, but not in a way that it could be moved and reused. The whole thing had to be totally reconstructed for the tour.)

The best thing about Istanbul was having our own live band. And after all the tension of Spice Camp, performing live on stage felt like freedom. Like I said, we are all performers and this is what we did best, being out there and giving it everything. And the audience loved us. Even the critics were soon eating their cynical words and coming up with the best in English tabloid puns: 'Istanbrill', 'Fab 5 Turk 'em by Storm' and 'It's good to turk'.

Getting off a treadmill isn't that easy. *Spiceworld*, our second album, was about to be released worldwide, so promotion was a word we couldn't ignore: soon it was back to the same old routine: plane, limo, hotel, studio, studio, limo, plane. Singapore, Thailand, India, Hong Kong and Japan. Looking back I don't know how I didn't crack up. David was wonderful. He was always there at the end of the phone, never too tired to talk. We talked eight, ten times a day. Though often I would just cry.

Breaking out of prison isn't that easy, particularly if you can't talk to the other inmates without a guard being

241

around. And that's how it felt with Simon. He never let us out of his sight. He literally came everywhere with us. The press used to call him Spice Boy and that's not far off the mark. Coming back from Japan, when we checked in at the airport they told us they only had five first-class seats. As part of our record deal we always flew first class: it wasn't a luxury, it was a total necessity with all the long-haul travelling we were doing. Now you would imagine that in those circumstances the band – the five girls – would travel first class and the manager would settle for business. No. One of us got kicked out of first class so that Simon could sit there. And who was the one who got kicked out? Me.

It was very rare that we were all five together without our hands-on manager busying around. No wonder we didn't talk.

At the end of October we were back in England for the UK launch which, as always, involved back-to-back TV and radio promotion. At least it was home. On our way back Geri had said that before we did anything we ought to talk to the lawyers. Did I want to do it or should she? I said she should do it.

I was only at home for a couple of days and then it was off again. We couldn't stop the tax-year-out clock ticking and I didn't even bother to unpack.

You don't have a life, you have a schedule.

This time it was South Africa and a charity concert for the Prince's Trust. If I'm being totally honest I knew hardly anything about Nelson Mandela and what he had achieved before I met him, which is awful I know. My excuse is that I come from a generation and a country who take freedom for granted.

We went straight from the airport to take tea with the President and his family. Geri and Melanie B went to the toilet and decided they had to have something as a souvenir. Obviously they didn't want to nick anything, but there was a plant in the corner of the toilet, so they tore off five squares of toilet roll, got some little pebbles from his plant pot, and wrapped them up in the toilet paper. One each for good luck.

Perhaps Simon realized how close to the edge we were – he had arranged for our mothers to join us for a break – we were going on safari. From Johannesburg we flew south for about two hours to a funny little airstrip just outside the National Game Park of Sun City where we met our mothers – in Geri's case, her sister Natalie.

I didn't think I was going to enjoy it as much as I did. But it really was fantastic. But even here there was something not quite right. At the lodge where we stayed, each of us had separate thatched huts as you would expect. But did we really need separate Land Rovers? Half the fun of being on safari should be sharing the experience.

It probably sounds really calculating that we got rid of Simon when he was in New York, totally bedridden, unable to move with back trouble, but one thing I learned from the game warden in South Africa was that to survive you have to be ruthless. There's no room for sentimentality in the wilds of Africa or the music business. It's kill or be killed.

The seed of the idea that had started in that laundry room in France talking to Geri had taken six weeks to take root but now everything was in place. Geri had talked to the lawyers who basically said, if we wanted to do it, we could. But it had to be all of us.

Remember, remember the 5th of November. The 5th of November 1997 was the day I got my friends back. We were in Rotterdam for the MTV music awards on the 6th. The night before we all sat up together in one room, just like the old days. First we talked everything over. It wasn't going to be easy, we knew that. But however difficult it was, we would be our own boss. We agreed to go ahead. Geri called our lawyer in London – in fact by this time it was so late we woke him up. It was two hours later before the poor man could go back to sleep. Sleep was the last thing the five of us could think of.

Simon might have been safely in his hospital bed but everyone around us from PAs to security was employed by 19 Management. We had no idea which way they would jump. Yet we had commitments to fulfil. We needed contact numbers, schedules. We had been given our mobiles by Simon – so on paper they belonged to 19 Management: if those went, then most of our contact numbers went, too. Geri's Filofax was our back-up bible.

It was arranged that the lawyers would notify 19 Management in London first thing in the morning. But they then had to tell Simon – which, unless they woke him up in the middle of the New York night, gave us four hours. But it was just a matter of time before Simon called and told the PAs what had happened. It was like, Hang on to your knickers, girls, and your diaries and your mobiles, and anyone else's you can lay your hands on.

You've got to give it to her, Geri had nerve. She had

taken Camilla's mobile and hidden it in the red and white carpet bag she always carried around with her. Not only would Simon not get through, but Camilla's mobile also had every single number we were likely to need stored in its memory.

We watched as the clock crept towards midday. Surely Simon must know by now. We're rehearsing on stage, and Geri is dancing around, clutching this carpet bag as if it held all her worldly possessions. She was like a refugee.

'Geri,' a voice from the control room would come over the tannoy, 'this is a serious rehearsal, you have to put that bag down.'

She didn't.

'Anyone seen my mobile?' Camilla asked.

In those days there wasn't the range of different rings that there is now, so until Geri got to turn it off, every time it rang one of us would say, Oh that's my mobile – can't be bothered to answer it.

It was actually a very very funny situation, in spite of all the tension.

We knew the bombshell had fallen when we saw that our normally cool and collected PAs were both in tears. They had been instructed to leave. Immediately. And security. Who needs 'em, baby?

In the dressing room, Jennie and Karin were wondering what the hell was going on.

'We've sacked Simon,' Mel B said, never one to beat around the bush.

And they both had tears in their eyes and they both hugged us.

'We're so, so glad for you.'

It was the first time we had any idea that they felt like that, too.

A few minutes before we went on air, we were told we had won the MTV award for Best Group. Often at these things you have a good idea of what you might get, but this time we had no idea, no idea at all. We just got into a circle, put our arms around each other and were just so excited. It felt like a new beginning. It came just at the right time. Because over the next few days the media vultures would be circling. Without Svengali Spice, the Spice Girls were finished. Dead. So they said.

It was the worst nightmare, but it was the best time. Because we had got back what had been stolen from us. Simon Fuller had always said a man will ruin this group – meaning one of our boyfriends from the outside. But the man who started to tear the Spice Girls away from each other was him.

Because our days in England were so limited, our flight from Rotterdam landed after midnight at Luton. To be fair, security had helped get us to the airport – after all, they were on the plane, too. But when we got to Luton, they just left. David was waiting for me and one other driver was there for the others. No one else had turned up. They were dropping like flies. In fact they were employed by Spice Girls Ltd but they also believed the myth, that Simon Fuller had invented us, and without him we were nothing.

As our record deal was directly with Virgin, they agreed to help us out – the last thing they wanted was the Spice Girls going down the pan. At least we had the advantage that it was our decision and we knew what we were doing. Virgin were quivering wrecks. We had recently found out that the Spice Girls' success in America had virtually saved their bacon.

So there we are in London, at the height of our fame, and back to driving our own cars, finding parking meters and pound coins and the rest of it. It was totally surreal. The most important thing when the news eventually got out was to continue our schedule as planned to reassure everybody from sponsors to fans that it was business as usual.

Our first big hurdle was *An Audience With (the Spice Girls)*, a TV show for London Weekend Television, which, luckily, was being produced by Andi Peters, who by that time was more of a group friend – a really sweet guy who was totally with us and did everything he could to help. God knows we needed it. We were so wired.

When we arrived for rehearsals there were two familiar faces waiting outside. Verne and JP our security.

'But we thought you weren't allowed?'

'Nobody tells me what to do in my own time,' Verne said with a smile like a lemon.

But Verne and JP were two of the few. Most of the people we'd worked with since the whole Spice thing began hugged us, said they felt really bad, wished us luck, then left. One of those who came to see us at the rehearsal was our TV plugger, Nicki Chapman (who went on to be famous in 2001 as part of the *Popstars* TV judging panel). She went on about how bad she felt but it made no difference. Her tears were followed by good luck and goodbye. And I felt like saying, fair enough, we've split up with Simon, but we're the ones who have been paying your wages for the last God knows how long. Like the others, Nicki probably thought that we wouldn't hack it on our own, that we would soon be back with Simon and then Simon would sack them for not being loyal.

And we genuinely hadn't expected the hey-sorry-girls-but-you-shouldn't-have-believed-your-own-hype negativity we were getting. People did not want to believe we could succeed on our own, did not want to believe that there wasn't some man behind the Spice Girls, did not want to believe that it could be just a bunch of girls. But it was. But what a bunch of girls. Stressful as it was, it was a great time for us. We were a gang again.

After the rehearsal we made our way to the lawyer's office. There was so much to decide, so much to do. Although we always knew it wasn't going to be easy, we had no idea just how much work was involved.

'Aren't you finished yet?' my mum said when she called me yet again to see when I was going to get back. It was Louise's twenty-first birthday and we had a marquee in the garden with huge great big heaters as the weather was starting to get cold and people were arriving.

Finally I could go. I was exhausted. I asked my driver to put on the radio. I've become practised over the years at just dropping off, taking little naps in the car, and having the radio on usually helps. But although I wasn't really listening, suddenly I heard the words Spice Girls and woke up. It was Capital Radio DJ Neil Fox, or Foxy as he is always known. We'd always had a good relationship with Foxy, he'd always been supportive and behind the Spice Girls a hundred per cent and we always got on well with him when we saw him.

'We've just heard that the Spice Girls have split from their manager, Simon Fuller.'

That's all we need, I thought, and closed my eyes again. It had to happen. We'd just hoped it would take longer than this.

The next few days were chaos. In twenty-four hours we had gone from having a busy office of ten people to just the five of us. We were on the phone to our lawyers every half an hour and we had paperwork coming out of our heads. We parcelled out the various areas of responsibility as much as we could. I was finance. Mel C was touring, Mel B was record company business, Emma was charity work, Geri was sponsorship.

There we were, trying to work, trying to perform, trying to do everything. We desperately needed someone to help us, if only to answer the phone. But who?

One name kept cropping up when we talked about the sort of person we were looking for: Victoria Williamson. Tor had once worked for Simon – she was the one who helped smuggle me out when I spent that night with David in Manchester – but she'd since moved to EMI. She was about our age – twenty-four – she was majorly efficient and we really liked her. By one of those incredible coincidences, when we got through to her on the phone she told us a copy of her CV was already in the post.

They were difficult days. In Barcelona we were booed off the stage by the foreign press. We had always said No Cameras while we were performing – I mean, who wants a lens taking pictures of their knickers? But this involved telling the photographers first, and Simon had always seen to all that.

I remember Simon saying fame can be taken away from you just as quickly as it has been given to you and this has stuck in my head ever since. After Barcelona we were really quite scared. But there was no way we were going to back down. Somehow we would do it. We had won all our other battles, why not this one?

Our first big meeting back in London was with Virgin. They couldn't allow anything like Barcelona to happen again. We were used to Virgin's laid-back style, but this was very different. They were scared. You could see it in their eyes. There were about forty people in the boardroom, lawyers, all the heads of department and senior management.

Getting the media back on our side was the biggest problem we faced. Virgin decided to get outside PR to handle it and called in Alan Edwards, who at the time was doing Janet Jackson's PR.

Next stop on the post-Fuller Spice schedule was Rome. Alan decided that attack was the best form of defence and put it about that the Spice Girls would be giving an impromptu concert on their hotel balcony at such and such a time. It worked. The British media turned up to discover the streets rammed with our Italian fans and the traffic gridlocked for miles. The recently announced death of the Spice Girls, they wrote, had been vastly exaggerated.

But that was only the beginning. When we booked into a hotel we'd ask for a conference phone. Because we were now managing ourselves, the five of us spent an hour every evening talking to the lawyers. Geri was really good at this while Mel B chipped in with naughty remarks about what kind of underwear these lawyers were wearing when she thought things needed spicing up. But these were major business decisions: sponsorship deals that could involve millions of pounds. And although me and Geri both had natural business instincts, we were still finding our feet.

In the end, after hearing all the arguments, getting advice and opinions, and looking at all the possibilities, we always came to a unanimous decision as a group, going on what we called gut instinct. One rule we always stood by was sticking to what was decided, not changing our minds. He might not have realized it at the time but my dad had taught me well.

One of the funniest experiences around this time was in Brazil. When we got there we found we were supposed to get in these five little boats filled with competition winners and go up and down the Amazon.

It might have seemed like a good idea to whoever thought it up sitting in an office in London or LA, but it was really dangerous. Didn't they know that the Amazon is the most piranha-infested river in the world?

So I called Paul Conroy, Virgin's managing director, and said, there's no way I'm going in one of these things made of bark with piranhas snapping around the oars. We'd already said no to the hotel we'd been put in, which was a real shithole – the walls of my room were a graveyard of mosquitoes. Someone said a friend of theirs had a big boat we could stay on. Done.

So what do five pop stars do when they're on a riverboat tied up to the bank of the Amazon when the weather is like an oven? They get out their Wham CDs and their Madonna CDs and they drink tequila. All I can remember of that day is dancing to an up-tempo

George Michael song and eating bowls of rice. Either the tequila or the rice didn't agree with me – personally, I think it was the rice – and I was soon making friends with the toilet bowl. The glamour of it.

What made things so hard was the bloody tax-year-out. If we'd been in England – or even had a proper base – it might have been easier. But we didn't.

Nor did we have an office for Tor. She basically had a mobile phone and sat in a car. How she coped I'll never know, but she certainly got us out of a lot of sticky situations. But it was too much for one person. And talking of too much, in December our single 'Too Much' went to number 1 – the sixth in a row. The Spice Girls were up and running.

Tor suggested that we meet Nancy Phillips, who she'd worked with at Brilliant, our TV pluggers, where Tor had been working before she joined Simon. Since leaving Simon Nancy had been working at V2, the label Richard Branson had started up when he sold Virgin to EMI. Nancy had previously been a partner in a management company that looked after the Undertones and Thomas Dolby, amongst others.

We met her at the Hotel Bristol in Paris. It was mid-December, just over a month since we had sacked Simon. And we talked, told her that we weren't looking for a manager but someone who would work for us, and run our office. Suddenly, she interrupted what one of us was saying, picked up a big glass ashtray and handed it over. 'Use this,' she said.

She'd caught one of us in the act of sticking their old chewing gum on to a posh china saucer. For a moment it was like you could hear an intake of breath. But from that we learned one very important thing. Nancy wasn't there to charm us. That she said what she thought and no nonsense. In the record business there's enough hot air to sail across the Atlantic. We wanted someone who was totally straight, totally down to earth. And Nancy certainly was that.

Right from the start she had this calm authority. She was in her late thirties/early forties, totally natural, well spoken and quite proper, though not prim. So we made her an offer we hoped she couldn't refuse and a month later she took over running the Spice operation, bringing Julie, her PA from V2, with her. She joined us in January 1998 and by April our office in Marylebone was open for business.

What we would do if we didn't have Nancy I don't know. She's like a fairy godmother, makes things happen, smooths ruffled feathers and has the patience of a statue. Nancy is fabulous, and just fantastic at what she does. If you ring the office at ten o'clock at night, she's probably still there.

That day we first met Nancy, I got another piece of brilliant news. Louise was pregnant. It was all a bit of a shock for my mum and dad, because although they've not exactly been strict, they've never let us sleep with boyfriends in the house, for example. Mark didn't sleep in my bedroom until we were engaged. Louise was incredibly nervous about telling them, but they were absolutely brilliant. I never doubted they would be, but they were even better about the whole situation than I imagined, my dad just so excited he was going to be a grandad.

The reason we were in Paris was the French première

of *Spice World*, which had already opened in the UK and America. It was a huge commercial success but a critical no-no. The problem was that some of the toffee-nosed pricks that write the reviews are so totally up their own bums they couldn't see that it was a total spoof from beginning to end. We set out to make a fun movie, kitsch, camp and a lorra lorra laughs. Frankly, I think we did.

Right from when the possibility of a tax-year-out was first talked about, we said we wanted to have a base and that Ireland would be the perfect place: we might not be able to visit our families in England, but at least it would be easy for them to visit us there. But Simon said no. Like I said, he didn't like the influence of our families and was happiest pretending we didn't have any.

A herd of rhinoceroses couldn't have dragged us back to the Gulag Riviera, but with the World Tour looming, we had to rehearse somewhere, so Ireland it was.

That Christmas, Emma and I stayed at the K Club, a fantastic country house-type hotel in County Kildare, about forty-five minutes from the airport. With Manchester only half-an-hour's flight from Dublin, David was less than an hour-and-a-half away, door to door.

County Kildare is famous for its horses, and as I'd always liked the idea of horse riding I decided to have a go. So when David was away I started lessons. And I'd been practising for a few days and I was so, Wait till David sees me. At last here was something I could do that David couldn't. I knew he'd never been on a horse because, like riding a motorbike, he's not allowed to.

So the first morning he's back, we go to the stables and I'm in all the get-up – the boots, the hat – and I even get to a trot and I'm thinking I've done really well and he says, 'Go on, let me have a go.'

So I get off, give him the hat, and would you believe it, he's cantering away like he was born on the bloody thing. That's the most sickening thing about David – he's a total natural.

The K Club was a great set-up. As well as the main house, there were little individual houses, probably a former stable block, each with a lounge, a kitchen, a bedroom, a bathroom and your own little garden. So why didn't we all come? With our first show of the tour on 24 February at The Point in Dublin it made total sense. We got five of these little houses in a row – or rather three on the bottom and two on the top. The only bad thing was that to get to where we had to rehearse, the other side of Dublin, took over an hour.

There was one thing I really wanted to do as soon as possible – get engaged properly with rings and everything. I spoke to the girls and they were all, Yeah, great, go for it. Now that Simon was history there was nothing to stop us. And where else but Rookery Hall?

The opportunity came when I went over to watch the FA Cup match against Walsall. Walsall aren't in the Premiership so nobody thought Man United would lose. And of course they didn't. We did everything right, the same room – only the view was different. In the summer everything had been green. This was winter and really very cold.

Unfortunately, the word had somehow got out that we were there. We got up next morning to find massed bands of photographers waiting outside. But this wasn't a day for feeling angry. I was too happy.

I miss my family so much when I'm not with them, that in a kind of way the people I work with become my surrogate family, which I think is why it hurt so much when they didn't stick with us after we left Simon. A few did – like Karin and Jennie. Rebecca Cripps, who ran our fan magazine, stayed with us and so did Richard Jones, who had been deputy to our original tour manager, Greg Lynne.

Richard had been with us in Istanbul, and it was great to have him back, this time in charge. He's about six feet tall, slender but not skinny. As for hair, he has a little bit of a stubble, which if he let it grow would be rather curly, but he chops it down. He's got one earring and little round glasses, a really nice guy, caring and good at his job. And he's always got time to talk to you.

Another person who stayed with us was our choreographer, Priscilla. This time, we all decided that we would like to have some dancers, male dancers. (Now that's something Simon would never have agreed to.)

And that's another reason why it was so great having Priscilla. She also knows all of the best dancers in the country and they all really respect her and listen to her. When you're on tour you have to be really, really fit. The sports centre at the hotel happened to be right by our little houses and they let us corner off half of the gym, so we put up mirrors and used them for rehearsing and training sessions with Jerry, a black guy who a few years earlier had had a car crash and been told he'd never walk again. Jerry's not tall, but he's all muscle, with legs that are so slender they're like a woman's. He may look a bit fey, but he's the hardest trainer. David loves training with him because he's such hard work. I did one lesson with him and then thought, Yeah, you're a really nice guy, Jerry, but you're just not for me because I'm such a lazy cow. This guy was me and Emma's worst nightmare.

'Ten more sit-ups, know what I mean, know what I'm saying,' he would say.

Luckily for us, directly behind the gym was the sunbed room.

Although we worked hard, it was a totally different atmosphere from the Spice Camp because it was our choice. We had been numbed by Simon and now all five of us were buzzing. We were like electricity flashing off each other.

The first of the male dancers to arrive was called Carmine Canuso. He came before the others to get us used to the pas de deux work, the spins and lifts, but in fact he was my dancer.

The idea was that each of us would have a partner who would have the same personality and dress to match, so Carmine (pronounced Car-min-eh) was the pouty designer one. He was a really good-looking bloke, half Italian and brought up in Switzerland. He wore black, tight clothes, and his hair all slicked back. Mel B's dancer was Jimmy Gulzar who she ended up marrying (and divorcing). Geri also got involved with her dancer, Christian Storm.

As soon as I saw him I realized that Christian was in fact none other than Christian Horsfall, one of the favourites at Laine's and who I'd really fancied at one time. He'd changed his name for Equity reasons, he said, though I can't say I've ever heard of anybody else in the business called Christian Horsfall, which you have to admit is not quite as cool as Christian Storm.

Then for Emma, there was Eszteca Noya, small and cute, and Mel C had Rob Nurse, a mixed-race guy. There were two extra dancers: Takao Baba (who three years later was one of my dancers with the True Steppers) and Louis Spence. They just made up the numbers and did acrobatics but were also stand-ins for all the Spice dancers.

I was closest to Carmine and Louis, especially as the tour went on. They knew how much I was missing David and used to come into my dressing room and we'd just chat. They were both so into clothes and could talk Gucci and Prada all day long.

We opened at The Point in Dublin on 24 February where we did two nights. Our first mainland European concert was in Zurich on Monday 2 March; from then on I totally lost track. Our final European date was Dortmund on 1 April. Then it was back to England and Manchester. While the other girls stayed at the Victoria and Albert Hotel, I was in Worsley with David.

One night, after a long day of rehearsals, we were in bed in the top room watching a video when Puffy and Snoop started making a hell of a noise in the kitchen. Puffy and Snoop (short for Puff Daddy and Snoop Doggy Dog) were two Rottweiler puppies that David had got me that Christmas. I had actually wanted more of a fluffy kind of dog, but David had been having trouble with some stalker and said we really should have something more like guard dogs.

Anyway, here they were doing their guard-dog thing and something had set them off. David immediately went to the window on the landing that looked out over the back garden and saw a man climbing the fence.

The same thing had happened once before when I

wasn't there. Again the dogs had gone completely mad. Puffy and Snoop were in the garden, and they were barking at the back gate. Behind the gate David said he had just been able to make out a man standing looking up at the window. So he opened it and shouted at him to piss off. But the man just stood there staring, didn't move, didn't do anything. And then David realizes he's standing there with nothing on – he'd been in bed when all the noise started. So he goes back upstairs, calls the police and within five minutes there's a helicopter over the house, three police cars outside and motorbikes everywhere. No sign of the man.

So obviously David had told me about all this, which is why the dogs now stayed in the house. Although they looked quite big, they were still only puppies really and I didn't want anything to happen to them.

This time we didn't bother to call the police. Ryan Giggs lived literally thirty seconds away so David gave him a call and another friend who lived about four minutes away.

'Where's that paint pellet gun, David?' I said.

He'd recently done this war games thing with the footballers where you shoot paint pellets at each other and David is one of these people who when he does something he'll get all the equipment. So he turned up to do the paint pelleting with a gun so powerful they wouldn't let him use it.

'It's in the top drawer. But don't bother to look for it,' he added, 'because there's no pellets.'

'Why not?'

'I used them all up firing at next door's roof.'

Now I can see the funny side, but I wasn't laughing then.

By now Ryan and his friends had arrived. Ryan had this baseball bat and the other bloke had a golf club. David grabbed another golf club from his bag in the hall. But it was too late. Whoever it was had gone.

I was really really scared. I wasn't spending one more minute in that house, I mean this nutter could come back, anything could happen. We didn't even bother to get dressed. I just put on a tracksuit over my pyjamas, got in the car, and drove to the Victoria and Albert Hotel, where the other girls were staying.

So we've just got into bed and suddenly I start thinking, But what if this nutter goes back and kills the dogs? Luckily Verne and JP were still up and they offered to go back and get them. As there was nowhere else for Puffy and Snoop to go, we put them in our bathroom in the hotel for the night.

Next morning, I woke to hear all this noise going on – I couldn't understand it: when David gets up early for training he creeps about like the SAS. But as soon as I saw what all the commotion was about I was the one doing the shouting. The bathroom was covered in guess what: all over the towels, in the bath, the floor, up the walls. It was just disgusting.

That was the end of Worsley for both of us. We couldn't go on living in that house. It just wasn't secure and there was no way you could make it secure. And anyway, after everything that had happened, I wouldn't want to live there even if you dug a moat round it and filled it with crocodiles. We decided to look for somewhere else, somewhere we could buy together, at the beginning of our married life.

15 losing a friend

We needed somewhere near the ground and near the airport. With me away on tour, David had to do everything, so every day after training he would go driving around looking for houses.

On one of these trips, he went to Alderley Edge, near Wilmslow, south of Manchester. He'd been sent details of some new houses being built there. No good. But on his way back he noticed a couple of Victorian mansions that were being done up, so he drove up to see if either of them was for sale. And that's how he found the flat. It was the whole of the top floor of one of these places, set right back from the road, at the end of a lane and surrounded by trees. Although it was just a shell when he first saw it, just a building site, it had a lift going up to it that was completely cut off and private. It was like a penthouse and the rooms were big and airy and full of light. Until then we'd never even thought about a flat but, in fact, it made total sense. None of the actual houses we'd seen had been secure so you'd have to start building walls and putting in an expensive security system and everything. And anyway, did we really want to spend all our money on a huge house when, at the end of the day, Manchester was only temporary? We're both Londoners and London was where we wanted to make our permanent home. And even if David stayed at Manchester United for his entire playing career (and not many footballers these days do that) you're still only talking single figures. No. When it came to our real home, the one where we'd bring up our family, then it would have to be in London.

Luckily I had a couple of days off around the time of my birthday, and went up to see it. Because it was so high up, it was nice and light and had lovely views over the countryside and generally had a good feel and I knew I could make it really nice.

Like Goff's Oak, Alderley Edge was once a village, but when the railways were being built they promised free train journeys into Manchester for life to anybody who built a house there worth more than £100 – which was a lot of money in those days, which is why it has lots of big old mansions like ours, and why, even these days, it's so old-fashioned and posh. Although only half-an-hour's drive from Old Trafford it's surrounded by countryside. The name comes from the hill that sticks up behind it, owned by the National Trust, so it's all very green and lovely for walks and things. The village has everything you need: butcher, baker, delicatessen, chemist, dry cleaners, restaurants, not forgetting a couple of handy car showrooms for David: Lotus and TVR.

Now if I said that in an interview, I can just see the headlines: Posh moves to Alderley Edge for sports cars. What is it about the press that they don't understand irony? I still get asked – like it was a serious question – does David wear my knickers?

That all started when I was on a television chat show called *The Priory* and when you have a record or whatever to promote, you do these shows. So this was one I did before my television interview programme *Victoria's Secrets*. (Some people even thought that was serious.)

The Priory's presenters were Zoe Ball and Jamie Theakston, and it's the kind of show where you have to be funny – the whole thing is supposed to be ironic, starting with the name. (For those who don't know, The Priory is this really expensive rehab clinic where pop stars go.)

Anyway, they have this plant in the audience, a young girl, not more than about nine, who asks the questions. So she asks if it was my idea that David wore the sarong that got everyone so hot and bothered in the south of France. Now remember I always like to have the last laugh – so first of all I say, 'I like a man in a skirt.' The audience laughs. So I then say, 'If you think that's funny you should see what he is wearing underneath – (Pause) – my underwear.' It was totally spontaneous, just a joke.

So we're all laughing, because that's what you have to do in these interviews, have a laugh and be a bit cheeky. And the next day it's front page news: 'David Beckham wears his wife's knickers'. And the world goes mad. I'm not sure they didn't even talk about it in Parliament. I mean, David wouldn't get one leg in my knickers, for goodness sake.

David's grandad Joe has worked in Fleet Street in the print rooms since he was a boy, and even he says he has never seen anything like it. Although he's well past retirement, he's still working and really intelligent; the work keeps his mind active, he says, and he enjoys it. He's like an encyclopaedia and he knows exactly what the press have been saying about us, who's been having a go, and who's backed us. We always try to drop in on them if we're in Islington and Peggy, David's nan, will always have tea or coffee and sandwiches for us. I think of them as my nan and grandad now because I don't have my own any more.

We managed to spend David's birthday together, before it was back to the European tour. Luckily the main football season had come to an end, and so on the weekend of 22 and 23 May he came out to join me in Copenhagen.

Although there was the show to do in the evenings, we at least had the days to just be together. On Friday it was beautiful weather and we went for walks around the canals and waterfront – all very romantic. On Saturday morning, we're still in bed, when the phone goes. It's my mum. Louise is going into labour and she's screaming for me. God knows why, but she was.

What could I do? They could hardly tell however many thousand fans, Sorry, but Posh can't make it, her sister's having a baby. What was really bizarre was that we had used the exact same scenario in *Spice World – the Movie*.

Anyway, there was nothing to do but wait. Even though it was a lovely day we didn't leave the hotel room, except for lunch, and then we just went down to the restaurant and I had my usual chicken and vegetables and David ate this great chunk of Brie with what looked like at least one whole baguette of French bread. And I said, 'God, if we had a baby we'd have to call it Brie.' All I could think of that weekend was babies. I so wanted to be with Louise, but here I was in Denmark, and on Monday night we were in Finland. So there's David stuffing himself with Brie and he comes up with the answer.

'It's easy, Babes. Just get a private plane.'

It's funny, even though I could afford it, I never thought like that. David had done it quite a few times coming to see me, but I was still Mrs Sensible and the idea of spending all that money on just getting somewhere never crossed my mind.

And it was a lot of money, because at such short notice we had to take whatever they had, and they only had a big one. Just as we were about to board my dad called. Louise had had a little girl, he said. He'd be waiting at Stansted to take us straight to the hospital. Although the plane was ready and we were ready we still couldn't leave Copenhagen until after eleven because I couldn't land in England before midnight, due to the tax-year-out. To make it worse we'd just been told by our accountants that the new Labour government had abolished the tax-year-out. We could either give up now, or if we carried on with it, we could only keep the tax from what we had made so far. In the end, by the time you take into account all the extra air travel, both for me and my family, I don't think I saved anything at all.

Poor Louise had had a really long labour and in the end they'd had to pull the baby out with forceps, so she had this strange, cone-shaped head. And everyone's saying, 'Isn't she beautiful?' and I'm thinking, No, she isn't.

It was around four when we finally got to bed. Early next morning, David flew back to Manchester so as not to be late for training, and I went back to the hospital, spent the day with Louise, then caught a flight to Helsinki. If I didn't get out of England by midnight, I'd be changed into a pumpkin.

On Wednesday, it was the same rigmarole: we had to be in London for the launch of the midweek Lottery, so we flew out of Helsinki to arrive in London (Heathrow this time) after midnight. Before midnight the next day we'd be back there on our way to Oslo, where the crew were already setting up for our next concert. But at least during the day I could get to see Liberty, as she was now called. The name came to Louise when she was on the way to hospital and 'Lucky Man' by the Verve had come on the radio.

So I'm on the way to the hospital on Wednesday morning when my mobile rings.

'Hi, Victoria' – it's Andrew Thompson, the Spice Girls' lawyer – 'can you talk?'

He wasn't usually this cagey.

'What is it?'

I could sense a pause.

'Geri's leaving the band.'

The words just sat somewhere in my head, like something you wish you hadn't eaten. This must be a joke. This had to be a joke.

'Yeah, right.'

'No, this is serious, Victoria. Geri is leaving the band. She's had enough. She doesn't want to come back.'

I. Literally. Could. Not. Believe. It.

'So we need to have a meeting. Twelve noon at my office all right for you?'

If anybody had taken a picture of me at that moment, it would not have been a pretty sight. A monkey's bum would have been more attractive.

'No, it is not all right for me. Do you know what? My sister has just had a baby and I'm on my way to see her now. And that's more important than anything as far as I am concerned and I'm not going to spend my one free day in England in a lawyer's office. I'm sorry, but we'll just have to do it tonight at the Lottery.'

So how did I deal with this? By being with my sister and ignoring it.

Back in Spice World all hell was let loose. Obviously we'd all tried to phone Geri, but her mobile was turned off and nobody knew where she was. And what with the Lottery being live, it was all so public. Finally after rehearsals somebody found her – I think she was at her brother Max's house. At least, he answered the phone. We all spoke to her, one by one. Things like – Come on, Geri, we've come this far, what on earth are you playing at? I remember having another go and asking Max to put Geri back on the phone, and him saying that she couldn't speak any more, that she was upstairs, hysterical.

'She doesn't seem well,' he said.

Geri not being well became the scapegoat for the evening. We agreed to say that Geri was ill. We even waved to her, to the cameras, smiling like our faces would break saying get well soon.

So how do you explain something you do not

understand? The last time I saw Geri was on the flight from Helsinki. I remember that flight because we were all in such good spirits – after all, we were going home, even if it was only for twenty-four hours. And I remember laughing so much it hurt. Then we hugged, and said see you tomorrow and that was it. I had no idea. Literally no idea.

Still the plan was to keep it quiet. Geri could be ill for a few days, even a few weeks. We only had one more show to do on the European tour, then there was a break while the stage set was transferred to Miami, the first stop on our American tour. This could just be put down as some kind of mad blip. Eventually she would see sense. But on my way to the airport Alan Edwards phoned. He'd had calls from the press saying that Geri had been seen at Heathrow getting on a plane to France. So not ill then. And the whole thing imploded.

The newspapers went into overdrive. Everyone had their theories. That there had been some great row on the flight back from Helsinki. That we'd even been hitting each other. (The truth is that we'd all really had a laugh on that flight back.) That there had been a huge falling out for months. That it was X's fault that Geri left, then it was Y's fault. I mean Geri leaving was like a crop circle or something. I'm sure there was someone out there who thought she'd been abducted by aliens.

It was a bit like how everyone wanted there to be a sinister reason why Princess Diana was killed – a conspiracy by MI5. Because the truth – that she was killed by a drunk-driver – was just too banal for somebody whose life was a fairy tale. I'm not saying that Geri leaving the Spice Girls was a tragedy like Princess Diana's death, but it was the same in the way that when Geri left everyone wanted there to have been blood on the floor. But there wasn't any. The truth is that Geri left because she wanted to move on. Nobody was to blame for Geri leaving except Geri.

Geri really had been under much more strain than the rest of us. It was always harder for her, the only Spice Girl who wasn't a trained dancer. It's not easy getting up there on stage night after night, six days a week. In spite of all the extra classes and rehearsals, she still found the pace of doing show after show more difficult to cope with than the rest of us. And she did get criticized for it, and it's horrible when people say you're the one with no talent, which they did. And I should know.

But the Spice Girls aren't just successful because they're good singers or dancers. At the original audition, Bob and Chris turned down better singers than us, because you need more than good voices. The Spice Girls are not only successful because of our vocals but because of our personalities. And you could never accuse Geri of not having a personality.

I don't know any more than anyone else, but the more I think about it, the more it seems to me that she had it all planned to the last detail: she would disappear for a while, then there would be that time when she appeared to be feeling bad, paying her debt to society if you like, working for the UN, keeping a high public profile while behind the scenes recording her solo album. And then there would be the sock-it-to-them comeback.

I remember seeing her on *Parkinson* in that Salvation Army grey suit, with the nice-looking ponytail and no make-up, looking really dull and boring, saying how

Ginger Spice is no more, Ginger Spice is dead. Blah blah blah. And I thought, you might fool Parkinson but you can't fool me. I know what you're going to do.

So her first single comes out and it's Goodbye Miss UN-Nice-as-Pie. Instead it's Geri the Vamp, with these hideous long extensions – I don't know what she thought she was doing, but it was vile. Bad-taste Geri was back. And then in the video there was a big car with a wreath on it that said Ginger. The Spice Girls have got a lot of young fans, and I thought that was so not right to do. Yet no one will criticize her for her music – at least the media won't – because they need her. People in the music industry are a different matter. Geri knew that, because her singing wasn't the best singing in the world, and her dancing wasn't the best dancing in the world; for her music to be accepted she had to get on a public sympathy jag so that everybody would be thinking nicely of her.

Geri tries to completely dismiss everything that she's done in her past. She likes to forget there was ever a Ginger Spice. Yet at the end of the day, we all know that we wouldn't be where we are if it wasn't for the Spice Girls. Yes, it can sometimes irritate me when I walk down the street and someone yells out, 'Oi, Posh'. I don't like it any more than someone walking down the street likes being called their professional name. Imagine – 'Oi, Builder' or 'Oi, Receptionist'. Because Posh Spice is my job. She's what made me. And for Geri to pretend otherwise is just arrogance.

In her autobiography she said we knew she was leaving. Perhaps she thought we were mind-readers. We didn't know. Why she said that I have no idea; perhaps because it made her look better, because otherwise it was like admitting she had left us in the lurch. Which, of course, was exactly what she did. Geri Halliwell had left us totally in the lurch.

We did the Lottery then went straight to Heathrow where we caught a plane to Oslo well before midnight.

The official Virgin line was to be: 'Geri is suffering from nervous exhaustion.' Yeah, right.

We knew that the place would be rammed with media in Oslo hoping to see us fall flat on our faces, just like they did after we sacked Simon. Then it was Svengali Spice who the Spice Girls couldn't survive without. Now it was Ginger Spice we couldn't survive without.

Everything was negative. History is against them, they wrote, going on about how the Supremes never recovered from Diana Ross going. We didn't care about history being against us, history said a girl band couldn't conquer America. What we didn't need was the press being against us.

We only had a few hours to re-stage everything. We had stand-in dancers, but nobody had thought to have a stand-in Spice Girl. Choreography-wise there wasn't a problem. As any dancer will tell you four is easier than five any day. An odd number always leaves somebody in the middle, at the back or the front. Even vocally, four is easier than five and we worked through the songs one by one. For me, there was one big plus. For the first time ever I got to sing on 'Wannabe'.

Once on stage we had to keep our wits about us. We could hardly go on clutching a piece of paper with our notes about who was singing what line. We just had to remember. And there was the odd glitch, the odd silence when whoever was meant to be singing Geri's line just forgot. It was a lot to cope with, and it was such an emotional time.

So we're all sitting in this hotel room in Oslo, saying you do this, you do that, and there's all the media saying it's the end of the Spice Girls, and we're just about keeping our heads above water, when Tor Williamson walks in and says she's leaving.

And it's like a terrible cartoon, four heads swivelling at once, and one thought in all four heads.

'But I swear to you all, I'm not leaving to work with Geri.'

A week later she was working with Geri.

We never found out if Christian (Storm/Horsfall: Geri's dancer/boyfriend) knew what she was up to, but as he was still under contract he was still with us, all dressed up in his Spice Boy costume and nowhere to go. It was a bit awkward, like, Yeah, your girlfriend's just walked out and left us covered in pigshit.

It was a really weird situation. In the end he had to go. Nothing vindictive, but he was a bit of a spare part, which was a shame because he was a really nice guy, but out of all the dancers I probably spoke to him the least. Because to me he was always Christian Horsfall from college who never looked twice at me. And there was always that thing – you were one of the favourites and you never looked at me, and now you're working for me – that put a distance between us.

He and Geri split up not long after and then he began going out with Shaznay Lewis of All Saints.

I was still in shock. I'd known Geri for four years, we'd shared a room in Windsor, we'd been through the most extraordinary experiences of our lives together. She was one of my best friends. And now she had walked out without a word. What I felt was first anger at the selfishness of it, then betrayal. Total betrayal.

In fact, that Oslo show was one of the best we ever did. Not that it was entirely uneventful. It was the last show of the European tour. We had two large screens at either side of the stage and these screens would often have close-ups of us on them. For one song – 'Spice Up Your Life' – which was towards the end of the show, these screens had computer graphics and fireworks projected on to them to add to the atmosphere and excitement. So there I am, dancing about, thinking how well it had all gone, considering, and singing 'Slam it to the left' and I just turn and can't believe what I'm seeing up on this screen. No fireworks, no computer graphics but footage of some of the crew in a sauna with condoms on their heads and topless women.

I was probably a fire hazard all on my own. I was fuming. Because remember the media are all out there desperate for something to throw at us and half the audience are just kids: you've got little Bjorn with his mum watching pictures of some fat bloke with a condom on his head and a topless woman and he's groping her tits.

When we came off I went berserk.

'I might be only half your age,' I said to the crew who were already looking sheepish, 'but what the bloody hell did you think you were doing? One of the band has just left and the media were out front in force just waiting for us to fall flat on our faces and this is what you do. I don't care if this is tradition. This kind of behaviour is totally and utterly unacceptable.'

They were all very quiet and later some of them were desperate, saying how sorry they were and begging all four of us not to sack them. We had grown men grovelling, but I'm afraid some of them did lose their jobs. We had no alternative.

I'd always been brought up to respect people who were older than me and I couldn't believe that I was having to tell off men who had been in the business since before I was born.

The other girls were quite shocked – mainly the surprise factor. I'd kept quiet for four years and this was the only time I had spoken up. In actual fact I quite enjoyed being on my soapbox. I was always quite capable of doing the Geri thing, but I had always let her do it. That was her talent. Her time to shine. And basically we let each other shine in whatever area we were strongest. And if mine was telling off a bunch of middle-aged idiots, the other girls let me go for it. We all stood strong together at this point.

On top of all this it was Mel B's birthday. In actual fact, it was just what we needed to take our minds off things and we organized a surprise party for her in the suite where we held a press conference earlier that day. It had a great big outdoor terrace with decking and a barbecue area, and because this was the summer and Scandinavia the night never seemed to get dark. Jimmy Gulzar somehow found a male stripper and he was completely vile, a real minger, all muscle and long curly blond hair, like Jean-Claude Van Damme crossed with Benny from Abba and whatever he was on should have a health warning on it.

We had a two-week break before we opened in

Miami for the first performance in the American tour. This was basically the time it took to get everything shipped over. We had one more show to do in Europe – as guests on a charity concert run by Pavarotti for War Child in aid of Liberia. I was so excited because along with Celine Dion, Natalie Cole, Vanessa Williams and Jon Bon Jovi was Stevie Wonder, my dad's great hero, whose songs I was literally brought up with. My first childhood memory is singing along to 'Sir Duke'. I used to put it on and dance round the lounge. In fact, the day of our wedding my dad called up Capital Radio for a request and asked for that as my favourite song.

That was my musical background – Stevie Wonder, Barbra Streisand, Anita Baker ('Caught Up in the Rapture') and a bit of Motown and the Beatles. The radio was always on upstairs when I was little – usually Capital. And downstairs my dad had his stereo and this great collection of sixties records.

They say you shouldn't meet your heroes, because you'll only be disappointed. But even though Stevie Wonder looks very different now, I wouldn't have missed it for anything, especially being able to introduce my dad.

But I had to drag him.

'It's a nice idea, but no, Victoria. I mean, what would I say to him?'

When the fans queue up to see us, you can tell that they don't know what to say. But to be honest it doesn't matter what people say. It's just so great to know that you're appreciated and to know that you've given somebody pleasure or made somebody's day. How many people have a chance to do that? To say it's a privilege is not an exaggeration.

So was my gorgeous fiancé with me for those two weeks of freedom? No. The English football season might have ended but there was this little thing called the World Cup. All we managed to get were a couple of snatched days at Elton John's house in the south of France.

I had met Elton John in the way you do in the pop world, at award ceremonies. Elton had even been in a scene in our movie. But I couldn't say I knew him, like as a friend. It was David who really got to know him first. Just like I had gone to the Versace show in Milan the year before, David was invited to the Versace Men's Ready-to-Wear and sitting in the front row next to him was Elton. Anyway, David is so shy and so not starry, so it was Elton who turned round to him and said that he'd met me and all that sort of thing and said to David that he knew how difficult it was being always in the spotlight and if we ever wanted to get away we could always use his villa in the South of France. So after Geri left, and we had the chance of a couple of days together (David had actually been in La Manga in Spain with the England squad), we called Elton and said, 'We don't mean to be cheeky but could we take you up on that offer?' I mean what a nice bloke. So that was the first time we went there.

Elton's house is so unbelievable. I had never been anywhere which was so totally my taste. It's in Nice and set in the centre of a park high above the town, so you look down over the Mediterranean. All hidden from the road behind high walls and high black electric gates, it's just so glamorous – even the garden is planted with flowers chosen not to clash with the house, which is a lovely lemony colour. Inside it's full of fantastic art. My favourite is two tables by Allen Jones – two women on their hands and knees wearing bondage boots, with a sheet of glass that they're holding up for the top. It's no exaggeration to say I could move into Elton's and I wouldn't even have to change the covers on the beds.

That time just after Geri left, and there was the football row about the manager leaving Gazza out of the England squad, was when the business of David wearing the sarong happened. A footballer (great arbiters of taste as we all know) couldn't have chosen to wear something so stupid, therefore it must have been me. The headlines were the usual example of British tabloid wit at its most brilliant: versions of Who Wears the Trousers?

In actual fact, David had been out shopping with Jimmy Gulzar a couple of weeks before and they had both bought these Jean Paul Gaultier sarongs. It was totally David's idea. He wore one because he liked the look. We were just going out to dinner one night and he decided to wear it, just wrapped round over a pair of trousers – I mean at resorts in Bali men wear them all the time. He's never worn one since, and who could blame him after all the flak he gets. But this was a summer's night in Èze on the French Riviera – what did they expect him to wear? A three-piece suit or a football strip? Or what about a nice line in Union Jack shorts with white socks, sandals and a beer belly, like the fashion icons that filled the screens in Marseilles when England played their first match against Tunisia on 15 June?

So how much do I love David? We were in Miami rehearsing the first show of the American tour when he called and said that the manager, Glenn Hoddle, wasn't playing him in that first game against Tunisia in Marseilles, telling him – and the world – that he was too preoccupied with his Spice Girl girlfriend to risk playing: he was so upset, I hired a jet and flew from Florida to Nice, where we spent literally a few hours together, then I flew back again.

The big concern for everybody after Geri left had been the American tour. Across the continent promoters were threatening to pull out. After all, they had been promised five Spice Girls, now they only had four. Everything depended on our first concert in Miami.

In fact, we weren't that worried – we were always very comfortable about our music and our performances. It was people like Virgin and our sponsors who were understandably nervous.

There was one thing that was a bit unnerving. We were used to having darkness and relying on the lighting to make it all extra exciting. But this was an amphitheatre concert in the open air where you step out on to the stage and you're squinting from the sun.

In front of the stage the grass rose up in a bit of a hill – the phrase grassy knoll springs to mind – covered in seats. As soon as I stepped out there I realized what it reminded me of: Blenheim Palace. All it needed was Barry Manilow and sheep shit. Instead I had mosquitoes stuck in my wig.

It was incredibly hot. A heatwave they said, the hottest weather for a thousand years or something. Where we ate was surrounded by sprinklers to keep the temperature down. I've never liked that much heat – it's all right if you're on the beach or by a swimming pool with no make-up on, but I felt sick and totally awful. But I knew I hadn't made things better by dashing off to France, so I just tried to make the best of it. When I was little my nan said horses sweat, men perspire but ladies only glow. Well, if I was glowing it was nuclear. Sweat was just pouring off me. The costume changes, bad at the best of times, became ridiculous as everything stuck and every movement made me feel worse. I mean, PVC is not exactly linen.

'You don't think you might be pregnant,' Karin said as she did my make-up for the nth time. It needed to be reapplied every time I came off stage.

Pregnant? Not very likely. Firstly, I had polycystic ovaries and the hospital had told me I had no chance of getting pregnant without help; secondly, David and I hardly saw each other these days – a fairly key ingredient in the whole procedure, so someone once told me.

'When was your last period?' Karin went on.

And do you know what? I didn't know. My periods had always been irregular and I hadn't had one for months. But as Karin went on asking questions, I could sense myself feeling really trembly and excited. As much as I didn't see how I could be pregnant, I kind of secretly wanted to be.

'I'll get you a pregnancy test,' Karin said. Well, I could hardly pop down to the Miami equivalent of Boots and ask for one myself.

Negative. But I was still feeling unwell. The jet lag had surely worn off by now. On 20 June we were in Charlotte, North Carolina.

'Perhaps it was just too early to show up,' Karin said. 'I'll get you another one.'

Karin had been with us since the early days, one of the first TVs we did for 'Wannabe'. It was on Sky, I think, and I remember her saying wouldn't it be funny if one day we could meet up on *Top of the Pops*? And she is just the nicest person to be around and she's very knowledgeable – and not only about pregnancy kits – she used to publish her own fanzine. She's always calm and matter of fact, perhaps because before she became a make-up artist, she had wanted to be a PE teacher. Now just imagine if I'd had a PE teacher like Karin at my school, how different my school life might have been.

The two Miami shows were better than anyone expected and very different from Europe. We were used to seeing our teenage fans dressed up as Sporty and Baby and Ginger and Scary (and even some as Posh, but not so many) but in America the mums dressed up as well. And let me tell you a fat fifty-year-old wearing bunches and a white miniskirt is not a pretty sight.

And whereas in Europe the audience would always crush down in front of the stage, even if they had got seats, the American audiences just sat there. Not that they weren't a great audience because the buzz was phenomenal.

We'd just heard that Madison Square Garden had sold out within minutes of going on sale. It was like a virus, everyone was catching the Spice bug. Merchandise was flying out of the window, every household in America from New Jersey to New Mexico had at least one Spice Girl in the family. From day one it had been our ambition as a band to crack it in America. And this was proof that we had done that. And there was a part of me that thought it's sad that it's not the five of us. Five of us started the journey and America meant as much to Geri as it did to the rest of us. And it was just so sad that she couldn't experience it with us. Sometimes when I was on stage I'd look out the corner of my eye expecting to see her cheeky little grin. We used to sit and have really good chats. I could tell her anything. I genuinely missed her.

When you're in LA or New York, there are always people to see you after the show. It's strange, like if they're famous they seem to have automatic backstage passes. It doesn't happen as much when you're in Palookaville. One night, after the show in one of these small southern towns, the door of the dressing room opens and in come four kids closely followed by Bruce Willis and Demi Moore. The last time we met in Milan I was signing autographs for her girls. Bruce and Demi are both much shorter than you would imagine. She was tiny, very tiny, beautiful and the nicest woman you're ever going to meet, really grounded. All the kids had drawn us a picture each. I got one from Scout which said 'I love the Spice Girls', and 'I love Victoria, love from Scout'.

All the time I was trying to work out if I could be pregnant. The only possible time was Copenhagen; I remember David eating all the Brie and remembered what I said. So that was four weeks.

By this time Karin is buying these tests in bulk and by now I'm not eating anything I'm feeling so sick. I'm living on fizzy water. And I still keep doing the tests. They work on your wee. It had got so every time I did a wee I'd do one of these tests, look at it, wrap it in toilet paper and throw it in the bin. So we're in Washington and I'm talking to Melanie C and Emma about whether I am or whether I'm not.

'You can't be waiting long enough,' Emma says. 'Have another look.'

So I go back to the bathroom, fish around in the bin, find it, unwrap it – and it's all soggy and covered in wee – and we all had another look. And there's supposed to be this line. And it looked to me as if there was a very faint line.

'So,' I said, dead excited, 'what do you think?'

They both shook their heads.

Later that afternoon the three of us were walking round the shops and every time I walked past a shop window and caught sight of my silhouette – I was wearing a gold sarong – I found myself quite liking the idea of being pregnant and patting this tummy that wasn't really there.

That afternoon everyone was watching the World Cup, England against Colombia. But I was just feeling so sick that I went straight to bed. And straight after the game I phoned David. The last thing I wanted was to worry him, so I didn't tell him how sick I was feeling. I didn't want to say anything about the possibility of being pregnant in case I was wrong, because I knew David really wanted children. And I felt so bad because I hadn't seen the game and he had scored this fantastic goal.

So then I phoned up my mum. She and my dad and my brother were coming to New York to see our show at Madison Square Garden and I asked her to bring out an English pregnancy test. I mean, perhaps I was doing something wrong, perhaps I hadn't understood the instructions. At least with an English one I'd know one way or the other.

I hadn't seen my family since the Geri business and I was really excited. That's what's nice about having money. I could bring all of them out, and not just once, and we didn't have to faff around looking for somewhere cheap for them to stay. The Four Seasons, darling. That will do nicely.

So I'm in my suite and they all pile in and my mum comes up to me, takes a pastel-coloured box from her handbag and gives me a look.

While they were admiring the view I went to the toilet, did the test. Basically the same – wee, look for the line. And there it was, this big luminous line. It was, Oh my God. Wo Wo Wo. Pregnant Pregnant Pregnant. This was pretty dead set.

My mum was waiting outside the bathroom door in such a state, she looked like she was waiting for someone to die. But one look at my face and she knew. She was totally over the moon.

And I was so, so happy. I would never have thought it possible to feel this happy and this ill at the same time. By the time I went back into the lounge they all knew. My little brother was really in shock, like, Oh my God, another sister having a baby and not married. And then there was my dad. He was still getting over Louise being pregnant and not married. Now he was going to be a grandad for the second time, and again I wasn't married. But I could see from his face that he was really really pleased and he cuddled me and everything.

I looked at my watch. Morning in New York, late afternoon in France. David would be on his way to the game. Should I tell him? I had to tell him. How could I not tell him?

I went into my bedroom and punched out the number.

'Can you talk, Babes?'

16 tangled up in blue

They'd just landed at St Étienne. The World Cup matches were being held all over France and the England team were based in La Baule in Brittany. It had only been a short flight, he said, and now they were on the coach from the airport to the stadium.

And that was where he was when I told him that I was pregnant. Exactly what I said to David, and what he said to me, no one else will ever know. But he was so, so happy. David had always wanted a family, we'd talked about it right from the start.

So, not long after that, we all set off to this English pub where they were showing the football. It was the quarter-finals: England against Argentina, one of the great football teams. At the beginning of the World Cup Glenn Hoddle had been attacked by the press for not playing his two young stars, David Beckham and Michael Owen. This time they were both there in the starting line-up: people-power the papers said (now that wouldn't have been said before the Spice Girls). Everyone agreed that the England team had hit its stride and it would be a great match. And, sick though I was, I decided to go.

No matter what you think about football, there's something about the World Cup – and the game against Argentina really was very exciting, particularly for me as David was playing so well. At half-time it was 2–2. The second half had only just started when the Argentinian captain goes banging into David from behind and knocks him flat on the grass. As he's lying there, David lifts one of his feet up and this Diego Simeone falls to the ground.

I saw it happen, but I didn't understand how serious it was and nor did anyone else. So when the referee went over and pulled out this red card nobody could quite believe it, and we could all see from David's face that he couldn't either – that little trip-up was nothing compared with half the things you see happening in matches. After all, this guy had run into David on purpose – that's how it looked to me.

A few minutes later my mobile rang. David, in the dressing room. He was very upset. Asked me what it looked like on television, and I said I didn't think it looked that bad. If England lost, he said, then in a few hours he'd be with me. Although a sending-off meant an automatic two-game ban he didn't think the manager would let him leave until the whole team left. And, as much as I wanted England to win the World Cup, I was pregnant and I wanted David to be with me. And David needed to be with me. It was all so emotional.

In fact, right to the end it looked as though England would win; amazingly, they were so much better than the other side even with David not there. But then they had the penalty shoot-out and two of them missed. England was out of the World Cup. But they didn't get the blame. Glenn Hoddle didn't get the blame. No, the person who got the blame was David Beckham. I'm not going to write the things they wrote about him, because even now I find it too upsetting. But it's funny that twenty-two other footballers got sent off during the World Cup but did anyone hear about them? Other countries respect their top players. England just likes to rubbish them.

British Airways sent a Concorde out to the England camp to bring the team home the next afternoon. At Heathrow David's mum and dad were allowed behind the customs area with his things and they were given the use of a private room to meet up in. He had literally an hour before the next Concorde to New York. It was one Concorde to another.

But somehow the press managed to get in behind customs – two camera crews and six other photographers, he said, ambushed him when he got to the British Airways transfer desk and started abusing him. Not just taking photographs, doing their job if you like, but literally abusing him personally. He was so shocked. David was used to the verbal abuse he got at Manchester United, but this was worse than anything he had ever experienced before because it was so unexpected. 'The thing that kept me going,' he told me later, 'was what Gary said.'

He'd been sitting next to Gary Neville on the coach on the way to the match, when I'd first told him I was pregnant, but he hadn't said anything then, even though he said he was nearly exploding. But after the match, after everything that happened, he said he just had to tell him.

'And Gary was brilliant. When I told him he just said, "Bloody hell, David, this is the best news ever." And that kind of puts things in perspective. From then on all I worried about was getting to be with you.'

We were just about to go on stage at Madison Square Garden and this man brushes straight past me. But then I caught my breath as I recognized that walk. I didn't dare shout – just waddled as fast as my tight skirt and high-heels would let me and flung my arms around him. We didn't need to say anything – just clung to each other and kind of rocked. Then I remembered what I was holding in my hand and gave it to him.

It was a Polaroid of the scan I'd had done earlier in the day. Because I didn't have regular periods I had no idea how pregnant I might be.

'Don't make me cry,' I said, as he held me in a bear-hug. 'You'll make my mascara run and then Karin will be cross.'

And we laughed and cried and laughed and cried. I was so, so happy.

The moment I found out I was pregnant I had called room service and ordered Dover sole, vegetables, potatoes and bread.

It had come like an electric shock: this baby is the most important thing to me. If you're pregnant and you don't eat then your baby won't get the goodness. I don't care if I'm fat. I don't care what I look like. Because although things had been better since I met David, once you have had an eating disorder – and I probably had, even though my weight was never dangerously low – to get back to eating proper food again is really hard. Being on the road hadn't helped, nor had being away from David. And whenever a headline screeched out 'Podgy

Spice' or 'Fat Spice' I'd reacted badly. And I would look at pictures of myself in the papers and say, Yes, you're disgusting. Society says you've got to be thin. I was completely obsessed. I mean, I even used to measure my thighs. It was so bizarre that all those years I had been desperately trying to get thin and nobody realized I was anorexic because of the polycystic ovaries. But as soon as I found out I was pregnant, everything changed.

At first it freaked me out that I was having to eat proper food because I began to realize that I hadn't really eaten properly since Maidenhead and Geri. Now it was three meals a day, carbohydrate, protein, even FAT: butter on my toast and on green beans and spinach (good for folic acid). But no chocolate or cakes or anything; I knew it had to be healthy.

David joined Spice World for eleven wonderful days – it was the longest time we had ever been together. It's unfortunate that I was too busy throwing up to actually enjoy it. Just having him there was wonderful. David being David, he seemed just as happy holding my head over a bucket or bowl as holding my hand.

Although the crew and stage sets travelled by road, we had this fifty-seater plane for the dancers, hair, make-up and any of our family who were with us. After Simon left, we had all agreed we would never be split from our families again. Three months is a long time to be away from home and sometimes you just want a mum. And because I was pregnant as well it was so nice there was always a caring mother there. Whoever it was, we would always make that person our mum and sit in our dressing room with her and just chat.

The problem with this plane was the smell: it must

have been the food they brought on. Nobody else could smell it, only me, but as soon as we got on I felt sick. And it didn't stop at feeling.

Before David arrived in New York I told him that I'd seen this really cool sweatshirt in Nike Town.

'What's it like?' he said.

'Bright yellow with Brazil written on it.'

As we were on the phone, I didn't see his face, but I could imagine it from the explosion that followed.

'Well, don't think you're having some Brazilian football top,' he spluttered.

But the first morning when he came back from shopping and I was having a bit of a lie-in, he threw this Nike bag to me from the door, laughing. A bright yellow sweatshirt with BRAZIL on it. But the first time I wore it was on a flight to Connecticut. I got on the plane, sat down, smelled the food, and was sick all down it. I never wore it again.

Life never ends at Manchester United and pre-season training began on Monday 13 July. We spent our last weekend together in Canada, and then we had to say goodbye.

I didn't see him again for six weeks and it was horrible. When he left, I hid one of his old shirts and slept in it for the rest of the tour. I would go to sleep and try to imagine what he was doing. Being in the same time zone is easy, you're both in bed, and I would know he was thinking about me. But being in different time zones he could be doing anything and probably not thinking about me, not at that precise second.

To keep me from cracking up I had on-the-road family, the girls, Karin, Kenny our stylist, the dancers

Carmine and Louis, Richard Jones, now the tour manager and, of course, our band who had been with us from Istanbul and were not only really talented but such good people to have around. They all helped keep me from going mad with David so far away.

So, in the best tradition of rock 'n' roll, let me introduce them. On percussion I give you Fergus Gerrand, a top-notch musician, a really sweet guy who used to change his hair colour quite a lot.

Then, on drums, Andy Gangadeen. Andy had a real image thing going on. He used to wear big skirts but with trousers underneath and big boots and long jumpery things. His speciality was weird hats and this frizzy kind of hair stuck out at the bottom. He was a strange combination: rather shy but also very opinionated.

On keyboards, put your hands together for Simon Ellis, our musical director. Now he was really, really funny. A real comedian, always taking people off and doing funny voices.

Also on keyboards please welcome Mike Martin, a black guy with a really good body. He always used to wear combats and tight tops. We called him 'Mr Lover Lover' because of the way he used to grind his hips. He really used to feel the music.

On lead guitar we had Paul Gendler, a fantastic musician who'd been in the business for years. Although he was quite a private person, he was really friendly with a really happy face.

Finally, on bass guitar, let's hear it for Steve Lewinson. He had long dreads and a really kind, sweet personality and when we were on tour I used to talk to him all the time.

I talked to David whenever I could but, especially when we were on the West Coast, it was hard to find a time when we were both awake. And if David was in an away game with Manchester United they wouldn't even put calls through. I just couldn't bear it.

I was so lonely. When I called my family I'd hear *EastEnders* in the background, and I'd hear my mum say, 'Turn the bloody television down, Christian', and then later I'd hear her say, 'Take the vegetables off the stove.' And when I put the phone down I'd cry. All those ordinary things. I missed them so much. And when I came home the little sister that I had left when I went on tour was now a woman with a baby, and the brother who was the baby of the family had stubble and under-arm hair and a girlfriend and was his own person and was working.

If you'd asked me four years ago how important having a view was out of my hotel room, I would have said I didn't care, whereas now I was spending so much time in hotel rooms, and I couldn't bear that feeling of being closed in. I had to feel free, even that small freedom of watching the sun set or looking at the moon. The same moon that David could see. I would just stand at the window and gaze whenever I got the chance. I've always been claustrophobic. I don't like toilets in trains or aeroplanes.

There were some nice things that happened in the States after David left. In Minneapolis even more people came backstage to see us, including Prince. He was sitting in this little room at the side of the stage and it's like, WOW. And with him was a guy called Jimmy Jam – a big black guy who is a producer and writer and it's like, DOUBLE WOW. He's done everything with Janet Jackson since the year dot and he's a songwriter and a producer I would have given anything to work with. And we went all silent and silly as you do when you meet your heroes.

'Say,' said Jimmy Jam breaking the ice, 'I'm such a fan. My wife bought me a Spice Girls T-shirt. But seriously. Would you want to work with me?'

I couldn't believe he was saying this. We're like, WOULD YOU WANT TO WORK WITH US? And in fact he ended up doing three tracks on our third album with his partner, Terry Lewis. Together they're known as Jam and Lewis.

In the meantime Prince was just sitting there, a silver-topped cane between his splayed velvet-trousered legs. I knew he was small. But he's not just small, he's tiny. Very very tiny. But every inch a true superstar. He wore high-heels and was really skinny with this pointy little chin, lots of make-up and curly, very-much-done hair. And I remember him looking like he'd just come offstage but of course he hadn't. We'd been the ones on stage. And he was saying in a very quiet, calming voice how great the show was and then there was another silence. Till Emma said: 'So, what do we call you, I mean now that you're not Prince any more?'

And he said, 'You can call me friend.'

Six weeks and 104 concerts later we were back in England. It had been the most phenomenally successful tour. We didn't realize quite how successful because we were so used to things going right for us. But no other pop band since the Beatles had done what we had done. One of the reasons was that there was no competition.

There was no American equivalent to what we were doing. There were the Seattle bands like Nirvana and Pearl Jam whose songs were all about death and drugs and that was it. Not since New Kids on the Block had there been anything in America that was what you might call pop. At the time we were just pleased that the concerts were a sell-out. We didn't understand the significance of what we had done.

But the Spice Girls showed there was an untapped audience out there of young fans who just wanted to have fun. And it was only after our success that pop music began to take off in America, with people like Britney Spears and 'N Sync. We opened up the door for acts like this.

The only other British bands to do well in America – apart from the Beatles – were hard rock bands, like Led Zeppelin and the Rolling Stones. And they had a very bad name from being badly behaved. We were the only band ever to tour America and totally fulfil our concert schedule. Not one cancellation. When we landed at Heathrow, having flown direct from Dallas, I felt like doing that Pope thing and kissing the ground. But decided to wait until I got through customs to kiss David instead.

The tour wasn't quite over. There were still a few more UK dates to do. But I was exhausted. We'd never done less than sixteen-hour days. By now the sickness had stopped, but for three months it had been relentless: morning sickness, afternoon sickness and evening sickness. Worst was side-of-the-stage-bucket sickness.

The flat in Alderley Edge was still a building site, so David was still living in Worsley. Doing a house up is difficult enough anyway. When you're four thousand miles away it's totally mad. I knew exactly the look I wanted and I wasn't having any interior designer doing it for me. So whenever my mum had come over to join me she'd bring suitcases of excess baggage full of tiles, samples of fabric, taps, doorknobs, for me to look at.

In America me and David had been pretty much left alone. But back in England, especially now I was pregnant, it was business as usual. One night after a show in Sheffield David picked me up. A lot of the time it was just quicker to take our costumes off, stick a bathrobe and trainers on, get in the car and beat the jam that followed any stadium concert. So that night we did just that. David had the car all ready to go outside the back entrance of the stadium and two minutes after leaving the stage we were on our way. To get to Manchester we had to take a remote road across the Pennines and about twenty minutes into the journey I had this feeling we were being followed – the lights of the car behind us were far too close. But it was hard to be sure because there was really only this one road. But whoever it was was driving really dangerously, coming up so close, trying to pass, which was ridiculous on a road that twisted and turned. And his lights seemed on full beam. Things like this are bad enough at any time, but when you're pregnant it's even more scary. You're not just worried about yourself, you're worried about your baby as well.

'What the hell does that idiot think he's playing at?' David said. 'Why doesn't he just pass or drop back?'

'Perhaps he's following us,' I said. Because I just had this feeling. There had been a straight bit when David had slowed down and if he had wanted to overtake he could have.

'Well, if he's not careful he'll get himself killed and take us with him.'

So halfway back we stopped at a garage hoping this driver would go past and also because I was desperate for a drink and some sweets: I had all these cravings for things I never usually ate.

So we're standing at the counter and I'm wearing my Spice tour bathrobe with Posh on the back that David got Adidas (who he has a sponsorship deal with) to make up for all of us, and I get this sense of someone behind me. Too close. And as I turn round I hear a sound I know only too well, the whirring of a camera motor. And although I never saw the driver of the car, I know it's him. Because this isn't just someone taking a snap of Posh for his mates at work, that motordrive says it's a professional. When we'd pulled in at the garage the other car had gone on. The oaf must have turned round and come back.

'What the hell do you think you're doing?' I said, or yelled probably. Anyway, it was what's called a rhetorical question, it was perfectly obvious what he was doing. Then I got really angry.

'Look, as you can see I'm pregnant. I don't need this. First you follow us really dangerously, then you start taking pictures. Why don't you just piss off and leave us alone?'

Then David stepped in front of me, grabbed this idiot's camera and handed it to me. Until now I had been angry rather than frightened. But now I began to shake. David told me to get back in the car and stood between me and this oaf to stop him following me. The idiot's shouting to me to give him his camera back.

And I felt so vulnerable, so aware of my unborn baby inside me that I had to protect, and suddenly I felt tears coming, and I just wanted to get out of that place and into the car, and then he starts shoving David and David has his hands in the air not wanting to mix it with this idiot who you just know will then claim he's been assaulted – and this bloke manages to push past David and it's one of those doors that you don't know if it pushes or pulls and I've got my hands full of this camera and I can't open it and the next thing I know is my robe is being pulled by this man, and I turn around and scream, 'Take your hands off me!', then David pushes him away and then gets the door open, then as I run to the car he points the remote key and opens the doors. He keeps the man away just by standing in front of him, like he was marking him, and once he sees I'm in he sprints for the car and we lock the doors. And the bloke's outside swearing and I'm calling the police.

When the police turn up, I get out of the car and put the camera down where some newspapers are stacked. Then we're off. I'm shaking and in a terrible state. It took all David's patience to calm me down. The next day the photographer phoned David's agent. The oaf was suing us because we'd smashed his camera. Which we hadn't. What really made me angry was that David's agent paid the money. For a quiet life, he said.

Wembley was bizarre. It should have been the high point of the tour – coming home in glory and all that. And in a way it was. Standing out there in front of sixty thousand people I remembered being one of them and seeing Michael Jackson. And now it was us. The atmosphere was truly amazing. Not doing Wembley Stadium is probably the one thing Geri regrets about leaving the band.

When we did Wembley Arena at the start of the world tour she had been standing next to me when Miss Laine, of all people, turned up, full of her wonderful-darling-I-always-knew-darling crap. I just let her ramble on. Didn't say anything. Didn't have to. Just looked at her. She knew.

This time there were much nicer visitors from Laine's: Maureen and Gwyn Hughes. My mum had heard that their daughter was ill and was in a wheelchair and so she organized access for them all and after the concert they came backstage.

There was no end-of-tour party. We were all too tired and our lives had already started to go in four different directions. Mel B was pregnant, and Mel C had started work on solo albums. As for me, I just wanted to go home and be a normal person. I was fed up with all the photographs in the paper. I was fed up with all of it.

First, David decided we needed a break, somewhere sunny, somewhere we could just slob around and where I wouldn't have to bother with make-up or anything: Elton's. So the second day we're by the pool and Elton's housekeeper, Laurent, says I'm wanted on the phone.

'It's Jerry.'

'Jerry who?'

'Geri Halliwell.'

I was completely shocked. Totally shocked. It was about four months since she left the band and although we'd tried to talk to her, we hadn't heard a word. So it's all a bit stilted. I say, How are you? and she says, Great news about the baby, and then she says, How about we meet up tonight at George Michael's, where she's staying at his house in St Tropez, and have dinner?

'Great,' I said. Because that was what I felt. I didn't have time to think it through.

The easiest way to get to St Tropez was by helicopter. So Laurent takes us to Nice airport, and someone from George Michael's picks us up the other end. And Geri meets us at the front door dressed in black and holding some kind of furry dog.

And it was all, How brilliant you're pregnant, and, How have you been, and I'm thinking my old mate really wants to be friends again. Then she says there's been a slight change of plan and that we won't be eating at the house.

'George has arranged for us all to go out to dinner,' she announces.

I mean, what was I to say? If I'd known we'd be going out, I wouldn't have come, because I would have thought: photo opportunity – Ginger and Posh's first meeting since the break-up – all that.

In the end there was nothing I could do. And the photographers were packed right round the door of the restaurant, snapping and flashing. Surely this wasn't a set-up. Was it?

But when the pictures came out over the next few days and she didn't call to say sorry, or anything, I began to wonder. Didn't I know she had a record out? No, I didn't know. She hadn't said anything. The sad thing was I had had a genuinely nice night.

At the end of September I was sitting having my breakfast in the kitchen in Goff 's Oak and my dad came in with the usual great pile of papers. I remember it was a Wednesday. A small part of the front page and double-page centre-spread in the *Daily Star* had some girl lying naked on her stomach with big boobs out, a pouty look, too much make-up, generally a bit of a geezer-bird saying how before David met Posh he went out with this girl blah blah blah. And she said how it was really boring for her, how she used to want to go to bed early and he would rather sit up and watch football with her dad. And how he was this and that in bed – they just have to do the seedy bit.

OK, so it was before I met David, and OK she said she had never heard from him again. But when you're pregnant you feel so vulnerable. I called him, and he said he felt really bad about it but yes, it was true. He had gone out with her, but it was long before he met me. But the damage was done: it's just not what you want to hear when you're pregnant and feeling like a pudding.

Two days later, on the Friday, I'm down at the gym with my sister and Maria-Louise and I'm on the running machine and I've got my mobile on the front of this thing, by the controls, and it rings.

David.

So it's, Hi, how are you? Fine. And where are you? Down the gym, on the running machine.

'So, what is it?' I say. Because I'm still not too pleased with the newspaper story.

'I've had a phone call saying there's a story going in the newspaper tomorrow.'

'Oh. What story?'

'Some girl is saying how when you were away on tour, she was having these phone calls with me.'

'Is it true?'

'Of course it's not true. But I'll try and find out more and I'll ring you back.'

I'm still on the running machine. I've upped the speed now.

Ring, ring.

'Well?'

'Bad news. This girl is going to make out that more happened.'

And instantly I felt my stomach turn over. I hit the off key on the mobile and burst out crying. By this time the whole gym is looking at me, still running on this bloody machine and totally hysterical. The man who owned the gym at the time, a guy called Danny, pushed all three of us into a storeroom, because by now everyone has stopped what they're doing and are looking at me like it's a road accident.

So we're in this storeroom and David phones back.

It was all to do with this friend of his, Tim, who works in this shop in Manchester where the team used to buy their clothes. I'd met him a couple of times and he seemed nice enough. He was really into the whole footballer celebrity thing. Tim and David had been out and Tim had been chatting up this girl. It was nothing to do with David.

Danny got us out of the storeroom and my sister and Maria-Louise took me back home. I was utterly distraught. And back in the house I'm screaming and shouting and swearing and going hysterical again. And my mum keeps on saying that she just doesn't believe

David would do a thing like that. That she's never seen anyone so devoted to anyone.

It seems Tim gave this woman his phone number but when Tim's fiancée found out, he decided to offload the story on to David.

And David's on the phone to me non-stop, saying he swears on the life of our unborn baby that he never did anything. But I'm five months pregnant, and my hormones are all over the place, I'm really emotional and I just don't know what to think and what to do. I'm literally thinking I'm going to kill myself.

So David's on his way down to Southampton by coach because he's got a match. And I'm getting worse and worse.

He calls me at ten o'clock. He's in his room. The team have been sent to bed in their camp like good little boys to get their beauty sleep for the match tomorrow. And I'm still totally beyond anything.

'You don't realize what you have done.'

And he was in a terrible state, swearing that nothing had happened, nothing at all.

'I can hardly remember the girl. Please, Victoria, you must believe me. I mean, what else can I say? I don't know what else to say.'

So it's about half-past two in the morning and I'm just lying in bed, and my eyes are so swollen from crying that I can hardly either close them or open them and I'm just lying there in the dark and sobbing into my pillow when David walks in.

He telephoned Costa – the driver who had taken us to the cinema – and got him to pick him up from outside the hotel, slipped the guy on the door fifty quid and gets out without anyone, especially Alex Ferguson, knowing. He'd phoned ahead and told my mum he was coming and told her not to tell me. He looked awful. He was just wearing a pair of shorts and flip-flops, like he was just off to the beach or something.

He tried to kiss me, but I just buried my head in my pillow and told him to go away and leave me alone.

'I'm not going anywhere, Victoria. We have to talk about this.'

And we did, until the light was coming through my curtains. And I did believe him. I finally became convinced that he was totally innocent. It wasn't anything he said. I could just tell from his face, he was absolutely devastated.

At seven there was a ring at the gate. Costa. David had to be back at the hotel in Southampton so that when the team had their breakfast, he'd be there.

And I've just about got the whole thing clear in my head. I know there are going to be these awful things in the paper but I just mustn't read it. It's just lies. All lies. And I go down to let Costa in. I've known Costa for years, he lives down the road in Barnet and so we have a little chat. He has no idea what's going on. So it's, Morning, Victoria, summer's nearly gone wouldn't you say? Blah blah blah. And then:

'Oh, and I brought the papers for you.'

I know I should have just binned them. But I didn't. For a start, it was on the front page of the *Sun*. A picture of me and David smiling, really happy, and this girl with permed, streaked hair looking vile. Then inside it had the whole story, two pages of it and pictures of this slapper with her twin sister. And it's all about how he squeezed her bottom and kissed her. And this was while I was throwing my guts up in buckets in America, pregnant with his child. How could he do this to me?

'So. Are you coming to the game, Victoria?'

My dad.

'No, Daddy. I'm bloody not going to the bloody game.'

And it's a bloody good thing I didn't. The crowd had a new chant now. 'Beckham can only score with a slag.'

But I did go out, to Marks & Spencer's at the Brookfield shopping centre in Cheshunt to get some prawns. I just fancied some prawns and I didn't want to answer the phone and I didn't want to hear it ringing, like some terrible playground taunt. So I've got my cap pulled right down and I'm walking so fast I could be in the Olympics but there they are, the press, screaming at me, great grins on their faces. 'Oi, Posh. Seen the papers, 'ave ya?'

It's a wonder England ever did away with public executions or throwing old cabbages and turnips at people in stocks. There's clearly a market for it.

And David and me had been talking and talking. Before the match, half-time, after the match. And he says we'll talk more tonight.

So in walked David that night after the match, and I went straight up to him and just slung at him, punched him in the face. Bang, bang, bang. I hadn't planned it. I have never punched anybody before. Just instinct. And I hit so hard I cut the inside of his mouth. And even then, with blood dripping down his chin, I just felt angry and hurt.

And outside the place is just thick with photographers.

Just waiting there, like vultures. I can see them from my bedroom window through the gap in the curtains. Why can't they just leave me alone?

The next day it gets worse. It's in every paper now, all the stuff about page-three girl Emma Ryan and pictures of her topless – so that's her career sorted. But now another one has crept out of the woodwork – how he had secretly been dating Lisa Hames, who he met in a wine bar in Southport. And she's going on about how often he used to phone her and how much time they talked on the phone. By now I'm just going berserk. The strange thing is that I did believe him. I knew that he was telling the truth. But I was angry at the situation he had got me into.

And now the papers are full of how incredibly angry I am. But I'm not having rumours and lies break up our relationship. It's nothing to do with them. This is personal, about as personal as it gets. I'd show them.

The only thing to do, I decided, was to brazen it out. After all, we couldn't stay in the house for ever. So I slapped on my make-up and just thought, Do it. Just do it. Like a job. So we went out, hand in hand, me smiling like a bloody gibbon, and just as I got in the car I gave David's bottom a squeeze. That's what she said he did to her. No chance these morons would get the irony, but it did me good.

My emotions are like a seesaw. It's a total torment, like torture. If you'd said to me: OK, here's the switch to end it all, I'd have pulled the switch. I just wanted out. I couldn't take it any more.

Then on Monday, it still carries on and it's the Disney Awards, David's won best sports personality or something and the Spice Girls have won something. Do I need this? And it's press outside the house, and it's press outside the Old Vic where the Disney Awards are held, and it's press inside. And it's Posh Spice giving the performance of her life. Don't anyone say I can't act.

By Wednesday the papers are bored with everything. My mum says we ought to go away. But how? David has an England match on Saturday at Wembley against Bulgaria. And everyone says I should go. If I don't go they'll be baying for blood.

Glenn Hoddle had arranged for the families and wives to go back to Burnham Beeches, where the England team always stays, for a celebration. As usual there's a coach laid on, but I just can't face sitting on a coach so I ask if I can go in my dad's car. So I'm in the car with my mum and dad and my phone rings. It's Alan, our PR. Another girl has sold her story, it'll be in the papers tomorrow.

So I rang David in the coach and David was hysterical down the phone.

'I swear to you, Babes, I swear I know nothing about it.'

And when I got out of the car at Burnham Beeches, David was waiting and he just walked straight to my mum, put his arms round her and cried. And said, I swear, I swear I have never had anything to do with these girls.

I just stood there frozen. Just frozen. And that night I didn't sleep, just waiting for the newspapers.

17 truth or dare

SANDY SLID THE ICE CUBE DOWN HER NAKED
BODY AND POPPED IT IN BECKHAM'S MOUTH.

P-l-ee-ee-se. According to the *News of the World*, this
woman at Stringfellows had done a lap dance for David
Beckham and he'd invited her to see him play against
the Italian team Juventus.

'I took an ice cube from the champagne bucket and
slowly ran it over my body. He was lost for words.'

David was just a wreck. He told me that he had never
been to Stringfellows and didn't even know where it
was.

To sue someone you have to have evidence, otherwise it's just their word against yours. This time we
had it.

The next day, there was an injunction against any
more stuff coming out, and in the end, after months of
meetings and phone calls, he won. Settled out of court.
For a lot of money (which went to charity) and an
apology, though you'd have to have had a microscope
to see it.

Finally it was over.

But not for me. Because how do you forget something like that? You think you won't remember, but it's there, a part of my life that will always be there. And these girls who sold these stories really have no idea. It was the most empty, nasty feeling, and being five months pregnant and going through all of this was the most awful thing that has ever happened to me. I wouldn't wish that on my worst enemy.

People are always saying, so why don't you sue if the newspapers print lies? But suing costs money for a start and usually it's not worth it. The trouble is, the newspapers are well aware of that, so they write what they know they can get away with. But, out of interest, here are a few lies that I wrote down once in a page of my diary.

- *Lie   That we paid £48,000 for a miniature Ferrari for Brooklyn at Christmas 1999.*
  Truth   We were visiting Santa Claus at Harrods and Brooklyn sat in this ridiculous Ferrari made for millionaires. Somebody took a picture and sold it to the press.

- *Lie   That I spend £60,000 a year on having my hair done.*
  Truth   The cost of having my hair done is practically nothing. It's often paid for by the record company or TV company or whoever I'm working for on the day. If I'm not working, Tyler, my hairdresser, does it free. And he does David's. Why, when we could afford to pay

him? Because it's good publicity for him. Thank you, Tyler, and everyone else who does things free for us.

- *Lie We bought an electric toy Jeep for Brooklyn that cost £2000.*
  Truth It cost £250 from Toys 'R' Us.

- *Lie That I queue barge.*
  Truth Once when I was pregnant, I was desperate to have a pee and I asked this woman in a toilet if I could go first otherwise I'd have wet myself, not to mention the floor. Another time, I was coming home, went into Tesco's to buy some cherries. There weren't many cashiers and the lady in front of me had a big trolley of stuff and she said did I want to go in front of her, because I only had this bag of cherries. Well, I said, signing another autograph, if you're sure you don't mind. The next day it's in the papers. Posh Spice was too posh to queue: she pushed in front of customers, gave everyone the hump and stuck her nose in the air. At airports people will always try and push us to the front of the queue and me and David will always say no.

- *Lie We bought an island off the Essex coast.*
  Truth I didn't even know Essex had any islands.

- *Lie I was in a bidding war with Madonna for a house that was up for sale in Notting Hill.*

Truth   Sadly not true, but any connection with Madge is cool, so who cares.

- Lie   I'm flying out to LA for a meeting with Kevin Costner to talk about Bodyguard 2.
  Truth   If only.

- Lie   David takes falconry lessons.
  Truth   David is scared of budgerigars, let alone falcons.

- Lie   David had a gold-plated snooker table made costing £50,000.
  Truth   He has an ordinary snooker table.

- Lie   David's parents and my parents don't get on.
  Truth   They get on fine but they don't live in each other's pockets, why should they?

- Lie   I tell David what to wear.
  Truth   David has incredible taste. There are things he doesn't like me wearing, but not often the other way round. David's a really strong character and he would never wear or do or say anything that he didn't want to. I would love to have taken credit for the sarong and the headscarf but I can honestly say that was all down to him.

- Lie   There's a big domed ceiling in Brooklyn's room in the new house.

Truth There isn't. It's just a normal flat ceiling,
with Disney characters painted round the walls
left from the previous people.

- *Lie That David is thick.*
  Truth So they let somebody captain England
  who's thick? Yeah, right. I have a very low
  boredom threshold. Does anyone really think I
  would want to spend my life with someone
  who didn't stimulate me, keep me on my toes?

- *Lie That I'm a man.*
  Truth There's no answer to that, except it
  makes Brooklyn even more exceptional than
  we like to think he is.

And this is just the start.

So does it matter? I mean, who out there cares
whether Brooklyn's car cost £2000 or £250? Most people
couldn't afford to buy their kid any kind of electric car.
And that's exactly why it does matter. Imagine some-
one reading their paper on a Sunday morning, and
they're probably struggling to pay their mortgage.
And they see this fairy tale. Me and David so in love.
And apparently I've got £50 million in the bank. And
David has paid £50,000 for a gold-plated snooker table.
You can imagine a person looking at that and thinking,
Bastard. And it's jealousy and you can't blame them.
And then they go to a football match and shout abuse.

And then there are the Bonk-Beckham lies. Or is that
just harmless fun?

★

I was still totally unstable. My dad said what about us going away together? But my mum wasn't so sure.

'You're a wreck, David is a wreck. Someone's got to come with you, stop you doing yourselves an injury. I'll come.'

'No, you won't,' I said. I love my mum but this was between me and David.

In the end we agreed that Louise and Stephen Lawrence, her boyfriend, would come with us. They'd been having a bit of a rough time lately, and Louise hadn't had a break since having Liberty. Stephen is a quarter Italian – that's where Liberty gets her dark looks from.

But where? What did I care? I was always in the same place, a dark place in my head. It came with me like a cage.

In the end it was just a question of what would fit in with David and what my mum could get: four seats on a cheap British Airways Go flight to Milan.

'You said you liked Como, Tor, when you went there that time.'

Ah yes. Donatella Versace: my first taste of celebrity life.

So we're both making an effort not to talk about it on the plane. But I am just so tense. It felt as if I was like one of those very thin glasses that you only have to put down on a table at the wrong angle and it will smash. But something takes over and I hear myself saying, Swear on my life it's not true. And I can see it's making David more and more hurt. But it's like when I bite my nails down to the quick. I know it's going to hurt but it's as if I need the pain.

A car picks us up at Milan airport and takes us to Como. So here we are on our let's-leave-England-behind-and-replenish-our-love little holiday. And I look out of the window and see nothing. Nothing except grey. Grey road, grey sky. And my mind is going round and round hearing the other three making conversation. Because that's what it is. Trying to cover up the fact that I'm not talking.

'Give it a rest, Tor,' Louise says when we get to the hotel and I just stand there at the desk while David does the checking-in thing.

I only wish I could. Why can't I switch my mind off? Why can't I just flick the off button and stop this terrible churning? It's like my head is full of ticking clocks.

The hotel is very old-fashioned and very expensive and we've got a suite with a balcony right over the lake. Forget the blue skies of the tourist brochures. It's October in the mountains. Como is grey and full of old people. And I think, right, the only way to get through this is to act. If I look as if I'm having fun, then perhaps I will have fun. And if I look as if I'm having fun everyone else will lighten up. So I'm really trying to have fun, but having fun here is like throwing a party in a crematorium, it's hard work. I remember walking to our room and I'm eating a banana, and outside our room was this statue of a naked man, so me trying to be light-hearted, I hung my banana skin over his testicles. Well, I laughed.

I was totally schizophrenic. One moment I was fine and happy; the next minute I did a complete flip. Sometimes I would instinctively put my hand on my tummy and feel the bump and instead of feeling warm and happy

313

I would feel so angry. Even though my baby was just a fuzzy image on a Polaroid, which, unless you know what you're looking at, could be anything, I was already like a mother hen and would have done anything to protect him. And we really were trying hard just to spend time together but because there wasn't anything else going on I couldn't get it out of my head. It didn't help that we couldn't understand the television. It got so bad one night David said he felt like killing himself. He was as desperate as I was; he was looking out over the balcony and he just thought, I've very nearly had enough of all this.

It's so hard to prove your innocence and it's amazing how harmful it can be to have that sparkle of doubt, however much the other person knows it's not true. And I knew deep down that it wasn't true. But I couldn't stop trying to catch him out even though I knew he hadn't done anything. Someone had put doubt in my mind that had never been there before. It was like a mosquito bite, sometimes it stops itching for a while, and then for no reason it starts up and you just have to scratch, even though your arm is bleeding and you know it's not going to help.

At least for my sister and Stephen it was great, because it patched up things between them for a while.

So now all you football fans that think I want David to move to Milan, with its Gucci and its Prada, you know the truth. As much as that part of Italy is a beautiful place, with its mountains and scenery and everything, I could never live there, because I could never go back to Lake Como again.

★

We returned to England as bad, if not worse, than we'd left. I felt ugly and horrible. Because Como had been such a disaster, we decided to try a weekend in the sun. So the next Saturday after the game we got on a flight to Malaga.

Now as much as the Marbella Club is full of celebrities, the pool is right by the beach and the beach is public. So it was an absolute nightmare. Photographers were hiding behind rocks, swimming out to sea, chasing us in cars. And there was a picture of us snogging taken at Puerto Banus where we went for dinner on the Sunday, and it's a close-up taken with one of those hideous long lenses.

And my dad says when he saw it my brother Christian said, 'Tell Victoria, it's so embarrassing seeing her tongue in the newspaper. I'm her brother, and it's really unfair that she does things like that.'

Through all of this stuff about the slags Geri was the one person who would have known what I was going through, knowing the kind of person I am and who I expected to ring me as soon as she saw it in the newspaper. She didn't. And I will never ever forgive her for that. All the other girls rang, even Mel B who was the other side of the world. And they did their best to make me see that it was a load of tosh, a load of girls trying to launch their tacky modelling careers.

In the old days, Geri would have been the first one on the phone saying, God, are you all right? and how awful and just rise above it. And it was then that I finally knew that the dinner in the restaurant with George Michael was what everyone said it was – publicity. And I had said, No, no, no. But I had denied myself the truth.

But when I didn't get a phone call when I really needed a friend, that proved everyone was right. And that was when I realized. And I thought, Yeah. You're my friend. Yeah, right.

So how do you get over something so devastating and public and hurtful? Answer, I don't know. I suppose with that old thing my nan used to say about counting your blessings. It helps if you love the other person as much as I love David. It helps if the other person loves you as much as David loves me. And also it was a bit of that other old thing about time healing. Each day that went by it was easier and the fear that it might be true didn't flash into my mind as regularly. At the beginning the only time I was free of it was the first few minutes I woke up in the morning but then it would pour in. Then gradually it wouldn't be till something triggered it, like me catching some perfectly innocent girl smiling at David, that I would be flooded by jealousy and anger. Eventually, a whole morning had gone by and I hadn't thought about it.

It wasn't as if either of us had an easy time. We were both so, so hurt in our different ways that it was easier for us to help each other than to just lie in a corner and expect it to just go away.

At the end of the day I had to remember that I could never wish for anybody as faithful and kind and caring as David. And it was up to me to stop being so bloody stupid and to realize just how lucky I was. I knew all along that he hadn't actually done anything. I was just being a spoilt brat because I thought someone was trying to take what was mine. Someone had tried to upset the one thing I actually had that was sacred. And I put David through hell but deep down I knew all along that he would never do anything that would jeopardize our happiness.

This wasn't the time to look back, it was all about looking forward to something so amazing, something money cannot buy, our baby.

It was when we were in Marbella that we came up with the name Brooklyn. We already knew he was a boy and so I knew he could end up a footballer, so it had to be a name that was a bit blokey. I had always liked the name Brooke and then we suddenly thought about Brooklyn. I'd always liked it as a place – it's very multi-cultural, very grounded. And it was only afterwards that I realized how appropriate it was because it was in New York that I found out I was pregnant and where David came after the World Cup.

Before Christmas we moved into the flat – real nest-building stuff – and I got bigger and bigger. But I wasn't well: I had a bladder infection that just wouldn't go away and, being me, I was convinced it was doing damage to the baby.

You know that joke about what do you give the man who's got everything? Well, the answer in David's case is a Ferrari. Although David has always been car mad, at that time a Ferrari had always been out of his price range. First I wanted to get him a Bentley, another car he'd always wanted and with a Bentley there's room for a baby seat. But as they didn't have one in stock, I decided sod being practical I'll get him a Ferrari. And Costa – the driver who did the midnight dash up from South-ampton that time, and who took us to see *Jerry Maguire* – who is a really sweet guy, helped me get it organized with Ferrari: ordering it, advising me on what colour. I just said I wanted the best of everything. The most difficult thing was to find one that was right-hand drive. In the end they had to bring it over from Australia.

Hiding a surprise piece of jewellery is easy. Hiding a Ferrari is more difficult. I actually got it delivered when David was training and they put it in the garage. It came with a red velvet cover and the cover even went over the little mirrors, and it just said 'Ferrari' down the side and I got a big bow put on the top. And I was really excited.

When he came back from training I said, I've had your Christmas present delivered but I've left it in the garage, so please don't go in there. I said I'd tried to get it upstairs but it was a bit difficult with me being so big and I didn't want to scratch the paint, and I made him think it was a piece of art. And for David that was such a tragedy.

And he kept saying, Look, maybe I should bring it up. And I'm saying, No, and trying to sidetrack him, asking him to make me a cup of tea.

So then it's Christmas Day. And David always makes a big thing of occasions and it's our first Christmas in the flat and so there's a big Christmas tree with so much on it. So we'd opened all of our presents and then I said, like as if I nearly forgot, 'Oh, and your present's in the garage.'

And so we both go downstairs and I hand him the remote.

'Don't cheat. Shut your eyes.'

And the garage door went up and he just saw the red cover with the big red bow – he couldn't believe it. And that's what's so nice about David. He would never ever take anything for granted. He would act exactly the same if I had bought him a pair of socks.

Just like he told me when we first met, Manchester United train on Christmas morning and everyone turns up in their cars and David Beckham turns up in a brand-new Ferrari, and everyone's like, My God, where did you get that from?

I have never spent so much money on anything. It was over £100,000. I would never have done that for myself. But it was just worth every single penny.

David's always loved cars. Half the photographs he's got of when he was little, he's standing in front of some sports car. At Manchester United they give you a car when you're seventeen and his was a red Ford Escort. Then when he got his first proper contract, when everyone else was buying sensible cars, David went straight down to the BMW showroom and bought this top-of-the-range M3, and had all the extras put on it. And that was the BMW we had our first kiss in, when I gave him the aloe vera leaf.

I was booked in to have my baby at the Portland Hospital in London, with the baby due at the beginning of March. By the end of February I was back staying with my mum and dad and I could think of nothing else but getting this baby out into the world. I'd had enough of being the size of a whale thank you very much. None of David's cars was big enough to fit a baby seat, and nearly not enough to fit me. Now we had a Range Rover: David clearly wasn't convinced I wouldn't get any bigger. So one Sunday we're down at my mum's and he says, 'Let's go for a walk.'

'David, it's like Siberia out there.'

'You could do with a breath of fresh air, Babes.'

I mean, I'm so big I even put off walking to the bloody toilet if I can; it's like parking a van without power steering.

So there I am waddling up the road away from the house when he suddenly stops in front of this garage belonging to some neighbours. Points the remote – and there it is, a beautiful grey Mercedes CLK. Since I had given my mum the little Mercedes SLK I'd got from MacLaren a year or so back, I'd been driving one of David's. Now he had got me my own car – a four-seater version, if you like, of the little Mercedes. The funny thing was, soon every footballer's partner seemed to have one: Teddy Sheringham's girlfriend, Nicola Smith, Julie Neville, Phil Neville's wife, and Hannah, Gary Neville's girlfriend, because they're perfect cars to drive, sturdy yet stylish-looking. What a trendsetter.

My obstetrician, Mr Gillard, had said that he would induce me about a week before my due date, because David had a lot of away games and international games scheduled, so that he could be there. But the baby's head had to be engaged, he said, before I could be induced. Every week I went down there, and every week he still hadn't dropped.

Then can you believe it, Melanie B goes into labour. And I thought, he's been in there cooking for nine months. I want him out now. I mean Brooklyn was meant to be here before Melanie's baby.

'If the head isn't engaged by the time you go into labour, then you'll have to have an emergency Caesarean,' Mr Gillard explained when I next saw him. 'The alternative is to have a Caesarean now and take him out straight away. That would probably be the safest for you.'

'Don't worry about me,' I said. 'What's safest for the baby?'

At a time like that you don't really care about your own welfare. The baby was fine, he said. But on balance he would rather do it now.

'OK. So when do you want to do that, then?'

'Shall we say seven o'clock?'

'What, today?'

My God.

'This evening. I'll arrange to get you admitted to the Portland now.'

'Have I time to go home first?'

I could just see my baby bag that had been sitting by the door for the last two months.

He looked at his watch.

'As long as you're there by about six, that should be all right.'

There was a clock above his head and it was 2.40 p.m. It was 4 March. David was already on his way down from Manchester but he wasn't expecting this. I was really nervous. And I really didn't want the press to find out. This was private, about as private as it gets. So I used my driver's mobile to call David. He was on the M6, eating a Lion bar at the time. I know because we always ask each other what we're doing.

'Don't worry,' I said, 'everything's fine, but can you get down as soon as you can because I have to go into hospital.'

David said he felt instantly sick.

We hadn't much time. I was in the bath when David arrived and I remember looking at the bump and thinking, Funny, this is going to come out tonight. And it was a really weird feeling. The knowledge that your whole life is about to change for ever. That nothing will ever be the same again.

We'd known that the baby was a boy right from the beginning. And at first it was quite a disappointment, because I found it very unnatural, being a woman and having a boy with all his boy-bits inside me. I think I was expecting to have a little version of me; having a boy didn't enter my mind.

Because my sister's labour had been complicated, my mum hadn't been allowed in for Liberty's birth. Usually they only let one person in if it's a Caesarean, but Mr Gillard gave permission for my mum to be there, too. So we headed off in the Range Rover. It had blacked-out windows and it was arranged that we could go through the delivery entrance. (Very appropriate.)

Nobody saw us go in. Or so we thought. Then it was straight up to my room, which was more like a suite. I had a big bedroom with a bathroom, and then there was an attached room like a lounge also with a bathroom of its own. It was quite high up with a good view over the street. And I couldn't believe it: two photographers.

So they put me in this blue gown thing, and really tight popsocks reaching up over my knees. And as they're doing this they're talking through what's going to happen.

First was the epidural, an injection into the spine that numbs everything but means you are totally conscious.

'So what kind of drugs do you want?' they said.

'Anything that's legal and vast amounts,' I said.

I remember Melanie C saying when Melanie B was giving birth, 'It's not like the cat getting stuck behind the oven, when you know it's got in there, so it's got to get out.'

And I was thinking, Shit. I looked down at this bump and I was so, so nervous. They give you the epidural with this massive needle. And the look on David's face when he saw the size of it was hilarious. When you can't feel your legs any more, they take you into the delivery room and put your legs into these stirrup things. I looked like that chicken in *Withnail and I*. I couldn't feel these legs, but I could see them flying everywhere. It was totally hilarious, or would have been if I'd felt like laughing, but I was absolutely petrified.

So we're just waiting for Mr Gillard, and David's sitting beside me holding my hand, all gowned up, looking totally ridiculous in this little hat to keep his hair from spreading germs. And he's saying, I love you so much. And my mum's there videoing everything. And then he looked at me, did something sexual with his eyes – like, Do you fancy a bit? – and I looked back at him and said with my eyes, Never again. Never ever again.

18 signed, sealed, delivered

'Is he all right?'

It's the only thing any mother is interested in.

A perfect baby boy, Mr Gillard said.

'What's his hair like?' I asked. Dark like me or fair like David?

'Ginger,' my mum said.

'GINGER?'

But it wasn't ginger. It was all the blood in his hair.

The whole thing was over in less time than it takes for David to take a free kick. Although I was totally awake, I didn't see anything because they'd put this tent thing up made of J-Cloth material. Every now and then David looked over and went green. My mum was videoing. I didn't feel a thing, except hungry. All I could think about was chicken korma. I pleaded with David to go and get me something to eat, preferably chicken korma.

Then in what seemed like only a couple of minutes they pulled him out, this little grey, squirming thing that would change my life for ever.

Brooklyn Joseph Beckham (Joseph after David's

grandad) was born at 7.46 p.m. on 4 March 1999. David was the first one to hold him, then me. I held him and looked at him like I had never seen a baby before. And he was a gorgeous-looking baby. That's not me being biased, he really was: the good thing about Caesareans is babies don't get all bruised and battered.

When we got back to my room it was like a party going on. There was my dad, my sister and Liberty, my brother and his girlfriend, David's mum and dad.

So I'm lying in my bed still woozy from all the drugs and there are all these people drinking champagne and I'm thinking that this is all really mad and I'm in a dream. And David leans over me and hands me a comb.

'Any chance you could do my hair, Babes? I've got to go outside and do this press announcement.'

Do David's hair?

I am in a dream.

The room was already full of flowers. The very first bunch to arrive was from Dominic Mohan, showbiz editor of the *Sun*, if you can describe something the size of a small haystack as a bunch. My room and the corridor outside were like the biggest flower shop in the world. No one wanted to be left out: I had flowers from all the newspapers and flowers from every single shop in Bond Street I'd ever wandered into. Next morning I turned on Capital Radio.

'And now we go live to the Portland Hospital where Posh Spice has just given birth to baby Brooklyn.'

In the next street there was a shop with a great big arrow in the window and a sign saying 'Brooklyn This Way'. Mad or what? From my window I could see the street below crowded with people. What was going on?

It was totally unbelievable. When we left the police had to shut the roads to let the car through. Frankie, Mel C's driver, came to pick us up and had the car all covered in curtain material to stop people getting pictures. We had police outriders all the way back to Goff's Oak.

My baby was perfect. He weighed 'a very respectable' seven pounds. He had my olive skin, my lips and my chin and nose. He had David's legs, thighs and feet. As Louise said, good thing he wasn't a girl.

The newspapers were full of anything they could connect with Brooklyn. Bookmakers were offering 10,000 to 1 that he would be sent off while playing football against Argentina, 500 to 1 that he would be a cabinet minister.

According to the *Evening Standard* the first picture of him would have a value of £250,000.

We weren't doing pictures.

Then a few days later we got a call from Alan Edwards. The *Sun* had been offered photographs, he said, but they were returning them. One was a Polaroid. They'd been handed over in a car park in Stevenage. They had to be fakes. But no, they were totally genuine – my mum remembered taking them herself. They must have been taken, we realized, by one of the workmen we'd had in the house at the time. They must have gone through all of them, the most private photographs I've ever had taken. What did they think they were doing? What kind of people would stoop to something like that? If that wasn't private, what was? We were like public property.

There was advice from the astrologers. Brooklyn was a Piscean, and we were going to have trouble keeping him under control due to the position of Mars, one

Richard E. Grant and one of his biggest fans on the set of *Spice World – the Movie*.

In a recent survey men voted for Dawn French over me in the desirability stakes.

Modena, June 1998. Reason for the huge smile is that I have just introduced Stevie Wonder to his number one fan: my dad.

October 1997. A creepy night in
Gianni Versace's bedroom.

Just heard we're number 1 in America.

Xmas 1997. Me and David with Puffy and Snoop.

Nice smile, shame about the suit. Me and David at Wembley just before an England game.

Aaaaaaah.

Good enough to eat.

Trick or Treat, 1998.

Ireland, winter 1998. It took me
a week to get up to a trot.
David gets on and it was like he
was born on the bloody thing.

In Vera Wang's shop in New York trying on the wedding dress that she used as the design template for mine.

Frocks away. Liberty, my mum, Louise, Christian, Brooklyn and David and a mystery parcel taking up the toilet and the aisle.

Mr Pearl and the soon-to-be Mrs Beckham.

If you don't like it, just sit on it.

On honeymoon at Andrew Lloyd Webber's house at Cap Ferrat.

wrote. I hadn't looked at the stars since Maidenhead.

The predictions weren't far off. Brooklyn wasn't an easy baby. He had terrible colic, always in pain, always crying. Perhaps he wasn't getting enough milk? When he was five weeks old I gave up breastfeeding. What a relief. David was pleased – it meant he could feed Brooklyn, too. Then we found out that he had carbohydrate malabsorption, a serious lactose intolerance. In other words, he was allergic to milk, any milk: mine, goats', cows', even soya for goodness sake. There was also the possibility that he had low fat absorption. The only answer was some ridiculously expensive stuff called Progestamil. There were only two babies in Hertfordshire who were on it. It smelled vile and didn't taste like any kind of milk. It just tasted like a chemical. He couldn't have anything dairy; if he ate a milk chocolate button he'd throw up. All he ever wanted was this chemical milk.

He didn't sleep during the day. At night he'd sleep for twenty minutes, then he'd be up for two hours, and so on through the night, and not just crying, but screaming with the most hideous colic. I don't know how he kept going, he was like a machine.

My mum was brilliant. After we moved back up to Alderley Edge she was always coming up, getting up in the middle of the night, letting me and David get some sleep.

So did the press back off? No. Just a few weeks after I'd had Brooklyn, the *Mirror* ran a photograph of me coming out of the house, and they'd drawn in arrows pointing to parts of my body where they said I had to lose weight. Even when Brooklyn had gone into hospital for a hernia they'd somehow found out.

Sometimes when I met up with Melanie B and her little girl I couldn't believe it. Phoenix would sleep during the day and she'd sleep at night and Melanie would always have her dressed nicely. I could never get Brooklyn dressed nicely. He'd look nice for five minutes then he'd throw up and we're not talking three times a day after meals. We're talking twenty times a day. He was just sick all the time. His speciality was what's called projectile vomiting.

I didn't have any friends in Manchester – since meeting David I'd hardly been in England at all. And much as I liked the flat, there's only so much clearing up and watching MTV you can do. I felt really cut off. Like there was this bubble around me and I couldn't hear through it and no one could hear me. And it is hard going from Spice Girl/Pop Star to a flat on your own with a baby, no friends, no family, no nothing. That's how it seemed.

Players' wives who I've got to know since who are with London clubs or have been with London clubs, say how different it is down there, how there's much more of a social side. In Manchester it's either a men-only thing, or the men will be at the bar with the girls sitting separately.

David did his best to make things better. For my twenty-fifth birthday in April he gave me this surprise party. Call me a sad cow but I've always had this terror of being given a surprise party. The official story was that David was going to take me to a French restaurant in Manchester. My mum and dad had come up and were looking after Brooklyn.

So we get dressed up, and David's driving and we're

halfway into Manchester when he says he's forgotten his credit cards and we've got to drive all the way back to the flat to get them. I say I'll wait in the car, but he says no. That it's too cold.

So up we go in the lift, then I walk into the lounge and a bunch of footballers go HAPPY BIRTHDAY. I didn't know what to do – I mean, it's very nice a load of people I don't know coming all the way out to Alderley Edge for my birthday party, but what must they have thought at the total absence of any of the birthday girl's friends? And, yes, all the men were on one side and all the women on the other.

For three months I lived in a tracksuit and cried. I cried on the phone to my mum. I cried on the phone to my sister. I cried on my own. I suppose it was some sort of post-natal depression. But what could I do? I never went out. I didn't have the confidence. When David was out training I would sit on the work surface in the kitchen, pull up the blind and stare out of the window over the countryside bathed in sunshine. That was the only thing that could get me out of my sadness.

David was so proud of his baby and I think maybe I was jealous of the way he could slip in and out; he didn't seem to be drowning like I was.

One of the first things he did was to get the tattoo done.

Jimmy Gulzar, Melanie's boyfriend, had loads of tattoos and David always had a bit of a hankering for one. It's a boys' thing. So Jim arranged for David to talk to this Italian called Claudio who had done all his tattoos. Then came the night when the tattoo was to be done. It was all quite rock 'n' roll even though both the children were there; Brooklyn was asleep in his bucket as we called it, his lift-out car seat, and Phoenix was in bed. The tattooing was being done in the next room and there was this really loud rap music blaring out 'That's Just the Way It Is' by 2Pac – to drown the screams I decided – and we've called it David's tattoo song ever since. There was smoke everywhere. David was bent over this beanbag and the guy was stripped to his waist and he was covered, absolutely covered with tattoos. It was quite scary actually. First the guy just wrote in pen. Luckily I looked in before they started the tattoo proper: Claudio had spelt Brooklyn with an I instead of a Y. David, of course, couldn't see anything as he had his face in this beanbag.

Obviously we had talked about his tattoo and I thought it was a great idea. It wasn't until Brooklyn was eighteen months that I had one done – three stars at the base of my spine. The same time as when David had my name written in Hindi on his arm.

'So, Babes,' he said, 'does this prove how much I love you?'

'So what do I have to do?'

He smiled that smile that's like the sun coming out.

'You have one done.'

And although I love the idea of having a big dragon on my arm, it's a bit limiting. But below my waist – I could handle that. So I had three stars. One for me, one for David, one for Brooklyn. And, as somebody pointed out later, it actually meant I could survive three months in a freezer.

Amazingly it didn't hurt at all. And the guy was very funny.

'At least Posh hasn't got a hairy arse,' he said.

Laughter is the best way of getting out of a depression and David is one of those people who can always see the funny side of things. When I was with David I could forget the emptiness I felt when he wasn't there. The other way to get out of depression is work – if you're busy you don't have time to think about how miserable you are.

What finally got me out of it was having to organize our wedding. We'd started thinking about it when I was on tour in America, before I was even pregnant with Brooklyn. I know I'm bad at delegating, and although I kept hearing my dad's voice saying, If I want anything done properly, I have to do it myself, even I realized I couldn't do this on my own. I didn't know the first thing about weddings, from what you did about the church to where you hired marquees or the chairs and tables. What I needed was a wedding coordinator.

It was our tour manager, Richard, who put me in touch with Peregrine Armstrong-Jones. I met him when I got back to London, along with a couple of others, but it was Peregrine I liked the most. He's really funny, quite small and has got the best personality. He's a half-brother or something to Anthony Armstrong-Jones, the photographer who married Princess Margaret, Lord Snowdon as he is now. Peregrine sounds even more posh than he does. But there is nothing patronizing about him. He totally takes the mickey out of the fact that he's connected. Like I'd call up and say, 'What are you doing?' And he'd say, 'Taking the corgis for a walk.'

I went to see Luttrellstown Castle before Brooklyn was born. I'd been looking for the right place ever since

331

the tour ended, but nowhere I'd seen had been right. It had to be somewhere not too near the road but easy for people to get to. I also wanted somewhere with nice rooms for guests and Luttrellstown had fourteen bed-rooms. Obviously I would have preferred to get married in England but nowhere we'd seen had been right, or else they'd heard the magic words Posh and Becks and asked ridiculous money.

In fact, by this time money was not really a problem. Soon after we got engaged, David's agent heard on the grapevine that someone was going to offer £1 million for the pictures. I was very much in two minds: this was our wedding and I wanted it to be as private as possible. Also I really didn't want to do *Hello!* magazine. It's known as *Hello!-Goodbye!*; everyone who has their wedding in *Hello!* ends up getting divorced. But at the end of the day if someone comes to you and offers you that amount of money you'd be stupid not to at least think about it.

What decided us was that getting a magazine involved was safer from a security point of view. They would organize everything, and it was like a weight lifted off my shoulders. My fears about fans being squashed were now out of my hands. They could organize things beyond anything I could attempt to do. Doing it on our own would have been an absolute nightmare. The £1 million paid to us was just the beginning of what it would cost them to make sure nobody gatecrashed the party. At Melanie B's wedding a group of photographers hid themselves on a little island and had been holed up there, dressed in camouflage, for quite a few days before they were found.

It must have been in January that we went to see Luttrellstown, and although it was cold and wintry I knew this was the place I wanted to get married in. Like all little girls I had imagined that my wedding would be a fairy tale. I would be the Princess and David would be the Prince and we'd get married in a castle. And David shared the same dream as me. Luttrellstown was exactly like I had imagined: it had towers and turrets and was covered in ivy and was Georgian Gothic. Inside it was rather old-fashioned as you would expect, but all newly decorated, whereas a lot of the places we'd seen were a bit grubby and grotty, chair covers with holes in them, that sort of thing. I wanted something that was really clean and sunny feeling. And Luttrellstown was exactly that. All the rooms where the family would stay were nice and sunny, big windows and a really happy atmosphere. Even the carpets were new.

The best thing about it was the folly – no more than a tiny stone ruin really, about five hundred yards from the house.

'Now wouldn't this be the most marvellous place to get married?' Peregrine said. You needed a bit of imagination to see it but, yes, if Peregrine could wave his magic wand, then it could be the answer to everything. There was actually a church down the road, but it wasn't particularly nice and safety-wise we knew it wouldn't be a great idea.

In actual fact, the folly was a wreck. It was built into the rock and was horribly damp. A tramp had been living there and there was no floor to speak of and you could hear the water running underneath. But if he could get it right, then it was perfect, completely going along with the romantic Robin Hood medieval theme that me and David both wanted. However, there was a teensy-weeny problem, Peregrine explained. For a wedding to be legal in Ireland you have to get married on blessed soil. Caroline McAteer, who works with Alan Edwards, comes from Northern Ireland and by one of those coincidences you never really believe, her father was something to do with the church and we were granted special permission. We'll probably find out one day that we're not legally married at all. Now wouldn't that be funny. The downside, Peregrine explained, was that it would only take a few people – thirty at the most – but for us that was a plus – the ceremony itself would be really intimate and then we'd have a big extravagant party.

The most difficult part was finding a weekend that fitted in with David's football schedule, and as Luttrellstown was already very booked up we ended up with just one possible date: Sunday 4 July 1999.

Because of all the preparations, we hired Luttrellstown for the best part of a week. We went out two days before the wedding, by which time it was already looking the way we had planned.

OK! magazine were so paranoid about a rival magazine finding something out, that they actually hired a private plane to take us to Dublin – us being our families and my wedding dress.

When I first got engaged, I thought it would be nice to go around the department stores, because that's the kind of thing you do, go shopping for your wedding dress with your mum. It made it a bit better that we were in New York: Saks, Barneys, Bloomingdale's. But I didn't see anything. They were all horrible.

It was Kenny, the Spice Girls' stylist, who introduced me to Vera Wang. Although she's based in New York she's very Hollywood and dresses people like Sharon Stone, Uma Thurman and Mariah Carey. Kenny came with me to her showroom in Manhattan and I really liked this one dress with a crumb-catcher front and decided that was the basis of what I wanted. Vera gave me the dress as a wedding present; it was very generous of her as the dress would have cost an absolute fortune. It was built around a corset made by a guy called Mr Pearl, who's English, very famous in couture circles, but rather strange. He actually wears a corset himself and has had two of his ribs removed to accentuate his tiny 22-inch waist. In actual fact, he can't talk properly, because he's had a corset on for so many years. He wears it all the time, he even wears it in bed. The only time he takes it off is to go in the bath, but he's so naturally talented and such a sweet person. How it worked, Mr Pearl would make the corset part of my dress – Vera Wang would send him the fabric to put on top of it – while she would make the skirt in her atelier in New York.

Another of Kenny's ideas was the after-wedding outfits made by Antonio Berardi. I had seen pictures of his clothes and always admired what he had done – he makes really good clothes for women. This time he would do both me and David.

My first idea for a wedding dress was a tight sexy number with a big slit up the side, but when I tried on proper wedding dresses I couldn't resist – you can only get away with all that flounce once in your life. I could leave the tight sexy number bit till the evening.

Antonio was a lovely person to work with, a really nice personality who would never be nasty about anybody. A lot of people in fashion are a bit lovely-darling bitchy. But he is so not like that. The other thing with the fashion industry is that they always leave everything till the last minute. And in this both Vera and Antonio were classic practitioners. They'd had a whole year to faff around, have fittings, get the sewing machines whirring, yet three weeks before the wedding and there's still no sign of either dress.

When Manchester United closed its doors for the summer, we decided to get away for a few days before the wedding. Very kindly Nancy Berry said we could go to her house in Tuscany. Nancy is married to Ken Berry who started up Virgin Records with Richard Branson and met Nancy there when she worked for him. Now Ken is head of EMI – he's based in London and Nancy runs Virgin in America so I've known them both for years. The house is very out of the way, the press wouldn't be able to find us and it was somewhere we could get a nice tan.

There was a huge amount of press attention over the wedding. They had even got hold of a copy of our wedding invitation. We knew it had been stolen because none of the invitations had been sent out at this point.

Before we left London, I had a final fitting with Vera Wang, who had flown over from New York. We met at the Landmark Hotel. It was exactly two weeks before the wedding and I was actually having a fitting while Sophie Rhys-Jones and Prince Edward were on the television behind me getting married. How surreal is that? The press were making such a meal out of the comparisons – which one was the wedding of the year and which one was the most royal – that ridiculous crap. And the tabloids were all being really nasty to Sophie, saying she's fat, she's frumpy. I thought she looked really nice.

Me and David have always said that we would rather not have a nanny and we both get so much pleasure from just being with Brooklyn, watching him grow, all the little milestones, neither of us wanted to miss anything. And the only way you don't is by being there all the time.

I don't say there's anything wrong with having one, but as we both have such supporting and loving families, we felt that we could manage without. However, as the wedding approached my mum said that it might be an idea to have someone around to look after Brooklyn for the Big Day and Peregrine very kindly said we could borrow his children's nanny, Lizzie. And she was a really nice girl, very golly, jolly hockeysticks and the rest of it.

'As you've booked Lizzie for the wedding,' my mum said, 'why don't you take her with you to Tuscany so Brooklyn can get used to her and give you and David some time together without worrying about baby all the time?'

So that's what we did.

Lizzie had been used to working with very wealthy people who wanted her to look after their kids all the time. But when I rang her to finalize arrangements I explained that wasn't what I had in mind. I just wanted her to help out occasionally at night. 'So me and David can have dinner together without jumping up the whole time.' Not to mention that unheard of thing in the Beckham household, a lie-in.

When she asked if she should sit at another table at the airport, I said, Don't be silly. It seemed unfriendly to have her sitting on her own. Lizzie was a very nice girl, and the first evening we said she should come and have supper with us. Mistake. The whole point of her being there was for me and David to spend time on our own, not make polite conversation with someone we didn't know.

My Berardi outfit hadn't arrived by the time we left for Italy, but as Il Maestro was based only two hours away from Nancy Berry's house, he said he'd come down and give us a final fitting there. Which, luckily, he did, because the dress was a bit of a disaster, though I loved the flowers he'd had made to go round the neck of the dress, a tight purple sheath with a high thigh-slash that revealed a red silk underskirt. Crystals had been sewn all over the petals to give the impression of dew on the flowers.

'Not a problem,' he said. He'd bring the dress over to me in London the following week.

Wedding Day minus 4. The Vera Wang dress arrives and it's fine. Antonio Berardi turns up about nine. We go upstairs – no peeking from the groom. I put it on, and the zip breaks. And it's not just that, the inside is rolling over.

'I mean, bloody hell, Antonio.'

'Not to worry. I will come tomorrow night, Victoria.'

Wedding Day minus 3. Antonio arrives at about seven, this time with a sewing machine, a seamstress and an assistant who will sew the flowers back on, because every time the bodice is altered, the flowers have to come off.

Wedding Day minus 2.

Antonio Berardi leaves the house at four in the morning.

Midday, Luton. The Antonio Berardi dress is in a suitcase. But it took a van to get the Vera Wang dress to the airport – encased in its own special box, with a hanging rail inside so as not to crease it in transit. So I was just trying to walk up the stairs without getting photographed when one of the crew loading our luggage says they can't get it in.

'What do you mean, you can't get it in?'

They're talking about my wedding dress. MY WEDDING DRESS, you landlubbers.

'There's no way that thing is going in that hold. You'll have to take it with you in the cabin.'

Given this thing is the size of a telephone kiosk, there's only one thing to do. My dad gets everyone off the plane, we all stand around the box, to hide what we're doing from any long lenses, take out the dress, get it up the stairs, with all the tissue paper flapping in the wind and drag it along the aisle through the plane into the toilet.

'Anyone who needed the toilet just had to tie a knot in it,' my dad says.

Glamorous or what.

And the two babies are going mad. Finally, David and the airline loader person fold up the box and put it in the hold: we'll need it at the other end.

So we get to Dublin airport and it's a really horrible day. And all I'm thinking of is the dirt and just praying it won't start pissing with rain because we've now got to do the same thing in reverse. So David's holding Brooklyn while the rest of us are all struggling to get the dress back in the box, because getting something that flouncy back in is not the same as getting it out. So we're out there on the tarmac, and it's like an episode of *The Vicar of Dibley*. Because of the *OK!* deal, we couldn't risk anyone getting even a glimpse of it.

It was such a relief to see Peregrine when we arrived at Luttrellstown. Although he looks like a posh elf because he's so tiny, over the months of meetings and ideas and decisions he had become more like an eccentric uncle, someone I could totally rely on. And when I saw the folly it just was so magical that I forgot everything else. There was this little Gothic window that I hadn't noticed before and a bridge where in the old days you would have had trumpeters standing on the top. He'd done an amazing job. The walls were all cleaned, the floor was covered with artificial grass, and the next day it would be scattered with pot-pourri, with fresh flowers in the stream that ran underneath. He'd got silver birch trees and put them inside so there were leaves and twigs over all the walls and ceilings. In actual fact, this was my idea – I wanted the whole wedding to be twiggy, all leafy, so that it matched the castle. The trees were completely covered with fairy lights and he'd made an altar out of old twigs.

My bridal bouquet followed the same rustic theme – apples, St John's wort berries, ivy, rosemary and unripe blackberries. My bridesmaids were Liberty and David's sister Lynne's little girl, Georgina. They were dressed as fairies, with ivy and twigs and gossamer-thin wings.

It was a fantastic day. For once I didn't have time to feel nervous. And anyway why should I? The wedding was safely in the hands of Peregrine and I was about to marry the man who I loved more than I thought it possible to love anyone.

It was nice, too, that the Spice family were together again. Not only the girls and their mums, but Kenny of course, and Jennie who did my hair and Karin my make-up. Only Geri wasn't there. I couldn't have invited her because it would have been just too public. But about an hour before the wedding, Kenny handed me an envelope. It was from Geri, who he still saw.

It was one of her poems – a bit scrawled – written in a car, she said. And it made me cry. Because so much shit had gone on, and I'm thinking she hasn't seen my baby, she hardly knows my husband, and it would have been so nice to have all my friends at the wedding. And it's so sad what happened, we were all so close. And it all started coming back to me about how sad it actually was.

The Bishop of Cork, who married us, was really sweet and fitted into the Sherwood Forest theme perfectly, he was just like my idea of Friar Tuck – thin on top, a bit round, and with jolly red cheeks. He was even wearing purple, which matched the colour scheme of purple, red and green.

After all the nightmares, our evening outfits were fantastic, though Brooklyn threw up over his daddy's shirt, so he had designer-sick splodges over it. Little did we know tie-dye would be the height of fashion a year later.

We had 225 guests and everyone was asked to wear

either white or black. My mum wore a dress made by Maria Grachvogel, who had lent me a dinner dress for the Brits in 1997.

David made a lovely speech, my dad made a lovely speech. David cried. I cried. My mum cried. Just like any other wedding really. Because this wasn't a starry wedding. Elton had a viral infection in his ear and at the last minute couldn't come. Apart from the Spice Girls, there were no stars. And that's what was so upsetting about the way some of the press talked about our wedding. We wanted it to be as romantic as possible, with me and David as the prince and princess of the fairy tale that got married and lived happily ever after. But a lot of it – a helluva lot of it as always with me – was totally tongue in cheek.

With the wedding being so close to when training was due to start up again, we knew we had a problem with the honeymoon. We'd been offered Magic Johnson's house on Hawaii but it took twenty-four hours to get there and unless David could get more time off, then it was just not worth it. So before the wedding David got his agent, Tony Stephens, who has always been really supportive, to ask the Man United chairman, Martin Edwards, if he could have two extra days' holiday which would give us ten in total – enough to get right away.

It was all a bit complicated. After the wedding, most of the Man United team were going to Australia for pre-season training, but the footballers who played for England weren't going because they'd been training with the England squad while everyone else had been on holiday. So they were having four extra days off before coming back to Manchester. But when Alex

Ferguson heard that David had gone over his head to ask for two days in addition to the four every other England player was getting, he went berserk. Not only could David NOT have the two extra days, he couldn't have the extra four days the other England players were getting either. He had to be back at Old Trafford on the first day of training.

'But, Gaffer, the rest of the team are either in Australia, or on holiday. The only people I'll be training with are the reserves.'

'You've got it.'

'What's the point in that? Basically you're calling me in for no reason.'

'Don't you talk to me like that.'

'Please, Gaffer, I've just got married. All I want is a honeymoon like anyone else. We're totally under siege here. We've just got to get away.'

'So get away.'

'But you're calling me in for next Saturday.'

'That's right.'

'But we can't go anywhere in less than a week.'

'That's your problem, David. I don't give a shit.'

19 nobody touch the baby

After Alex Ferguson's outburst on the phone to Luttrells-town, David felt frustrated and angry. I'd known for some time that 'the Gaffer' wasn't an easy person. But his behaving like this was a real turning point for me. Not giving David the extra days he asked for was one thing, but not letting him have the four days that every other England player was having was just vindictive and, as far as I am concerned, unforgivable.

We were both totally shattered. That's why people have honeymoons these days – not to get to know each other in the sexual sense, just to get over the tension and stress of getting married. We'd just had this amazing wedding but, suddenly, no prospect of a honeymoon.

I called the Spice Office. Somebody thought Andrew Lloyd Webber's house in the South of France might be a possibility. The office spoke to his PA, who said I should ring his wife, Madeleine, and she very kindly said we could go.

It was a godsend. But with David having to be back in Manchester by the weekend we only had four days – one day getting there, one day getting back, two days actual honeymoon, so we asked Lizzie, the nanny, if she could come, too; the idea of sleepless nights on top of everything else was just too much. As much as I found it difficult to hand Brooklyn over to somebody else, it would only be at night. This time I would make it work.

Andrew Lloyd Webber's house was on Cap Ferrat, the peninsula that juts out into the sea near Nice. You drove in through a huge gate and the house itself was at the end of a lovely long gravel drive. There was no one else there except the housekeeper and the kitchen staff. Inside it was quite old-fashioned with high-backed chairs and mirrors with swirly gold frames. Nothing like Elton's. But everyone was very welcoming and, even though the time we had was very short, I gradually began to relax. At the end of the day I was married to the man I loved, I was Mrs Beckham.

Although there was a room where the staff of the villa had supper, it seemed a bit mean to ask Lizzie to eat there, so I said she should come and eat with us. So we're sitting there having our dinner and Brooklyn starts crying and who goes to settle him? Me. I got up without thinking. Just instinct. But was it really right that the nanny was having dinner with my husband on the first night of our honeymoon? It was at this point I decided that nannies were not for me.

On our last day David arranged a surprise. He'd called Elton's housekeeper, Laurent, who we'd got to know when we were staying there, to ask him about hiring a boat. And Laurent, who is this classic Frenchman, quite short and round with a really smiley face, said he'd organize everything.

So on our last day we drove to Antibes and went on

board this huge white speedboat. Just the three of us this time. It was very film-star luxurious with two cabins and a large saloon. We didn't have anywhere in particular we wanted to go, so we just cruised up the coast passing Nice and Monte Carlo on our left (Port Out Starboard Home) towards the border with Italy where the mountains come right down to the Mediterranean.

The day started off with blue skies, and the cook did us a fantastic barbecue on deck with langoustines and prawns and sea bass. It was so relaxing just to lie there and sunbathe. I remember looking at the sky through my sunglasses and watching as a few fluffy white clouds gradually went over. Suddenly the sun went in and the sky turned a really dark purply colour and without any real warning we were right in the middle of a storm. All I could think of was that we didn't have a baby life-jacket for Brooklyn. Although we were by now downstairs in the saloon, we were both just hanging on to him. However difficult our baby was, he was everything, the most precious, wonderful thing in my life. And I knew I would do anything to keep him safe.

The storm blew over as suddenly as it blew up. Little did I know that there were other storm clouds massing that would not blow over so easily.

After only four days, we flew back to Manchester and David went back to training – twenty-five minutes every morning with the reserves. What a farce.

When the rest of the team returned from Australia David's life returned to normal.

While I was being a mum in Alderley Edge, the other Spice Girls were getting on with their solo projects.

Even Melanie B was working on an album – all right, she had an easy baby compared to me, but I felt very left out.

I knew I wanted to do something, but I didn't know what. As I didn't have the confidence to do my singing, I thought I'd have a go at acting. I had kind of been pushed into that area anyway: Simon Fuller always said I would end up as a Liz Hurley-type actress. I'd enjoyed making *Spice World – the Movie*. It was a lot of early mornings and late nights, but it had been a good laugh and although it was generally panned by the critics, personally I had come out of it quite well.

The Spice Girls had lots of dealings with William Morris, the big theatrical agency in LA, so when the possibility of my going into films came up, William Morris's London office was the obvious choice. My agent there was Tara Joseph. I had visions of myself starring with Bruce Willis and saving the world. Or a horror film; at least then I wouldn't have to worry about a sequel. Seriously though, I wanted something that had a good cast and a well-respected director. What I didn't want was to have to carry a whole movie on my shoulders.

My first screen test since *Tank Girl* and Geri stealing the popcorn four years before was for the film *Charlie's Angels*.

This time I did dress for the part: I wore tight trousers, spiky shoes with matching handbag. I'd been sent several scripts but this was the only one that really got me excited. And I was excited. But also a bit scared: for the screen test I had to play a scene with somebody else giving me the lines off-camera. This is more difficult than it sounds: like playing football with a balloon.

Anyway, it went really, really well. The tape was being sent out to Hollywood and I would hear in a few days. I so desperately needed something to get my teeth into. Workaholic that I am, I become really irritable if there's nowhere to channel my energy. Because we didn't know what time I'd be finished at the screen test we were all going out for a Chinese when I got back.

As the security gates of my mum and dad's house slid open, David and my mum were standing at the door. Which was quite odd.

What happens next I remember like stop-frame animation. I go in. The television is on in the lounge. Brooklyn is lying in his bucket asleep. I bend down and kiss his head very gently so as not to wake him. My mum says they've got something to tell me. David puts his arm around me and kisses me.

'So, what is it?' I say as my mum tells me to sit down.

'Now, don't panic,' she says, 'but we've had a threat that somebody is going to try and kidnap Brooklyn.'

And instantly my heart races and pounds. It's the worst thing I have ever been told.

My breath started coming in bursts. No tears. My mouth went completely dry. I tried to say something but the words wouldn't come.

'The police say it could be just a hoax,' David said. But I could tell from his eyes that he didn't think it was. There had been a phone call to the shop in Manchester where Tim, David's ex-friend, still worked and who still had my mum's number. The caller had said he would phone back a fortnight later.

All they knew was that the man had a Manchester accent. The police had tried tracing the call, but it was from an off-the-supermarket-shelf mobile. My family had known for hours but they hadn't called me because it wasn't something they could say over the phone.

My whole world was imploding.

Just the name of Tim made me angry. After the business of the slags, David had said he would never speak to him again, and he hadn't. But I couldn't help thinking that it might all be something to do with him, getting back at me.

And my mind flashes back to stories about people being kidnapped, how the kidnappers prove the person is still alive, like sending bits of them through the post, like their ears. Am I the only one who reads newspapers here? But then he just puts his arm round me and I begin to cry.

But we couldn't stay in the house for ever, we'd have to get security. Since the end of the tour I'd not needed a driver. When I did – like the *Charlie's Angels* screen test – there was this friend of my parents who would come and drive me.

Who to call? The first name I thought of was Frankie, the driver who got us out of the Portland Hospital safely. So professional, a really smooth operator you could trust with your life.

I tell him what's happened. I think I'm being calm and organized but he can tell I'm verging on hysteria.

'Don't panic, Victoria, we'll sort something out.'

Next I call Nancy Phillips – still at the office – and tell her what's happened.

My mum is organizing a takeaway.

What would I like?

They must be joking.

An hour later Frankie calls.

'Do you remember Dougie, Victoria?'

Yes. He'd driven for the Spice Girls a few times.

'OK. Dougie will drive you, Victoria, and he knows somebody who can provide twenty-four-hour protection. Ex-SAS. If that's all right with you, he'll bring him round in the morning.'

Brooklyn had slept through all of this. I so wanted to wake him, hug him, see him smile. But I knew I couldn't. His sleeping still wasn't great and he needed all he could get. I kept looking at his ears, so perfect. I looked at his tiny little hands open as though asking for something. And I felt the anger in me bubbling up that somebody could want to harm him. Because that's what it meant. I tried to look at him as if I was a camera, his long eyelashes on his cheeks, the tiny little veins in his eyelids, the little hollow in his forehead which just pulsed up and down. His little mouth puckered up as if he was about to have a drink. I just looked at my baby thinking, *This is the last time I'm going to see you.*

That night Brooklyn slept between me and David. From now on I wasn't letting him out of my sight. David had to leave early next morning to get back to Manchester and I could hardly bear to let him go. He slept but I didn't. Just lay there listening to them both breathing.

At eight o'clock Dougie arrives. He's in his forties. Smartly dressed. He's all: Can't believe this has happened, Victoria, but don't worry we'll sort you out. Then he introduces me to this other guy he has brought along, the one who can give us twenty-four-hour protection, Mark Niblett.

You have to make your mind up quickly at times like this. Yes or no. I looked at him. Mid-thirties, but his receding hairline made him look a bit older. Although he was small – no more than about five foot seven – he was built like a bulldog. He was wearing a suit and small round glasses that made him look incredibly intelligent. It was a good combination – I could tell that he was really taking on board everything that I was saying. It turned out he was actually living with Dougie; they shared a house in Bow.

I had to make a decision. OK. I'd try him for two weeks. See how it worked out.

Every morning Mark and Dougie arrived together in Dougie's Mercedes. Most of the time I would go with Dougie, and Mark would take one of our cars because they were already fitted up with baby seats and my mum or David's mum would go with him.

I did go with Mark a few times – he said it was best that Brooklyn didn't always go in the same car – and I was very impressed with him. He was so professional, always looking in the mirror.

'To check if we are being followed,' he explained.

Mark Niblett was an answer to my prayers, my White Knight. Myself, I felt totally secure with him, and it made all the difference knowing my baby was safe when I had to go off to work.

He used to joke that he was bulletproof. He actually said to me once, that if anyone tried to do anything to me or Brooklyn, 'I would dive in front of a bullet.'

One day I said I was surprised he wore glasses rather than contact lenses. Oh, he said, he didn't actually need to wear glasses. 'I wear them as a bit of a disguise.' To give the impression that he wasn't as hard as he actually was.

But in fact I didn't talk to him much.

'If you don't mind,' he said, 'I won't talk when we're out. Because if I'm talking to you my attention isn't on the surveillance.'

It was about three weeks later that Mark spoke to my mum about working for us permanently.

'Victoria is paying through the nose for her security,' he told her, which was true. When you get a driver through an agency you pay an hourly rate plus mileage and petrol. On top of that there's the commission to the agency. Mark was suggesting that we employed him direct. Also, he said, we really didn't need him and Dougie. Brooklyn was only six months old so it wasn't as if he was being taken out all the time, and I wasn't working every day by any means.

My mum was all in favour. The two weeks were up and there had been no more threats.

Although it wasn't directly a Spice Girls matter, Nancy Phillips at the office did the final negotiations with him. I didn't want to have to deal with the money side myself. Mark had asked for £800 a week going up to £1000. A lot. But he was very highly qualified. His CV was very impressive – he had been involved in high profile personal close protection, surveillance and complex electronic security systems. He had even worked for the Kuwaiti royal family.

As well as our individual projects, we were now working on the third Spice Girls album. Now that we didn't spend all our lives together it was all taking a bit more time: time to get used to each other again, time to get the Spice vibe up and running and just the logistics of getting our diaries into sync. Whenever I wasn't working with the girls or reading film scripts I was working on getting the house done as soon as possible. As I said, I'm always happier when I've got a project on the go, and Rowneybury House was about as big a project as you could wish for.

We had been looking for a place in London ever since we bought the Alderley Edge flat. In Manchester there were only so many locations we were interested in, but when it came to somewhere in London we really didn't mind where it was, as long as it was in the country, had enough land for privacy, and was reasonably close to the M25, and preferably north, to be near to my family and David's. I didn't want a house that was already 'done' – I wanted to have the opportunity to play around, but then again I didn't want something that was falling down. No rivers for Brooklyn to fall into. Somewhere, above all, that was light and spacious and had a really nice, homely feeling.

The kind of houses we were interested in don't often show up in estate agents' windows. It's all word of mouth and if you don't have much time it helps to get someone on the case for you. Melanie B and Geri had both used the same housefinder so I got in touch with her and I also had a guy Elton put me in touch with called Johnny.

It's surprising, but even when you're talking over a million, properties like this are thin on the ground. I saw houses in Buckinghamshire and Surrey and one near Epping. The boxing promoter Frank Warren's house was so enormous you'd have needed a huge staff just to keep it going. I wanted somewhere where I wouldn't rattle around and feel vulnerable when David wasn't there.

The moment I drove up the drive of Rowneybury House, I loved it, just from the look of the outside which was like a huge doll's house, red brick with pale-coloured pointing between the bricks. It was set in the middle of twenty-five acres so all round the house there was nothing but garden. Although it was big, it wasn't like, Where are you?, it still had a homely feel. It was early summer when I saw it and sunlight flooded the main rooms at the back through the huge, floor-to-ceiling windows.

The decoration was not me at all – a bit mumsie – but there was nothing unpleasant, it just meant I could have fun redoing it. I really liked the layout of the rooms – the kitchen was the only one I would have changed. We wanted a kitchen we could entertain in if we wanted to – just a matter of knocking down a few walls, I decided.

As soon as I saw it I was on the phone to David. The location could not have been better: under an hour up the M11 to the West End, twenty minutes from my mum's, half an hour from David's parents and ten minutes from Stansted.

Ever since my dad changed the windows in the house in Hoddesdon where I was born, he has always loved doing up houses. There have been a couple over the years – one in Tottenham, I remember – and he was as excited as I was at the idea of getting his hands on something this big. I wanted to keep everything as much in the family as I could, and so I asked Del, my mum and dad's friend, to do the work.

One Friday in early September I finished work really

late at the studios where me and the girls were recording 'Holler' for our third album with big-time American producer/songwriter Rodney Jerkins.

Mark had dropped me off in the West End in the morning then gone back to Hertfordshire to be with my mum and Brooklyn. Mark was adamant that Brooklyn should never leave the house unless he was with him, not even in the garden. 'Anything could happen when you're least expecting it,' he said. Most of the time Mark would just hang about or there would be little errands to do. Although Sandra and Louise sometimes took Brooklyn out, it was my mum who took the brunt of the babysitting. She always said, 'Don't worry about Brooklyn, he's fine here, just leave him with me.' But the truth is that for months she didn't have a life.

Around ten o'clock, when I came down the steps of the Whitfield Street studios, Mark was waiting with my little green Mercedes SLK, as always really smart in a sharp navy-blue suit, looking just like the soldier he had once been. A true professional, he didn't even ask me how my day had been. In actual fact I was completely shattered. On the way home I called David who was at Burnham Beeches with the England squad. The next day they were playing Luxembourg at Wembley. I said I would see him after the match. Although Burnham Beeches is less than an hour away around the M25, it might as well be in the Outer Hebrides. Once inside the camp, it's like being in a convent.

The first thing I did when I got in was to go to the fridge by the back door. I hadn't eaten properly since breakfast and I was absolutely starving. My dad was on the phone looking serious. I remember I made a funny face. He didn't respond. I got some chicken that my mum had cooked for dinner and took it into the lounge where she was sitting with Dee and Del.

'Victoria,' my dad said when he'd finished on the phone, 'can you come in here a moment?'

Now that he was in charge of the house, hardly a day went by without another decision having to be made. The door frames were all being changed to a Gothic shape that suited the size of the rooms but there was a problem with the ones going out to the swimming pool.

I went back into the kitchen. But it was nothing to do with the house.

'That was the police,' he said. 'They've had a tip-off.'

'Brooklyn?' I said numbly. I could hardly get his name out. My dad nodded and put his arms around me, but it must have been like hugging a statue. It was as if I had been turned to stone. It was like some terrible nightmare when you wake up and realize it's a nightmare then go back to sleep again and you go back into the nightmare. This couldn't be happening. Still holding me my dad told me what had happened. That the police had heard from a reliable source that Brooklyn was going to be kidnapped the next day, 4th September, and taken to an address in The Bishops Avenue, in Hampstead.

Tomorrow. My mouth was dry. They'd chosen tomorrow when they knew David was away. Tomorrow. I looked at my watch, a watch David had given to me. How many hours left till tomorrow. Tomorrow started tonight at midnight. Then the adrenalin kicked in.

The chicken never got eaten. It was still there in the kitchen three days later.

The first thing I did was run upstairs and check that Brooklyn was all right. He was fast asleep in his cot. Then on the landing outside his room I called Mark. He said he'd grab a change of clothes and get back as soon as he could. He told me to close all the curtains and lock all the doors and that nobody in the family should leave the house.

Then I called David on his mobile. The switchboard at Burnham Beeches often don't put through calls on the night before a match. At this point I didn't care about England, I didn't care about anything except Brooklyn. And there was no way I was not telling David. So it's sod the bloody football.

I tell him what's happened, and at one point the signal begins to go, the line crackles and I just can't bear it. David says he'll call me back. He's going to speak to the England manager, Kevin Keegan. Hearing David's voice should have calmed me down, but it didn't. I felt as if I was talking into a huge echoing cavern. The house might have been full of people, but when I put the phone down I felt so alone.

Half-an-hour later Mark arrives, a changed man from the one who had dropped me off a couple of hours earlier. He was dressed more casually for a start, but everything about him said, I'm in charge.

The first thing he did was check the doors and windows. Lighted windows made easy targets, he said. If they were coming with guns he wasn't going to make it easy for them.

I was shaking. Quivering. I could feel my blood throbbing in my neck. My mouth was totally dry. Why didn't David call? I must do something. If I don't do something I'll go mad. So I go around checking the windows, windows I've already checked, that Mark has already checked. But Mark isn't family. You can't trust anyone but your family.

It's like I'm a machine, just checking windows, waiting for the crash of glass, waiting for men to come crashing through windows with guns, in masks, come to take Brooklyn, the chosen one.

NOBODY TOUCH THE BABY.

I'm upstairs in Brooklyn's room, just watching him, when David calls back. My mum answers it. I just sit there like I'm catatonic or something. She whispers to me from the door. He's on his way with the manager 'to sort this out'. I remember thinking, Alex Ferguson wouldn't do this.

Downstairs I can hear my mum and dad talking to Dee and Del in quiet voices. I just pace up and down the landing outside Brooklyn's room while Mark moves around from window to window in the dark, looking outside for movement.

NOBODY TOUCH THE BABY.

When I hear the car at the gates I feel such an intense rush of relief as I never remember having before. David. With him was Kevin Keegan and Terry Byrne who is the England masseur, and in fact more of a friend.

By now it must have been about one o'clock in the morning. David looked terrible. I'd barely met the England manager before, but I cannot heap enough praise on him. He was just totally incredible, the nicest man you're ever going to meet. He said he knew just how I was feeling; when he was living in Germany he and his wife had received death threats.

Although the police had said it was OK to stay in the house, Mark said that according to his reading of the situation we should get out. A safe house.

It was Kevin Keegan who suggested we all went to Burnham Beeches. When it's not being the England team training ground, it's an ordinary hotel. Like I said, the England squad's training ground is run like a nunnery. No one can get in.

'Give us half an hour,' Kevin said as he and David left. 'And by the time you arrive, all your rooms will be ready.'

I thought me and Brooklyn should go with them, but David hugged me and said that in an hour we'd all be together and it was better to do as the boss said, that everything would be ready and my dad's 4WD would be safer.

I went upstairs and threw Brooklyn's and my things into a couple of bags. I was shaking so much I could hardly get the drawers open. We went in my dad's Cherokee Jeep and Mark followed in my Mercedes in case anyone tried to follow us, he said. On her way out, mum went back to the kitchen and got a knife out of the drawer. She didn't even tell Mark. Unless you're in my family, I would never totally trust you.

Forty-five minutes later and we're passing through the security gates at Burnham Beeches where David and the chief of security were waiting. Kevin Keegan had said me, David and Brooklyn could all stay in one room together – unheard of the night before an England match. The rooms weren't great, but there was nowhere I would rather have been. With David. And Brooklyn asleep between the two of us.

We had about four hours' sleep. The manager said he would leave it up to David to decide if he felt fit enough to play and said he didn't need to make up his mind until the morning. When we woke up David was still um-ing and ah-ing but I said I thought it would do him good, take his mind off things. After all, Kevin Keegan had been amazing and David couldn't let the England fans down.

So he played.

We had been put in a separate wing to the footballers, the wing where management and the staff stay. None of the footballers had to know we were there, so the next day we just stayed in our rooms or used the dining room.

After this latest threat the police decided we should have a new security system with panic buttons. It would take a bit of time to install. Was there somewhere we could go for a few days?

I gave Elton a call. His house in Nice was ours for as long as we wanted, he said.

'Just tell Laurent what flight you're on and he will arrange to meet it.'

But Mark said just installing in-house security wasn't enough. This latest threat, he said, was very serious. We needed twenty-four-hour personal protection and it was too much for him to do on his own.

'To do this job properly and for Brooklyn to be safe, I'll need to take on someone else.'

If Mark thought it necessary, then that was enough for me. At the house in Bow where he lived with Dougie, he said, there was another security driver who had worked in Northern Ireland with him. It would cost us an extra £1000 a week, he said, but with Brooklyn's life at stake, he knew that money wasn't the issue.

David said, Do it.

20 you're going to die

Only my dad had stayed to oversee what was being done. Me, Brooklyn, my mum, Louise and Liberty flew down to Nice with the two security. By the time we got back there were panic buttons all over the house backed up by a twelve-minute response from Scotland Yard. Outside there were cameras covering every last inch of the garden. They'd put taps on our phone and police cars would regularly cruise up and down the lane outside the house.

But that wasn't enough for me. The nightmare fear every parent has that something might happen to their child was now total terror. Like the man said, paranoia strikes deep, and it had struck right down to the roots of my confidence and I had lost all sense of proportion.

Mark said that he and the new security driver should take it in turns to sit in the kitchen every night just to watch the security cameras. This went on for a few weeks but in the end my dad said we couldn't carry on living like this. We agreed to three days on, two days off, which meant they would overlap for a day. That was the only day that my mum had any real freedom to go out.

Over the next nine months Brooklyn hardly ever left the house. Mark said it wasn't even safe for him to go in the garden, he didn't even get to feed the fish in the fishpond. My mum says now that she doesn't know how they lived. She couldn't just pop to the chemist, couldn't just pop anywhere. Neither my mum nor David's mum dared even go to the shops with him in his buggy like any other grandmother would. Mark said it was too dangerous. We all lived in this bubble of fear.

To make travelling easier we offered Mark and the other security use of the flat over the former stableblock at Rowneybury House. The flat had been used by the builders for making coffee and things, so it needed a bit of tidying up. As well as getting new carpets laid, me and my sister went shopping and came back with everything, from a sofa to matching curtains, duvets, bar stools and microwave, kettle, TV and video. It was rent-free, of course, and we'd pay all the bills, and they had use of our cars.

By the beginning of November there hadn't been any more kidnap threats so we decided we didn't need two security guards, and to be totally honest the other guy didn't really have Mark's edge. He was often more of a hindrance than a help. I thought Mark might be uneasy about taking sole responsibility again, but in fact he seemed desperate to stay with us, although I pointed out that we'd be going back to the old timetable now that the other guy had left. Mark's father had been ill and he'd been having a lot of extra time off.

Yet here he was saying things like, are you happy with me, Victoria, is my job secure? I was generally more than happy with him – it wasn't his fault that his father was ill. But I did take the opportunity to point out that he hadn't always been totally straight with me – like when I'd first interviewed him he'd told me he spoke fluent French. The few days we spent in Nice were enough to show that that was pure fantasy. Also, when we were in France I found out he had been taking photographs of Brooklyn. You just don't do that if you're working as a bodyguard. And then there was the business of the glasses he wore just being a disguise.

'You must think I'm stupid, Mark – anyone can see they've got lenses in them,' I said.

The next day he turned up and I'm thinking there's something different but I can't make out what. And then I realize. No glasses. And his eyes are this incredible blue like an ad for a Caribbean holiday. Contact lenses. Before they were a kind of nothingy grey. Now they were so blue that he looked in a constant state of surprise. I didn't say anything, he was quite sensitive. He was good at his job; the last thing I wanted was for him to leave. As he was always reminding me, anything could happen at any time. Let down your guard and that's when it would happen.

In December the Spice Girls had a series of concerts in Manchester and London. It was all a bit weird, like slipping back into Spice World. We rehearsed at Elstree studios where the set had been built. It wasn't far from where we all lived and for the dress rehearsal we invited all of our family and friends to come.

I had been really looking forward to performing again, but when I saw the costumes I was totally horrified – short skirts, skimpy tops – all I wanted to do was cover up, as I just knew what the papers would say. Because from being Podge Spice pre-Brooklyn I had now become Skeletal Spice.

It had started when me and David went out to dinner at Michael Caine's restaurant, Langan's, and the papers were going on about how thin I was looking. Skeletal Spice came when they ran pictures of me at the birthday party of David Furnish (Elton's partner) leaving the Ivy.

I was going to be dancing in heels and it was like, What if I fall over? They'll say I'm collapsing because I'm anorexic, whereas I was probably more healthy than I had been for years. And I'm thinking, it's sod's law that I'm going to fall over when there's nothing wrong with me.

The papers weren't wrong about me being thin, I was. Since having Brooklyn I had begun losing weight and gone on losing weight and I was getting thinner and thinner. I genuinely didn't know what was wrong with me. It was the first time for years that I was actually eating properly. It was getting to the stage where if I didn't have sugar, I would nearly pass out. I was eating tins of mango, lychee, mandarin segments, pears, anything. I was eating five tins at a time. I was eating like a bulimic would, but not throwing up.

Eventually, I was persuaded to see a Chinese doctor who did a strange test to check for allergies and food intolerance. The whole thing sounded so totally ridiculous but in the end you'll do anything. You had to hold a little bottle of whatever the guy thinks you might be allergic to, then you have to try and stop him pushing your arm down. It's seriously weird, but amazing. With some things I held my arm up, no problem. With other things my arm might just as well have been made of felt for all the strength I had.

It turned out that I had a zinc deficiency and candida. This was something similar to what Mandy Smith (who used to be married to Bill Wyman) had when she was so ill. I got to know Mandy through her sister Nicola who is engaged to Teddy Sheringham. They're both lovely girls and Mandy has been through such a lot.

The Chinese guy gave me some medication and said I had to cut out all sugar, including alcohol, fruit, all carbohydrates, dairy products and Diet Coke. When I discussed this with my family doctor he said it could be that I also had slight hypoglycaemia – which is the opposite of diabetes – but blood tests never showed it up. To this day I'm convinced this is what I have.

It was awful. I did try to stick to the diet, but it didn't last long. I had a migraine for a week, which I'd been told was a sign that I was detoxifying. The tablets weren't doing anything and my body was craving all the things I was allergic to, especially fruit. I had no energy and was just lying in bed the whole time. To make it worse we weren't even at home. We were staying at Gary Neville's house in Bury because the flat in Alderley Edge was being fitted with extra security. Even though it was at the top of the house and the way to reach it was by lift, when David was training I was there with Brooklyn on my own and I was terrified. After all, the first kidnap threat had come from someone with a Northern accent and the bullets had been sent to the house at Worsley. It was Manchester United fans who hated me, everyone knew where David Beckham had moved to, all they had to do was come and get me. We had wanted to get security gates fitted but the other residents didn't want them, even though we said we'd pay for everything.

By now my mum and dad's house felt the safest place in the world so I was pleased when the Christmas Spice Girls concerts meant I could spend some time there and it meant Brooklyn had Liberty to play with. Brooklyn wasn't even crawling, whereas Liberty being nine months older was rushing around. But Mark still said they couldn't go out, not even into the garden unless he was with them.

Although my mum tried to make me eat what she called proper food I still wasn't putting on weight. So when it came to the concerts I wasn't surprised that most of the press ran pictures that made me look as thin as possible. But not everyone had a go at me. The *Mirror* (the paper which a few days after Brooklyn was born published a picture of me with arrows drawn on it where they decided I had to lose weight) wrote that the only disorder with Posh Spice was the thousands of fans loving what she was doing at the concert. Others weren't so kind.

With David away playing football in Brazil with Manchester United after Christmas, I could feel the terror set in again. I wasn't about to be in the flat on my own so I decided that rather than stay in England down at my mum's, why not just get out, get away from everything and get some sunshine? They had suffered as much as I had. For the first time in my life I wasn't interested in how much it was going to cost. All I wanted was for us all to be safe.

In fact there wasn't much choice – at that time of the year many of the best hotels were already taken up by rich people with the same idea. Also a lot of places won't let you take children. I could have had Bali or the Seychelles, but the flights were too long for Brooklyn and Liberty. Also I needed somewhere that wasn't miles and miles away. I only wanted to be away for the same amount of time as David was out of the country.

I first heard about Mustique from Peregrine Armstrong-Jones. It was when Princess Margaret built a house there that it began to be known as somewhere celebrities could go to get some privacy and apparently sometimes you could see her toddling around in her shorts. The Cotton House was the only hotel on the island – everywhere else was private villas.

The most important thing for me was how they prided themselves on not allowing any press on the island. If they didn't even allow press they weren't going to allow kidnappers and murderers. I even decided that Mark didn't need to come with us, though I knew he was disappointed at not going to the Caribbean. I didn't tell anyone else we were going – not even Alan Edwards. I told him we were going skiing. If no one knew where we were going, we were safe.

Mustique is tiny – only three miles long and two miles wide. The airport is more like a shack on a landing strip and you have to fly in while it's still light because they don't have radar. From Barbados, where you fly to from London, you take a little plane to Mustique, it just takes forty minutes and it is beautiful. You fly really low and the beaches of the islands we skimmed over were pinky-red from the setting sun.

The moment I stepped off the plane, I felt instantly relaxed. And a sense of relief swept over me. The Cotton

House was only five minutes away and was perfect for what I wanted. Me and Louise shared one of the little houses that were dotted about the grounds and my mum and dad were in another. The restaurant was in the main house. It was all very low-key, not majorly luxurious but with big old wooden tables and handmade distressed, limewashed furniture and lots of cream-coloured hangings.

The place itself was absolutely beautiful. The beach was a two-minute walk away and there was a little private sunbathing area by the pool. Most people went to the beach, which was just as you would imagine: palm-fringed white sand and sparkling blue sea that not even the best photograph can capture.

But the best thing for me was being left alone. In England it had got to the point where I was so tense the phone only had to ring and I would jump. Any sudden, unexpected noise would make me grab Brooklyn. Sometimes he would be so startled he would cry. Here the phone didn't ring, there were no unexpected noises. Only funny little blackbirds came visiting, looking for food. The only decisions I had to make were whether to have mango or pawpaw for breakfast, whether to stay at the Cotton House for lunch or go to Basil's Bar down by the jetty, only five minutes away in our little golf buggy thing, where the local food included lots of fresh fish.

Everyone on the island knows that Mustique can only keep its reputation if celebrities can rely on being left in peace. We saw Mick Jagger and his daughter Elizabeth and Pierce Brosnan and Michael J. Fox – though we were never sure that it wasn't in fact his lookalike.

The good thing was, nobody at the Cotton House had recognized me. Unless I'm dressed up as Posh Spice, I don't look like Posh Spice. And anyway, half of the other guests were foreign. To them I was just a young mum on holiday with her family. We kept ourselves to ourselves.

Although my mobile was turned off, I picked up my voice mail every night. It was on the third day, I think, that I got Alan Edwards's message to call him.

'So,' he said, 'hot enough for you, is it, Victoria?'

'Sunny,' I replied, remembering how I was meant to be skiing. 'But not what I could call hot.'

'That's odd,' he went on. 'From the pictures in the papers it looks as if it's baking.'

My heart missed a beat.

'What pictures?'

'You in a bikini and a baseball hat. In Mustique.'

I couldn't believe it. Just could not believe it.

My body went rigid. My first thought was, where's Brooklyn? He was sprawled out asleep in his cot.

Alan said he would fax me the pictures. In fact they weren't too bad. What was frightening was that the photographer had got so close. There was a close-up of my hip bone that they claimed was 'sticking out', and a close-up down my top.

They had been taken by the pool, but I hadn't been aware of anything or anyone. None of us had. And – as any woman knows – the idea of somebody taking pictures of you in your bikini without you knowing is just horrible. But that was nothing. There was a photograph of Brooklyn naked on the front page. How dare they. If someone could smuggle in a lens long enough to take close-ups like that, what about guns? I shook with fury. For a few days I'd been perfectly calm and happy. Now, once again, the paranoia had kicked in. I had an enemy on the island. Not only that, I had an enemy in England. Someone had told the press. Who could it have been? It must have been the travel agent. I was furious at myself for not bringing Mark.

Mark had told me he thought he ought to come. But I had genuinely thought we'd be all right. It turned out that there had been a man on his own who had stayed one day. He had originally booked into the only other place you could stay on Mustique, a restaurant with rooms called the Firefly, but had come to the Cotton House claiming there was something wrong with it. So he'd been given a villa just across the pool from ours. All he had to do was lean out of his bedroom window and click, click, click. And we remembered how we'd seen this man on his own one night in the restaurant and joked how he looked like a photographer. By now he was long gone. We stayed on another four days, but basically my holiday was in ruins.

Shortly after we returned, *Victoria's Secrets* was screened on Channel 4, one of the projects I'd got involved with when I was looking around, trying to get my work teeth into shape after the wedding. The office had received a proposal from a TV company called Swing Productions for me to do an interview show – where I got to interview friends. The whole thing was pretty much a send-up. It was all coordinated by Julia at Spice HQ who is a lovely girl who mainly looks after Mel B. She appears quite shy but underneath is very strong and incredibly organized.

Luckily, everyone I asked – a fantastic lot of A-list celebs that included Valentino, Elton John and Richard E. Grant (not to mention a certain famous footballer) – were completely up for it and we had a great time. As any performer knows, having a great time when you're doing something is usually the kiss of death for the finished thing. Not this time. *Victoria's Secrets* (a joke in itself – Victoria's Secrets is a famous American sexy underwear shop) got amazing reviews, along the lines of: Who would have thought that Posh had so much fun in her.

One of the people I interviewed was Guy Ritchie. It was on the set of *Snatch*; he had already done *Lock, Stock and Two Smoking Barrels*. I had met Madonna when we were on tour in America; she had come backstage just before the show to say good luck with a couple of her friends at Madison Square Garden and her daughter Lourdes (pronounced Lourd-ez) was with her. With these cute little pigtails and big brown eyes and olive skin, she looked unbelievably like Liberty – they could have been twins.

It was the same day that David had come back from the World Cup and everything was just too much. And I'm thinking, David's home, Madonna's here, my mum and dad are here, and I'm pregnant and I've got a picture of my baby five weeks old.

So we were all there with the girls and doing the introductions and suddenly she notices David.

'And you must be the famous soccer star,' she said.

And David just went red from his toes up. And later he still couldn't believe it.

'Madonna knew who I was . . . Madonna knew who I was.'

Not long after me and David got married we were in the Ivy with my sister and a couple of our friends and we got sent over two bottles of champagne. 'That's nice,' I said to the waiter, 'who's it from?'

'The lady over there.'

I wasn't wearing my glasses, I couldn't see who he was pointing at, so I just walked over.

The last person I was expecting to turn round was Madonna.

'This is my friend from London,' she said throwing her arms around me. 'I want you to meet my friends from America.'

It was so weird, having a conversation with Madonna. I have always been such a big fan and I was like a kid meeting Father Christmas for the first time. Who would have thought when I was in John Lewis with my mum pretending people were asking for my autograph that one day Madonna would know who Victoria Adams was, the spotty little teenager from Goff's Oak. NOBODY wanted to talk to me when I was at school, not to mention Madonna.

The first person she introduced me to was Michael Jordan who is a huge man. So we shook hands and his hands are the biggest hands alive, the size of dinner plates. And I looked at David and he is just frozen to the spot, totally in awe. And I'm like, David stop embarrassing me. Shut your mouth and pick your tongue off the floor.

And then she was showing everybody my wedding ring and she was so full-on.

There was another bloke there, but we were so amazed to see Michael Jordan that I didn't catch his name. Later we realized it was Ricky Martin, who – to put it politely – is a little bit larger in the flesh than he is on television.

I think that the place where you feel most alone in the world must be the fashion catwalk. And looking back I must have been either mad or a total masochist to agree to do Maria Grachvogel's show at London Fashion Week that February, but it was a debt of honour if you like.

Back at the Brits in 1997, Maria had lent me a fantastic dress to wear when we picked up our awards. It was beautiful, with a spider's-web top and chiffon skirt with big slits. To buy it would have cost something like £20,000. She was scared I was going to rip it because it was so incredibly fine – and to be honest I was, too. But I promised to take really good care of it – it would just be for the awards ceremony, I wouldn't even wear it to the party afterwards. I was talking about how fragile it was just before we went on and Caroline Aherne, who was then really big with Mrs Merton, was listening – she was right behind us because she was presenting the next award – and as I walked on stage to collect the award, she stood on it. A total accident I'm sure. Luckily there was no damage.

Maria made my mum a fantastic dress for my wedding, so when she asked if I could do a fashion show I really felt I owed her one. She'd first asked me a couple of years back, but I just hadn't had time. Now I had a different problem, given all the fuss about how thin I was, the last thing I wanted was to put myself up on a bloody catwalk during London Fashion Week.

It wasn't as if I needed publicity, quite the reverse.

Everywhere we went there were photographers, for everything we did. We seemed to have been in the papers literally every single day. It was as if the nation had this unhealthy obsession with 'Posh and Becks'. But how these reporters and photographers knew where we would be was something none of us could understand. This time what was worrying was not the lies, but how accurate so much of it was. But whenever we sat down and really thought about it, there would always be someone outside the family who knew, a driver, a travel agent, someone who could have told someone. We put it down to the fact that everybody has a price.

Even the press realized that something odd was going on, that there was a leak. Matthew Wright in the *Mirror* claimed it was Louise and that she was tipping off *The Times*, for goodness sake, that she was 'the family friend' they were quoting. Poor Louise, it was so, so hurtful. But there was someone. Someone who must have been close to us. I began looking at everyone around us, searching their eyes, wondering, is it you? It was a horrible feeling.

No, I needed publicity like England needed rain. This was to help Maria Grachvogel. And it wasn't as if it was the Alexander McQueen show with the whole fashion world there. Maria was a young designer, she's fantastic at what she does, but at the time she was still quite new. Nobody would even know. I made clear that I'd only do it as long as nobody was told in advance. I also wanted to be involved in the design process – I'm not a natural clothes-horse who can look good in everything. And Maria was quite happy about that.

She makes me lots of clothes even now, particularly

when I'm going to a big do and need something special. What I love about her designs is that they are very feminine. She likes women to look like women, her clothes are sexy but in a classy way.

I told hardly anyone what I was doing except my family. I didn't even tell the girls. It would be the first thing I'd done on my own and if I was going to fall flat on my face (possibly literally) I didn't need the world's press there to take photographs and write about it.

So I'm in the car on my way to the Natural History Museum, where it was being held, and listening to Capital Radio when I hear that 'Posh Spice will shortly be arriving at London Fashion Week and she's going to do a fashion show'.

Instantly, I got this pain in my stomach, and the first thing I do when we get there is dash to the toilet. What is happening? I had told no one. God knows how long I was in there. I just remember sitting in this Portaloo thing in a courtyard behind the museum with Louise banging on the door, telling me to hurry up. I was petrified. This was supposed to be totally low-key. I'd had no rehearsal, nothing. I hadn't even tried the clothes on.

I mean, I'd never done anything like it before.

So I walk into the tent and it's freezing. And there I am, the only model with spots and a pair of tits. In fact, I realize for the first time in my life that I'm a pygmy, not even five foot eight, not to mention five foot eleven. So I go Hi, but I might as well have been talking to a row of Christmas trees. They completely ignored me. Fashion is a really bitchy industry I've decided. Maybe they were shy, but I don't think so.

Maria had cornered off this little area for me. My first outfit was hot pants and a little top. And I remember standing at the side of the stage and feeling so vulnerable: I have no running order, no idea when I'm supposed to go on, what I'm supposed to do. All I can think of is pirates and walking the plank. Maria says she'll just give me a push. Great.

And then the music starts up, nothing I recognized, something Moroccan-y. So I'm standing there and I imagine it's like waiting at the gaping door of a plane when you're about to do a parachute jump. And I'm thinking, how difficult can it be? I've been practising this thing called walking for twenty-five years, so I should have mastered it by now.

'OK, go.' Maria gives me a push and I'm on.

And it was like, Bloody hell. As I walked in these four-inch heels and hot pants the lights went psychedelic and it took me a second or two to work out it wasn't pyrotechnics, it was photographers.

Oh great. That's it, then. And my shorts are riding up my crotch but with the world's press looking at you, you can hardly start pulling at them.

It was on the front page of every newspaper, including the *Independent* and *The Times*. It even made the front cover of *The New York Times*. It was amazing. And yes, a lot of it was about what I looked like. But most of it was actually quite positive. Some people said, yes, she does look too thin; others said things like I must go down the gym every day (which I didn't), her legs are quite muscly.

There's one fantastic picture that is one of my all-time favourites and I'm going to have it blown up for the new house. It's not really of me, it's of the photographers all shouting with me just a dark outline facing them. All you see is the photographers and my bum with my hands on my hips – and my mum and dad and sister in the front row clapping.

By the next morning, Maria had calls from Harrods and Harvey Nichols wanting to stock her clothes, so it did the job.

Another of my guests on *Victoria's Secrets* had been Michael Parkinson. There was me, the absolute beginner, interviewing the king of interviewers. But he is just as nice in real life as he is on television and although it was nerve-racking, in fact we got on really well, to the extent that he asked if I could go on his show.

Parkinson is recorded a couple of days before it goes out, so that it's still newsworthy but they can take out the boring bits and also use clips for trailers.

About an hour before the start he came to my dressing room and we had a chat and he asked if there was anything I wanted to talk about or not talk about and I said no. Personally I don't like to know what they're going to ask because I think it's nice if it's spontaneous. Also I never like to highlight things I don't want to talk about because you just know that'll be the first thing they'll ask you.

It's a really big deal doing *Parkinson* and while I was sitting in the dressing room in front of this big bowl of fruit that they give you, it was like, Oh my God, Michael Parkinson. But I've always enjoyed watching the show – I like the fact that they still have a live band – and being on *Parkinson* is a real honour.

I'm always being told how at ease I look in front of the camera. This couldn't be further from the truth. I have always suffered from terrible stage fright – sometimes when I'm dancing I completely blank out. But it's just as bad sitting on a sofa in front of a studio audience.

To make it even more nerve-racking, when I went on I found I was sitting next to one of the Two Fat Ladies from that cooking programme, Clarissa Dickson-Wright. And I just knew there would be questions about my weight and what I ate – and just being next to her made me feel really embarrassed even before I was asked anything. And I knew as soon as I saw her, that's the way the questions would go.

'So, Victoria,' Michael Parkinson began, very smiley, patting my knee like a kind uncle, 'there are three questions everybody wants to know.'

And out they came: 1, 2, 3. Does David still wear your knickers? Have you had a boob job and are you anorexic?

At first I was quite on the defensive. And as much as it came across really well, it really wasn't an easy interview. I had never done anything like this on my own – without the other girls – and while I was doing it I was really quite shocked at how frank the questions were. The knicker question was easy. As for the boob job, I said if I'd had a boob job I'd have given myself something bigger than a B-cup. And no, I wasn't anorexic.

At this point, Clarissa Dickson-Wright turned to me and said something along the lines of so do you eat anything else except lettuce leaves? And everybody laughed. And I wanted to stick up for myself and yet still be respectful. What if I'd turned round and said to her so do you eat anything except chips and pizza? Imagine the public outcry. You're allowed to take the piss out of being thin. You're not allowed to say anything about people being fat. She was actually a nice woman – a natural comedian. So I took it with a pinch of salt. But it was hard to defend myself.

Overall though it went well. Michael Parkinson is one of nature's gentlemen. He's not trying to trip you up, like some of these younger interviewers who think that making you look small will make them look big, all he wants is to get the best out of you – and again, the show got really well reviewed. But I still found it very hard to believe that anyone could be interested in having me on my own.

Over the last few months, the threats to me, David and Brooklyn had got progressively worse. Kidnap threats and death threats. They'd usually arrive in the post, with cut-up photographs or drawings, usually involving nooses and necks, or bullets with blood spurting out of our heads. I mean, imagine it. Imagine what it feels like. Imagine someone hating you so much, someone who you have never even met. Or someone you have met.

One of my worst fears has always been that I would be shot on stage. With so many people screaming and the music being so loud, you wouldn't even hear the bang.

On 1st March, two days before the Brits, a letter arrived at my mum and dad's house, written in what looked like a child's handwriting. But this wasn't a child. I'd been sent things by this person before.

Victoria, you bitch. I hate you, you're going to die. See you at the Brits at Earls Court on the 3 March.

21 low life

Four years after we first went to the Brits as guests of Virgin, the Spice Girls were being given a lifetime achievement award and performing a set.

My first instinct after opening the letter was to phone the police. But Mark said no.

'Are you crazy?' my dad said when I told him. 'You have to tell the police. I mean, what if something was to happen and we hadn't told them?'

'But Mark says the leak about the kidnap probably came from the police.'

(The story had somehow found its way into the papers.)

'I don't give a shit what Mark says.' My dad was really angry by now because he never swears. 'There's no way you can keep something like that from the police. They'll know what to do, put a guard on you or something. I'm going to tell them whether you like it or not.'

The police were round within an hour. I gave them Richard Jones's contact number. Our tour manager would be the best person I reckoned to liaise between them and the people at Earls Court. I also told the girls and they were really concerned for me.

I was in a terrible state. The night before I barely slept: Earls Court is a big old place – not somewhere you can keep majorly secure. But what could I do? Say I had a cold?

In order that Mark could concentrate on the security aspects, I had a different driver for the day who came down from Manchester called John. By the time we turned up at Earls Court I was shaking like a jelly. John said, stay with me all the time. Mark had said, stay with him all the time. I didn't know who I could trust. I didn't know if I could trust anybody.

As soon as I arrived at Earls Court we went to my dressing room where the police put me in the picture about what was going to happen. The whole place had been thoroughly checked out, they said. But there would be some of them shadowing me all day, wherever I went. They'd also be there at the performance.

And for all that I'm thanking God I didn't listen to Mark about not telling the police, I'm thinking, What did I ever do to deserve this? I had kissed Brooklyn goodbye when I left and as the car pulled out of the gate I looked back to the door where my mum was holding him and he was waving his pudgy little hand and I thought, I'm never going to see you again, and my eyes filled with tears. I very nearly didn't go. But it was my dad who said, this is what these people want. They want you not to turn up. They want to turn your life upside down. You mustn't let these people rule your life.

Around midday I had lunch with the other girls, if

you can call a packet of crisps and a peach lunch. I couldn't chew. Not enough saliva. I explained to them exactly what was going on. I didn't want them to think it was me being theatrical, the only pop star in the place walking around with a security man glued to her side. But all of this sounds quite rational, quite matter of fact. It didn't feel like that at the time, it was totally unreal, the feeling that you sometimes get when you haven't slept for days and days.

The dressing rooms were just flimsy partitions really, built for the show. There was carpet on the floor, a bunch of flowers in the corner to make you feel important and a little fan heater, because it was bloody freezing. We had some time to wait because at the Brits, if you miss your rehearsal or are late, you're fined.

'Spice Girls on stage.' The tannoy echoed all over Earls Court and I began to shake. It was a four- or five-minute walk up a huge great ramp, then a sharp right on to the stage. Mark stuck to me like glue. There we were joined by our dancers and also by our band as we were singing live.

Everything went well. But it was like only half of me was connected. This was just the rehearsal so the lights weren't as bright as they would be for the performance, and in the shadows I couldn't shake off a sense of things moving in the auditorium, people who shouldn't be there.

So then we go back to the dressing rooms where hair and make-up are already setting up, so I'm just walking back down the ramp, when for some reason I lower my chin and see a red light shining on my chest, and without thinking I follow it up, up to the gantry that runs round the top of Earls Court where the lights are, and I could see this red light shafting down.

I looked at Mark but he was looking somewhere else. And everything seemed to last a very long time. It was like *The Bodyguard* all over again. And I'm thinking, I've got policemen, I've got Mark beside me, but no one can see this thing shining on my chest. So this is how it ends.

And I went cold. Completely cold and stiff. And I turned round to Mark, in what felt to me like slow motion, and I just pointed at this thing, and he got hold of me, and pushed me, literally pushed me down the ramp which ended at the door into the dressing rooms.

I sat at the dressing table, just shaking and staring through the mirror as this terrible film unfolded behind me. The police coming in. Mark telling the police what had happened. The police going out. The sound of their feet running up the ramp then racing up the ladders to the gantry echoed round the hall. They found that the fire escape had been wedged open.

I rang David. But I knew he thought I was exaggerating. But by now I know that it's only a matter of time. Today, tonight, I am going to die.

Winning a lifetime achievement award, the Spice Girls were the last ones on. We were hidden in this giant egg quite high above the side of the stage. At the cue of 'And now – the Spice Girls' the egg started to vibrate, then there was this loud boom that made it sound as if it was going to erupt, lights were flashing over it and everything, then the egg opened and there we were – the Spice Girls. Emma looking all cute with her pigtails, Melanie B standing there going *Grrrr* in a scary kind of position. Mel C was doing a karate kick thing, and me with my arm out in front doing the Point. Everyone's smiling. And all I see are the red lights on the cameras, on the floor, on cranes, each one moving to its own choreography, and I feel my stomach knot.

There's a long pause then the band strike up 'Spice Up Your Life'. And we *La la la la*, doing our Spice Girls thing down the staircase that took us down on to the stage where we were met by our individual dancers. Usually I try to make contact with the camera. But this time I just want the whole thing over. Every second I'm alive I'm thinking that the next second I'm going to be dead. All I could think of was David and Brooklyn, Brooklyn and David, David and Brooklyn and how much I loved them.

After 'Spice Up Your Life' we did 'Holler', which we had sung at the shows before Christmas. And all the time I'm thinking, What the hell am I doing up on this stage? Finally 'Goodbye'. It had been our last single, and our last number 1 the previous Christmas. So we're singing 'Goodbye' and then on the last chorus I heard the shots ring out – BANG, BANG, BANG, BANG, BANG. I just clutched at my stomach. I'd been shot. I knew I'd been shot. And Mark started to run up on stage, and although I could feel myself going, I could see policemen starting to run, everyone all wired up, people starting to run towards the stage. I was bent over and I'd stopped singing. But the shots hadn't stopped. BANG. BANG. BANG. Over and over again. And out of the corner of my eye I realized what had happened. The roof of Earls Court had been covered by what must have been a thousand balloons and for the finale they were somehow bursting them. They hadn't told us that this was going to happen. And as each one burst it went BANG. Hundreds of them – BANG, BANG, BANG.

Tears of relief were pouring out of my eyes as I realized that I wasn't dead.

Then Will Smith came on stage and presented us with the award. And the next day there are pictures of me bent over on the stage with tears in my eyes and it was 'Posh gets emotional' because they assumed I was overcome with having won this award. My emotion was simply from the knowledge that I was alive. I was so convinced I'd been shot that I actually looked for bullet holes. It was without doubt the worst performance that I have ever done; the one occasion when 'Posh Spice can't sing' might even have been true.

The day after the Brits was Brooklyn's birthday party. We had it up in Manchester because most of the other babies we know are children of footballers. But a few people came up from London including Mel B's little girl Phoenix, David's sister Lynne's daughter Georgina, and of course Liberty.

Liberty and Brooklyn are like brother and sister. They were born only nine months apart, and when some new houses were built backing on to my parents' house, I managed to buy the one right next to theirs, so Christian, Louise and Liberty now live next-door. You just have to go through a wrought-iron gate in the wall. Liberty calls Brooklyn Bibbin and Brooklyn calls Liberty Bibbi. So they're Bibbin and Bibbi, and probably always will be. When we're staying in London the first thing Brooklyn does when he wakes up is look out of his bedroom window at the door in the wall and begin calling out 'Bibbi, Bibbi', literally waiting for her to walk through. And of course Liberty is doing just the same the other side. They are very cute together and always hold hands when they are out.

The rather funny-looking baby that I saw when she was only a few hours old has grown into a lovely little girl – the complete opposite of Brooklyn in many ways – a real girly girl who loves things like putting on make-up and dousing herself in hairspray. I look at her and recognize myself at that age. Not only does she look like me, but she's a real show-off. For her last birthday I bought her a little pair of sparkly toy high-heels and she just loves them and she loves having her nails painted to match and to parade up and down. But when it comes to being brave, Brooklyn is a real boy. Like when me and Louise and Brooklyn and Liberty go to visit a farm near my mum's, Brooklyn will go straight up to big pigs, whereas Liberty stands back and hates it if a fly goes anywhere near her. What we would have done if Louise and Liberty hadn't been next-door I don't know. It meant that Brooklyn always had someone to play with.

Because I'd been so busy, Mark had arranged most of the birthday party – a friend of his managed a hotel that did this sort of thing. He was in charge. He got in all the extra security we were going to need and had them all sign confidentiality forms.

Everyone who works for us always signs a confidentiality form – it's the only way we can rely on the things we say in private not turning up in the newspapers. Coming only a day after the Brits, Mark was totally obsessed with the security aspect and even said he would get the hotel swept for bugs, though why anybody would want to tape-record a children's party I don't know.

I wanted it to be like a kind of circus, so we had clowns, jugglers, conjurers and people dressed up as characters. It was great. However, the strain of the past few weeks was beginning to tell, I was tired. So tired. But that was mainly down to the travelling up and down to Manchester, but there was no avoiding the travelling – if I wanted to work. And in myself I was much better than I had been when Brooklyn was still a real baby, when I spent my entire life in my tracksuit, never leaving the flat.

The way we have to live apart so much of the time, it's David who gets the worst of it. He is such a hands-on father, saying goodbye to Brooklyn can be unbearable. David will do anything to be with him.

It was David's decision to put Brooklyn first that led to a terrible and public row with Alex Ferguson. It happened a few days before a premiership match with Leeds in February. David was down in London and he planned to get up early and drive up to Manchester. Well, he wouldn't be driving, Mark would – David would sleep in the back.

So Brooklyn has one of his nights. And this time he's being sick and we're changing nappies every ten minutes and his screams are literally blood-curdling. Not even David's back-rubbing works. He's just walking around holding him. So around two in the morning we call out the doctor. It's gastroenteritis. The doctor gives Brooklyn some medication, but it's several more hours before he finally settles.

Because David had to leave early next morning to get

back to Manchester, I took over the walking up and down and rubbing Brooklyn's back to let David get some sleep. The only thing that seemed to calm Brooklyn was holding him close to my heart so he could hear it beating.

At six David left with Mark. Less than an hour and a half later he was back.

I was in the kitchen when he walked in, having a cup of tea. Brooklyn was lying across my lap asleep.

David tiptoed across the floor and kissed my head. He couldn't just leave me like that, he said, with a sick baby. He'd take over for a bit, he said, and I should try to get some sleep.

'But what about training?' I said.

'In nine years I've only missed one day of training,' he said. I went to bed and slept while David stayed with Brooklyn. When I got up, Brooklyn was asleep in his cot. It must have been around midday. So we had a bit to eat, then David set off again for Manchester.

With all the diarrhoea we were right out of nappies. The laundry basket was full of dirty babygros. My mum said she'd look after Brooklyn while I went to Marks & Spencer's to get some more.

When I get back he's awake and looking perfectly happy and calm. I could hardly believe this is the same baby who was nearly delirious a few hours earlier. But babies are like that, as every parent knows. Every parent except Alex Ferguson that is.

The next day David went to training as usual and was totally attacked by Ferguson who called him a disgrace and worse. What he took exception to, he later told the press, was that David had missed his training because he was looking after his son while his wife was out gallivanting at London Fashion Week. Strange to relate, a photographer managed to witness all this and it was all over the press like a rash.

Yes, I was at a reception at London Fashion Week, but long after David had gone back to Manchester. It was a long-standing engagement and I don't believe in letting people down. I wouldn't have gone if Brooklyn had still been ill. But he wasn't. I waited for him to go to sleep, showed my face at the do, presented an award and then left immediately. I'd only been gone a couple of hours and Brooklyn was still asleep when I returned.

The point is, that Alex Ferguson had been waiting for any excuse to have a go.

David had known for some time that 'the Gaffer' was angry at all the travelling he was apparently doing, saying that it was affecting his game. But that was just rubbish. David had had a fantastic season and as anyone who's ever had anything to do with David Beckham will tell you he would never do anything that would affect his game. Football and Manchester United are everything to him.

So after Ferguson had a go at him right there on the pitch, telling him to get out, David went to find him in his office.

I wasn't there, so all I can do is recount what David told me when he got home. As we've had Alex Ferguson's version of what happened in the paperback edition of his autobiography (after he'd said in public that it was dead and buried and he wouldn't refer to it again) it seems only fair that I put our side.

David was really, really upset: Ferguson told him he wasn't committed to the club; that he wasn't doing this, doing that. And that as a punishment he wasn't going to play him at the Leeds game the next Saturday, and he fined David £50,000.

David said how he loved Manchester United. How he was working hard. How he always puts in a hundred and ten per cent when he's on the pitch. How he's always in bed early before a game. Then Ferguson told David that there was no room for someone who wasn't committed to the club. That no player was bigger than the club and that he wanted him to leave.

When he came back he was in a terrible state. The man who had guided him for so many years, who had been like a second father to him, had basically said, eff off.

And if it wasn't for me saying, no, David, you've just got to grit your teeth and stay, he would have done as Alex Ferguson said and left. It's not as if he wouldn't have had anywhere to go: read the back page of any newspaper in the world and you'll see they're queuing up, cheque books at the ready to sign David Beckham.

So why didn't I jump at the chance of moving away from Manchester? Because that's what everyone seems to think I spend my life plotting to do. I'd be lying if I said I wouldn't prefer to live in London, but when I started going out with David, I knew that was something I had to sacrifice. I'd live in a dustbin if it meant living with David. Manchester, Scotland, Delhi, Dubai, I'll live wherever is best for David.

So when David comes back from the meeting in Alex Ferguson's office, totally distraught, I know I have to persuade him to stay. Why? Because he's basically happy there, his friends are there, he's been there since he was sixteen. I can't blame the Man United fans looking at me and thinking, you horrible cow, you're trying to take David away because that's the line they've been fed. But it's just not true.

Alex Ferguson is the most fantastically successful football manager there has ever been. He's fantastically talented at what he does. He does this through controlling his players and that's the key to his success. Though I imagine he would prefer to think of it as being protective. But what do I know? He has never said more than 'Hello' to me in the four years I have known David.

It wasn't the first time we'd fallen foul of the manager – if the media are to be believed.

When you've been with a football club for ten years you get a testimonial year. This always includes a match where the whole game is dedicated to you. You get all the takings and don't pay any tax. It can also include other things. Alex Ferguson had a golf day, for example (which David did), and a testimonial dinner and dance.

It was held at Nynex, a huge sports arena. And literally thousands had paid for a ticket. Only the players didn't have to pay. They just had to be there – and donate something to be auctioned. In David's case a signed shirt, which went for £15,000.

Anyway, myself and David were a bit late. Next day it was front page news. Posh snubs Fergie, all that.

I didn't snub Fergie. In fact quite the reverse. I postponed a trip to LA by a day so that I could be there. What happened was Brooklyn. I had arranged for a friend of my mum's called Pat, who lives in Stockport, to babysit. And it was one of those nights when he just wouldn't stop crying. If possible, I like to get him settled before I leave him with anyone. And he was so bad he was hyperventilating. I couldn't just go and leave him.

So we arrived late. But only by a few minutes: the dinner hadn't started, people weren't even sitting down. And neither had Sir Alex made his grand entrance accompanied by Scottish pipers after highlights of his career were shown on a giant TV screen.

The next day it's all over the newspapers, how I am disrespectful at his dinner and dance. I just don't understand.

At the beginning of April I was off to LA for meetings with songwriters, taking Brooklyn, my mum, Louise and Liberty, and, of course, Mark.

Over the years since I'd met up with the girls I had been so demoralized by always being told I was the useless one, the one Spice Girl who had less talent than a coconut, I had never had the confidence to think about a solo singing career. But gradually David had persuaded me to think about recording my own album and Nancy at the office was very supportive and set everything up for me. This was a toe-in-the-water trip, to meet people and get ideas rather than actual songwriting.

After LA we flew down to Miami to join up with Emma and Mel B to work on the new album. Mel C was in New York and would be adding her vocals later. We had under a week to finish off the album with Rodney Jerkins, only twenty-two, but one of the hottest songwriting names in music, with a whole string of hits for people like Whitney Houston, Toni Braxton, Destiny's Child and Michael Jackson.

It's a family thing; as well as Rodney there's his brother Fred, his father the Reverend Jerkins and his cousin Le Sean. They don't smoke, they don't drink and they don't swear. You'll always recognize their songs because somewhere in the lyric will be Darkchild, the name of their record and publishing company – like a kind of subliminal advertisement. They don't usually let you write with them, but for the Spice Girls, they were making an exception: we only ever sing songs that we have co-written. In fact the first time we worked with them in London, I really found the whole set-up a bit scary. But I knew it was going to be a good few days, although vocally they do push you to the max.

We arrive late and downtown Miami Beach is Miami Uncut: flashing neon, bars everywhere, girls walking down the street in cheeky bikinis. And where is our hotel? You got it. Right on the main drag.

At the entrance we have the opportunity to have our photos taken with a boa constrictor for $1.50. I'm thinking it can't be as bad inside as it is out. Wrong. Concrete floors everywhere, just what little knees and knuckles need. My room overlooked the street at the front. Brooklyn and Liberty were supposed to be sleeping but the noise from the club across the road was loud enough to dance to and every few beats set the window rattling. I called Sara, Emma's PA, who would be looking after all three of us on this trip. Where were they?

'That hotel was so terrible,' she said. 'We're looking for somewhere else.' Surprise, surprise.

I decided I'd rather stay the night in the car than in that place and we left. Mark was still downstairs with the car and the bags so we did a tour round all the nice hotels, like the Delano, places like that. Completely full. It turned out it was some kind of holiday called the spring break when all the college kids let rip and everywhere is booked. And it wasn't as if we'd just got ourselves to worry about: Melanie had Phoenix and we had Brooklyn and Liberty.

Then one of the drivers suggested we try an island off the southern point of Miami Beach called Fisher Island – an exclusive resort you can only get to by plane or private ferry. It's so exclusive the sun still shines on Fisher Island when it's raining on Miami Beach. (Boris Becker has a house there.)

We drove to the end of the causeway then got on a ferry – they wouldn't even let us on until they checked our booking. It took less than ten minutes to get there. Even though it was incredibly expensive the hotel itself wasn't that luxurious – you're paying for it being so exclusive and private. In fact it was perfect for us – the accommodation was more like villas, and when you have children it makes all the difference having a kitchen.

We had three songs to write and record, so we worked all day and most of the night. Then it was goodbye Miami, except for Emma who was staying on to work on her own album. Melanie B was flying to Vancouver to meet up with her boyfriend, Max, and we were going home: my mum, Louise and Liberty to Heathrow, Mark, me and Brooklyn going on to Manchester.

We got back on 16 April, the day before my birthday. That is, we arrived, but the luggage didn't. As usual, everything of mine had gone under Mark's name for security. I couldn't believe it. Round and round went the carousel but no sign of my luggage, none of Mark's, not even a sign of Brooklyn's buggy. I mean, who needs this after a transatlantic flight?

Mark said that he would deal with it.

A couple of hours later he calls. Some of the bags have turned up, he says. Which? All of his, two of mine: a small Louis Vuitton suitcase and a black Nike sports bag I'd got in Miami that I'd filled mainly with Brooklyn's washing. All that was in the Louis Vuitton bag were baseball caps I'd bought for David in LA, which I hadn't wanted to get squashed.

Hours went by and nothing. Eventually I decided to call the airport myself. From Miami to London we'd flown British Airways, but from London to Manchester we'd gone British Midland. It was the fault of British Airways, said British Midland. No, it was British Midland's fault, said British Airways.

'Bags never get lost,' a helpful person told me. 'You'll probably find they never left Miami.' Yeah and my name is Pamela Anderson.

April 17th, my birthday, and I've got nothing to wear. It sounds ridiculous but I'm one of those people who pack everything when they go away. Travelling first class you rarely have to pay excess baggage, and anyway, even if you do, it's better than finding you've left something crucial behind. The easiest thing to do is take the lot.

Then I get a call from British Airways in London.

Another item of baggage has turned up. Mark goes to get it. The bloody buggy. Mark's done enough, and as I was now dealing with British Airways myself I said he should have a few extra days off – his father was now in hospital in Manchester.

My birthday treat was a trip to Chester Zoo, about forty minutes' drive from Alderley Edge. I can't say I felt like going – I had nothing to wear, no clothes whatsoever except what I was wearing on the plane and an old tracksuit hanging around the flat, plus it was pissing down with rain. But Brooklyn has this thing about animals, he absolutely loves them and even if I wasn't exactly in the right mood, seeing Brooklyn having a good time would be enough to make it worthwhile.

But when we arrived I just couldn't believe it: photographers at the gate and there were probably another five or six in the grounds, they told me. The people at the zoo had gone to so much trouble, they had even made me a birthday cake. They were hugely apologetic and swore blind that they certainly hadn't told anyone at all, they'd even said the cake was for somebody else. This was becoming a familiar story. It couldn't just be coincidence. Someone must be leaking all this information.

The next day it was all over the papers. Goodbye Skeletal Spice, Hello Misery Spice. And OK, it's true I wasn't exactly beaming. I had no clothes, no make-up, and I'm thinking even the bloody animals aren't coming out today, it was so pissing down with rain. Poor David, he so wanted to make my birthday special, he'd hung disco balls up all over the flat to welcome me back.

They said I'd shut half the things in the zoo, how – because Posh Spice had wanted to go into the monkey hut – I had stopped other people going in at the same time and how I had preferential treatment. And it was all crap. Total crap. We walked around like everybody else – what did they think we did, go by stretch limo from cage to cage? There were some bits that were enclosed – like the monkey hut – but we went inside with everybody else.

What got me really wound up was that the newspapers had been there in the first place. How could they have known? I couldn't work it out. I called Mark.

'You couldn't have mentioned us going to Chester Zoo to anybody could you, Mark?'

'Absolutely not, Victoria.'

'But, Mark, think about it. You and my mum were the only ones who knew apart from the zoo people. And the zoo man swore blind it wasn't them.'

'Victoria, I swear on my children's lives, I never told anybody.'

I hated having to ask him, but it's like, What can I do?

Anyway, I had other things to worry about, like my luggage. I had written a list of everything I could remember that had been in them. My clothes, Brooklyn's clean clothes, a few faxes about a sponsorship deal David's agent was sorting out and my lyric book – the notebook that goes with me everywhere where I jot down lyric ideas and it even had in it a piece of Brooklyn's hair. I usually keep it in my hand baggage but because I had so many things to carry to keep Brooklyn amused on the plane – not to mention nappies – I'd shoved it into a suitcase.

A couple of days later, David had an away game at Southampton, so I went down to London. Waiting for my cases to turn up was getting beyond a joke and I'm such a funny size it's difficult to get clothes to fit me just anywhere; at least I knew I had some things at my mum's to be getting on with and I could always borrow from Louise.

So it's Saturday and I've been out shopping trying to

replace things, shoes, socks, make-up, everything. It's a long, slow business. Some people – like Vivienne Westwood – are being incredibly helpful, she just replaced what I had lost and didn't charge me a penny.

My mobile goes. It's Jo, the girl who does my nails up in Manchester, and what she tells me is possibly the most bizarre story I have ever heard.

A couple of days earlier she'd called me to say she'd had a phone call from some guy who said he'd found a notebook and a CD belonging to me in a skip at Heathrow and that Jo's telephone number was scrawled in the front of the notebook, which was why he had called her. She'd thought it was a wind-up and told him that if he really had these things he could post them to her. He was called Mark and she gave me his mobile number.

So I gave it a try, but nothing. Obviously a hoax.

Now she was calling to say that a package had arrived from this guy with a notebook and CD and it was definitely mine as she recognized my writing. I must have written down the wrong number when I called him.

The notebook was my lyric book, the CD I knew, from the way she described it, was three demos, songs written by a couple of the writers I had seen in LA and recorded by a session singer. I couldn't remember if it had been in the same suitcase. I called Mark Niblett, who was still in Manchester, told him what had happened. Jo shouldn't put them in the post he said but he'd send a close friend of his to collect them personally.

Only at this point did the penny finally drop that my suitcases had actually been stolen. British Airways never used any words except lost or mis-routed. It was an awful feeling. All my stuff being rummaged through.

I rang the woman I'd been talking to at British Airways and went berserk, absolutely berserk. Later that day the guy who was actually Managing Director got back to me, and I went totally mad. Poor man. He'd probably never ever been talked to like that in his life.

As for my lyric book and the CD, what was all that about? It was like some Miss Marple mystery. You don't just find a notebook and a CD in a skip. I mean, it's not as if they had been held together with an elastic band. I decided to call this Mark the skip guy myself.

There are times when being a famous person can help – he might be so unsettled to be talking to a Spice Girl that he might make a slip-up.

'Hi,' I said, 'it's Victoria Beckham, and I just want to say I really appreciate you sending my things back.' Oscar time again.

And then I went on to ask how he had found them. He told me he had a rubbish collection company at Heathrow and he happened to see the notebook and the CD in one of his skips. His family had told him not to get involved and to just dump the stuff, another friend had told him to put it all on the internet, but his mother who was a born-again Christian told him to give them back. And of course, as he was *such a nice guy*, he felt really guilty and decided to hand the stuff back.

And while he's saying all this, and I'm coming out with Oh really, and How thoughtful and all that crap, I'm thinking, This guy is low life.

But the nicer I am, the more I keep him talking, the more chance there is of getting more information out of him.

'So anyway,' I said, 'if you find anything else . . .'

'I won't,' he said.

'Well, if you do.'

'Believe me, I won't.'

'You see, clothes are one thing, but there's one special thing I can't replace.'

David had got me a silver-framed picture of himself and Brooklyn for Valentine's Day, and he scratched down the side of the frame with a penknife or something, *Love You Lots, David and Brooklyn*.

'It's just sentimental value,' I explained, 'but me and David spend a lot of time away from each other so if anyone finds that I would really appreciate it. I'll give you my security's number just in case. I really would like to get it back.'

'Tell you what,' he said, 'seeing as it's so important, why don't I go back and have a look now. Give me a call in five minutes.'

22 betrayal

I wait five minutes, then ring again.

'OK,' he says, 'I'm at the rubbish dump.'

'Thank you so much for going to all this effort, it really means a lot to me,' is what I'm saying. What I'm thinking is, WHAT'S THIS ABOUT A RUB-BISH DUMP? Last time it was a skip. Already the story was changing.

'I'm just climbing over the wall now,' he says. And then, 'Oh, yes. I can see something shining.' And then, 'It's your picture frame.'

But there's no picture in the frame, he says. I say that doesn't matter. I can get another picture but the frame's irreplaceable. But can he see anything else that might be mine?

'No.'

'Are you sure?'

But he says there's nothing. For all I know he's just crashing about in his back garden.

He agreed to hand over the frame to Mark Niblett, which happened. But by then the police were involved and they took it away for testing. The next time I saw it was in court.

The end of April 2000 and the football season was coming to a close. When David found out he wasn't playing at the second-to-last game of the season he didn't tell me but decided to arrange a surprise. Me and David were always arranging little surprises for each other.

We'd often talked about getting another dog. Puffy and Snoop were now fully grown and were serious guard dogs – I wouldn't even put my fingers through the mesh of their run at the new house and I certainly wouldn't let Brooklyn near them. What I really wanted was a fluffy white poodle and we had often talked about getting one from an animal shelter.

So when David told me he had arranged this surprise, I was sure it was a dog. Of course I asked him, but he just smiled that smile which didn't say yes and didn't say no. But I was convinced it was a little dog. So that night I could barely sleep: half excited – how I could take it everywhere – and half terrified: I could barely cope with a baby, how was I going to cope with a fluffy white poodle as well? Next morning, David said that before he told me what the secret was, we had to take his mum to the airport – she'd been up helping with Brooklyn.

We did go to the airport, but we didn't go to the animal rescue place. Instead we flew to Tuscany, to Ken and Nancy Berry's house, where we had gone the week before the wedding. That was the surprise. David had secretly packed the few things we needed beforehand and sent Mark on ahead with them to the airport and loaded them on to this private plane he'd had standing by. He'd been trying to arrange something for days — somewhere we could rely on the weather was his first priority. His first idea was Dubai, but then he decided it might be too hot for Brooklyn. He'd only been given the green light for Tuscany late the night before.

When we landed in Pisa, guess what? Photographers and people waiting for autographs. I just couldn't bear it. I signed the autographs, trying to smile but all the time knotted up thinking, How could they possibly know? It was like someone had taken over our lives, knew what we were doing before we did. It made me feel completely sick. I hadn't known. Even David didn't know for definite until that morning. Even the people we hired the plane from — who we totally trusted — didn't know.

Mark knew.

The words dropped into the pit of my stomach like the fruits on one of those old-fashioned slot machines. Clunk.

At Chester Zoo there had been other people who knew we were going, like the zoo staff. But this time, there was literally nobody else. Just Mark. And then my mind flashed back to Mustique. I'd always thought nobody except the travel people knew we were going to Mustique. But Mark knew.

And there was another odd thing. When we got on the plane I'd asked David why Mark wasn't coming with us. Mark had said it wasn't necessary, David told me. He said, 'You'll be fine in Italy.'

Fine in Italy? Everyone knows that Italy is the kidnap capital of the world.

Mark knew.

Clunk.

But although the piece fitted the jigsaw I kept going back to how he'd sworn on the lives of his children that it wasn't him. I hadn't met his children, he was divorced. But no parent would say that if it wasn't true, would they? I mean, this was the man who said he would dive in front of me or Brooklyn to stop a bullet.

I put it out of my mind. I'd always had this imagination. I could make two and two make ten if I set my mind to it. And we were going to have a wonderful holiday. The sun shone, Brooklyn was at the age when he could really enjoy the pool – he already went swimming with us at the sports centre in Manchester – and for once it was really nice not having any security around.

'Had a good time?' Mark said when he picked us up from the airport.

'Fantastic thank you. Really great.' And it had been. As a surprise for David's birthday, which he'd had while we were out there, I had secretly arranged for both our parents to come out and join us for a couple of days.

We'd been out to Ken and Nancy's villa a couple of times and every time we'd said, wouldn't it be great if our parents could experience something like this? Because although obviously they'd been in smart hotels, this was something entirely different. The food, the decor, it was all just so amazing.

I also had to get some presents sent out because I'd had no idea we weren't going to be in England for his birthday, so of course hadn't brought anything with me.

At first, I couldn't think what to do but then I phoned William Hunt, the men's fashion designer who David really likes, and I got him to send some suits out. Then I spoke to our friend Bruce, who works at Theo Fennell, the jewellers, and arranged for an earring that I had previously designed to be sent out as well.

David knew nothing about any of this, and it was all I could do to keep it secret. Everything had to be done without him knowing. So the morning of his birthday, we walk down the stairs and the staff have been brilliant – the front room is filled with balloons – and it's like, Surprise, surprise. Not only balloons, but his mum and dad and my mum and dad. They had arrived late the night before and David hadn't heard a thing.

It was a perfect birthday. First we all had breakfast together then we spent the rest of the day just lazing around the pool. In the evening I'd organized a big birthday dinner with David's favourite food – a dish that he's only ever had in Italy: pasta and creamed peas, with tiramisu for dessert. There was so much you'd have thought they were cooking for forty, but Italians are like that, so generous in everything they do. Afterwards we asked the staff who had made everything so perfect to join us for a drink.

The evening after we got back David was out getting a takeaway when the front door buzzer went. Mark. Could he come up? he said through the intercom. He wanted to talk about something.

'He'll be back in a minute,' I said, when he'd come up and found that David wasn't there.

Mark had an envelope in his hand.

'Look,' he said, 'I really hate to do this, because I love working for the two of you, but this is my letter of resignation.'

I was shocked. We'd come to totally depend on him. He did everything from driving the car to picking up the dry-cleaning. A lot of the time he was more like a PA than a security driver.

'Have you got another job?'

Nothing like that, he said. It was his father. 'When my mum died I wasn't there, and I don't want that to happen this time.'

'If having more time off would help, you've only got to ask,' I said.

He shook his head.

'I just need this time to be with him. But I won't leave you in the lurch. I'll come to the States with you and when we get back I'll find you a replacement.'

We were due to go back to LA two days later. Me, David and Brooklyn. I was going to be working on my album – even saying the words 'my album' was something I was having to get used to without feeling a complete fraud – and Mark was meant to be coming with us.

'But if your dad's really ill, the last thing you want is to be traipsing around LA.'

I was feeling really panicky and kept hoping to hear the sound of the lift – but David still wasn't back.

When Mark left, I realized I was shivering.

David was as shocked as I'd been when I told him. But what about LA? We'd already paid for Mark's flight, so we decided he might as well come.

LA is always quite social because a lot of the people who worked at Virgin when the Spice Girls first started out are now based in California. Most of them hadn't met David, so this was a good opportunity for us to do the couple thing. I usually go to those kind of parties on my own or with my mum or Louise.

And as it turned out I was really pleased Mark had come along. He did all the organizing of cars and booking restaurant tables – things that David gets really shy about. Also he said he was quite happy to babysit Brooklyn when we went out, which was good for Brooklyn who was at the age where if he woke at night seeing a stranger in a strange room could have frightened him. Mark said he'd only be watching a video anyway, and he could do that just as well in our room as in his.

On our last night we were invited by Nancy Berry to a big glitzy Hollywood party and Mark offered to babysit. But when I let him into our suite there was something that didn't add up. As he went in, I turned around and saw him go up to David, and I looked at what he was wearing: baseball hat, white T-shirt, and this pair of grey combat trousers lined in yellow, all ruffled up round the knees and bunched over, just like David sometimes does. And suddenly it came to me – he's dressed like David. And I could feel my skin crawl. It wasn't just that Mark looked ridiculous, which he did – David can dress like that because he's young but Mark Niblett was thirty-five and looked forty. It was more than that. It was as if Mark Niblett was trying to take over David's personality.

I looked into his eyes and I felt very very odd. There's this expression when people say you have a ghost brush past you. And it felt like that.

As soon as we were safely out of earshot in the corridor, we both burst out laughing because David had realized what was happening, too. Mark Niblett – a David Beckham lookalike. I mean, pl-eeese. But as we got in the car I felt cold. Something that weird, I decided, wasn't really funny at all.

The party was at Nancy and Ken Berry's house in Bel Air – the launch for Lenny Kravitz's new album. And it's real Hollywood, loads of glamorous people walking about, casual but cool, quite rock star-ish – Lenny Kravitz walked through the crowd in shades, the full bit. I'd often told David about these kinds of parties, but he'd never been to one before. And it was nice just to be out at a party enjoying it together.

While David was talking to Lenny, I was chatting to someone I knew at Virgin who, after a few minutes, said she hoped I wouldn't take it the wrong way but there was something she wanted to tell me.

'That man who works for you,' she began.

'Mark Niblett, you mean?'

'Well, I think you ought to know that he has spoken to my assistant twice and both times he asked her if she, or anyone who she knows, would go to the hotel and have sex with him. I'm sorry to have to tell you this, Victoria,' she went on, 'you can't imagine how embarrassed I feel but I thought you ought to know.'

Embarrassing for her? I mean, I'm trying to be taken seriously as a solo artiste here.

Of course I apologized and she said I really had nothing to apologize for and all the rest of it. But I was stunned. Totally shocked. I just didn't understand. I mean, what was wrong with the guy? The more I thought about it, the more I realized how strangely he'd been acting recently. The David Beckham lookalike outfit was only the tip of the iceberg. He'd taken to talking to me, making conversation. Very unlike him.

On one of the trips to the States he told me how he'd bought these fantastic diet pills and did I want some? He knew I'd had an eating disorder and offering someone who's had an eating disorder diet pills is like offering a recovering alcoholic a bottle of vodka. Fortunately I'd put all that behind me, but you just don't do it. And he'd become forgetful, always nipping off, saying he'd left something somewhere – in the room, in the car. He even said he'd left his Filofax on the plane one time. And this was Mr Totally Organized. What was going on? It was a total mystery.

I decided not to say anything to David. He was having such a good time and I didn't want to spoil it. It could wait till we got back to London. And anyway Mark Niblett was leaving. I was beginning to think it wasn't such a bad thing.

Me and David were only going as far as London while Mark was going on to Manchester to see his father. He'd be down again on Wednesday, he said, with someone he had lined up as his replacement so that I could interview him. I asked him whether I should arrange for security to tide us over the next few days.

'No need,' he said. And laughed.

As soon as we got into Heathrow I called my lawyer. I'd had enough of people leaking private information to the press. I'd had enough of just hoping that whoever it was would go away. I didn't mention my suspicions about Mark Niblett. I'd look bloody silly if I was wrong. And I probably was wrong.

That afternoon we were at the local garden centre buying Brooklyn a little red pedal car and my mobile goes. It's my lawyer. A colleague had put the word out, he said, and dealing through a third party had informed him that someone called Mark Hayes had some information. Another Mark.

'Hayes claims that he knows who the leak is, but it'll cost ten thousand pounds.'

I can hardly believe what I'm hearing. First, it's blackmail; second, how do we know this Mark Hayes knows anything at all?

Naturally, my lawyer said, they had no intention of getting involved financially, adding, however, that it would be prudent to continue talking to him in order to find out as much as possible.

Mark Hayes had implied that he and the leak had been working together and that when the leak found out he'd been sold down the river, he'd be after him, which is why he needed the money – to disappear. And I thought I was melodramatic.

He said the leak is ex-SAS.

Mark Niblett.

It has to be.

I feel my mouth go dry as the lawyer carries on talking. Everything makes sense. It's like a Polaroid getting clearer as you watch it develop.

But proof? What proof did I have?

That evening we went out for a drink with my mum and dad and Dee and Del. They were all chatting away – David was telling them all about LA – but I was just sitting there thinking, thoughts bouncing around inside my head like balls, trying to see any holes in my Mark Niblett Is The Leak theory. And there weren't any, not one, apart from swearing on his children's lives and the fact that he'd signed the confidentiality agreement.

Like my dad said, when I went over it all with him later that night, it's the bloody Marx Brothers: Mark Hayes, Mark the skipman and Mark Niblett.

Next morning, Wednesday, a ring on the doorbell makes me feel sick to my stomach: Mark Niblett and the guy he's bringing as a replacement. I'm really not looking forward to this. He's standing looking totally creepy at the bottom of the stairs as I come down. There was something different about him, his hair was darker and his face was paler. I'd not realized until now that he dyed his hair. He introduces me to Tim. Another Tim.

There's no way I am employing anyone who has had anything to do with Mark Niblett but I have to go through the motions of interviewing him. In fact, Tim seems like a nice guy, but he could be the Archbishop of Canterbury and he wouldn't get the job. I say thank you for coming and I'll let you know.

Tim went out and waited in the car.

Mark came in.

'So, what do you think?'

'He's OK,' I said. 'But to be honest with you, Mark, I'm interviewing people myself this week and in fact I've got someone in mind and with things being quite quiet at the moment I'm thinking maybe it's best – what with your father being ill and everything – if you go after today.'

I was very polite, because you never know. Sandra, David's mum, would be arriving shortly, then they would all go off with Brooklyn shopping or whatever she planned to do for the day, so a cheery wave and I would never have to see the little toe-rag again.

David had a photoshoot for his book, so I was going

to work with him, which was nice for a change, because I didn't have to be anywhere till the afternoon.

So I'm in the studio watching David do his stuff when my mobile rings. My lawyer again.

'Any news?'

'Possibly. Hayes has just told me that you interviewed somebody called Tim this morning and you've sacked Mark Niblett. Is this true?'

My heart gave a lurch. I felt sick. It shouldn't have come as a surprise, but it did. No one else except Mark Niblett knew the name of Tim. I had told no one, not my mum, not my dad, not a single soul in the world, not even David.

I can't remember saying yes, but I must have done.

'Well, we may have a serious problem, Victoria.'

I look over at David looking so cool under the lights and he gives me one of his smiles. I smile back like there are two strings being pulled up at the corners of my mouth, like a puppet.

'So what else did he say?'

'He said Niblett has got documents belonging to you and David. Most worryingly for us, Hayes suggests these include his confidentiality agreement with you.'

It was as if somebody had punched me in the stomach but at the same time turned a light on inside. Suddenly everything was falling into place.

'As you can see, Victoria, whatever the truth of any of this, it would be wise to exercise extreme caution in your dealings with him. By the way, do you know where he went after he left you?'

It was only then that I remembered where Mark Niblett was. With Brooklyn.

I can't believe the nutter I've been trying to avoid is the person who's been looking after my baby. It was like being in a film, a horror film.

All I can think of is Brooklyn. I call David's mum.

'Hi, Sandra, it's Victoria.' Keep calm, keep calm.

The sounds in the background tell me she's still in the car.

'Is Brooklyn all right?'

He's fine, she says. They're about five minutes away from the house.

'Sandra, now listen carefully and hold the phone close to your ear. Can Mark hear what you're saying?'

'I expect so.'

'OK. When you get home, tell Mark to take the rest of the day off, then lock all the doors and shut all the windows. Now if you understand just say "Yes". Did you get all that?'

'Yes.'

'I'll ring you later to explain.'

Then I called my dad. He was on his way to sort something out to do with the builders at the house in Sawbridgeworth, but he turned straight round and went to Chingford to pick up Brooklyn from Sandra's and bring him home.

Over the next few days the lawyers continued to talk with Mark Hayes. One of the things he said was that Mark Niblett had taped eighty-three hours of our conversations and was planning to write a book.

Write a book?

And I'm nearly having a nervous breakdown thinking about what I might have said over the nine months. I mean, occasionally I sound off, have little arguments with people, like we all do. I just thanked God that there were no nasty skeletons in the cupboard. But when I thought about it – why worry about Mark Niblett writing a book when he could barely write a shopping list?

It's hard to remember exactly what happened over the next few days. Everything that this Mark Hayes had said was turning out to be true. As soon as we heard about Mark's confidentiality agreement, Louise checked his file in my dad's snooker room, which is where we keep all that kind of paperwork. There was nothing in it except his CV. Then we called the Spice office but it turned out the copy held there had also disappeared. So no confidentiality forms then. And without a signed confidentiality agreement, the lawyers warned, life was going to be a lot more complicated if Mark Niblett did try writing a book.

Then I had an idea. David still had a couple of days before he joined the England squad for Euro 2000. Mark had asked him for a signed shirt. So we decided that David should go up to Manchester with this shirt, and take with him a release form for the documentary that ITV had been making about David – the sort of form you have to sign if you are used in a documentary, and Mark had appeared in parts of it. And these release forms include a confidentiality clause. So, as the lawyers explained it, whether or not he signed it would be a test of Mark Niblett's good faith.

So that's what happened. First, Mark arranged to meet up at the airport, but then he called to say he had to go to the hospital to talk to the consultant about his father and he suggested meeting somewhere near the hospital.

So David went home, picked up his car and drove to where Mark had said. No sign of him. He keeps calling and saying he'll be there in half an hour and the rest of it. Eventually, Mark Niblett sends a friend of his, John Bagnall. David doesn't give this guy the shirt, but does give him the model release form, which of course was never returned. He then flies back to London. A whole wasted day, bless him.

Mark Hayes, in the meantime, says he's got back things that belong to us but that he'll only hand them over to a member of the family. No police to be involved. In fact, by now the police were majorly in on everything.

Louise agreed to go up to Birmingham to collect whatever it was. She was under strict instructions not to touch anything because the police would need to take fingerprints. Anyway, she met this Mark Hayes in a car park where he handed over a white carrier bag full of our stuff. Neither of them said anything apparently. Then she drove back down to Goff's Oak where I'm waiting to go through it all.

It must have looked a strange sight. Me on the floor in the lounge, going through this bag of David's and my things wearing black leather trousers, black leather top and a pair of pink bridesmaid's gloves that had little buttons all the way up to my elbows – the only gloves we had in the house. It was mainly documents – papers relating to Puffy and Snoop's pedigrees, bank statements, personal pictures, snapshots that might have been lying around, Polaroids from photoshoots, cards and things that I had written.

There were also photocopies of papers that had been in the stolen suitcases, documents relating to David's

Adidas deal and David's internet deal. And an unmarked gold-coloured Kodak CD. That was odd, because I don't have any Kodak CDs. I put it in my personal stereo player and recognized it immediately: it was a copy of the CD that had turned up in the skip/rubbish dump in Heathrow. I had the original upstairs – three tracks with a session singer in Los Angeles that a couple of writers had given to me. Then I remembered how Mark had insisted on picking up the lyric book and CD from Jo, my nail technician, and it was three or four days before he gave them back to me, plenty of time to get them copied.

Meanwhile the lawyers are trying to piece together this whole story and it's getting more and more bizarre every day. Like the fact that Mark Niblett changed his name by deed poll to James Marti in December.

I decide to call Mark Hayes myself, using the approach I was becoming familiar with: 'Hi, this is Victoria Beckham. I just wanted to say thank you for helping, and handing over the things in the carrier bag, I really appreciate it.'

I asked him why he was doing this – and this is where it becomes totally surreal. This Mark Hayes says how he really wants to work for us, that he runs his own security company, although he was actually a physiotherapist.

'So I'd love to be head of your security now that Mark's not with you. I figured if I helped you, you might employ me.'

Ple-eee-se. But I lead him on to think that might be a possibility, and we're getting quite chatty.

I said was there anything else he could tell me? And he said yes.

'You've got some vibrators in your flat in a drawer in your bedroom.'

And I just laughed, because a couple of years back Melanie B had bought all of us in the band a pack of vibrators for Christmas, the idea being that we'd open them in front of our families and be very embarrassed. Her idea of a joke. And in fact it was quite funny at the time, which was why I'd laughed.

'I shouldn't laugh if I were you,' he said. 'And don't whatever you do use them.'

'Look here, mate,' I said. 'I'm married to David Beckham, I don't need to use them. They were given to me as a Christmas present.'

'Victoria,' he went on, 'how do you think I know this? I hate to tell you but Mark has got keys to your house.'

That was it. I didn't think it could get any worse but it just had. The flat was my home. Someone – people – had been in there doing goodness knows what. I was in London when I heard this, and when I put the phone down the idea of going back there made me feel sick. It was like some terrible nightmare. What's going to happen next? If Mark Hayes is right, Niblett's writing a book, he's taping my conversations, he's going through my underwear drawer and it's getting worse and worse and worse. What was he trying to do to me? I was a complete wreck.

I tried to think about what a terrible life Mark Niblett must have had to need to do something like this. But it was hard not to just hate him. I tried to do that thing I did when I was little, close my eyes, put him on a boat and watch it sail away towards the horizon. But it didn't work. I couldn't help feeling that part of the fault was mine. After all, I had employed him in the first place. How could my instincts have been so wrong? I couldn't believe I had put my trust in someone who had let me down like this. Why? What had I ever done?

It's the kind of thing you see in films. But in real life? Could it really happen in real life? I'd always treated him well. What had I done to make him do this?

23 great timing

Throughout my life I've always been able to sleep. But that changed when the kidnap threats started. Now any noise inside or outside the house would wake me up. And I'd just lie in bed, my head buzzing, my heart racing. Now me and David never went anywhere if it meant getting in a car with someone I didn't know. And as for Brooklyn, I watched him as fearfully as if every moment was his last. I knew I should be enjoying every second with him, but how can you enjoy anything when you are knotted up with fear? The only escape was to throw myself into work.

While David was in France with the England squad for Euro 2000 I started a new project. In early May, Nancy Phillips at the Spice office had been contacted by a guy called Nick Raphael, an A&R man from Arista Records in London. He wondered if I would be interested in singing on a track with Dane Bowers, formerly of Another Level, a follow-up to his hit single 'Buggin'' earlier in the year.

Nancy put the idea to my A&R man, Paul McDonald, and he and everyone at Virgin loved the idea. And so did I. Because I did have a problem: all the other Spice Girls either had solo albums out or were about to release them whereas I had only just started work on mine. Yet if I didn't get something out there soon, by the time the album was ready, it would be Victoria who? But there was no point in releasing a single from my album if the album itself wouldn't be in the shops for a year. I knew I wanted to do something, and this could be it.

Nancy sent me over a copy of the track when I got back from Tuscany – it wasn't perfect but nothing that couldn't be changed and I really liked it. The song was called 'Out of Your Mind' and what made it so exciting as a one-off single for me was that it was like nothing the Spice Girls had ever done and like nothing any of the other girls had done individually. It was dance, not pop.

Dance is the music of clubs, not music of the charts. Or hadn't been until very recently when one or two tracks had escaped the dance charts and crossed over into mainstream pop. 'Buggin'' was one of those.

Dance music had been around since the late eighties, but it's only in the last few years that it's become heard outside clubs. Dance tracks are made using synthesized sound, and they're so quick to make, styles are changing all the time. I first went clubbing when I was fourteen at the Tottenham Ritzy; then it was mostly techno, electronic dance music with no vocals at all. Then there was house and drum and bass, then garage came in from America which added vocals with more of a soul feel. What Dane and the True Steppers were doing was UK garage.

Conventional dance music focuses on what's called

Photoshoot in New York, trying to hide the fact that I was pregnant – not easy when you're throwing up every few minutes.

The first time in my life I was ever proud of having a big tummy.

After Brooklyn was born I was so hungry I'd eat anything.

At Elton's after the second kidnap threat. I was so terrified of losing Brooklyn I never let him out of my sight.

What a little tiger.

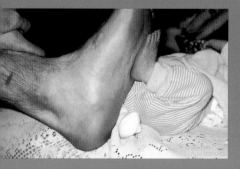

My two boys.

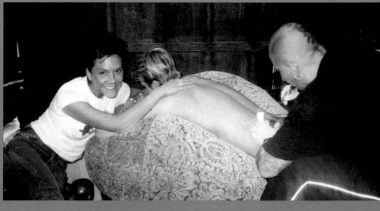

At Mel B's, getting scarred for life.

Tyler giving David his all-or-nothing haircut. Who looks the more confident?

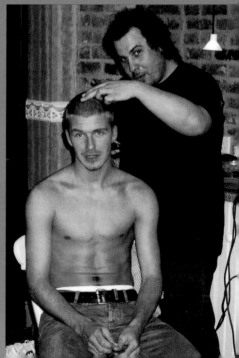

Shock horror. Personally I love it.

Surprise party for David's 25th birthday at Nancy Berry's house in Tuscany.

My mum, without whom . . .

Still in a state of shock at the post-Brits party,
March 2000, with Louise and Christian.

My white knight, Mark Niblett.

'Oh my God, it's Posh Spice' – 'Oh my God, it's Britney Spears.'

Los Angeles, recording 'I Wish' for my solo album.

Working Mummy.

A future footballer with rhythm. That's a first.

four to the floor, which means four basic drum beats. UK garage only has two major drum beats on the bass line – more of a two-step thing (True Steppers: a play on two-step). This makes it sound a bit syncopated, which gives it more of a skippy feel, like early Beatles if you like, except they used real instruments. In other words, as my dad would say, it swings, which four to the floor music doesn't and that's what makes it much more interesting to dance to, which is why in the summer of 2000 everyone was saying how UK garage was going to be 'the biggest British musical export since the heyday of Brit pop'.

Yes, there were bits of the demo track that I thought could do with improvement, not so much the melody, but the lyrics were a bit repetitive. But that's one thing I've always been quite good on: knowing when something doesn't quite work and then coming up with the answer.

Before I agreed to anything, however, I said I would have to meet them all. I'd met Dane at the MOBOs six months before and liked him.

It was after I had presented an award with Maxi Priest and was back in the audience with David. David's view at the time was that boybands were totally up their own arses, thought they were bloody chocolates, good enough to eat. But when Dane actually came up and said that he and his dad were big Manchester United fans and his dad would never forgive him if he didn't come up and say Hi, that kind of changed his opinion. It was clear that he was a really bright guy and not up his own bum at all. And I had always thought Another Level were great and had done a lot for British R&B.

But that was just a five-minute chat, and mainly me listening to Dane talking football to David. Recording the song is the easy bit; at this stage a few hours in the studio would do it. It's the weeks and weeks of promotion that take it out of you and if we didn't get on, it wouldn't work.

When I walked into the Roundhouse Studios that afternoon, I was so nervous. I probably didn't look it: the pop star, shades, chauffeur-driven to the door. But the worlds of pop and garage are very different. Pop was my job if you like. Garage is what I danced to. It didn't help my nervousness that when I told Louise I was off to meet the True Steppers, she went completely wild, OH-MY-GOD-ing and saying, you better put something different on.

The True Steppers are two DJ/producers Andy and Johnny. They look the ultimate in cool but in fact are really sweet guys who would never dream of forgetting their mums' birthdays. Andy Lysandrou is quite round with no hair, Johnny Lisners is tall and thin with bleached, cropped hair, earrings and a few tattoos – they call him the skinny rocker. They are incredibly different and yet really complement each other. Andy's quite subdued, thinks everything over before he does anything. Johnny is totally wired, all Yeah, Yeah, Yeah we're gonna do this, we're gonna do that, like he's on fire all the time.

Once you get to know them, they're complete puppy dogs, but on that first afternoon in May 2000 I was just a bag of nerves. One Spice Girl faced with a room full of cool DJ-type dudes.

And it was like, What the hell do I wear? I didn't

want to turn up all pop starry with my tits out, so in the end I went really street, a pair of big, baggy blue jeans, a tight little T-shirt, denim jacket with the collar up, blue NY Yankees hat and Timberlands. But I still had my Posh Spice Louis Vuitton rucksack, for luck.

As I pushed open the door and walked in, saying 'Hi, guys' brightly and looking around, I realized I was the only woman; this was a room full of smoke and men. And as much as I knew they were just sitting there trying to be cool and not impressed because Posh Spice is about to walk in, it was really intimidating. So they're all sitting there doing and saying nothing, except for Dane who's walking about showing off his vocal ability – he has a really good voice.

As well as Andy and Johnny and Dane there were the guys working the desks. Spoony, a big-time DJ with Dreem Teem, Nick Raphael, Dane's A&R man, so slight you feel he'd fall over if you bumped into him, but with so much energy he's like a bullet coming out of a gun. I got to know him really well over the next months and he's just great: same attitude to work as me, always on the phone, when he wants something done, wants it done right away, doesn't want to wait for anything. Ambitious, really excitable. He can really visualize things and make things happen. And he really shared a dream with me and Dane on this.

Anyway, I said what I thought about the track, and the changes I would make if it was up to me. And Dane and me sat down and reworked the lyrics and some of the melodies. And that was cool. Everything was so easy and natural that before I knew what had happened, they said, OK, into the booth and let's do it. I still hadn't made a decision, but then I thought, you know what? I'll go in, sing it and if I don't like it, scrap it. In fact it was quite a difficult song for me to sing because it wasn't in my register and I hadn't ever done anything like it before.

So after the session I went back and joined the boys for a drink and I was still feeling quite shy and reserved, but I could hear everyone getting really excited. I told them that I still hadn't made up my mind. But I think I had. And I remember catching Dane's eye as he prowled round the room in his big baggy trousers and big baggy coat and a really badly shaped cap. I already saw that me and him had a very similar Ali G sense of humour that I could see was lost on some of the others. Yeah, I thought. This could work. This could work.

For the next seven days I ummed and aahed about whether to do it. Because the truth was I still couldn't believe that anything I did on my own would be of interest to anyone, let alone worth spending hard-earned money on.

The success of the Spice Girls should have changed all that. But it hadn't. In actual fact I think it made it worse. In the time since we had been together I'd heard the same thing: I was the useless one, only there to make up the numbers. I had always longed to do something on my own, but you need confidence to stand up by yourself on a stage. The last time I'd felt totally confident about being up there on my own was before I went to Laine's. When the audience are with you and everything is going right being on stage alone can be like nothing else on earth – you feel connected with everyone: other performers waiting in the wings, the audience, everybody – which is why it's such a drug and why people go on performing just for the chance to get that high. But against this is the fear that something terrible will happen: that you'll fall, will forget your lines – when things go wrong the stage can be the most terrifying place on earth, when everyone will see who you really are. Imagine that you're standing on a street and find everyone's looking at you and you then realize that you don't have any clothes on. It's like that.

The anxiety that stopped me saying yes straight away was probably also a form of defence. If I said yes, and they said no, I might not be able to handle it. A week later I heard that the True Steppers were booked in to the Whitfield Street studios where we had done most of the Spice Girls album. 'Out of Your Mind' was going to be properly recorded and mastered. I taught Brooklyn to do a high-five.

Any doubts I still had disappeared within the first few minutes. They are all such nice guys and so talented. And this time there was another girl, Jo Charrington, Dane's manager, though I didn't really get to know her properly until we were on the road. Majorly mad, never off the phone, but majorly efficient and I really liked her.

Before we began Andy said to me, 'Look, is there anything else you'd like to change?' And I'm about to say, well, there's this bit where it sounds as if the speakers blow and there's a kind of thud, when they start going on about 'this really wicked bit in the track' and I realize that 'this really wicked bit' is the one bit I was going to say I really hated. And there they all were, going, 'Wicked,

wicked, man, drum and bass', and I just thought, OK, I'd better shut up and stop being so poppy and dweeby here. They know what they're doing.

And Nick Raphael their A&R guy was being so complimentary. About me, about my ideas, about my singing, for goodness sake. I couldn't believe it. It was like a cartoon where I'm looking around wondering who he's talking about. Here was this guy who really knew his stuff and for the first time in my life here was someone who believed in Posh Spice – no, not in Posh Spice, in Victoria Beckham. Someone who believed in Victoria Beckham.

And I remember thinking this was what it must feel like when David scores a goal, surrounded by other members of the team, hugging you and wanting to be part of it. To feel that someone has total faith in you.

Anyway, that afternoon suddenly everything felt so right. We talked about tactics, how it would be played first in the clubs and picked up by pirate radio stations, but with no mention of my name (this in actual fact did happen and I was extremely flattered when I found out that the betting was that the unknown woman on the new True Steppers track was Madonna). Then Dane said how wouldn't it be great if we did Party in the Park? Every summer the Prince's Trust has a big open-air concert in Hyde Park. And that was the moment for me when everything crystallized.

If we do it, I told them, it's got to be done properly. And I explained what I meant by properly. Loads of dancers, loads of pyrotechnics. Fantastic costumes. I was a right madam: I want this, I want that. But I knew that was the only way it could be done. I had so much to prove and Victoria Beckham wasn't going to be some scaled-down Spice Girl. I was a dancer so we'd give them dancing like they'd never seen. Not a hint of a totter, not a hint of a heel – I saw it already: great biker boots, leather, lots of gold, silver – a space-age look. I'd get Priscilla Samuels to do the choreography. (It later turned out that Priscilla had worked with Dane when he was with Another Level and Dane felt just like I did about her.)

I wanted to shock. With everyone expecting a long dress and a ballad I wanted people to not believe it was me up there. I wanted to do something that no one would expect. I could feel the excitement bubbling, charging through my veins.

'All this is going to cost money,' I pointed out. But I think Nick Raphael recognized a fellow perfectionist. He knew exactly where I was coming from and that afternoon he got it straight away. Over the next few months, Nick, me and Dane really shared a dream. The song was Dane's. I had helped make it better but I would never want to take anything away from what he and Andy and Johnny had done. What I could do was get the rest of it right. I knew there were going to be a lot of cynical people out there waiting for us to fall flat on our faces.

I hadn't danced for nearly two years and I had writers coming over from the States to work on my solo album that I couldn't cancel. But there are moments in your life where you just have to take everything a notch higher and go for it.

From then on until Party in the Park on 8 July I would be literally working from dawn till midnight,

429

taking Brooklyn with me whenever I could. Brooklyn loved being in the studio – the loud music and the dancing. He used to dance with us.

Every morning I was rehearsing with Priscilla, Dane and the dancers in Camden, then a car would take me across London to Barnes to work on my album. Then it was an hour and a half back to my mum and dad's house. I rarely got in before ten at night when David would have supper ready. I was exhausted, but I didn't care. I thrived on it and felt better than I had done since before I had Brooklyn.

So often in relationships one of you is up and the other is down, but no two people could have been so in sync as me and David that June. He was as up as I was. Everything was coming together in France – the England manager, Kevin Keegan, was such a nice guy that the atmosphere at the camp was totally different to how it had been with Glenn Hoddle at the World Cup two years before. And Euro 2000 was the chance David had been waiting for to put all that behind him. I knew he wanted me to go to the opening match but I was under such pressure, rehearsing with Dane and the dancers in the mornings, and working with songwriters in the afternoons. And then there was Brooklyn to think about.

The paranoia that I had been feeling over nine months wasn't about to disappear overnight. It would take time – and if I'm totally honest I don't think I will ever be quite free of it completely. David understood all this.

But then driving in to work that Friday morning I was listening to Capital and they had picked up on a story in the *Daily Mail* about how I was snubbing the other England wives by not going. All the media was so bloody negative. On television they kept showing footage of poor Gareth Southgate missing that penalty at Euro 1996 and shots of David getting the red card at the World Cup and asking is he going to do it again? Pictures of Alan Shearer saying is he too old? Are Paul Ince's injuries going to play up? And I'm thinking, hang on a minute, shouldn't they be showing clips of all these fantastic English players, scoring their goals, saying England can do it? What is it about this place? I need to live in some patriotic country. I was just praying that David didn't have to take a penalty.

Since getting rid of Mark we'd hardly been in the papers at all. If ever proof were needed that he was the leak, as far as I'm concerned that was it.

But now that David was a 'legitimate target', why not bring in his wife, too? The *Daily Star* said research showed that foreign players were actually encouraged to have sex with their wives before big matches as it made them play better. So this Dr Whateverhisnameis says how Posh needs to go and give her husband a good seeing-to. How tacky is that?

So I decided I'd go. I'd show them. But it would be very much head down, don't tell anybody, because, you know what? This is David's day. And anyway if the press got pictures it would be what's she wearing? what colour's her hair? how much does she weigh today? does she look thin? where did she wear that before? why is she wearing that again? So that's why I went secretly. But once I was at the airport away from photographers, then I'd sit with the wives and I'd go on the coach like everybody else. I called Dane and told him I wouldn't be at Monday's dance rehearsal. Football fan that he is he said, 'I never thought you would be. Have a great time.'

I didn't have a great time. All the other wives were done up in their short skirts and because David said dress down I'm there in my jeans and looking a right bloody mess. The horror of that walk back from the VIP lounge to our seats was something that will live with me for ever. I was literally terrified. The second time in a year that I thought I was going to be killed. And then when David told me that the press had a picture of him giving one finger to the crowd as he made his way down the tunnel, I just remember the total bewilderment. What had we done to deserve this? How could we go on with the whole world hating us?

Then when the *Mail* ran the headline – Is This Man a National Liability – I didn't think things could get any worse.

But then came the phone call from my lawyer telling me that the book Mark Hayes had said Mark Niblett was going to write was in fact going to be written by Andrew Morton, the man who wrote *Diana: Her True Story*. Mark had apparently spent weeks talking with him in London. And that's what had happened to the hours and hours of tapes that Mark Hayes said Mark Niblett had recorded secretly. He had sold them to Andrew Morton as part of this book deal. He had also kept a diary.

None of us could believe that this could happen, that someone could buy bits of our life like this. I felt totally betrayed. Luckily we had no terrible skeletons in our cupboard but the next worry was that Mark Niblett would end up saying anything he felt like, inventing things to justify whatever fat fee he was being paid.

The only hope of stopping it, the lawyers said, was to take him to court. The fact that we didn't have a signed confidentiality form was going to make things more difficult.

By an incredible stroke of luck, a week or so later Louise went to the flat above the garage at Rowneybury House where Mark had lived. In a cupboard she spotted a blank confidentiality form in an empty box of Teach Yourself French tapes. At first she thought it was just a blank one that Mark had left. He was supposed to use them whenever we had to employ temporary staff, like for Brooklyn's party, for example. Then she noticed that it had a fax transmission date on it. The 3rd of November 1999, right at the time when we had got rid of the second security guard and when we got both of them to sign confidentiality forms. And although there was nothing on it, no writing that you could see, she happened to notice the indentation of a signature. Whose was it? Mark's. The lawyers said send it to them immediately. They then gave it to the forensic people.

The lawyers weren't very hopeful, but I just said do whatever it takes to stop him. I was so angry. So, so angry. To think that this man who I'd given time off to see his father in Manchester was all the time gathering information for Morton's book, going over everything he could remember about the time he worked for us. There isn't a word in the English language that could describe what I feel about him.

He was arrested on 23 June in Warrington. The *Daily Mirror* described him as 'personal bodyguard and close confidant of the couple'.

It turned out that the police had been investigating

him about the death threats. He was arrested 'on suspicion of inciting threats to kill'.

After that, people started telling me things that Mark Niblett had done and said, but they hadn't thought they could tell me at the time. It probably wouldn't have made any difference. By then we all believed that none of us were safe unless he, Mark Niblett, was there to protect us. I remember once my brother saying how he thought Mark was out of order and I'd done nothing.

It was one afternoon when Christian brought his new girlfriend, Lucy, to the house; Mark had been sitting watching television in the lounge with his 'bits' hanging out of his shorts, Christian said. And it wasn't the first time it had happened. But I'd chosen to ignore it. I mean what was I to say? 'I can't help noticing your meat and two veg are hanging out, Mark. Could you kindly put them away?'

It had started after that trip to Elton's place in the South of France in September when he had begun wearing shorts. But it hadn't stopped when we got back to England. Even though it was a cold autumn, he just wore a fleece on top. But I was so frightened of upsetting him, of risking losing the gladiator who would dive in front of a bullet to protect me and Brooklyn, I was literally terrified he'd leave. I might not have liked his dress sense, but he was really good at his job, wasn't he? And wasn't that all that mattered?

He may have made me think he was good at his job, but in actual fact he wasn't. I know now that true professional bodyguards are taught not to personalize relationships with their employers. I also found out that if the police had been confident of his ability, they could have issued him with a gun on the quiet, but they didn't. Lastly, I found out that anybody who claimed to be ex-SAS wasn't. And why did he sell out to Andrew Morton if he was so good? Because, make no mistake, he'll never work again in the security business. He sold out because he was past it. To be taken seriously as a bodyguard you need to be able to hit the ground running. He could barely keep up with me and David when we were strolling through Beverly Hills. And as for those glasses – without them he was blinder than I am. I don't have to wear glasses all the time – he did.

The news about Mark Niblett being arrested came one afternoon when I was over at the Olympic Studios complex in Barnes, working on my solo album with Andrew Frampton. I was just getting a coffee in the canteen when I bumped into Paul Wilson and Andy Watkins the producers also known as Absolute.

I hadn't approached them about working with me because when Geri left the group and wanted to do her own album a lot of people who'd worked with the Spice Girls felt they had to choose, if you like. And Absolute went with Geri.

So it's all a bit awkward.

'Oh, what are you doing here?'

'Oh, I'm working on my album. What are you doing?'

'Oh, we're working on Geri's next album.'

'Oh, yeah? How's it going?'

'Oh, good. In fact Geri's coming in later.'

And I sensed they were expecting me to say, Oh God, don't let me see her. But I didn't.

'Oh. It would be really nice to see her. So how's the album coming along?'

'Oh, good. No big-time ballads. But then you know Geri, and you're not going to find Geri doing a big ballad, are you?'

Anyway, I'm in Andrew's studio singing one of my songs and David's there with Brooklyn and another writer over from America, Steve Kipner. And Geri bursts into the studio, and the booth where you actually sing has got sliding doors, and she pushes back the doors and comes in and throws her arms round me.

'So,' she said, after the So-how-have-you-been? stuff. 'Your first album, eh? It's really great that you're having a go. Don't let anyone tell you that you're no good. I know it's easy for me to talk because I've had three number 1s and that does change things, but don't let anyone put you down.'

Then she rushed over and tried to pick up Brooklyn, who of course didn't know her from Adam. And he completely froze. And David was as stiff as a board. I was completely cold. We were like a family from Madame Tussaud's.

Even though none of us were saying anything, she carried on like a clockwork toy.

'God, Tor, you're really thin, though not as thin as they say, but still really thin. Now make sure you watch your weight.'

Finally she got the message.

'I really ought to go now, I feel I'm intruding. Wouldn't want to do that now would I?'

And she just waved goodbye and left.

★

The 8th of July was not only Party in the Park, it was also my brother Christian's twenty-first birthday. Christian is not into the celebrity thing at all so that people are often surprised to learn that I have a brother. He hates all the publicity and he's always been the shy one.

When we were little the three of us used to stick together like glue. People used to come up and say, 'Hello, little boy, what's your name?' And me or Louise would always go, 'Christian'. We always spoke for him and bossed him about. In many ways he deserves a medal for putting up with us.

Even now Christian keeps himself to himself. He's so not like me and Louise. He's very organized and tidy-minded, one of those people who books his summer holiday at Christmas and always remembers to keep a supply of Alka-Seltzer in the bathroom cabinet.

When I joined the Spice Girls he was only fifteen, a boy. Even when I met David he wasn't much more grown up – I remember how the only thing that really interested him was what car David had. But by the time I came back from the tax-year-out the baby of the family had become a man.

He doesn't earn a lot of money – he's not ambitious but he's not lazy either and he has never asked me for a pound and never takes anything for granted. He'll make someone a fantastic husband some day.

It still surprises me how different we all are when you think that we have the same parents. When Louise was younger she looked like a little Shirley Temple, all red curls and dimples and smiles. She was a right mischievous little madam and was always getting into trouble at school, totally hyperactive, always the one to go out and have fun whereas all I've ever seemed to do is work – Victoria, the steady sensible one.

There are times when Louise must be sick of the sight of me because I'm not so thick-skinned that I can't imagine what it must be like, one sister always getting the attention, the other sister who gets hardly any attention at all. And people are so insensitive. Like the other day I bumped into the mother of a friend of Louise's who's getting married and this woman said to me, 'Are you coming to the wedding?', and I said, 'Yes, so's Louise.' But before I could finish what I was saying, she interrupted and said, 'Yes, but are you and David coming?' And she walked away. And when that happens you just feel terrible.

But on the surface at least I think Louise quite enjoys being Posh Spice's sister. I know her well enough to know that she would not like to be me. Louise likes having fun too much to be a workaholic. In fact she goes to far more celebrity parties than me and David do, because when I'm working I don't have a social life in the conventional sense. My family is my social life. But it can be a bit annoying when I'm really tired and I come in at eleven totally exhausted and I say, 'Where's Louise?' and my mum says, 'Out.' I do find myself thinking, God, I'm working my butt off, but everyone else is out having a good time. But the truth is, that's how I like it.

I think of the three of us I have probably changed the most. Not because of the money or anything like that, but because being a Spice Girl gave me the confidence to be myself. I was always sensible and careful but I wasn't naturally a moody cow. I realize now it was just a defence mechanism that came from being spotty and not having friends.

Four days before Party in the Park was our first wedding anniversary. Great timing. Instead of going away for a really long holiday (which means two weeks) as I had planned, it looked like now we'd only be able to take a week off after Party in the Park. There was a Spice Girl video shoot scheduled for our double-A-single 'Holler' and 'Let Love Lead the Way'.

Everything seemed to be happening at the same time. 'Out of Your Mind' was scheduled for release on 14 August when David would be back in Manchester, but most of the hard work of promotion came before the release date when David was with me.

Capital and Kiss FM took up the song earlier than we expected and were soon playing it big time – which, as much as it's positive, made things really hard because it wouldn't be in the shops for six weeks – all that air time and no one would be able to buy it. As problems go, it's a nice one to have but somehow we had to keep the momentum up. First we had to make the video.

It was Jake Nava, the director of the video, who said he wanted me with long hair. He wanted this Mad Max futuristic look with a wind machine that had my hair billowing out. We had already done the cover for the single and some other promotional stuff like magazines and I just had a spiked-up version of the cut I'd had since before the Spice Girls tour when I'd got Jennie to get rid of the bob.

So Tyler, who I'd met at the MOBOs when he was doing Mel B's hair and who now did mine, got yards of it on strips. The way it worked, he would make a parting, cut off a couple of inches of this strip and stick it on to my scalp. It took hours. Literally. It didn't really hurt, just felt cold for a few seconds, but it was incredibly boring.

It was when we were shooting the video that Brooklyn first saw me with long hair. At least he saw a woman with long hair that he didn't know. He looked very strangely at me. Dane even called me Ghetto Spice, which made a change from Moody Spice. But there was no denying that the long hair did suit the costumes and when the wind machine got going it looked great.

Our stylist was a guy called Wale Adeyemi. It was Dane who brought him in, he'd done stuff for Another Level. And I knew he'd worked with Missy Elliot and Puff Daddy but Wale is a pure south London. I'm not one of those people that can hand everything over to a stylist but Wale was great, full of really good ideas yet totally unpushy and always open to suggestions.

We shot a promotional interview during a break in the video shoot and so we were in full costume and make-up and, in my case, hair. So after people saw that, everyone wanted the long hair look. It was such a pain. Take the Ant and Dec shows on Saturday mornings on ITV – *SM:TV* which then becomes *CD:UK*. To be ready for ten o'clock, me and Tyler had to be at the studio at 6.30, which meant leaving my mum's at 5.30. They had to be redone every time. I could have said, no, let's just go back to the short hairstyle, and saved myself hours every day. But I knew it was right for the song.

I must be terrible to work with, because just like

my dad I'm convinced I know best. I'm not saying I am the best, I'm not arrogant in that way, or at least I hope not. It's just that I want to oversee everything, so if things go wrong I can't blame anyone afterwards except myself. Whether we're in a TV studio or a photographic studio, I want to know beforehand what the lighting's like, what the camera shots are like, what the dancers are wearing, what I'm wearing. It's just that I've been working in studios and on stage for quite a while now so I know what shapes work best for me. I know what looks good. I know what fabric will work under what light. I know how I want to look, I know how I want to sound, I know how I want to be marketed. I worry about all these things and always will do if it's my neck on the block, because I believe that it shows: the costumes, the dancing, the performance, the music, the sheer professionalism.

And that all takes time, and that's why I'm so busy.

In the old days you released a record and then waited for it to climb the charts, only very rarely did a record go straight to the top, whereas now you can often get to number 1 the first week of release. In reality the record companies usually know by the second day after release whether it's going to be number 1 on the following Sunday.

Which is why I was determined to give it my all. Geri had made number 1, so had Melanie B, so had Melanie C. Emma was the only Spice Girl not to because she had been up against Geri and Geri being Geri was determined to win. Not content to see whose song the fans genuinely preferred, Geri had conveniently found love in the arms of Chris Evans. Or at least publicity. That week it was wall-to-wall Geri. Emma didn't stand a chance and only made it to number 2.

I say only, but in fact that is ridiculous. Sometimes we forget in this industry that to get anywhere in the top 5 is an incredible achievement.

Me and Dane weren't up against Geri, but around the time we made the video we found out we would be up against an Italian DJ called Spiller and a song that had been played in clubs for months and months called 'Groovejet (If This Ain't Love)'. It had been on compilation albums, as these club dance tracks often are, but hadn't been released as a single. Until now, when the record company realized they were sitting on a winner.

Like 'Out of Your Mind', 'Spiller' – as we always referred to it – was a dance record. The vocal on 'Spiller' was sung by an unknown. It had been around for so long that I knew it, and in fact quite liked it.

We were told by everyone that we didn't stand a chance if we released ours the same week. But what could we do? We couldn't go back a week because Mel C was there and there'd been a verbal agreement between the record companies that we wouldn't go up against her. Put it forward a week and we'd be up against Madonna. (As it turns out, we sold 40,000 more than Madonna in the first week.) There was nothing we could do, except give it a hundred and twenty per cent.

At least no one was expecting a number 1.

The weeks of rehearsal were nearly over and I was really scared. We'd done the routine for the video, we'd done it for *Top of the Pops* but in front of a crowd of a hundred thousand people was different. As for promotion – radio interviews, print interviews, television interviews – it was wheel 'em in, wheel 'em out, I was so wired; how David put up with me I don't know.

On 4 July: last year it was our wedding. This year a day like all the others, non-stop promotion. That night we drove an hour north of London to a health club which was my surprise for David. An anniversary treat. And we had everything there was time for, facials, body massage, the lot. The next day was David's surprise for me – dinner by candlelight on the terrace of our new house – a bit of a mad idea as it was still a building site and would be for months. He had to buy everything, a heated trolley, table and chairs, white tablecloth, candelabra, bowls and plates and chopsticks. As he didn't have time to do everything himself, my mum and Louise got to pick up the furniture. It was only when they got it back to the house and undid the boxes that they found out it was self-assembly. So they called Dee and Del to help them. It was like *Challenge Anneka*, my mum said, running up and down the stairs with bits of table, spring rolls and champagne. But it was worth it. The weather stayed fine and we sat on the terrace lit by fifty candles which kept going out, but it was so romantic. Just us, looking out over our garden and imagining what it would be like when it was finished.

Three days later was grey and the weather forecast was for worse to come. Storms over England. Although we would be under cover the crowds wouldn't. Would anybody even bother to come?

Although I was as nervous as I can ever remember being, even I had to laugh when the concert started with Travis singing 'Why Does It Always Rain on Me?' In fact the rain stayed off, but the clouds got darker all the time.

Hair and make-up had been in the Mandarin Hotel in Knightsbridge and I didn't really see anybody else until we arrived backstage.

Watching the bands before us go on, I was just so pleased we had gone for an entirely different look: it seemed like all the girls – from Steps to Destiny's Child – were wearing scarf tops.

The band immediately before us was Savage Garden, who are two Australian guys. By this time I was so nervous I had even stopped going to the toilet. I was completely empty of everything. Through the panic, I heard odd lines of the song they were singing which said things like you can't appreciate love till you've been hurt, it's only when you lose something that you know what you had, and that your family is worth more than anything else . . .

Then it's us. First Dane sings 'Buggin''. All I can see is wires and cables and holes in the stage and all I'm thinking is, Don't fall over. With Dane and all his dancers and me and all mine, plus Andy and Johnny, there are about twenty-four of us on this stage, which is a lot of people in a comparatively small space, particularly when you haven't had a chance to rehearse, which none of the bands had.

Then I walk out and I'm hit by this huge wall of sound. The stage is about ten feet above the ground and I look out over thousands and thousands of heads. I have never performed in front of so many people before, even with the Spice Girls. And there among the photographers in a semicircle just beneath the stage is a face

I know so well, smiling at me, that wonderful smile. He gives me a wink, puts the camcorder to his eye and the music begins.

24 time out with the wizard of oz

Victoria Beckham, wearing a white futuristic leather outfit, goldy-coloured belt, a little bit of glitter, long flowing hair, and a bar code on her arm – which Karin, who as always did my make-up, had cut off a plastic bag – was front page news next morning, from the *Observer* to the *News of the World*. And most of it was really positive, except for one or two who wrote that I mimed.

Of course I bloody mimed. This was a dance track and to make it sound like a dance track you have electronic effects on your voice, every single dance track has that – including 'Spiller'. And who's going to be able to sing live sounding like that? And it's not exactly new. Joe Meek – who signed my dad – invented reverb recording John Leyton in the bathroom of his flat in Holloway ('Johnny Remember Me', 1961, you pop pickers). Now they do it on computer consoles. And what about Cher? Even Madonna on her latest album has effects on her voice.

Also I knew when I first did this song that I wanted to have lots of dancing and if you look at great artistes like Janet Jackson, Michael Jackson, even Britney Spears, they don't sing live when they're hoofing it up. Why didn't they just come out and say what they meant, which was POSH SPICE CAN'T SING? I sang live on every single show I did with the Spice Girls – 104 of them. I'm fed up with having to say, 'Yes, I can sing.' But my album will prove that.

They did it because they couldn't criticize anything else about our performance, and the performance to me is the most important thing. It's not just a question of standing up there like a stick of wood in front of a mike. A performance was what the fans wanted and as far as I was concerned, a performance was what they were going to get.

Because that's what I am, a performer, a trained dancer, and I've never been able to show that before.

At around 8.30 me and David were back at the Mandarin Hotel having a drink with Dane and his then girlfriend waiting for my family to turn up. We were all going to the Mirabelle to celebrate Christian's twenty-first birthday. And the Corrs were there. And that week they were actually number 1, so me and David went over to say congratulations and have a drink with them. We left when my family arrived at about 9.30.

The next morning, I get a call from Caroline McAteer, my PR. 'So,' she says, 'bit of a rowdy night last night, was it?'

And I say, 'What do you mean?' She told me she'd been up all night dealing with this story that the newspapers had got hold of saying how me and David had stayed the night at the Mandarin and how we were so rowdy and throwing things around the room, how all the guests were complaining that we were having a party and how we got thrown out. She'd told them it was complete rubbish and so managed to keep it out of the papers.

Caroline works so hard. She used to work for Versace and is rather trendy and is very good about that side of things. What I would do without her I don't know. It doesn't matter if it's me or David or my parents or Louise. Anything to do with our family and she'll do anything to help. When Louise started to get modelling and TV work, Caroline helped her with stylists and contracts.

But why were they making up stories like this? They just totally had it in for me. I couldn't bear it. What made it worse was that me, David and Brooklyn had been due to fly to Majorca for a week's holiday the next day. Everything had been booked under false names, but the day before we'd had to tell the airline it was us — it's the law — and somebody there had decided to make a couple of hundred pounds by just lifting the phone.

Alan Edwards had called and told me the press had all the details. He's another one who deserves a medal for everything he does for us. And it's not only when things go wrong. When it came to my solo album, Alan was supportive right from the start. Whatever we pay him it's not enough. (Only kidding, Alan.)

So I cancelled. Because this wasn't a private villa we were staying at, it was Richard Branson's hotel La Residencia. Any photographer with the price of a meal could just walk in through the gates and make our lives a misery.

By chance we'd been in Harrods earlier in the day

buying champagne to give the dancers and Mohamed Al Fayed had said that if ever we needed to get away we could always stay at his place in St Tropez.

I called him.

Two days later we were in St Tropez, but nothing was going right. For a start our flight had been cancelled – we'd had to spend a night at Heathrow. Great.

Mohamed Al Fayed has about five houses in St Tropez and we were staying at one he uses for guests, and it was great – chefs, everything you could want, except somewhere safe to put a baby by the pool. So while I'm on the phone to the lawyers for about two hours every day going over affidavits by everyone involved in the Mark Niblett case, David is rushing around saving Brooklyn from knocking himself out on glass tables or drowning.

On our second day Mohamed Al Fayed called to say that his children really wanted to meet us, and would we like to have dinner on his yacht? The yacht was about as child-friendly as the house – his own children are much older. With Brooklyn careering about like a tornado, we couldn't relax for a minute.

I was so tired, I just wanted everything to stop. I remember once being on a roller-coaster at Alton Towers and hating it and sobbing that I wanted it to stop and I wanted to get off. It was the same now. There I was, one of the richest and most successful women in the country, so the newspapers said, and I couldn't even have a bloody holiday. The next morning I called my mum and just cried and cried. I later found out that she was at the Acropolis in Athens when I phoned. I was too upset even to ask where she was. 'Just get back home as soon as you can,' she said. 'Sandra and me will sort something out with Brooklyn, don't you worry.' Louise and Liberty would be at home, so Bibbin would have Bibbi to play with.

So that's what we did. I was supposed to be doing a photoshoot with the Spice Girls the following week. I called Nancy at the office and she could tell what a state I was in.

'Please, Nancy, see what you can do. Because if I don't have a holiday where I can get away from everything I'm just going to crack up.'

Then came the magic words.

'I'll sort everything out. Just have a rest and don't worry about anything this end. I'm sure the girls will understand.'

Getting back to London was no easier than leaving it. Brooklyn threw up in the taxi that took us to Nice airport and we ended up having this terrible row with the taxi driver, not made any easier by him not speaking English and us not speaking French. I can see the funny side now, but at the time it was like living in a terrible dream where you can't get home. Two days later we were back at Nice airport, but the lovely Laurent was waiting for us, not a miserable French taxi driver.

What I'd done was call Elton. He'd always said we should 'just treat the place as your own', but me and David are not people to take anything for granted. He'd said it was fine, and as long as we didn't mind that there were going to be a couple of other people there we could stay as long as we liked. It was just going to be three days.

We always have the same room, on the same level as

the swimming pool. The great thing is, it's totally private. In France now it's actually against the law to take photographs of people on private property without their knowledge and publish them in England.

The other guests turned out to be Patrick Cox and Janet Street-Porter. David Furnish was there to introduce us. We met them the first day when we came out of our room and they were already sitting round the pool. Patrick Cox is a total sweetheart and he's really good friends with David Furnish. I'd met Janet Street-Porter before and she's a bit unnerving at first: very, very intelligent and really, really tall with seriously red hair. So as we walk around the swimming pool to our chairs she stands up and she's got this Louis Vuitton swimming costume on and these big Versace diamond earrings, and then on her feet she's wearing five-inch high-heeled ruby-encrusted shoes and pop socks rolled down to her ankles. She was Dorothy. She really was the Wizard of Oz. And I'm thinking, Blimey, I'm a bit underdressed here in my Nike trainers and my bikini that's been through the washing machine so many times it's lost most of the colour it ever had.

The next person to arrive was Joan Collins of all people. They were all going to a party that evening, which was in fact why Janet Street-Porter was wearing the shoes – Elton had brought them for her from New York three months before and she was wearing them in for the party.

Anyway, Joan Collins had come round early to have a swim and there she was, going up and down the pool, big black sunglasses, red lipstick and a white turban with a big hat on top of the turban. When she got out she put

451

on this long white sarong covered with little white sequins. So glamorous, so Hollywood. And I was sitting there in my losing-its-elastic bikini, hair everywhere and sunburnt in really un-designery places – like the backs of my knees. Ms Collins, on the other hand, sat in the shade, though her legs had to be in the sun. She looked fantastic. I don't know how old she is, but I would be more than happy to look half as good at her age.

There was a bit of an atmosphere at first, because she was the only person who refused to allow me to use the interview I did with her on *Victoria's Secrets*, which really upset me at the time. I had always loved Joan Collins and she has always been a big influence when it comes to my jewellery and my approach to shoulder-pads.

So, we're at this do for something or other, and the camera crew said to me, 'Go and interview her.' We'd written and asked her, but she hadn't got back to us. They said if she agrees on camera, then it's fine. So I just went up to her and said, 'Could I just do a quick interview? I've never done this before but I think you're fantastic.' It was all very well lit, so she had nothing to worry about on that score. So she said, 'Yeah, that's fine.'

I did this quick, snappy interview and it was all very positive and nice.

The next day, we had a call from her agent to say we could only use the footage if we paid Joan Collins £25,000. Now I'd interviewed Elton, Ruby Wax, Blondie, Valentino, Richard E. Grant – all sorts of famous people – and they'd all done it for nothing. I even did it for nothing. It was a little company that approached me, and I did it for the experience and because it sounded like fun, which it was. So we explained all this – I mean, this wasn't a half-an-hour interview, it was literally five minutes. They wouldn't even let us show a clip.

At the swimming pool, she was obviously aware that it was a bit of a situation but she was very polite and so was her boyfriend. She made up for it by being very funny, especially when the talk came round to the press.

'Darling,' she purred. 'You'll just have to get used to it and play them at their own game. I had an interview the other day with Joan Rivers, and Joan Rivers said to me, "Who's the best man you've ever slept with?" and I turned round to her and said, "Your husband, darling."'

On Patrick and Janet's last day they said how about us all going out for dinner? So we went to this little family-run French restaurant that Elton has been going to for years. Nothing flash but really nice. You didn't actually order anything, things just came along. I mainly had prawns, more prawns than I have ever had at one sitting. Another dish I had was truffles. I'd heard of truffles, but I'd never had them before and I absolutely loved them. You usually have little shavings of them because they're so expensive but the owner of the restaurant came over and shaved this whole white truffle on to my plate. He didn't only not charge me for the truffle, he gave us the whole dinner free. Elton couldn't believe it when we told him later.

'I've been going there for twenty-five years,' he said, 'and they've never even given me a free drink.'

We were having such a fantastic evening that we all wanted to go on somewhere else.

By now there was nowhere open except a gay bar called the Blue Boy, just like the Blue Oyster Bar in *Police Academy*. It's not like a cool, trendy gay bar, it's a proper gay bar. And it was so eighties camp it was hilarious. As usual, I was so drunk on my one glass of wine. Patrick was quick to get me up on the podium where I gave them my Kylie impersonation. How I didn't fall off I don't know as I had on the highest heels I had ever worn in my life, green slingback sandal things. Then Patrick jumps up on the stage beneath me and we're both going mad whirling and twirling. And then all the gay men start to recognize who we are, and because of the music you can't hear what they're saying but you can tell it's, Oh my God, Posh Spice and David Beckham. They say I pout, but I had nothing on this lot. It was as if every gay man in the place was thinking 'I've been given five minutes by God to turn David Beckham.' So they're all dancing in front of him with their tight vests and their tight little bums, hands on hips, groins thrust out and giving it everything. And he's the only one of us not on the dance floor because he never dances. Usually he isn't fazed by anything like that, he's not homophobic at all, neither of us are. I love the campness of places like that and I had one of the best nights I've had.

But he turned around and there were five of them standing there, big butch blokes and it was like, Bloody hell, what's going on. I could see he was absolutely petrified. He wasn't about to take a trip to the Gents tonight, thank you very much.

Janet Street-Porter, Patrick Cox, Victoria and David Beckham are such an unlikely combination, you just wouldn't think of putting the four of us together except on that show of Ruby Wax's. But they were so great, such nice people. For once we felt really, really relaxed.

I got back to the UK for the postponed photoshoot for the Spice Girls' third album while the build-up to the release of 'Out of Your Mind' continued to grow.

My decision to go down the radical, they-won't-be-expecting-this route had paid off better than I could ever have hoped. *Music Week* wrote:

Who would have thought that Posh Spice would re-emerge as the most credible of the Spices? Although not as immediate as 'Buggin' ' . . . the True Steppers' second release is a sure-shot contender for the top of the charts. This is a triumphant release.

A trade paper like *Music Week* wouldn't just write that because they liked the colour of my lipstick. And the airplay it was getting was amazing and the video never seemed to be off MTV. (Fans call in to ask for particular videos.) However, it was still two weeks before it could be bought in the shops.

For the Spice Girls' shoot they used a hairdresser I didn't know and I looked terrible, like I'd been thrown out of Abba. Virgin was anxious to keep the short look for the Spice Girls – to avoid confusion, they said; the long hair was for True Steppers. In actual fact I was getting seriously fed-up with having to start my day three hours before everybody else.

'I'm going to have permanent extensions put in, Tyler. I've decided.'

'No, Victoria. I really don't think you should.'

'But it will be so much easier.'

Tyler is fantastic at doing my hair, but he is incredibly stubborn. He just gets into a groove and stays there. It was Tyler who said David should have all his hair cut off in the spring. David would have been quite happy with just a bit of a crop.

'It's all or nothing,' Tyler had said. And David trusted Tyler enough to agree – Tyler's a real lad from Manchester, though in fact he comes from Lytham St Annes, the posh bit of Blackpool.

At the same time as David and Brooklyn had their hair cut really short, I was desperate for a change as well, and I had this deep-seated need to go blonde. Tyler said, 'No, don't do it.' But I went ahead anyway. But that time I had to admit he was right.

My thinking now was that I needed to have my hair image changed by the time my album came out the next year. You can't do anything with short, spiky hair so I had to grow it out, but I'm thinking I can't go through that awful in-between stage because I can easily look like a soldier with a busby on my head. So why not grow it without anyone noticing? Like underneath fake long stuff?

I really prefer my hair longer, just because you can do more with it. I only had it cut in the famous Posh Spice bob because at the time Louise was training to be a hairdresser and she'd be the first to admit that she wasn't very good, one side was always longer than the other, so she just went on cutting so it got shorter and shorter. It wasn't what I was intending.

So two days before the release, I got someone Tyler

found to do the extensions. It had been a long day of radio interviews ('Hey, guys, loved the song. So, what do you think your chances are against "Spiller"?') and I was shattered. Felanie, as she was called, was coming at six o'clock. So imagine the scene. Felanie arrives with her assistant and sets everything up in the kitchen at my mum's. My dad's there on his mobile, and my mum and Louise and Liberty and Brooklyn are playing around together, being noisy and happy. Then David arrives, having just driven down from Manchester, and Brooklyn goes wild when he sees his daddy as he always does. Then some friend of my mum's turns up and she stays for a chat. Then Judy, who does my St Tropez tan, arrives from Nottingham. I'll wait till Felanie wants a break, then I'll have the tan done, I tell her. You can't get a better fake tan, look at Jennifer Lopez. Did you know, Jennifer Lopez is really pale-skinned and those lovely golden skin tones are as natural as my nails? Very sensible I say. Who wants skin tough enough for a handbag by roasting it in the sun?

In the meantime I suggest that my mum has a tan. Then Wale comes in with his assistant for a fitting for the outfit I'm wearing in Ibiza. Straight after tomorrow's *CD:UK*, which goes out live in the morning, we're all flying out to Ibiza and Louise is coming with me because it'll be a laugh and she's never been. Nor have I for that matter.

Then Tyler arrives – he's going to cut the hair when it's all in. At that point I counted fourteen people in the kitchen. Felanie takes a break around ten, when I have the St Tropez tan, which takes about forty-five minutes. Then it's back to the gluing, because that's what it is –

it's called a weave, but it's not woven. Strands of hair are just glued to the ends of my own hair and set with heat.

At one o'clock in the morning there's only Tyler and me left. Everybody else has either gone home, or gone to bed. And he's keeping me awake with stories about his two cats called Sid and Frizling and his dad, who was a genuine Teddy boy with a Brylcreem quiff, 'a real cool dude'.

At least, because I now have permanent extensions I won't have to be at the studio as early as last week: 8.30 rather than 6.30, which means leaving the house at 7.30 rather than 5.30. Which gives me four hours' sleep, because before I get to bed I get my clothes ready for tomorrow. We're not only performing the single on *CD:UK*, on *SM:TV* I will be there as myself, with Emma standing in as a female presenter and Mel C performing her single, which is this week's number 1. Bloody Louise, I mutter, as I creep round my room trying to be quiet. She's borrowed the skirt I wanted to wear on the show and not given it back.

'Out of Your Mind' was released on Monday 14 August. Now that people could actually buy the record, tactics changed – record signings: one in London on Monday, one on Tuesday in Oldham, near Manchester. This is the best part of doing promotion for me, it's the one time we get to meet the fans, the ones who go out and buy our records and who have made us what we are.

When the car arrived in Piccadilly Circus, I quite literally could not believe what I saw. The whole place was seething. For a moment I imagined that they must be there for someone else. But no. It was Dane Bowers and Victoria Beckham or Posh and Decks as we now styled ourselves.

After forty-five minutes they ran out of CDs. After fifty minutes they ran out of tapes and vinyl. The manager said he had never seen anything like it.

I called Nick Raphael, told him I thought we really had a chance.

'Look,' he said, 'I hate to tell you this, Victoria, but you don't.'

I was exhausted. We had got back from Ibiza late the previous night. And frankly the legendary Balearic vibe had not done it for us.

At seven next morning we were in Manchester 'talking up' the record signing on the breakfast show. I had gone for the Pocahontas look and tied a bandanna around my head. This was because without Tyler to do the straightening, I can look a bit of a witch.

I don't have a problem with early starts, not like David who is so bloody miserable in the morning it's ridiculous. I'm quite perky really. I'm used to getting up early with Brooklyn and I'm one of those people who don't need a lot of sleep – I seem to thrive off stress, though every now and then I do get really really tired. But as for lazing around, I just can't do it. If I'm not doing anything on a Sunday, for example, I'll sit down for about three or four hours going through paperwork. The most relaxing thing I'll do is clear up my bedroom which, when I'm busy and working, becomes a complete tip. Or best of all playing with Brooklyn. What I won't do is do nothing.

However, I know I'm a bit weird in this. Dane is like

the rest of the world, and doesn't really get into his stride until about ten. But with me there to give him hell, we were soon into our well-honed double act, wise-cracking away like we were Skinner and Baddiel. Then on to the BBC and another radio interview, then a TV. Someone asked me how long it had taken me to grow my hair. I told him I just sprinkled it with fairy dust.

'She was only kidding,' Dane said when the interviewer looked surprised. 'Actually it's manure.'

Dane is really quick. Like when I told him about sunbathing with Joan Collins, he said, 'Did she melt?'

Most of the time these interviewers didn't discover his great sense of humour because they insisted on focusing on me and David. I always tried to steer them away, saying, look, it's about the music. How Dane put up with it, I don't know. He didn't complain, he didn't moan. He just does not seem to have an ego problem.

The truth was we complemented each other.

On to another studio to do a few 'down the lines' to local radio stations in the area. And it's 'Hi, guys, love the song. So how did you two meet?'

At about eleven we had moved to another studio in BBC Piccadilly doing 'down the lines' when the call came. Jo, Dane's manager, was making faces through the studio door. Because it's soundproofed I couldn't make out what she was saying. Dane was talking to the interviewer on the other end of the phone and didn't see.

I mimed to the engineer that I was desperate for a wee and went outside. Jo looked like she'd swallowed a firework.

'You're two and a half thousand ahead,' she shrieked.

'What?'

'Nick's just called. He's just had the figures for yesterday and you're two and a half thousand ahead of "Spiller".'

That was just the kick up the arse I needed. From then on I was like a machine. First I phoned Nick Raphael to hear it from the horse's mouth. It was true, but we shouldn't get too excited, he said. Two and a half thousand wasn't that big a margin and we still had five days to go.

If I thought Virgin Piccadilly was good, it was nothing compared to Oldham. A crowd of six thousand were waiting for us; barriers kept them back and police on horses. In fact it was so incredible, I suddenly felt my eyes pricking as if I was about to cry. The queue for the signing snaked right through the shop and out the back. The shelves around were quite high, and every time a new lot of people came to the front and saw us, there would be shrieks and screams. It was incredible.

We sat at some tables in front of the big windows covered with posters. Behind us the crowds showed no sign of getting smaller. There were kids up lamp-posts and the balconies of the flats opposite were crammed.

And still they came.

'Could you put "For John"?'

Sign, smile: 'There you go.'

'Could you give this to Brooklyn?' (toy hedgehog)

'Thank you.' Sign, smile: 'There you go.'

'Could you sign my top as well so I can show everyone in the office?'

'Could you sign it for Zoe?'

I signed T-shirts, Spice Girls' albums, arms. I even

signed a £10 note. We did pictures with gap-toothed kids, pigtailed twins. I always felt a pang when a mum would tell me that her baby was the same age as Brooklyn, Brooklyn who was upstairs being looked after by my mum.

One little girl found she didn't have the money to buy the tape – lost it or something. She was totally hysterical.

'Don't worry,' said David, giving her a big smile. 'How much do you need?'

'Fifty p.' She squeezed it out through the tears.

He put his hand in his pocket, pulled out some change and gave her a £2 coin.

We signed over 1500 records – all they had.

25 helterskelter

From then on life was phone interviews, signings, flights, cars. I had no idea where we were half the time. I just remember a week of the most amazing sunsets, fiery gold skies, through aeroplane windows, or the smoked glass of whatever car I was in. The headline in Wednesday's *Sun* was 'Desperate' saying how I was travelling thousands of miles doing all these signings just to get a number 1. That I was so desperate I'd had to force David to come along with me. It was nothing to do with that. David had been away on some training thing, and we spend so little time together that he always comes with me if he can. People are often surprised when all three of us turn up together. But we're not pulling stunts – most of the time the public doesn't ever know.

As for travelling thousands of miles, I was only doing promotion in the old-fashioned way. I could have invented some terrible row between David and me – that would have cleared everything off the front page. Or how about sparking up a relationship with someone else – like other people I could mention? But I didn't. All the publicity I got was through genuine, on the road, hard work. That's how we did it at the beginning of the Spice Girls and, call me old-fashioned, that's how I feel it should be done.

On Thursday we all met up at Paddington Station for the journey down to Devon for the Radio 1 Roadshow. It was the first time we'd all been together – the dancers, Andy, Johnny, Karin and Tyler and Jo – the True Steppers family – since Ibiza. We'd heard that we were the mid-week number 1. But that didn't mean anything.

While Tyler tried to do my hair in the train – with the guard constantly telling him not to use the electric socket – Dane kept us all laughing with his Ali G routine. He is that rare combination – really funny, really intelligent and a really sweet guy. It's so nice to work with a man and there be no sexual chemistry to get in the way. Dane – the man who singlehandedly made duffel coats nearly cool. He's so professional and he loves what he does. I can sit next to Dane and talk to him like I would my brother and I feel really safe, though that might have something to do with the fact that he got a karate black belt when he was thirteen. What with Tyler having been a schoolboy boxing champion we were well set up.

Paignton was an old-fashioned seaside resort, beach-huts the colours of a paintbox, seagulls, a fairground wheel in the distance. It was the second Radio 1 Roadshow we'd done. They're such an institution and have been going for ever. I remember when I used to listen every week and long to go to one of these towns where they went.

The presenter Chris Moyles can be very sarcastic. When he'd interviewed me and Dane a couple of weeks earlier, by chance his parents were visiting the studio.

Anyway, when we were doing the interview I said to him on air, 'Now don't forget, Chris, if you're nasty to me, I'm going to tell your mummy.' And his mum was so sweet, gave me a cuddle and everything, and she and his dad had bought me a bunch of flowers.

But throughout our campaign he'd always been very supportive and just before our performance in Paignton he did a little interview with us.

'If you all go out and buy the single,' he said on air, 'next year I'll do the show naked.' It must be admitted that this wasn't much of an incentive – he's not called Big Belly for nothing. But when it comes to having a big mouth, there's no one who can beat me.

Like when I said how David was an animal in bed and how he'd be streaking around Old Trafford if I got to number 1, it was just me trying to make the whole thing fun, that's just my personality.

Me saying that David would streak around Old Trafford was probably because that morning we'd been offered £10,000 by *Playboy* to pose naked, as a couple. In fact, we were both quite up for it, but we agreed we'd rather do it for nothing. I mean, only £10,000 for me to get my bits out? But seriously, being photographed naked by *Vanity Fair* or *Playboy* is really quite classy these days. Demi Moore's done it, and Bo Derek and so has Elle MacPherson. They use top photographers like Mario Testino, photographers who do *Vogue*. It's not, 'Cor, come on, luv, show us your crotch.' But you do have to show a slight bit of hair nowadays, I've heard. David could do that, I decided. Like underarm. But in the end we decided it wasn't for us.

Getting out of Paignton was just like being back in

Spice World. Security had the car engines turning over, doors open, and the moment we left the stage to the shout of 'Go Go Go', we ran to the back of the Porta-kabins that did for dressing rooms, leapt into the back-seats, roared out of the ground through the crowds with Security shouting, 'Shut the windows.' Hundreds of people were still waiting for autographs. I didn't feel too bad: we must have spent twenty minutes signing on the way in.

We had an hour to kill before the train. So one of the local drivers took us to a pub where me, Dane and the dancers could at least get out of our space-age costumes.

It was the Hare and Hounds at Kingskerswell.

'I feel a bit overdressed,' I said as we went from the bright sunlight into the gloom of a hundreds-of-years-old English pub. 'Is there a dress code?'

A group of girls started screaming 'Oh my God'. The rest of the regulars looked at us in shock, as if we had just arrived from Mars. In actual fact we wouldn't have looked any more extreme if we had just arrived from Mars.

But as soon as we showed we were happy to sign autographs they calmed down and we had a little chat. Dane totally agrees with me: always make time for kids, without them we'd be nothing. Security are always trying to get me away quickly and into the cars, but if young fans have been waiting for autographs, I always try and stop and sign whatever it is they want me to sign. Because we owe them everything.

Seeing young children or talking about children always makes me think about Brooklyn. I called David's mum, who was looking after him that day.

'Hi, Sandra, it's Victoria. Is Brooklyn all right?'

When I'm away from him I'll probably call at least ten times a day.

Brooklyn was fine. I wondered what time I'd be home.

Champagne, I decided, was what was needed. After all, work was over – until tomorrow.

A woman came up to me and said that her daughter was doing media studies at university studying me and David. I mean, how weird is that? The world was going mad.

But being famous does have its pluses. On the train I persuaded the guard to let everyone come up to First Class to join us.

'You see,' I slurred, because – as usual – one glass of champagne and I was already a bit wobbly, 'without the dancers, we'd be nothing. Absolutely nothing.' Jo found a spare publicity photograph, and me and Dane scrawled our names over it, and David offered this guard a toast.

'This one's for your massive, this one's for your crew, we're here to feel good, through and through.'

Ali G had become our patron saint. We decided to have a party. Dane put a copy of the single in his laptop and we were off. It wasn't the best sound reproduction, but who cares.

'Haven't I seen you on *Cliff Richard*?' This was directed at Dane by a rather proper old lady who was sitting behind us, with her granddaughter, thank goodness, who was a fan. And – Dane had to admit that, yes, it was true. Then when the dancers went into their routine in the aisle, I think she thought we'd all gone mad. But it didn't seem to worry her.

It was time, I decided, for a little speech so I stood up, as the train sped across the countryside, through yellow fields dotted with rounds of hay.

'It's been a really good week,' I said. 'We don't know what's going to happen on Sunday, but even if we're not number 1 on Sunday, we are today. And without you lot, it wouldn't have been the same.' Then I saw Tyler. 'And I really think the hair made it.' And then there was Karin, thirty-four today. 'Happy birthday, Karin.' And wasn't that Wale hiding behind her?

'And forget Armani, forget Versace, we got Wale.'

Cool like dat.

'Ibiza was the pits and we're really sorry and thank you for being with us. Devon was great, and it really is the whole thing that makes this. We couldn't do it without all of you.'

And we all clapped and cheered and Dane put the CD back in the machine again.

'Out of Your Mind'.

I slept all the way back to London and, in the car back to my mum's, sparked up a really intimate relationship with the car door handle.

Number 1 or number 2 – I just had to hand it over to the universe. There were plenty of much more talented people than me out there who are signing on the dole.

The worst part for me about doing all that promotion with the True Steppers was not being able to spend as much time as usual with Brooklyn. Since we'd got rid of Mark Niblett, Louise had got me doing all those ordinary things every young mother wants to do with her baby, like swimming and going to the park to feed the ducks. I so wanted to be with him all the time, in a way to make up for the time I'd lost, but it wouldn't have been right to put an eighteen-month-old through all that rushing around the country and often I just had to leave him at home.

Seventy per cent of mothers in this country work, and I know that they all feel just as guilty as I do when I have to leave Brooklyn. It's hard to cope, no matter what your job is. At least it was nearly over now and life would soon get back to normal. I'm so lucky that Brooklyn's got such wonderful grandparents, and also Louise – it's not as if I was having to leave him with a childminder or anything. Even so, it's just one huge juggling act. Bringing up a child is the hardest job in the world.

Saturday morning *CD:UK* had us at number 1 and me and Dane went up and accepted the little trophy thing, but still I couldn't let myself believe it.

Sunday and I'm up in Manchester. Nick Raphael said he'd know at one o'clock. At 12.15 I'm in our bedroom – David's sister was helping me with my hair – and I hear my mobile ringing in the kitchen, the only place we can get reception in the flat. Joanne still has the straightening tongs on my hair, so David goes to get it. Then he walks back and I watch him in the mirror.

'That was Nick.'

A pause while he thinks what to say. As if I don't know already.

'He says you're number 2.'

'By how many?'

'Sorry, Babes, I didn't ask.'

It could wait.

So how did I feel? Half of me felt I'd let everybody

down, my friends, my family, the people we'd been traipsing round the country with, the fans who had gone out and spent their pocket money on it. But the other half of me was really proud. I never expected to have a successful record on my own, without the other girls. And how can you feel that you've failed when you've sold 180,000 in one week and had a number 2 record?

Not that I ever felt that I'd failed. That was the media: they said I'd failed, not me. In fact, after the first rush of disappointment – after all, I am very competitive by nature – I wasn't that bothered that we hadn't got the number 1. Because don't let's forget that we were one of the top-selling records of the year. And when I started out with the True Steppers I never imagined we'd make the top 5, let alone number 2. To me this was a triumph. All along I'd been thinking how lucky I was to be with the True Steppers, but I began to see how I had brought something to the party as well. Slowly I was beginning to realize what they all knew: that I wasn't the useless, talentless piece of shit everyone said I was.

That afternoon, during the interval at Old Trafford, I called Dr Fox at Capital Radio as arranged.

'It was so close and it was one of the biggest-selling records this year,' he said. 'Any other week you'd have done it. It's unbelievable.'

'You're dead right,' I said. 'How anybody managed to outdo us by 25,000 in one day is a miracle. How did they do it I wonder?' Because by this time we knew that 'Spiller' hadn't just pipped us to the post by a couple of hundred as had been the case every other day that week, but by a massive 25,000.

We may not have made number 1 in the UK, but

we still had European promotion to do. Two days later we were in Majorca and I took Sarah Bosnich with me. Sarah is married to Mark Bosnich and I met her first when he was a goalkeeper for Man United. Although I had never been particularly close to her I'd always liked her, and when I heard she'd been going through a bit of a rough time I decided to call her.

'So how about you come to Majorca with me?' I said. All of a sudden it was sod number 1 or number 2, I'm going to Magaluf with Sarah and we're gonna have fun.

Sarah Bosnich is a real girl's girl, so not like me. Her day might be go out to lunch, go shopping, buy a Louis Vuitton handbag. She'd never go around like me, dressed in a tracksuit with my nails half coming off and my extensions falling out. She'll sit there and tickle your hand with her perfect nails and say are you all right? And as for swearing. Oh no, no, darling.

As we weren't on until three in the morning, we had dinner in a nice little restaurant in Palma: the dancers, Tyler, Karin, Jo, all of us. When we arrived at the club, the first thing we saw was a girl standing under a waterfall, wet clothes, tight Lycra skirt, white legs, and mascara all down her face. Her top had been ripped off and she had love bites all down her neck.

Right, I thought, we're going to have a good time here.

It was a big club called BCM which, funnily enough, I remember was where Geri used to work once upon a time as a podium dancer. Inside and out, it was rammed. It's nearly the size of a football pitch on two floors and there were literally thousands and thousands of people. The upper floor was hardcore garage, underneath it was a bit poppier – a bit more what I actually like. We did our show in the hardcore bit. The crowds were unbelievable – all we could see from the stage was a sea of heads.

'So,' I said when the whoops and screams had quietened down enough for me to be heard, 'apparently there's a few people here tonight who are *Out of Their Mind*.'

And they erupted. We couldn't have had a better time even if we'd gone to number 1.

After the show, Dane had said he was going to DJ on the floor below, so we both went down and ended up in the DJ box with wave after wave of people asking us to sign T-shirts they'd been giving out.

'OK, guys' – this was Dane in DJ mode – 'we've got a guest DJ here who wants to do some scratching. It's POSH SPICE.'

So I put these headphones on and I had never done it before. Total silence. You're supposed to scratch when the record is on. I started scratching before the record had started.

Because this was so acutely embarrassing, Dane said, 'Here's a song that you might know.'

And it's 'Spiller'. And Dane scratched it to bits, literally broke the record, then segued into 'Out of Your Mind'. And the crowd roared.

I jumped down from the DJ box on to the stage and started dancing like a nutter. The crowd went wild. Security weren't happy, but I was. Then one by one my dancers came down on to the stage and started freestyling. It was absolutely fantastic.

Then Dane said, over the microphone, if you want

an autograph you've got to take your clothes off. All of a sudden, thousands of people take all their clothes off and some of them, let me tell you, were not a pretty sight, knickers that had been washed a hundred times, bras that looked like they were left over from the First World War, everything a horrible shade of underwear grey. It was all quite gross – like *Ibiza Uncut* but a million times funnier.

This time when security suggested we leave we didn't argue. It was getting quite ugly. The last thing I remember is this girl shouting to Dane from the floor below to sign her chest, as she calmly and coolly stripped off. I can't remember if he did.

We were in Majorca for less than twenty-four hours, but I came back feeling ready for anything the world could hurl at me, which was just as well as the next day was the key hearing in the civil court case of Beckham *v* Morton. It was held in the High Court and fortunately we didn't have to go.

I had spent an afternoon a week or so before at the lawyers' offices reading through the load of shite that Andrew Morton had cobbled together from press cuttings and sneaked titbits from Mark the traitor Niblett. Frankly it was pathetic. Perhaps because from the moment we'd heard that Andrew Morton was involved my lawyers had got an injunction out against all of them: Andrew Morton, the publishers and Mark Niblett – so even when he was writing it Andrew Morton had known his hands were tied by the court. Among the things Mark Niblett had handed over to Andrew Morton – which the court later insisted got returned to us – were six rolls of film, including pictures of Brooklyn, pictures

473

of Mark and another man in our flat, pictures of our new house, carefully captioned on the back. He had started taking photographs right from the beginning. It was only because of the injunction that Andrew Morton wasn't able to use them. Even though he wasn't allowed to use anything from Mark Niblett that was confidential, it was still upsetting seeing your life put on the slab like that and I came out of it like a bitch cow, but David came out like Persil: Mark Niblett wasn't about to point the finger at his golden boy, because I had come to suspect that was half the problem: jealousy. There was nothing particularly libellous in the book – the usual things repeated from newspapers that weren't true in the first place – but just said in a bitchy way. He really hadn't done his research. Andrew Morton considers himself a modern-day historian but in this book he is nothing more than a cuttings collector.

The only thing that really upset me was how he made out that my parents and David's parents didn't get on. That was so hurtful.

As the court hearing approached, our objections to certain passages of the book were sorted out and we settled the case against Morton and his publishers. Both sides gave undertakings to the court and so, much as I may want to, I cannot say what the settlement terms actually were, but that didn't stop Morton's side claiming it was a victory for them and using the court hearing to publicize the weasel's book. They had to apologize afterwards for comments they had made.

So our case against Morton and his publishers was over, but our case against Mark Niblett went on.

The next day we were off to Germany. I was feeling

about as fresh as a week-old lettuce. But you know, 'the show must go on'.

Adrenalin saw me through the performance but the lights were really getting to me and suddenly I had this terrible headache and felt sick. I couldn't stand the light and I was all curled up in a ball in my dressing room. And I'm just groaning and saying, 'I don't know what's wrong with me', and Dane's saying, 'Are you all right, Vic?' And I said, 'No, Dane.' I was so far from right.

Dane got me back to the hotel and meanwhile security had managed to get hold of a doctor.

'I've got this terrible headache, I feel sick, my neck aches, I'm a bit spaced. I can't quite work things out,' I told her.

'You've got a virus,' she said. 'I'll give you an injection.'

'No, no injections.'

She probably thought I was some sort of religious nutter, but David had said whatever you do, don't let them give you an injection. I was in no state to argue.

So this doctor gave me a prescription for some medicine, which turned out to be a little bottle with a dropper that you squeezed. Twenty drops.

When I was really young I used to get terrible headaches. I was a terrible worrier and if I got upset then I'd cry, shut my eyes, squeeze them really hard and I'd hear things, noises in my head, things like sirens and echoing sounds. And I used to say to my mum, what are these things in my head driving me mad? And then the headaches would come.

I don't know what the drops were supposed to do but I couldn't sleep, tossing and turning from side to side. I was sweating buckets. Every time I saw light, it was like a stab in my head. And I could hear myself screaming this high-pitched noise, not a usual pain noise, but the noise of a cat. I knew I had to have some more of this medication, but I'd left it in the lounge part of the suite. I was in the bedroom and the idea of getting out of bed and walking those few feet – you might as well have asked me to swim the Channel.

I picked up the phone. Reception answered. They only had night staff on who didn't understand. What I asked for was 'one of the True Steppers party' – they thought I was complaining about a party, heard nothing, and so did nothing.

Eventually I found Fiona, who was doing my make-up on this trip. She got the paramedics out and the same doctor.

It was awful. I felt sick, I couldn't talk, I was shivering – hot and cold at the same time. I was convinced I'd got meningitis. I've been a patron of the Meningitis Research Foundations, a national charity 'fighting to prevent death and disability from meningitis and septicaemia', for a couple of years – and in fact had recently been nominated for some award for my work. Anyway, that was why I knew all the signs and tests. One sign is a rash. But I was at that stage where I was feeling so ill I couldn't be bothered to look for rashes. I just thought, if I've got it I'm going to die anyway.

I got the injection but, frankly, it didn't make any difference. I couldn't move because my back and neck were hurting so much – another meningitis sign – and I didn't sleep all night.

Everything was cancelled and the next day we got a

private plane home. My mum had booked me in to my local GP. I couldn't stop shaking. I was staring like a mad woman.

'You're under a lot of stress,' he said. In his opinion it was a bad migraine. My mum wasn't convinced. She made an appointment for me to see a craniologist first thing in the morning.

He took an hour to check me out. His verdict was different. 'You've got viral meningitis,' he said.

No treatment, just rest. It wasn't life-threatening but could stay in my system for up to a year.

Next day it was front page news, though half the newspapers missed out the viral bit. But then who cares about accuracy?

26 getting my life back

'If you don't like it you're going to have to sack me,' Nancy said when she told me she'd cleared my diary for two weeks. TWO WEEKS? Didn't she understand – I had songs to write, people I was working with flying in from America?

She and David had obviously been talking: he had this idea that I needed looking after and the only person to do it was him. Nancy agreed.

In the end I was up in Manchester for nearly three weeks. For the first few days I felt terrible, and on top of it all one newspaper even asked for a sick note. But gradually I began to get a bit of energy back. And something was different. For a start, I didn't have a phone constantly clamped to my ear. For the first time in my life it felt good to have nothing to do. Good to be there when David got back from training, to have the house tidy and lunch on the go. Good playing with Thomas the Tank Engine and Postman Pat, and their little friend Brooklyn. Good to get in the car and go swimming as a family. Good taking long lazy baths. And I began to realize what people had been telling me for years: that I didn't do enough for me. I never went out to lunch with friends, never went down the gym. Because there was never enough time.

So why do I do it? Why do I feel this need to work, work, work? I've always had goals ever since I first started at Jason's. First it was grade 1, then grade 2, and on it went. Every certificate was just a stepping stone to the next and the next and my ultimate goal. Fame.

Those few weeks were the best I've had in my whole life. It gave me time to think. I wish more than anything that I didn't want to do what I do. I wish I could be happy living up in Manchester and not working. I've been living out of a suitcase since I was sixteen. I just want to unpack my clothes and have a home really. But something so simple, that most people have anyway, is just a dream for me. I say to David sometimes, tell me we're going to have that. Tell me.

As well as thinking hard about what my life was doing to me, David and Brooklyn, I also began to weigh up its effect on my parents. People outside must think, Oh, nice house, nice cars, loadsamoney, flash holidays. But they don't realize what goes with it: the fact that my mum can't listen to the radio or pick up a newspaper without hearing something bad about me. It wasn't until I had Brooklyn that I understood how hard it must be for them. If anybody said things like that about my child, I wouldn't be half as controlled. Before I had Brooklyn, when they got upset, I used to lose my temper and say, I don't see what you're so worried about. They're not writing about you. But now I understand.

When I was living at home, whereas I'd spend the whole day trying to be humorous and lighthearted with the people I was working with, when I got back, I'd take all my stress out on my dad or my mum. And I shouldn't have done that; it should have been the other way around. The people who are closest to you shouldn't have to get it in the neck.

And no amount of money can make up for that. And although I've always shared everything with them, like they've shared everything with me, you can't just pay all the time, it's humiliating for people. And it must be a hard thing for a parent to come to terms with, especially a dad. Because my dad's always been the breadwinner in the family and now I'm a lot richer than he is.

None of my family has ever been jealous and they never ask for anything, which is why I enjoy giving them things I know they would really love and appreciate. But the only way I can buy things for them is as a surprise present. Christian won't even accept £20 for petrol.

I mean I've bought my dad a Porsche and I've bought my mum diamond earrings, I've bought houses for my sister and my brother and I've bought them all watches – all that kind of thing. But you can only get them so much without them feeling that they're getting handouts.

But when we're out at dinner as a family and I offer to pay and my dad says, no, he'll pay, I feel guilty then. Guilty because without my family, I wouldn't have any of this. They supported me in my dream right from the beginning. My mum driving all those hours from our house into Broxbourne, making costumes all through the night sometimes, my dad giving me a real template for running a business, always reminding me that I was his daughter and he knew I wouldn't give up. And Louise and Christian, always there for me, telling me the truth when nobody else would, and Louise for being my best friend.

When Brooklyn was born, people said, you know it's going to be really difficult bringing him up. But I didn't understand. He could be taught to say please and thank you like anybody else, I decided. And he does. But now I'm beginning to see what they meant. It's nothing either me or David do or don't do. It's just our situation.

Of course I can bring him up to be a nice little boy – and he's already turning into a really nice little boy. The first words he learned were 'pees' and 'ta' and he knows what 'no' means.

It took something quite little to bring home to me how hard it was going to be to get the balance right. The summer when I was rushing around Europe with the True Steppers, my mum's friend Dee took him shopping in Enfield. Nobody knows what Dee looks like so they didn't know Brooklyn was Brooklyn, he was just like any other little boy. And anyway, it started to rain. And Dee said he just stood there in the rain, his little hands held out trying to catch the drops, amazed. And everybody else was staring, wondering why he didn't take shelter. And she told me this – like here's a funny story for you – but I was suddenly overcome by guilt. He did it because it was a new experience for him. He'd never been in the rain. He went everywhere by car.

The kidnap threats had made me feel so vulnerable that I was living how somebody else wanted me to live. Now I have security only when I need it. But it took a long time. It is only now that I feel I can live a normal life and because I can, Brooklyn can.

When Mark was around I used to stay in the flat all morning until David got back from training. Then one day last spring I just put Brooklyn in the car and drove to the local McDonald's. Summer was coming and I love that time of year. It was lunchtime and we sat there, just the two of us, among the other mums sitting there with their children and Brooklyn was really having fun. Such a simple thing, just going to McDonald's and I thought, I can't believe I haven't done this before with my own baby.

Instead of seeing these women as people who would be on the phone to some paper or other saying how they'd seen me looking terrible in McDonald's, I saw them as mothers like me. And when they looked at Brooklyn they smiled and when another little boy wandered over I didn't grab Brooklyn and feel my heart nearly break out of my body because it was beating with fear. I just watched and laughed with the other mums as the two solemn little boys looked at each other. This was what being a child was about. This was what being a mother was about. This was what being happy was about.

Brooklyn is his own little person now and he'll come and give me a cuddle, but then he's off. He's so independent. When I see friends with tiny babies, I just long to have another one. I have this dream of having four children. And it shouldn't have to be just a dream. David has already proved he is a wonderful father and I know from having a brother and sister myself how important it is not being the only one. And although Brooklyn has got such a strong personality and he can entertain himself, I know he needs a brother or sister.

Once I have proved what I can do, then I plan to take time out and have another baby or another two babies and really get settled as a family. But I can't get settled in myself until everything's done.

The Spice Girls' third album, *Forever*, was released at the beginning of November 2000. Leading up to the release of the single, a month before we'd done a week of promotion. We'd all been very busy with solo projects and having babies, so it was quite strange being back together again.

We'd spent a week that summer doing the videos for the single – two because it was a double-A-side. 'Holler' – two very long days – was a lot more work because the director was Jake Nava, who also directed 'Out of Your Mind' and that's just how he works. 'Let Love Lead the Way' was easier – two very short days – directed by Greg Masuak, the same guy who did 'Who Do You Think You Are'. In fact it was all rather lovely. My Winnebago became the crèche, with Brooklyn and Phoenix running around everywhere having a great time.

We spent a long time working on the Spice Girls' third album, but it wasn't as intense as the first two because we were all working on our solo careers as well. With *Spice* and *Spice World* having done so well, it was always going to be a hard act to follow. The first tracks we wrote for the new album were with Matt and Biff, and we recorded at Abbey Road Studios. Then our A&R guy, Ashley Newton, who is now based in LA, arranged for us to work with some American producers – Rodney Jerkins and all of his crew, Le Sean and his brother Fred Jerkins and Jimmy Jam and Terry Lewis, who in fact we had first met with Prince when we were on tour, and they had said they wanted to work with us way back then. Usually when you work with writers at this level, you have to go to them, but we were in a very lucky position: because we were the Spice Girls writers would come to us.

Without our realizing it, working with Rodney Jerkins and Jimmy Jam and Terry Lewis was taking us in a new direction. It was still pop music but with an R & B influence. Virgin were so pleased with the Rodney Jerkins tracks that six months later we went over to the States and recorded another three songs in Miami.

When we got there we found out that Mel C wasn't coming but would be putting down her vocals later. At first, we thought it was just that her schedule clashed, but it wasn't long before we realized that there was more to it.

It had been two years since the end of the American tour and we had all grown up, but Mel C had also grown away – not least in terms of her music. She was always more rock 'n' roll than the rest of us, but that was what she brought to the group.

It wasn't easy for any of us when we finished the world tour at Wembley. It's very difficult to go from being a huge superstar performing live in front of a crowd of seventy thousand to being just a normal person.

When we came back from America, while the rest of us were quite happy to escape from Spice World for a bit – me and Mel B to our boyfriends and pregnancies, and Emma to spend time with her mum – Melanie C didn't have anything like that to anchor her. She didn't want to stop. All she has ever wanted to do is perform.

So that's what she did. She went straight into working on her solo album.

It was when we began talking about the third album that I began to sense she wasn't really comfortable. Maybe she thought she didn't need to compromise any more – after all she'd had success on her own.

But you do have to compromise when you're not just you. And, make no mistake, it's not easy. Take me. I've got a husband and a baby, do I really want to have to ask three other people if I can wear a certain thing, do a certain thing? But that's what you have to do if you're part of a group.

Emma probably doesn't want to wear her pigtails any more. I don't particularly want to wear little skirts. And as for Mel B, no normal person would want to go on wearing leopardskin prints year after year. Well, would you? Melanie C obviously decided that she didn't want to wear a ponytail and Adidas trainers, being sporty, when she'd rather be rocky. She may want to be Rocky Spice but it doesn't work like that. She can be as rocky as she wants on her own, but she can't be Rocky Spice.

At the end of the day I think being a Spice Girl is a bit like a marriage. Compromise is a central part of it. You get the 'for better' and the 'for worse'. But even though you may have your disagreements, the truth is that you're in for the long haul. And my own feeling is that in time Melanie C will realize that she can do both. Like marriages that go through bad patches you just have to work your way through it.

When we got everything back it became clear that the tracks we'd done with the Americans had taken us up a level and the songs we'd done with Matt and Biff no longer fitted. There was no natural flow and so in the end they didn't make the album.

The feeling was that the Spice Girls had really matured. Rodney Jerkins did an amazing job. Jimmy Jam and Terry Lewis did an amazing job – the quality of the tracks, the production, the way they were mixed, everything about it was first class and the vocals were a million times better than on our first and second albums. I still listen to our third album and think it's fantastic.

But either people in Britain don't know how to digest music like that or we just got it wrong. *Forever* was called a flop because it 'only' got to number 2 in the album charts. Thinking about it now, the chances are whichever way we'd gone we'd have been criticized. If we'd stuck to what we originally did – very poppy – they'd have said we hadn't moved on. As it was, they said we were trying to be something we weren't. But that just wasn't true. We were just taking our vocals and our songwriting ability to another level and as far as I am concerned *Forever* is the best album the Spice Girls have ever done.

The truth is the Spice Girls have been so huge, sold so many albums, we could never top that. And it doesn't matter how big you are, if you want a number 1 you have to do massive promotion and this time around we just weren't prepared to do that. Two of us had children, we all had solo careers and there's only so long you can live in the Spice bubble. But whatever we do individually, now and in the future, we're still Spice Girls and we always will be; it's part of our DNA if you like.

For both the earlier albums we all lived and breathed Spice Girls. We were in America, we were in England, we were in Europe, we had a movie out, we'd won an unbelievable number of awards, we had an unbelievable number of number 1s. We were on a roller-coaster. And the truth remains that if you want people to buy your record, they've got to know it's out there.

And Simon Fuller really understood that. For years I said how much I hated him – and he did do things that were wrong – but now I have a lot of respect for him. It's taken a long time for me to come to the conclusion that – in some aspects at least – he had to do what he did. It was hard to admit because I had been hurt, we all had, and that made me angry. But the constant promotion that nearly pushed us over the edge with exhaustion helped make us as successful as we were, and the only way you can keep five such strong people together is to rule them with a rod of iron. Now that I can stand back I understand how it happened.

So *Forever* got to number 2. The only sad thing about not making number 1 was the press saying that the Spice Girls were over, forgetting that just a month earlier our single 'Holler' got to number 1. They can't have it both ways. As one of the papers said: Why are the British media so intent on killing their most successful export?

The week of promotion was at the beginning of October 2000 – *Top of the Pops, SM:TV, CD:UK, The Lottery*. In the old days I used to get slightly frustrated when we did promotion. Compared to the other girls I was quite shy and reserved. I would have liked to say more but the truth is my personality was always squashed between the other personalities. That was Posh, if you like. It was never done on purpose, I let it happen, but I always felt frustrated. And I think that's why people have been as interested as they have in my solo career, it's because I never shouted my head off about what I thought, what I did, so no one knew much about me and they were curious. Being the Greta Garbo of the group allowed this curiosity to build up for years.

When you're in a group, you have to keep clear of controversial things, even what appear quite trivial questions such as what pop group do you hate? As Posh Spice I can't turn round and say I hate the Venga Boys – because as a Spice Girl I represent all the Spice Girls in a way, and people would then think the Spice Girls hate the Venga Boys. If we say controversial things, it has to be in our solo environment. Or that's what I believe.

But when I did 'Out of Your Mind' it was entirely different. With Dane it was the first time I'd been able to say what I wanted. I found I enjoyed talking in interviews, saying silly things. After that you would think that it would have been difficult going back to taking a back seat with the girls, but funnily enough it wasn't.

I'd proved I could do my own thing and that gave me the confidence to just sit there and let it all roll over me. In fact, I remember a few interviews that we did and when I did decide to open my mouth, it was, Oh, my God, Victoria's going to say something.

But it would have totally altered the balance of the group if I had suddenly changed and become mouthy. That wasn't my role. As a Spice Girl I was the one at the back who looked pouty and didn't say a lot. There's a big difference between Posh Spice and Victoria Beckham. Posh Spice is part of me and always will be. But only part.

★

In November 2000 I was named fashion icon of the year by *Elle* magazine. Although I think I've always had quite an eye for a look, my only trick, if you like, is that I never follow fashion – not through any kind of arrogance, but I'm not a clothes horse and not everything looks good on me. I've always known how to dress in a flattering way for me – which in the old days was black, black, black, black and black. But what looks good on any particular person depends on their body – emphasizing the good bits and trying to disguise the bad bits. In my case my legs were always long and thin, even when I was much bigger, but against that I had no boobs to speak of.

What I love more than anything is things that make women look like women. That's why I love corset tops really sucky, sucky, that push your boobs up, hold your waist in and flatter your hips. I like women to wear make-up, do their hair and wear tight sexy clothes, and I like it when people are individual and do something a bit different with fashion.

One reason why basques were always so great for me is that as much as I've got a small frame I've never had the smallest waist. If there's anything that needs work with me it's my waist and my tummy muscles. That's not just because of having a baby, it's because I haven't got hips, I just go straight down, so I need a bit of help to make me look as though I've got a feminine shape. It was only a few months ago that I had combats on and a hat pulled down and somebody came up and called me 'Sir', thinking I was a young boy.

I think that's why I love high-heels; they shift your centre of gravity and make you walk in a womanly, sexy way. If you wear four-inch heels it's impossible to look like a boy even if you've got no chest at all.

I also love glamour, I love matching handbags, I love short skirts – as far as I am concerned the shorter the better – and I won't wear heels unless they're majorly high-heels. I must have more high-heels than Imelda Marcos. My favourite shoe designers are Gina and Manolo Blahnik. Manolo Blahnik made my wedding shoes as a present for me. The head designer at Gina, Aydin Kurdash, wears suits like he might work in a bank, but he's a really nice guy – if I need something special he'll make it for me. For my birthday last year they surprised me with a pair of high-heeled denim boots, with snakeskin toe and heel and 'Victoria' up the side in diamanté. They were just so camp in a really classy way. Now they even have a boot they call the Victoria Beckham boot. Young and fresh at the minute, but after a few wearings it won't look the same; dare I say, an old boot.

When my suitcases got stolen Gina replaced all my shoes and didn't charge me. He's great, and I've been going to him ever since the beginning of the Spice Girls; the heels were always so high it was difficult to do any more than just totter, which is why I never had an opportunity to dance properly.

I like to think what I've brought to the party is glamour. I am very very camp in my personality – which is why I loved it when we performed 'Out of Your Mind' at a gay club called G.A.Y. in London because they love the campness of my act and the glamour behind it, which is why I feel so relaxed in that environment.

Being all dressed up is a bit like a performance in itself

– but I would like to think I have a certain way of dressing in a dressed-down way during the day. The other day I went out in a pair of men's 32-inch-waist trousers that are huge and I wore them slung low on the hips with a nice little tummy chain and a tight little T-shirt with my boobs up around my neck. I'm not saying that I am the most credible dresser, but I do have a side to me that is more casual now, and that's thanks to David.

Make-upwise I'm in the lucky position of hearing about all the new things and all the new ideas from a professional make-up artist. So I can try things out and see what works and what doesn't.

Also with hair, I'm lucky I have a top hair-stylist who can try things out on me. Just because someone tells me to do something, doesn't mean to say I'll do it. I'll listen to what people say and take it on board. But I like to learn by my own mistakes and follow my gut instincts. I've always done that, and of course I've made mistakes, everybody has. But at least they're mine. I had the hair extensions for a very practical reason, but then one day I woke up and thought, How did I ever think that suited me? I wanted to get them out straight away. So I did. Apart from anything else, although it was real hair, the extensions felt vile, and David couldn't stand having it near him on the pillow.

Me and David have got very similar ideas about how we look, although my skirts are often shorter than his ideal would be and my tops may be more plunging than he might actually like.

The first time we dressed alike was at a Versace party. We had just come back from abroad and so hadn't bought anything special but knew everyone else would have had their outfits planned for weeks. So I said to David – we both have black leather trousers and black leather biker jackets and black boots and white tops – let's go and coordinate.

We couldn't have caused much more of a sensation if we had gone totally naked. Couples weren't at that time going out dressed the same. I remember my auntie and uncle used to have his and hers clothes, and I used to think bloody idiots, what do they think they look like? And when my mum and dad told me they used to have matching T-shirts, all I could think was that's so uncool. But then I would never claim to be cool. I almost enjoy taking the ridiculous and making it fashionable.

We always discuss what we're going to wear if we're doing anything where we're likely to get photographed together. David would never wear pink and orange and me wear brown and red for example – unless we were trying to make a statement.

Since the spring of 2000 David had been involved in two projects of his own, one was his book, the other a documentary for ITV. They both came out in October and proved another milestone in how people came to think of him. It wasn't the book itself, which was mainly a coffee-table book full of pictures of David looking fantastic, it was doing *Parkinson*.

I had done *Parkinson* in 1999 and I think that helped me get rid of the Anorexic Spice tag. Unlike a lot of interviewers out there, Michael Parkinson seems to think his job is to make you look interesting. The day after David's interview it was, My God, who would have thought he was such a nice guy? I think the media had come to believe their own pathetic prejudice that David's brains were located somewhere around his ankles.

The documentary a few weeks later was the same story, praise from everyone. This was broadcast only a week or so after David was chosen to captain England against Italy. It came completely out of the blue. He was staying at Gary Neville's house that night as he often does when I'm away – I was working in London and staying at my mum's. He called me straight away. Peter Taylor, the Leicester manager who had taken over managing England when Kevin Keegan pulled out, had just called and asked him to be captain. I can't remember when I heard him so excited. To captain England had always been David's dream. A couple of weeks before he'd captained Manchester United but this was only because nobody else wanted to do it, he said, and as David is always so matter-of-fact, I don't think he was just being modest.

But England was different. This time David had been chosen to lead his country. For David this was the most incredible honour and I just felt a great surge of love and pride. This was the man who in July 1998 had been the most hated man in England and even six months before was being seen as 'a national liability'.

I couldn't go to the match in Italy because the Spice Girls were performing at the MTV Video Awards in Stockholm but we spoke on the phone throughout the day as we always do, or sent text messages, me telling David what was happening in Sweden, him telling me what was happening in Italy.

I watched it later, with David, on video at home. Not

the same excitement perhaps, but a silly grin on my face the whole time. I felt so, so proud. And after four years, I am actually beginning to enjoy watching football. I kind of understand the offside rule.

In the old days I would switch off when the talk turned to this footballer and that footballer but now I find myself listening. Did you know that Eusébio, one of the greatest footballers of all time, only had size 4 feet, the same size as mine?

I'm not saying that I could ever be as committed to football as David's mum and dad – I don't think anyone could be. I don't think Ted has missed one match that David has played in since he began and even Sandra has only missed one or two. Football is their life. They come up to Manchester whenever there's a game – sometimes twice a week – and they go to all the away matches, wherever they are. But if Brooklyn became a footballer, I know I'd be the same.

However, if I'm being totally honest, I think I would rather Brooklyn did something different, because the pressure on him would be huge. People would always be comparing him to David – one of the greatest footballers in the world. And that would always be so, so difficult. You wouldn't wish it on anyone.

But Brooklyn really is unbelievable with a football even now, and that is something I am obviously going to have to let him get on with. The first few steps that he took in the kitchen, he stood up and kicked a teddy bear that was lying there across the kitchen floor. He loves to go and watch his daddy. I don't know if Brooklyn associates what he does with a football and what David does on the pitch as the same thing, all I know is that he just loves it. Kicking a ball is second nature to him.

David's documentary was filmed over about nine months. We kept Brooklyn out of it as much as we could because – unlike what the newspapers say – we want Brooklyn to keep his anonymity as much as possible. It's going to be difficult enough for him anyway. I was hardly in it either – just a couple of sessions at the flat. In actual fact, it was quite funny because the crew kept making me change into different clothes so that it would look as if I'd done more sessions.

They asked us about our careers and anybody could see that both of us are really supportive of the other. I know that for David to be happy he has to play football at the highest possible level. And I want David to be happy. The fact that where he works may not be entirely convenient for my life is just one of those things you accept. It's the same for David. He just wants me to be happy and, although I think he would love for me to just be there every day and have baby after baby, he knows that will happen, that's something to look forward to.

The suitcase saga came to an end in January 2001. Mark the Skip turned out to be Mark Oliver and he was found guilty on two counts of handling stolen goods. Some of my clothes had turned up in his sister's wardrobe. I was called to give evidence for the prosecution, but half the time I felt I was the one on trial, with the barrister for the defence trying to catch me out about the business of finding the photograph frame in the skip/rubbish dump/back garden.

My heart was pounding I was so nervous. And I'm thinking, Hang on here, some toe-rag has nicked my bloody suitcases and that's the bottom line. You've raided that guy's house, found my clothes in his wardrobe and now you're trying to make me sound like I'm guilty and that the guy is such a nice guy for telling me that he's found my suitcases and some of my books.

Another witness for the prosecution was Mark Niblett. Fortunately I didn't have to see him – they put us in separate rooms. The criminal case against Mark Niblett – he was arrested remember back in the summer on suspicion of inciting threats to kill – had been abandoned because of lack of evidence.

Things were turning out much better with the civil case. Mark Niblett said the reason we couldn't find his confidentiality agreement was because he had never signed one but he didn't know about the indentation of his signature on the blank confidentiality form from the beginning of November 1999, the time we said he had signed. And forensic tests the lawyers had organized showed that it was his signature.

This was done through the same technique that resulted in the Guildford Four's conviction being quashed, something called Esda, electrostatic detection apparatus. They make what is called a 'lift' and this image of the signature can then be used in evidence in court. At the end of the day it might not make a whole load of difference – being loyal is part of the job of a bodyguard – but at least it shows that Mark Niblett lied.

Later on, we got judgement against him for damages and our legal costs, and the temporary injunction that the lawyers had got in the summer to stop him talking to the media about our private life was made permanent – a gagging order, as the press called it. It came too late to stop him talking to Andrew Morton, but at least it has stopped him making a full-time career of it. But perhaps the greatest crime he committed was not one he could ever be arrested or sued for: inducing nine months of paranoia. He made me think that I could trust no one. He made me doubt everything and everyone.

27 i owe you

It's not just a bit of PR hype that it was David who encouraged me to do my album. I really had given up all idea of a solo career – but he just kept on at me. I know it's hard for people to believe that Victoria Beckham has low self-esteem, but it's true. If you're told that you're a talentless piece of shit for long enough, then that's what you believe. When I get depressed my mum always says, 'Ignore the bad stuff, just remember all the wonderful letters from the fans, after all they're the ones that really matter.'

But it's so much easier to believe the bad stuff somehow. It's like exams. You might forget the subjects you pass, but you never forget the subjects you fail. It stays with you like a sticker on your back.

But gradually, as I worked on my album, I began to discover that songwriters and producers were very happy to work with me, and not just because I was a Spice Girl. The stories Melanie B had been telling me about working in America were a bit scary. I needed to start closer to home to build my confidence. When it comes to confidence-building Elliot Kennedy is king. He did it for all five of us when we first left Bob and Chris, now he would do it for me. The big difference between working with the girls and working on my own is that I can take Brooklyn wherever I go, and that week in Sheffield working with Elliot my mum came with me to help with him.

I had no idea which direction I wanted to go. At the start of working on this album it was real trial and error and that week with Elliot, who I've always liked so much, was a great learning experience for me. We did three tracks, one ballad, one up-tempo and one mid-tempo – quite guitary, but I wasn't convinced.

So then I decided I'd try Matt and Biff. I already knew that I wanted to stay true to myself. It might have been great for Melanie B to be doing R&B but that's not where I'm coming from. I want to make pop music.

But Matt and Biff don't work together any more. Biff now works in Ireland with a guy called Julian, and I heard they'd been working with U2, so I spent a week over there which was great – I love Ireland and Biff is such a lovely guy it was almost like going home, there was no pressure and he was great for me. But I still didn't know which direction I was going in. Again, I wasn't convinced.

I was also being introduced to writers I didn't know by my A&R man, Paul McDonald. He had only recently joined Virgin from London Records so he had to get to know me and I had to get to know him. There was something not right about the music I was writing. I still hadn't found the right direction. But Paul helped keep my confidence up. He really stuck by me and had faith. When the music's great it's easy for people to be interested and get on the bandwagon but Paul's been interested from day one.

Nothing seemed to work and I was getting quite despondent. I can bring melody ideas to the party, I can bring lyric ideas to the party, what I needed was somebody who was great with music. I can't work the equipment, it's not what I do.

Then we tried another tack. Virgin and Nancy set up some meetings with songwriters in LA. (This was the trip when my luggage got stolen.) The first person I met up with was Rhett Lawrence and I talked to him about ideas that we'd had and we just clicked. He wrote 'Never Be the Same Again' with Melanie C, which was a huge success in the UK and around Europe. He's also worked with 98 Degrees and the Backstreet Boys. A few months later, I went back to work with Rhett and we wrote and recorded a song called 'Unconditional Love'.

There's something about American artists – Britney Spears, Christina Aguilera, 'N Sync, Janet Jackson and Madonna – everything is polished. It's strong, the image is there, the videos are amazing, it's like WOW! And as soon as I started meeting more producers and song-writers in America, it was, Do you know what? This feels right.

Next, I met a guy called Steve Kipner, though I very nearly didn't. I'd spent the whole day pinballing across LA and I was exhausted and he lived the other side of the city in the Hollywood Hills. And I thought, Do I really need to go and see yet another songwriter? I knew he'd done 'Genie in a Bottle' with Christina Aguilera and that really impressed me, but I could always come back another time. Couldn't I? But then that Dad side of me kicked in and it was No, come on, get back in the limo, we're going to meet Steve Kipner.

The door is opened by his wife and the first surprise is that she's English, from Sheffield, with two lovely children rushing around. The second surprise is Steve himself, who is Australian. And he's got this lovely smiley face and with his lovely happy family all laughing and joking, I immediately felt at home.

His studio was out the back behind the house and as soon as he played me some music, I knew instantly that this was the guy who was going to make my album work. And in fact that's exactly what happened. Working with Steve was fantastic, he understood that it had to be poppy, but a cool poppy with a slight feel of R&B but not a lot.

When I first started work on the album, I was co-writing everything, just as I had done with the Spice Girls, but then after the success of 'Out of Your Mind' I had songwriters coming to me with amazing songs. And as much as I wanted to write as much as possible myself, turning down a great song that somebody else happens to have written is a sort of arrogance. So what if I haven't written it? It's a great song. My nan had this phrase: 'Don't look a gifthorse in the mouth.'

When I got back to the hotel I was incredibly up. Steve had also given me a CD of songs which I listened to on my way back on my personal stereo including 'Not That Kind of Girl', which he had co-written with David Frank. Another of his co-writers he told me later was English. Perhaps I knew him? His name was Andrew Frampton and he worked at Olympic Studios in Barnes.

This was so funny, as I had so often been to Olympic but had never come across him.

Steve told me he planned to come to England to work with Andrew later in the year and perhaps we could work together? And we did. On two songs, 'No Tricks No Gain' and 'Mind of Its Own'. We met up again in spring 2001 when I recorded another Kipner/Frampton song 'Innocent Girl' which went on to become my first single.

The music business is a very small world and sooner or later you find everyone has a link somewhere along the line to somebody else. Andrew Frampton also wrote with Chris Braide – and I wrote a song with them called 'I Owe You', which is a ballad all about David.

A&R stands for Artists and Repertoire and one of the things an A&R guy does is to find you great songs. I had only just got back from one of these trips to LA when I had a phone call from Ashley Newton, the Spice Girls' original A&R man, who is now based in LA.

'I've found this song,' he told me. 'It's a hit. I love it. Let me know what you think as soon as you hear it.'

And he was right. 'I Wish' was a good song, but the session singer on the demo was a real black R&B singer. Could it really sound right for me? The truth is that if you've got a great song, you can do anything with it. You can make it more poppy, you can make it more R&B, you can make it slower, you can make it faster. If you have the core of a really great song, it can sound like anything you want.

I wanted to change the key.

No, the songwriters said, when I arrived at the studio in LA. You can't change the key. They were called Soul

Shock and Karlin, and were originally from Denmark but had lived and worked in LA for years, writing for people like Whitney Houston.

I had felt really comfortable with Rhett Lawrence and Steve Kipner. But this studio was the other end of the feeling comfortable scale. It was totally awe-inspiring. The sign on the armour-plated studio door said: Victoria Beckham Session. No Entry. This was Big Time.

I'd asked Ashley to tell them that the song wasn't in my key. That it was too high for me. He had obviously forgotten. So they played the track again and it was really great.

They were both very smiley. Soul Shock dresses very similar to David and if you looked quickly it was David – trainers, big baggy jeans, big baggy T-shirt – which was very disconcerting. Karlin is a lot smaller and a bit rounder. Both very cool.

'But I think it's a bit high for me.'

'It's not too high, it sounds great in this key' – and basically just go in there and get it right, was what they said. They had decided that this was how it was going to work. And as much as I felt sick and all I wanted to do was run away, I decided at least I should go in the booth and try it.

And to cut a long story short, I went in, got it right and it sounded great and I went on to co-write another two songs with them, 'What Are You Talking About' and 'Into My Heart'.

It was a great week, I have never worked harder in my life, but I really pushed myself. It helped that I had Brooklyn there. Both my mum and Sandra had come out to help me with him. And the truth is I couldn't have done this third album without them. David's mum is amazing with small children, so patient, always playing with and reading to them. She says now that she wished she had trained as a children's nurse. She has three grandchildren now. As well as Brooklyn, there are David's sister Lynne's children: Georgina, about the same age as Liberty, and Freddy, born early in 2001. The best thing for Brooklyn on that trip was going to Disneyland where we went all together on my day off. You only really appreciate the magic of it when you go with a little person.

At the end of the week, Soul Shock and Karlin took me out to dinner and confessed that at the beginning they hadn't wanted to work with me at all.

'We can respect you for the amount of records you've sold but the Spice Girls wasn't our kind of music,' they explained. 'But Ashley is such a great A & R man and he persuaded us to work with you.'

He had doorstepped a restaurant where they were having dinner and sent them a copy of *Elle* magazine with a page marked where I'd been photographed with two Dobermanns. And I'm standing there in cashmere knickers basically and these two dogs. And there was a note attached saying, 'Are you sure you don't want to work with this person?'

They were hugely complimentary, said they had been completely bowled over by my professionalism. And yes, I really could sing.

A few months earlier when I was on a train with Dane coming back from a Radio 1 Roadshow, we started writing down a few lyric ideas, a few melody ideas, and suddenly we had the makings of a really great song. Who should we get to produce it? I thought immediately of Harvey Mason Jnr. who I had first met with Rodney Jerkins. I had recently been sent a song of his by Paul McDonald, called 'Always Be My Baby' which I really wanted to record. It turned out that Dane had worked with Harvey with Another Level. Harvey is an incredible musician; his father, Harvey Mason, was a really famous drummer.

So Dane's record company got on the case and we were booked into a recording studio in London in September. And then I got meningitis. The studio was already booked, so Dane and Harvey did as much as they could without me actually being there, although I was in spirit. My body was up in Alderley Edge, in bed, curtains closed and sunglasses on. But I was able to talk, and so Dane would call up every five minutes or so, with 'What do you think of this, Vic?' There was nothing else we could do.

Then I'm just on my way back from the session in LA with Soul Shock and Karlin and my mobile rings. I'm at Heathrow, in transit, waiting for the shuttle to Manchester where David is going to pick us up. Brooklyn is rushing around, so excited that he is going to see his daddy. And it's Paul.

'Victoria, you're really not going to like this, but I want you to fly back to LA tomorrow. Harvey Mason Jnr. has a few clear days.'

I couldn't bear it. I was so tired. I still wasn't totally normal after the meningitis and I hadn't seen David for nearly two weeks and he was so looking forward to seeing Brooklyn and I wanted the three of us to be together.

'Just ask them if he can do any other time. I just need a few days off.'

But Harvey was booked up with another singer.

'Look, I'm really sorry, Paul, but I'm going to have to say no. My family is just too important. I can't do this to any of us.'

As much as these songs really meant a lot to me, they would just have to wait.

When you're one of four or five, it's difficult to give your family the priority they deserve. But now I was on my own it was different. While I had been ill I had decided that whatever I did with my solo career it would have to be scheduled around David and Brooklyn.

I couldn't have been home more than half an hour when my mobile went again. Paul again. Harvey had decided to cancel this other singer and would be over in a couple of days.

We were recording at Whitfield Street studios, where we recorded most of the Spice Girls' third album. And Studio 3 is my favourite studio. There's a car park at the back and it's just past Camden so it's perfect for me. And we worked bloody hard. Usually you record two songs in a week, we did four, but it meant working all day and half the night. The guy working with Harvey was Damon Thomas who used to work with Baby Face. I was a huge fan of Damon who has co-written so many class R & B hits. So we recorded 'Girlfriend' and 'Always be My Baby' and a song about Brooklyn called 'I'll Walk with You'. And that's the great thing about working on your own, I had Brooklyn there a lot of the time. It's my session so if I want a baby running around, then that's fine.

I'm not a diva and I never set out to be a pop singer, I set out to be a performer, and that's what I do best, entertain people. But now that I've had the chance to show exactly what I'm capable of, I hope a lot of people are going to be surprised. I have spent half of my life trying to defend myself, but this album shows that I really can sing. It's all me. And what my fans want is the whole package: it's the choreography, the costumes, the lighting, the video, the performance. And they're going to get it.

And then I'm just hoping I can sit down and say, right I'm going to have another baby now.

New Year's Eve is one of those times when there's so much pressure on you to have fun that usually it's awful. So, with David playing on New Year's Day 2001, it was a relief not to have to go out.

For once, Brooklyn went to bed really early and at half-past eleven he woke up. So we're in our bedroom in the flat at Alderley Edge and doing what everyone who isn't at a party is doing: watching television.

And it's one of these tributes to the West End kind of shows (which being a bit of a sad cow I rather enjoy) where Elaine Paige is singing everything from *Cats* to *Starlight Express* and *Phantom of the Opera*. And we're all quite tired but it's that thing where you have to stay up.

So it's getting close to midnight and David goes into the kitchen and gets the clock that usually hangs above the breadbin off the wall, puts it on a tray and brings it into the bedroom with three silver goblets, which he'd had made as a New Year's present from Brooklyn and each one is engraved: *Mummy*, *Daddy*, and *Mine* on the miniature one.

So as midnight approaches, David sets up the video camera at the end of the bed and Brooklyn is racing around being really really funny holding his goblet with his little finger stuck out and suddenly I can't stop laughing. Because I realize we look exactly like people would imagine Posh, Becks and Baby Brooklyn would look like – a total self-parody. So then the countdown begins, Brooklyn opens the cards he made for his daddy (with help from his mummy) of our handprints and David hands me my goblet, which he's filled with 7 UP (not even a thimbleful of champagne the night before a match for any of us), and at the stroke of midnight we clunk our goblets (silver doesn't clink) and I neck my drink and suddenly I realize that I'm choking. And at the same time I realize there's this string hanging out of my mouth. Flapping around my chin is something cold. So I pull at it – it's like a tag that you get on teabags – and feel something in my mouth coming out. David had only put a diamond ring in the goblet and had the tag made in white gold with the date on it – my New Year's present.

Brooklyn climbed up on the bed and we all hugged and we all laughed and had the best time. It was so funny and so romantic. The best New Year's Eve I have ever had.

A few months later me and David did one of the most terrifying things we have ever done – an interview with Ali G. It was for Red Nose Day. Apparently Ali G said he would only do it if he could get either the Clintons or the Beckhams. And although we both really love

Ali G, it must be said that watching somebody else being made mincemeat of is not the same as being under the hatchet yourself.

In fact, I had met Ali G about a year previously before he was really famous. I was doing a casting and he sent me down a bottle of wine and a signed photo with a note saying, 'Dear Scary, Do me show and de bottle is yours'.

I went up to see him and he was completely different from his TV character. He was wearing a nice shirt with a nice jumper, very clean-looking, quite well spoken. If you had walked into him in the street you'd never have known it was Ali G.

Anyway, the BBC called and asked if we were interested. And we said yes, we like to do as much for charity as we can and luckily it fitted in with David's footballing schedule. But as we drove into the BBC, David said to me, 'What the hell are we doing? What the hell do we think we're doing?' He was terrified.

The Ali G who came to see us backstage before the show was nothing like the person I'd met a year before. I think he has spent so much time being Ali G now that he has taken on a lot of the mannerisms of his character. Before, he was very public schoolboy, now there's a bit of Ali G in him all the time.

Obviously we knew that when it came to the interview he'd go on about the whole sex thing, because this is what he does. But it was for charity so you have to not worry about things like that. We both decided that we couldn't actually compete with him so we didn't try. Ali G is very very funny, so we're best just to laugh, send ourselves up if you like and enjoy ourselves. So many people take the piss out of me and David, we may as well show that we can do that ourselves just as well.

Before we went on, David was very very nervous so while we were on camera I had my arm on his leg to make him feel a little bit better.

In fact, I really enjoyed it, we both did, although I was surprised that Ali G's questions were so scripted — they were all on autocue.

When it went out on Red Nose Day — which we watched like everybody else — I was actually quite disappointed that so much had been taken out — mainly the bits where me and David had come back at Ali G. In the broadcast version David says practically nothing. But in the original interview — which we've got a copy of so I know it's not just my imagination — David actually said quite a lot. And there were a couple of times when he was playing up to the gay stuff that Ali G was throwing at him. And you could tell Ali G was caught off-guard. The laugh was on him and at one point I looked at him and knew he had stepped out of character and I could see he was put out that, perhaps for the first time, two people were standing up to him.

And I was so proud of David because in real life he's really shy. I have learned to give as good as I get. I'm not afraid to stand up for myself and say what I think. Even though sometimes I shouldn't. I wouldn't think twice about saying to someone on live television, 'Oi'.

But the feedback afterwards was amazing. Everybody loved it. David stuck up for himself really well and I do wish people could have seen it. The sheer fuss that everybody made around us when we were there quite astounded me. It was far more than we had with the

Spice Girls. And it's only me and him. And it did feel really weird, because I've never had that before and David doesn't get that when he's on his own. I'm not saying we don't both get a lot of attention individually, but it's nothing compared with what happens when we're together. It's kind of crazy, people go to pieces around us. It's not as if we're the kind of people who need fussing, we don't need a hundred people around us telling us we're great.

When I was with the Spice Girls, I was never the favourite, I was always the one in the background. But then when I met David and then fell in love with David it was as if the chemistry of us together did something nobody expected. It was like a snowball, it got bigger and bigger and bigger until really it was out of control.

And now there's virtually nowhere we can go when we're not followed by paparazzi. And I can accept that. But I'll accept it a lot more when I have had success on my own. Although I am famous because I've been in the biggest band in the world, people still say, what can she do? And this can be frustrating.

Being famous for tottering around in high-heels and wearing designer clothes is not enough. I don't want to be famous for being famous. I want to be famous for what I do best. Performing.

When I was young I thought fame would protect me from feeling empty inside, from feeling I was nothing. But without ability to back it up, being famous just makes you more vulnerable to attack, because people feel that you're public property.

What I really wanted all the time was to be taken seriously, not to be mocked as being spotty, or thick, or a rich kid who wasn't like the rest of them. David understood me right from the beginning. He'd had the same thing when he was little. It's not enough that your parents think you're the best thing since sliced bread, if the people around you – teachers, other kids – treat you like shit, because you're different. The hurt you feel is something no amount of your family saying you're lovely can overcome. I'd say Brooklyn was lovely even if he had three heads. Because he's mine.

And sometimes it's made even harder for me because David so obviously does have ability to back it up. It's not that I am jealous of David, I'm not and I never have been – I'm nothing but proud of him. But it's quite hard for such an insecure person as I am, going out with someone like David. OK, people might sometimes be bitchy about him but the bottom line is no one can criticize him for what he is famous for.

I'd often heard other footballers' wives talking about the strain it puts on the marriage when your husband isn't playing. There aren't many footballers who play every single club game and every single international game, but it's like that for David. He hardly ever gets a rest.

So it came as a bit of a shock when in March 2001 Alex Ferguson decided to rest him. David was tired because he'd had flu after Christmas and hadn't had time to really get over it. And as much as David knew that was the reason, it was quite stressful. For several weeks before this, the papers had been going on about him not being in good form, and it was getting a bit hairy, particularly with the crucial World Cup qualifier against Finland coming up.

We never thought he wouldn't be in the team, but because his confidence had been bruised by the press, it wasn't a foregone conclusion that the new England manager, Sven Goran Eriksson, would make him captain.

For the first time we were really feeling it. There has never been that kind of pressure before. Until now I'd always taken it for granted that David would be up there. In actual fact I call him golden bollocks.

When David heard he was going to be captain he was so happy but it also put him under a lot of pressure. This was a really important game and I really wanted to be there and take Brooklyn. But because of the reconstruction of Wembley – where England internationals are usually played – the Finland match was being played at Anfield, home ground of Liverpool FC, Manchester United's deadly rivals. It's the Liverpool fans – together with Leeds fans – who have made David's life a misery with their abuse over the last few years, so Anfield was the last place he wanted to be playing.

So David said he didn't want us to come. He was worried it wouldn't be safe and he decided he would play better if he wasn't worried about us.

Because my mum had had flu, I'd been down in London while David was with the England squad. Unfortunately, in order to get back up to Cheshire for the dinner being organized for the wives and children there wasn't time to watch all the game.

I'm a bit superstitious about watching important games, and I just turn into a bag of nerves and I can never relax till the end of the game. And David knows that my thoughts are always with him.

So I'm in the car going north with Brooklyn and

calling David's friend Dave Gardner every five minutes to find out how David's playing. And they're 1–0 down but I wasn't too upset because Dave said that David was playing really well and that's all I really wanted to hear.

So then it's half-time, and it's 1–1 and Dave tells me that David helped make the goal. Then a friend of mine calls and we're having a chat and I can hear the television on in the background and suddenly the phone just explodes in my ear. And she's shouting *Arraghghgh!* Oh my God, David's scored. It's 2–1 to England. And I can hear the noise from the television and I can imagine him running up to whoever is near him and I can imagine the television cameras going in tight on his face and it was only then that I realized that my own face was wet with tears.

Because David needed this. He so needed it. He has played thirty-nine England games and had only scored one goal before, the game I didn't watch in the World Cup against Colombia. And I can hardly believe it. He scored. And in the front of the car I can hear the driver's phone going, and voices saying to tell me David's scored.

And the last time I spoke to him when he was on the way to the game I said, just imagine that the ball is Mark Niblett's head. And he said I'd kick it out of the bloody stadium. And we laughed. For the next few days it was incredible. I felt like wearing a T-shirt that said Mrs Hero. The papers were full of it. Page after page after page. In 1997, when David was sent off in the World Cup, the front page of the *Daily Mirror* had the headline, TEN HEROIC LIONS AND ONE STUPID BOY. That following Monday morning they printed that photograph again, but this time with a different headline. How the stupid boy grew up to be a true England hero.

'Fatherhood made a man of Beckham,' they wrote. And again I cried.

More importantly perhaps than the press reaction was the manager. When I got up to the hotel where the dinner was being held, David had just walked into our room which I had filled with candles and little drawings and congratulations from the two of us. We were hugging with Brooklyn, when I saw Sven Goran Eriksson walk along the corridor – David was just so happy to see us that he hadn't bothered to close the door.

And Sven looked at me and gave a thumbs-up sign and said softly, 'He did really well.' And that was so nice. Such a friendly face, such a friendly smile.

And that's another reason why I have to go on until I've proved myself. David is so obviously talented and fantastic at what he does but I want Brooklyn to be as proud of his mummy as he is going to be of his daddy.

David is one of those people who can wake up in the morning and he looks great, with stubble, without stubble. He never has spots, never has a bad hair day. But I am very insecure about the way I look, and when I'm out sometimes find it really difficult to talk to people because I feel they're judging me, what I wear, what my hair looks like, the expression on my face. Which is why I often go out wearing a cap and sunglasses: the less of me people can see, the less they can criticize.

Every woman knows what it's like to make an entrance when you're all dressed up, like at a dinner and dance. And you walk in and you just feel everyone's eyes on you. And you're thinking, what do I look like?

Am I going to fit in with everybody? I go through that every single time I walk out of the front door to the football, to Tesco's, to Marks & Spencer's. The only time I feel comfortable is when I'm on stage performing, or when I'm in combat trousers with no make-up on, hair not done and I'm just me at home with my close friends and family.

And at the end of the day, it's just Brooklyn and David who make me happy and nothing else is important, certainly not chart positions. I know I would sacrifice anything for my boys, including my career, even though I also know that they would never ask me to. Sometimes me and David just sit down together and look at Brooklyn in wonder at the miracle of him, at his amazing little character that surprises us every day. When he kicks a ball, he's just like David. And when it comes to food, he's me. What other little boy would turn down a piece of chocolate for a piece of haddock? Sometimes we just look at each other and say, aren't we lucky. Aren't we so, so lucky.

And although we don't have another baby yet, we do have a puppy, Simba – a fluffy white Japanese spitz – who is promising to be just as much trouble. Soon after we got him we were driving down to London, sun shining outside, *Jungle Book* blaring out on the stereo, Brooklyn gazing adoringly at Simba and Simba gazing adoringly at Brooklyn. And then suddenly Simba just throws up and it's everywhere.

'Well, Babes,' I said as David passed me a load of baby wipes, 'we're a proper family, now.'

A trip to the zoo or the park used to be something that had to be planned and thought about. Now it's something we just do because we feel like it. The other day, David had the day off and we went to a farm a few miles away and showed Brooklyn the pigs and the cows and the lambs. He loves animals so much. It was a lovely English day, sunny, blue skies, no clouds. Afterwards we went to this place down the road where they have climbing frames and slides and the children rush around and the mums and dads chat. And they're used to us now, just another mum and dad.

I'm at the bottom of the slide, my arms out waiting to catch him and David is at the top, ready to let go. I give my boys a wave. And they both smile. And I'm noticing the prams, and I'm thinking, Soon that will be me, hopefully.

And we have the best time. Not being Posh, Becks and Baby Brooklyn, but David, Victoria and Brooklyn, and of course Thomas the Tank Engine and the Tweenies. And don't forget Postman Pat.

TO MY FANS

I owe all my success to the support of my family and my fans. You've stuck by me, you've made the Spice Girls who they are, and I really want to say a big THANK YOU.

There have been ups and downs and people haven't always been positive. But for every negative thing that has been written about me, there are a hundred fan letters that have picked me up. Throughout it all you have really stuck by me.

And sometimes when I have felt like giving up, it's you who have given me the strength to carry on. And no matter what anybody says, I will keep making music for as long as you want me to. I love you all and I love what I do. You've given me the opportunity to express myself and be who I am.

Thank you.
Victoria XX